W9-CAV-947

Healing Fear

New Approaches to Overcoming Anxiety

Edmund Bourne, Ph.D.

MJF BOOKS
NEW YORK

Publisher's Note: This publication is designed to provide accurate and authoritative information in regard to the subject matter covered. It is sold with the understanding that the publisher is not engaged in rendering psychological, financial, legal, or other professional services. If expert assistance or counseling is needed, the services of a competent professional should be sought.

Published by MJF Books
Fine Communications
Two Lincoln Square
60 West 66th Street
New York, NY 10023

Healing Fear
Library of Congress Control No. 00-130537
ISBN 1-56731-382-5

Copyright © 1998 by Edmund Bourne, Ph.D.

This edition published by arrangement with New Harbinger Publications, Inc.

Edited by Carole Honeychurch
Text design by Michele Waters

Guidelines for simplifying life, pp. 30-31, from *Voluntary Simplicity* by Duane Elgin. Copyright © 1981 by Duane Elgin. Reprinted by permission of William Morrow & Company, Inc.

Right attitudes, pp. 230-233, and meditation exercises, pp. 238-239, adapted from *Full Catastrophe Living* by Jon Kabat-Zinn. Copyright © 1990 by Jon Kabat-Zinn. Used by permission of Dell Books, a division of Bantam Doubleday Dell Publishing Group, Inc.

"Beliefs That Hold You Back from Growth and Change," pp.343-345, adapted from *You Can Heal Your Life*, by Louise L. Hay. Copyright © 1984. Hay House, Inc., Carlsbad, CA. Used by permission.

Excerpt pp. 354-355. Reprinted with the permission of Scribner, a division of Simon & Schuster from *Coyote Medicine: Lessons from Native American Healing* by Lewis Mehl-Madrona. Copyright © 1997 by Lewis Mehl-Madrona.

All rights reserved. No part of this publication may be reproduced or transmitted in any form or by any means, electronic or mechanical, including photocopy, recording, or any information storage and retrieval system, without the prior written permission of the publisher.

Manufactured in the United States of America on acid-free paper

MJF Books and the MJF colophon are trademarks of Fine Creative Media, Inc.

10   9   8   7   6   5   4   3   2   1

Grateful acknowledgment to:

Matt McKay, for his patience and flexibility in working with me throughout the project

Carole Honeychurch, for skillful and sensitive editing

Kirk Johnson, for his contribution to the cover design

Michele Waters for the text design

Tom Rucker, Sita Packer, and Steve Prakken, for reviewing early versions of the book

and to

Jane, my partner who processed the entire manuscript, made valuable editorial contributions, and has been a healing presence in my life.

In moments of separation,
Adrift from ourselves or each other,
Our restless minds
Too quickly conjure fearful images—
Like bad dreams we mistake as real.

Though we see it not,
Each of us seeks to return
To a common ground
That lies deep within and beyond us.
A place—long remembered—
Where we all can meet
Beyond visible and verbal differences
Where each may feel safe,
Take heart,
And remember the quiet love
That enfolds us all.

Contents

Appendices

Introduction

This book begins with a story—my own personal story. When I'm asked how I originally got involved in the field of anxiety disorders, I usually say that it was to help people recover from anxiety by teaching them what I've learned in the process of my own recovery.

Having been born to parents both of whom had anxiety difficulties, I realized early on the challenge that anxiety could present. Later, I had my own anxiety challenges to face—including panic attacks, obsessive thoughts, and social phobia. In seeking to help myself, as well as the many clients I've worked with, I've learned quite a bit about how to overcome problems with anxiety. Much of what I've learned was incorporated into my first book—*The Anxiety & Phobia Workbook* (1995). The concepts and strategies described in that book provided wide-ranging resources that both my clients and I have found to be quite helpful. I still draw on the *Workbook* almost every day in my counseling work. I'm happy that this book has been able to help so many people.

Five years after the publication of the first edition of the *Workbook*, my own anxiety disorder took a turn for the worse. This happened in spite of all the knowledge I had gained about how to treat anxiety problems. The resulting crisis led me to reevaluate everything I was doing and to redirect the course of my life. This book—*Healing Fear*—is a result of that reevaluation. It includes but also goes beyond the mainstream strategies described in *The Anxiety & Phobia Workbook*: cognitive behavioral therapy and medication. In my own case, I found that the conventional approaches, while very helpful, were not quite enough to permit me to overcome my difficulties. Something more was needed. Cognitive behavioral therapy and medication seemed helpful in managing symptoms, but these interventions did not seem to address the underlying issues for me. Certain basic changes in my lifestyle, values, and priorities were necessary.

Many of my clients in recent years have voiced a similar need. Cognitive behavioral therapy and/or medication is quite useful in enabling them to handle symptoms and resume a functional life, yet these approaches do not resolve all of the issues that contributed to their problem with anxiety in the first place.

A true *healing* of anxiety involves more than symptom management. Healing, in fact, requires understanding the *meaning* of anxiety symptoms. Such symptoms are not a mere random occurrence but a *signal* that calls for some kind of change. An anxiety disorder functions in much the same way as a psychosomatic problem like ulcers or migraine headaches—the body and brain are throwing up a warning sign that some kind of change in priorities and attitude is needed. The change required may be to deal with a long-standing personality pattern, to resolve an interpersonal conflict, to take life more slowly and easily, or to make a major shift in your personal values. In my own case, I needed to learn to simplify my life, let go of perfectionism, build a better support system, and rely on a more spiritual approach to dealing with my situation. To this day, I cannot say categorically that I'm "100 percent cured," yet I have a significantly more fulfilling and peaceful life than I ever had before. Recovery, in my experience, is not synonymous with "cure" but with a desirable quality of life—as well as with peace of mind.

As you read through this book, it's important to keep asking yourself whether your difficulty with anxiety is calling you to make some basic changes. What sorts of changes? What risks do you need to take?

The guiding metaphor for this book is "healing" as an approach to overcoming anxiety, in contrast to "applied technology." I feel it's important to introduce this perspective into the field of anxiety treatment since the vast majority of self-help books available (including my first book) utilize the applied technology approach. These books present—in a variety of ways—the mainstream cognitive behavioral methodology for treating anxiety disorders. Cognitive behavioral therapy reflects the dominant zeitgeist of Western society—a worldview that has primary faith in scientifically validated technologies that give humans knowledge and power to overcome obstacles to successful adaptation. This paradigm is evident in the titles of many of the leading books and programs in the field, for example, *Triumph Over Fear* (Ross 1994), *Mastery of Your Anxiety and Panic* (Barlow and Craske 1989), or *Attacking Anxiety* (Bassett 1985).

I don't want to diminish the importance of cognitive behavioral therapy (CBT) and the applied technology approach. Such an approach produces effective results in many cases, and I use it in my professional practice every day. In the past few years, though, I feel that the cognitive behavioral strategy has reached its limits. CBT and medication can produce results quickly and are very compatible with the brief therapy, managed-care environment prevalent in the mental health profession at present. When follow-up is done over one to three-year intervals, however, some of the gains are lost. Relapses occur rather often, and people seem to get themselves back into the same difficulties that precipitated the original anxiety disorder. Of course, relaxation skills, cognitive restructuring and exposure—along with interpersonal therapy—are very helpful at these times to overcome relapse. Yet, they often don't go the whole distance. If you have entrenched personality patterns, expectations, priorities, and values that are incompatible with living peacefully and in harmony with yourself, anxiety may tend to keep coming back. In fact, I believe the problem goes even deeper than this. Some of the difficulty lies not just in personal habits, attitudes, and values but in the larger society from which those habits and values derive. If you live in a family, society, and environment that does not support recovery from anxiety, your problem may return in spite of your best efforts.

My impression is that *anxiety arises fundamentally from a state of disconnection*—a disconnection of each individual from self, significant others, environment, community, society, and spirituality. My intent in writing *Healing Fear* is first to describe this disconnection (or alienation) in its various forms and then offer specific approaches to remedy the basic problem. Again, the purpose of the book is emphatically not to replace cognitive behavioral therapy and medication as treatment approaches. Rather, it is to offer a range of strategies that allow the reader to heal the sociocultural and existential roots of anxiety—the state of disconnection from self, others, and the world that is prevalent in modern times. Such an approach, *in combination with CBT and medication*, can offer a more integrated, comprehensive path to healing anxiety in its deepest and most intractable aspects.

In the first chapter of this book, I tell my own personal story. My purpose in recounting my story is to offer some hope. It's no exaggeration to say that my particular problem with anxiety was, for several years, chronic and severe. There were certainly times when I felt hopeless about it. Not until I decided to make healing my first and full-time priority did I begin to see any change. Today, I enjoy a level of peace and ease with my life that I had never experienced before. I've come to believe that there is no problem with anxiety, no matter how severe, that cannot be substantially helped if you have the desire and faith to do what is needed.

Following my own story, the remainder of this book offers a range of strategies that have been helpful to myself and many of my clients. The book is divided into two parts. Part I, "Basics," describes a series of basic approaches for overcoming anxiety that can be useful to everyone. Part II, "Beyond the Basics," presents alternative approaches that are not usually found in other books addressing anxiety disorders. These approaches were vital to me personally and have been helpful to many others. Take from them whatever you find to be personally useful. A brief description of each chapter follows.

Chapter 2, "Restoring Lost Connections," provides a short overview of some of the sociocultural and existential roots of anxiety in the twentieth century. This chapter suggests that anxiety arises fundamentally from a condition of separation—separation from family, community, nature, the cosmos, and oneself. This is not to deny that brain imbalances, conditioning, and erroneous cognitions (false thoughts) play a role in causing and maintaining anxiety disorders. However, I believe such factors themselves arise out of a sociocultural milieu that creates excessive stress and alienation for large numbers of people. The intent of Chapter 2 is to briefly outline a number of ways to heal some of the difficulties unique to modern society. Later chapters elaborate on some of these possibilities. Chapter 3, "Simplifying Your Life," offers some concrete strategies for living more simply and thus creating more time to heal some of the alienation inherent in modern life. This chapter echoes a trend prevalent in recent years for people to downsize the scale on which they live. A simpler life was one of the most important changes I needed to make in order to overcome my own difficulties. Even one or two such changes can make a significant difference. Chapter 3 concludes with a list of suggestions for making your life less complicated.

The next two chapters (4 and 5), "Caring for Your Body: Relaxation, Exercise, and Energy Balance" and "Caring for Your Body: Nutrition," make a strong case that taking care of your body and physical needs will help reduce anxiety. These chapters provide a counterpoint to the emphasis on cognitive therapy in treating anxiety disorders. Cognitive therapy rightfully stresses the importance of changing thinking patterns and beliefs to alleviate anxiety difficulties and depression. In short, thinking better leads to feeling better. The two chapters on caring for your body stress the converse point, which is equally valid: When you feel physically well and vital, you'll naturally tend to entertain more positive thoughts.

Chapter 6, "Tools That Work: Help for Overcoming Panic and Phobias," summarizes what are, in my opinion, the most useful aspects of the cognitive behavioral treatment paradigm currently used to treat all anxiety disorders. The cognitive behavioral approach will continue for some time to be at the forefront of effective treatment for anxiety problems. It is particularly helpful to people struggling with panic attacks and phobias. Some parts of this chapter are based on material in my first book, *The Anxiety & Phobia Workbook*, while other parts are entirely new. Although the purpose of *Healing Fear* is to provide a range of approaches that go beyond cognitive behavioral therapy, I felt it was important to include one chapter that covers the most important basics.

Chapter 7, "Medication: Healing Your Brain When Anxiety Is Severe," covers the topic of medication in depth and reflects a number of changes in my view of medication from the short chapter that appeared in *The Anxiety & Phobia Workbook*. Medications, particularly the SSRI (selective serotonin reuptake inhibitor) antidepressant medications, have come to play a major role in the treatment of anxiety disorders, particularly panic disorder and obsessive-compulsive disorder. For milder difficulties, cognitive behavioral therapy may be sufficient; yet when anxiety is severe, the combination of an SSRI and CBT can often be quite helpful. The timely use of medication at the onset of severe anxiety can forestall a "runaway" effect whereby acute anxiety turns into a more chronic, long-standing disorder. There is no conflict, in my opinion, between appropriate use of medication and the more holistic approaches presented in this book.

Chapter 8, "Addressing Personality Issues," is the first of several chapters to suggest that recovery from anxiety difficulties may require more than symptom management through cognitive behavioral therapy or medication. After an initial course of therapy is complete, some people experience a relapse months or years later because more enduring personality and self-esteem issues have not been dealt with. This chapter describes five "core fears" and associated personality traits that can underlie panic, phobias, and anxiety symptoms: fear of abandonment, fear of rejection, fear of losing control, fear of death/injury, and fear of confinement. Strategies are described for addressing each of these basic fears and associated personality issues on an *emotional* as well as cognitive level.

As previously mentioned, Part II of this book offers a series of perspectives on healing fear that have been profoundly helpful to me as well as many of my clients. These perspectives have been written about elsewhere, but are not addressed by the majority of books specifically intended for people struggling with anxiety disorders. Such approaches go beyond established and well-known methods of treatment. Yet, they are intended to *complement*, not replace, conventional treatment. In various ways, all of the chapters in Part II embrace holistic concepts and values. They also emphasize the importance of the spiritual dimension in recovery. In my own experience, spirituality has been important, and I believe it will come to play an increasingly important role in the psychology of the future. Holistic medicine, with its interest in meditation, prayer, and the role of spiritual healing in recovery from serious illness, has become a mainstream movement in the nineties. I believe there will be a "holistic psychology" in the not too distant future that, like holistic medicine, *integrates* scientifically based treatment approaches with alternative, more spiritually based modalities. (The twenty-five-year-old movement of transpersonal psychology has already made a start in this direction.) Part II of this book was written in the spirit of this vision of the future direction of psychology.

Chapter 9, "Developing Your Observing Self," considers the applicability of mindfulness meditation (or "awareness meditation," as I prefer) to problems with anxiety. Meditation is the oldest methodology humanity has devised to overcome anxiety and cultivate inner peace and equanimity. Regular meditation practice enables you to develop a different stance toward your own inner experience. It allows you to gain an increased ability to stand back and witness the reactive and conditioned thoughts that make up your moment to moment awareness instead of being caught up in them. Ultimately you develop more acceptance and compassion for your personal limitations, rather than struggling with them. Chapter 10, "Finding Your Unique Purpose," addresses the problem of *existential anxiety*—the type of anxiety that arises from a sense of meaninglessness or purposelessness about your life. The chapter begins with the premise that everyone has unique creative gifts and talents to offer. By developing and expressing these gifts, life can take on a new dimension of meaning. Much anxiety can be healed in the process. If you feel that a sense of meaninglessness or lack of purpose contributes to your problem with anxiety, this is an important chapter to consider.

Chapter 11, "Enlarging Your View of Life," introduces spirituality as an important means of "cognitively restructuring" (changing your basic viewpoint about) your way of understanding both your anxiety problem and life in general. I believe that exploring your spiritual values and beliefs can be regarded as an extension of cognitive therapy—cognitive therapy at a *philosophical* level. I have kept the chapter relevant by discussing a number of specific ways in which spiritual principles and values can help heal anxiety disorders. Although you may not agree with all of the points made in this chapter, I hope it may help stimulate your thinking. Chapter 12, "Letting Go," consists of two parts. The first addresses how to let go of worry and an attachment to perfection in day-to-day life; the second addresses the process of relinquishing an intractable problem to the care of your god or Higher Power (however you define such a power). It is something I often did when my own problem with anxiety seemed out of control. Throughout, I emphasize that relying on a Higher Power for assistance in no way diminishes the need for taking responsibility to do all within your power to work on your problem through available methods. Healing can be fostered through a combination of doing all the necessary footwork and trusting in help from a Higher Power. This seems to be valid for the twelve-step approaches to healing addictions, and I think it is equally applicable to persons struggling with anxiety disorders. (I am not alone in this, since there are now twelve-step groups in certain areas for agoraphobia, obsessive-compulsive disorder, and post-traumatic stress disorder.) Chapter 13, "Affirming Your Recovery," elaborates on the recently popular notion: "You create your own reality." This idea has dominated a number of books in the contemporary self-help literature and is widely discussed these days. I have found it to be helpful to me personally, although I feel it's overly simplistic to assume that *everything* that happens to us is an outward manifestation of our beliefs. Chapter 13 offers a hypothetical model of how "creating your reality" might actually take place and then offers step-by-step methods for applying this principle to overcoming problems with anxiety. If you truly believe in your capacity to recover—and affirm it with conviction—you will indeed invite healing into your life.

The final chapter, "Learning to Love," begins with the idea that love and fear are opposites, and that authentic love (in all of its diverse forms) is ultimately the most profound and enduring solution to the problem of fear. The capacity to love is not an acquired behavior but an innate potential that need only be brought out. *Learning* to love means deliberately practicing actions that foster the expression of this inherent capacity. This chapter reflects on and suggests ways to enhance important dimensions of love such as self-love (self-worth), forgiveness, compassion, and generosity.

The purpose of this book is to provide a wide range of approaches to healing fear and anxiety that include yet go beyond existing, mainstream methods. In my experience, such a comprehensive strategy has the best chance of helping people achieve a true *healing* of fear—a more fulfilling and peaceful quality of life over the long-term. Rather than replacing cognitive behavioral therapy and psychopharmacology, this book seeks an integration of the current treatment paradigm with an alternative model based on the metaphor of healing. I believe that such an integration is needed not only in the field of anxiety disorders, but in psychology in general, in medicine, politics, international relations, and particularly in our attitude toward the earth's environment as we enter a new century. Scientific and holistic perspectives on ourselves and our world no longer need to clash, but can best complement each other. I, for one, believe that it is through a collaboration of both types of perspectives that we as humans can find lasting solutions to our problems, both at the individual and collective level.

How to Read This Book

There are at least two different ways to read this book, depending on your previous experience with books on anxiety and anxiety disorders. If this is the first book you've read on the topic of anxiety, I suggest you read the first eight chapters in order. Chapters 4, 6, and 7, in particular, cover the most important basic concepts and approaches that are employed in treating anxiety, panic, and phobias at the present time. Relaxation, abdominal breathing, cognitive behavioral therapy, and medication constitute the foundation of conventional treatment; the remaining approaches described elsewhere in this book are powerful and effective, yet they can be viewed as complementary to the basic approaches.

If you've read previous books on anxiety disorders, including my own (*The Anxiety & Phobia Workbook*), you may already be familiar with the foundational strategies for overcoming anxiety and phobias. In that case, feel free to read the chapters of this book in whatever order you prefer, depending on what interests you most. If you feel you're already thoroughly familiar with the cognitive behavioral approach, you may want to read the chapter on addressing personality issues or some of the later chapters in Part II for a fresh perspective. If you're particularly interested in meditation, see the chapter "Developing Your Observing Self." If you're interested in spiritual perspectives on overcoming anxiety, see especially the chapters "Enlarging Your View of Life" and "Affirming Your Recovery." All of the approaches described in this book can contribute to healing your particular difficulty with anxiety or fear. Let your intuition guide you in choosing which ones to read first.

Finally, keep in mind that in using this book you do not have to go it alone. You may find it beneficial to use this book as a basis for an ongoing support group. Or you may want to work though the chapters with the assistance of a therapist.

References

Barlow, David, and Michelle Craske. 1989. *Mastery of Your Anxiety and Panic*. Albany, New York: Graywind Publications.

Bassett, Lucinda. 1985. *Attacking Anxiety* (audiotape program). Oak Harbor, Ohio: Midwest Center for Anxiety.

Bourne, Edmund J. 1995. *The Anxiety and Phobia Workbook* 2nd ed. Oakland, Calif.: New Harbinger Publications.

Ross, Jerilyn. 1994. *Triumph Over Fear*. New York: Bantam Books.

Part I

Basics

1

My Story

Each one of us has a story. I decided to tell mine in order to impart what I've learned from my own experience with a chronic anxiety disorder. Some of you may wonder why the author of a popular workbook on anxiety should have been personally challenged by anxiety. Shouldn't I know enough to be able to overcome my own problem? If anxiety disorders were merely the result of a lack of knowledge, combined with maladaptive thoughts and behaviors, then surely diligent application of all the strategies described in my previous book, *The Anxiety & Phobia Workbook*, should be enough to ensure recovery. The reality is that anxiety disorders, in some instances, appear to involve more than this. We now know that in some cases anxiety disorders have a genetically predisposed, neurobiological component. Because of this, such cases may be only partially responsive to cognitive behavioral therapy (CBT), and indeed only partially responsive to CBT combined with medication. My own difficulties with anxiety have been with me for over thirty years, and I'm convinced that they are in part biological. That emphatically does not mean I or anyone else should feel resigned and give up hope. The primary purpose of this book is to argue that there is much you can do and much to be hopeful about, even if you feel you have a chronic and disabling problem. My own problem reached disabling proportions a few years ago, surprisingly after I had been a successful therapist and published my first book. Today, as a result of implementing everything described in this book, I feel I have attained considerable serenity and optimism. I'm freer of my problem with anxiety than I've ever been at any previous time in my life. I've learned through my own experience that there is no challenge with anxiety that cannot be helped.

The difficulty I personally experienced was an unusual form of obsessive-compulsive disorder (OCD), although I have also suffered panic attacks and certain types of social phobia. My particular form of OCD involved intrusive thoughts only, without any compulsions. To my surprise, I have never encountered my type of OCD in anything I've read or in any client with whom I've worked. That is fortunate, since I wouldn't want anyone to experience what I've been through. There was nothing violent or offensive about my particular obsessive thoughts, but they still were very persistent, intrusive, and bothersome. It was my decision in writing this chapter not to talk about the details of my own problem because of the potential suggestibility of some of you who might read this book. Suffice it to say that my problem periodically reached a stage where it felt quite frightening for days at a time. It also caused periods of depression that could last as long as two or three months.

In order to manage my difficulty, I incorporated all of the methods described in *The Anxiety & Phobia Workbook*. These methods certainly did help. What I found most useful were:

- Abdominal breathing

- Relaxation in the form of meditation

- Daily physical exercise

- Using panic-coping strategies and countering unconstructive thoughts and beliefs

- Identifying and expressing deep-seated feelings

- Inner-child work

- Improving nutrition

- Medication

For a long time, all of these strategies were useful. By practicing them consistently, I was able to maintain a busy life of teaching, counseling, and writing. These strategies allowed me to keep my symptoms at bay while I led a complicated and often stressful life. However, for many years I felt a lack of genuine contentment or satisfaction with my life. During any given week I would have good days and bad days, and the bad weren't much fun. Then there were occasional times when my problem would get out of control to the point where, for days at a stretch, it was hard to function.

For a long time I asked myself why I couldn't make a full recovery. Given all that I knew and was doing, why couldn't I overcome my problem to the point where I could truly enjoy life?

As I look back over my life, I now realize that two circumstances continued to seriously aggravate my problem. The first I was well aware of for some time, yet, for many reasons, was unwilling to do much about. The second was very subtle and escaped my understanding until much later. I'll describe each of them.

First, for many years I created a high-stress lifestyle for myself. Although I practiced deep relaxation, aerobic exercise, good nutritional habits, and routinely worked with my own attitudes and negative self-talk, I was unwilling to simplify my life and live at a more relaxed pace. Like many of my clients, I was a product of a society that emphasizes personal achievement and accomplishment over taking care of oneself. I was caught up in the values of that society—not so much the materialism as the part about working hard and being successful. Having grown up in a family where both of my parents were medical professionals, I automatically lived out a script that defined personal fulfillment in terms of achievement and professional success. I believed that keeping up with the pace and the norms of modern society was necessary, no matter what the cost.

Again and again in my practice, I saw people who themselves were not able to keep up indefinitely—people who eventually burned out from the cumulative stress of modern life. Many of them came to therapy hoping I could offer them a quick fix so that they could go back to their previous lifestyle. Often I tried to do this. The managed-care programs that would only pay for six to ten sessions supported this type of approach. The problem, for me, was that I was unwilling to break out of some of the very patterns I saw in my clients. Periodically I would burn myself out, take time off to recover, and then go back to my life, which consisted of two different private practices a hundred miles apart, along with numerous teaching and speaking obligations. I also allowed myself to become isolated, choosing to live alone, with most people I knew available only by telephone.

By the early nineties, serious warning signs were beginning to appear. My response was to take a four-month break from work. That break certainly helped, but then I went back to the exact same lifestyle I'd had before.

The second and subtler problem that I was unaware of at the time was the effect of using sedatives and tranquilizers to help manage my anxiety over a long period of time. Although antidepressant medications such as Prozac, Paxil, Zoloft, or Anafranil were the drug of choice for my particular difficulty, I was not able to tolerate the side effects of these medications even at the lowest possible dose. So I fell back on tranquilizers and sedatives to help manage my anxiety during the day and my insomnia at night. These medications, together with implementing all the strategies described in *The Anxiety & Phobia Workbook*, certainly enabled me to get by. The problem was that I was doing only that—just "getting by"—and wasn't very much at peace with myself or with life.

My personal experience with long-term use of benzodiazepine medications may or may not be unique. I do not believe long-term use (more than five years) of medications such as Xanax or Klonopin is necessarily harmful. Certainly I know of clients who have used benzodiazepines for as long as twenty to thirty years without significant problems. However, in my own case, long-term use of benzodiazepines led to complications that offset any benefits I was obtaining. I found that benzodiazepine tranquilizers made me depressed, and I would tend to feel better when I reduced the dose or actually stopped taking them for a while. Even worse, they had a peculiar way of aggravating my OCD. To reduce the dose, I wouldn't take them daily (as prescribed) and consequently did not keep a steady amount in my system. Almost every time my body cleared the drug, I would have rebound anxiety (see Chapter 7) which showed up as a new twist or form of my OCD. Thus, for several years I felt in a bind with regard to medication. I couldn't take any of the antidepressant medications recommended for my particular problem, so to help manage my anxiety I relied on the benzodiazepine tranquilizers. And yet the very medication I was using to try to help was actually aggravating my problem. Several times I succeeded in not taking any prescription medication for a period of a few months. During these times, I redoubled my efforts to rely on natural methods and felt well and optimistic for a while. Unfortunately, natural methods always proved insufficient to manage my problem over the long-term. Sooner or later the stress of my complicated lifestyle caught up with me. Then I would go back to using low doses of the benzodiazepines, only to suffer the same complications. My life went on in this fashion for about five years.

The Turning Point

It was in 1995 that I came to a major crisis point. Just after the publication of the second edition of *The Anxiety & Phobia Workbook*, my problem with intrusive obsessional thoughts suddenly became much worse. In fact, the problem became so difficult that I could no longer function professionally and had to stop working. In two months I informed all of my clients that I was discontinuing my practice and would transfer them to other therapists who specialized in treating anxiety disorders. It felt as though my entire life had come crashing down on me. For a period of about four months, my anxiety reached a level where I was in an almost continual state of dread. Tranquilizers were of little use to me at this point. It is no exaggeration to say that there were times when I wished I could just go quietly to sleep and not wake up. The combination of still being perceived as a national expert on anxiety disorders while having a problem so severe was devastating to my personal sense of identity. For a while it felt as though my life, at least as I had known it, was over.

I have no idea how long I could have gone on this way. Fortunately, through what I now view as a form of spiritual grace as well as my own efforts, I found a way out of my predicament. Three things contributed to this shift.

The first was discovering an antidepressant medication that I could tolerate. After numerous trials with various different types of antidepressants over a period of five years, I finally found one I could take. In order to do so, I started with a very low dose and very gradually worked up to a therapeutic level. It took about twelve weeks before I began to experience any benefit.

While the medication helped, it was not sufficient to give me back my life. The second factor that contributed to my recovery was a decision to simplify my life as much as possible. After twenty-five years of living in large metropolitan areas (Chicago, Los Angeles, San Francisco Bay Area), I moved to a small town of about ten thousand (Kona, Hawaii). My decision to move to Hawaii was based on the fact that I had suffered from seasonal affective disorder (SAD) for many years. (Seasonal affective disorder is a disturbance involving an increased predisposition to depression and anxiety during the winter months, primarily because of reduced exposure to sunlight.) From November through March of every year, I had experienced a significant aggravation of my difficulties to the point that it was sometimes difficult to work despite using light therapy and engaging in a rigorous exercise program. In moving to Hawaii, I sought a climate where there is very little seasonal variation.

I decided I needed to take a full year off from work. During this year I did everything in my power to minimize stress and take life at a slow and easy pace. I realized that I needed more than just a month or two break. There had been too many years of accumulated stress to offset by just taking a few months' vacation. I had already tried that before. It was necessary for me to "wipe the slate clean," stop everything, and focus solely on my recovery for an extended time—as long as it took. During this time my days consisted of sleeping, eating, meditating, swimming and snorkeling in the ocean, and taking long walks. There was no TV, no movies, no computer, very little use of the phone, and occasional light reading. I simply stopped—"got off the merry-go-round," as one friend put it—and decided to just rest for as long as necessary.

I realize that most of you reading this book may not be in a position to move to Hawaii or take a year off from work. Such measures are, in fact, unnecessary to heal a problem with anxiety, even one that is long-standing and severe. What is important is that you understand the *meaning* of your anxiety and then make a sincere commitment to do something about it. By "meaning"

I'm talking about focusing not just on your symptoms, whether panic, phobias, or obsessions/compulsions, but coming to terms with the underlying causes of your problem. Your difficulty with anxiety is calling you to make certain changes—changes in your lifestyle, your behavior, your personality, and perhaps even cherished assumptions about yourself and your most important values. *Your responsibility is to understand what changes are required and then to sincerely commit to making them.* This usually requires moving out of your "comfort zone" and taking risks. In my own case, simplifying my life, letting go of perfectionism, valuing personal serenity before most other things, and cultivating spirituality were some of the most important changes called for. Your own situation may involve these types of changes or others. Perhaps, for example, your life already seems "too simple"—you're at home and afraid to go out into the world and become active. In this case the change you are being called to make may be to develop autonomy, assertiveness, and find meaningful work that can empower you. The point here is that healing anxiety often involves more than simply learning how to control symptoms with breathing techniques, constructive self-talk, and exposure strategies. More fundamental changes in attitude, lifestyle, personality, and your basic perception of life may be required. When you get in touch with what it is you need to change, you need to commit yourself and take the risks to make that change, if you truly want to recover.

In my own case, I realized that I had to make my daily life about recovering from my problem if I was going to get better. I set up a healing program that included not only cognitive behavioral strategies and medication, but all of the approaches described in this book. This book is, in fact, a summary of what has helped transform my life from being challenged by a serious anxiety disorder to functioning in a healthier and happier fashion than I ever had before. Certainly the basic, well-known strategies such as relaxation, exercise, working with self-talk, and medication contributed significantly to my recovery. Three chapters in this book review these important approaches. However, I feel deeply that these methods alone would not have made the difference without incorporating several additional perspectives described in eight of this book's chapters:

- Simplifying my life

- Taking care of my physical well-being

- Developing a capacity for self-observation through meditation

- Recognizing and being true to my unique purpose in life

- Enlarging my view of life to include spirituality

- Letting go—relinquishing control enough to let others and my Higher Power help

- Affirming and believing in my ultimate recovery

- Learning to love

For me, these additional perspectives went well beyond the concepts, skills, and techniques I had been using with my clients and advocating in my first book. Through them I experienced a deep personal transformation from the inside out—a "healing" from fear. In the process I decided that it was important to write about what had been helpful to me, in the hope that it might also be helpful to you.

The last four perspectives mentioned above incorporate spirituality. The chapter called "Enlarging Your View of Life" (Chapter 11) introduces a universal spiritual perspective, not associated with any particular religion. The chapter on letting go (Chapter 12) talks about relying on a Higher Power (God) for guidance and support at those times when your own efforts seem inadequate to the task. I believe that my own healing process was assisted by my Higher Power and that, without such assistance, I would not have recovered to the level of inner peace, ease, and confidence I experience at present. The chapter called "Affirming Your Recovery" (Chapter 13) elaborates on the idea that what you believe in and commit to with your whole heart tends to come to you. This idea, that humans draw to them what they believe in most strongly, can best be understood from a spiritual perspective (conventional science tends to view such an idea as childish "magical thinking"). My personal experience was that when I truly committed to my own healing, I entered into a relationship with a Higher Power that assisted and guided me on a daily basis toward recovery. I still had to do my homework, but I consistently received inspiration and guidance at those very times when I despaired of ever having a normal life again. The kind of assistance I received is well known to the many persons who've recovered from addiction through twelve-step programs, and I felt it was important that the millions of persons who suffer from anxiety be aware of it. When you sincerely commit to something, and that something is for your highest good, your Higher Power (however you choose to define such a power) will assist you to achieve it.

Finally, Chapter 14 ("Learning to Love") describes an area that I'm still working with. By love, I mean the kind of unconditional love that is sometimes called compassion. Cultivating compassion toward yourself and others is the most direct way to overcome fear, because such love is the exact opposite of fear. Love cancels out fear in the same way light dispels darkness. Love arises when you fully accept a connection with or inclusion of something (or someone) other than yourself; fear, by contrast, arises out of a disconnection or separation from others—or within your own being. As you open your heart and deepen your ability to love, it becomes easier to dispel fear. In those very moments when you're afraid, if you are able to come from your heart ("take heart"), your perception of things becomes clear and any unrealistic fear is exposed as an illusion.

It is my hope that the spiritual perspective developed in the last few chapters of this book may be helpful to you. As you read through these chapters, take what fits for you and discard what does not. The diverse religions and creeds of the world reflect the countless ways in which human beings have approached the spiritual dimension of life. I believe there is no "one right way," and that each person must define the nature and scope of spirituality for him- or herself. In my own case, a combination of conventional and spiritually based approaches was necessary in order to recover. The approaches described in my first book carried me a long way down the path of recovery, and I know that these approaches are quite often sufficient for many people. Yet, for me, they weren't quite enough. For several years my particular problem with anxiety was severe. It took everything described in this book, in addition to the conventional, mainstream approaches, to overcome it.

What I learned from my experience is that any problem with anxiety—even one that is chronic, severe, and has a genetic-biological basis—is not intractable. There is always hope for recovery. No matter how difficult your situation, you can reclaim your life and find peace—if you truly want it.

2

Restoring Lost Connections

The twentieth century has often been referred to as the "age of anxiety." Over the past thirty years, writers from Rollo May to Scott Peck have pointed out that anxiety is endemic to modern society. What is it about the twentieth century that has contributed to increasing anxiety in Western society? What made life in the twentieth century particularly conducive to anxiety in contrast to life in previous centuries—which were dominated by war, famine, plague, persecution, suppression, and so on?

My experience with anxiety (both professionally and personally) has led me to believe that anxiety, at its roots, arises both individually and collectively out of a state of *separation* or *disconnection*. This separation can occur on many levels, including separation from family, from community, from cultural institutions, from nature, and most essentially from one's self and one's Higher Power or God. Security lies in connection with something larger—in a sense of unity with yourself, others, and the universe at large. Anxiety arises in that moment when you have lost touch with a larger sense of connection and perceive something (almost anything) to be a threat to your sense of security or stability. The threat may sometimes be real, but in many cases is imagined. Feeling disconnected and isolated enlarges the sense of threat. Feeling connected and supported fosters a sense of safety and comfort.

While people living in previous centuries certainly had to confront fear and threats in many forms, I believe that they weren't subject to the kind of anxiety experienced in the twentieth century. This is because society was neither as complex nor as fragmented (primary factors in human alienation) in such a variety of ways as it is today.

It seems likely that the industrialization and urbanization of modern society have played a large role in promoting this multileveled condition of separation. Although in recent times society has reached a "postindustrial" phase (high technology and communication have superseded manufacturing in the economy), I believe that the types of separation and alienation created by industrialization are still with us. Each type of separation is described in what follows.

Separation from Family

Most preindustrial societies raised their children in the context of an extended family. Mothers had sisters, aunts, and their own mothers living nearby, if not within the same home, to assist with child rearing and daily chores. Fathers had brothers, uncles, and their own fathers to assist with hunting, farming, or craft trades. Particular skills such as tool making or construction were often passed down within a single family line. The support provided by close family ties has tangible effects. For example, an Italian community in rural Pennsylvania baffled medical science because it had no cardiovascular disease in spite of a high-fat diet. Researchers concluded that family and community solidarity in this group was strong enough to offset the usually detrimental effects of such a diet.

In modern society people frequently move away from parents and siblings and raise their own children within isolated nuclear families. And with divorce rates close to 50 percent, the nuclear family is often split, with children shuttled back and forth between mothers and fathers living at a distance from each other. The mental health consequences of divorce and single-parent families are well documented—anxiety and mood disorders in adolescence being one common outcome. Apart from the family, primary and secondary education focuses on acquisition of cognitive skills with little preparation for facing the demands of life. Without explicit and sanctioned rites of passage within the community to guide them from adolescence to adulthood, young people often rebel and may even run away from their families.

Separation from Community

In preindustrial society (and in many developing countries today) people lived in small villages where they knew one another and were tightly interdependent. When someone got married or died, the entire village showed up to acknowledge the occasion. If someone was unable to work due to accident or illness, the community pitched in to help.

By contrast, a sense of community is often hard to come by in modern urban society. People who live in single-family homes or in apartment complexes may barely be acquainted with their neighbors. If someone has an accident or needs help, people frequently drive by oblivious to their plight. No one in the community pitches in to help if you lose your job. In short, the basic human need for community cannot usually be satisfied in one's immediate neighborhood. Instead it is most frequently sought through church, twelve-step or support groups, or community service organizations. When modern people don't utilize these kinds of resources, they can feel very isolated.

Separation from Nature

In preindustrial society, people lived in small villages. The primary occupation was farming the land. Food was obtained locally or grown at home. To wash clothes, people went to the local stream or well. To heat the house, people had to go out and get wood from the forest or oil from fish. To go anywhere one either walked or rode on an animal. Life was intimately and immediately connected to nature.

Contrast this image with modern society where people commute on freeways to get to work, eat food and wear clothes that come from thousands of miles away, and may spend much of their time in front of their TV or computer screens. The highways around urban areas are jammed every Friday afternoon with thousands of people seeking refuge from the city in the countryside. There is no immediate and simple connection with nature in the urban environment, most of which is paved over. It's necessary to create such a connection in the form of a garden plot, picnic in the park, or an occasional vacation to the mountains or beach.

Separation from Self

A deeper and more serious form of separation peculiar to modern society is that which exists within the individual's own psyche. In preindustrial society, roles were very clearly defined and, by and large, people knew their places in their families and communities. Stresses occurred in the form of war, disease, or inclement weather leading to famine, and people simply did their best to contend with these unplanned aspects of life. Work consisted of farming, homemaking, skilled crafts, going to war, or joining a religious order. One's work served an immediate and obvious purpose for the community.

In modern society, work often doesn't have an immediate and obvious connection to either your own sense of self or to helping the community. Instead of meaningful work, you often have a routine job to help pay your bills. If you work on an assembly line or in a large corporate setting, what you do is simply a small link in a large system whose beginning or end is often hard to see or appreciate. After days of such work, combined with morning and afternoon commutes, all you may want to do is to get the kids to bed and escape into the TV, perhaps with an alcoholic beverage to soothe yourself. You may be just too hurried and stressed to even feel your innermost feelings; and why bother to feel the pain anyway, when it is easier to escape?

Over time stress accumulates. As it does, your inner pain grows and with it the need to escape. Addictions become convenient. Whether your addiction is work, alcohol or drugs, the TV screen, or taking care of someone, the alienation from your innermost self can grow. Then one day, finally, the separation and stress become so great that you panic. The panic may seem to come "out of the blue." But it has been a long time in the making.

Separation from a Higher Power

In preindustrial society, religion was often a part of daily life. Homes had spiritual relics or talismans with which people prayed. There were frequent ritual celebrations within the community honoring the god of their chosen religion. Attending church, the temple, or other sacred rituals was a major part of community life that no one questioned.

In modern society, the biggest part of community life often tends to be shopping at the mall. In a secular, materialistic culture, religion is something you do for an hour on Sunday (if at all), while the rest of the time you are striving to make ends meet and keep your children out of trouble. Rarely are there altars in private homes or community ritual celebrations where you directly experience the numinous reality of Spirit within yourself. God is often externalized and sometimes trivialized, as in the case of praying to obtain your dream home or help your favorite football team win. The consequence of alienation from spirituality is a sense, conscious or unconscious, of emptiness or meaninglessness about life. You're not sure what you truly want to do with your life because the creative inspiration and guidance simply aren't there.

It's difficult to confront this meaninglessness and very common to deny it. Often it's much easier to escape into various forms of addiction or compulsion, which may ease the pain but perpetuate the inner split. After years, however, you may finally panic, get seriously depressed or be stricken by some other serious illness. Something deep within is finally demanding a change—that you let go of a life of isolation and begin to search for connection.

Rebuilding Connection

You might ask yourself whether you have experienced any or all of the types of separation just described. Do you see a connection between them and your problem with anxiety? There is hope for healing the alienation created by modern society, yet it requires action on the part of each individual. Society will change when each of us changes. As you read through the remainder of this chapter, think about ways in which you might rebuild lost connections within your own life.

Communing with Nature

For many people working in cities or suburbs, it's not possible to live in remote natural settings and still commute to work. Often it's possible to get closer to nature by finding daily forms of recreation or exercise that are done outdoors—from walking in the park, to cycling on back roads, to merely jogging through a quiet residential neighborhood. Within your own backyard, you can plant a flower or vegetable garden. Working with plants and soil is a fine way to reconnect with the earth. Perhaps on days off or weekends you can travel out to the country to county or state parks, or further, to mountain or seashore recreational areas. You are likely to find that making direct connection with nature once per week will help relieve a good deal of the stress of urban living.

A more radical solution is to find a form of work you can do out of your home and to relocate to a natural setting. This is a healing choice from two standpoints. Not only does it more directly overcome a separation from nature, but also it eliminates the stress of a daily commute. I have personally been able to make such a choice and have found it to be very beneficial.

Finding Community

Work schedules and other constraints of modern life often make it difficult to get to know your neighbors in an apartment complex or on the same block. Creating community occurs more easily along lines of common interest rather than physical proximity. Support groups for men or women are perhaps the most viable way to find community in a fragmented society. While some are paid therapy groups, others are freestanding groups that may advertise in local papers or on bulletin boards. Among special interest groups, support groups for persons with anxiety disorders will be most relevant to many readers of this book. A list of networks offering support for persons with anxiety disorders can be found in Appendix 2. A great number of persons are subject to addictions, which may or may not necessarily involve a substance. Beyond the very numerous groups for persons recovering from alcohol and drug addiction, there are twelve-step groups for workaholics, those addicted to romance or sex (SLA), codependency, overeating, and many other issues. Phobics Anonymous offers twelve-step groups in many areas for persons recovering from anxiety disorders.

Service organizations offer a different path for healing the split between individual and community. While fellowship and affiliation are important goals of such groups or clubs, there is a strong emphasis on collaborating on projects to help the community.

Finally, the church remains an important place to find community, as well as to reconnect with a deeper spiritual life. Often it is the weekly classes at larger churches that offer the best opportunity to make friends and obtain support.

Connecting with Family

Rebuilding a sense of connection within the family first requires making time to do so. Allocating time away from work or household responsibilities for the family to be together as a whole is vital to building cohesion. Some of this time can be devoted to recreational activities, and some to what family therapists speak of as a family "conference" or "roundtable." The latter is a time when each family member has the opportunity to get a hearing about what they'd like to see change for the family as a whole or in a particular individual's behavior. Children are given an equal voice with parents, although parents get the final say on deciding family policies.

Basic communication skills are critical to enabling families to function in a healthy and intimate fashion. Family members can benefit themselves and each other by learning and practicing at least three basic skills: 1) the ability to listen and to *hear* each other without interruptions, 2) the ability to respect each family member's individuality and right to their point of view, whatever it may be, and 3) the ability to distinguish behaviors from persons—asking another family member to change a problem behavior rather than blaming or judging them personally. Communication skills can be learned through classes, workshops, or by working with a family therapist. As long as there is a commitment to heal family difficulties, these skills can be acquired in a relatively brief time.

Finally, creating an atmosphere of caring and mutual respect within the family requires a willingness to forgive. It is necessary to acknowledge and forgive mistakes from the past and then go on. Nothing works like forgiveness to overcome alienation and allow the potential for love that exists to emerge. You can make a difference in your family by being the first to initiate a process of forgiveness. See the chapter called "Learning to Love" (Chapter 14) for a more complete discussion of the role of forgiveness in healing fear and separation.

Connecting with a Higher Power

The church or spiritual organization of your choice is often the first place to go to search for a deeper connection with your Higher Power or God. The company of other persons exploring spirituality can go a long way to motivate and inspire you to make your own search. To maintain and deepen your commitment to spirituality, daily practices at home are also very important. Prayer is one such practice. Taking out time daily to ask for strength, support, guidance, or inspiration may help attune you to a spiritual power that can offer a deeper sense of meaningfulness in your life.

Meditation is another excellent practice. By quieting your mind, you can access an experience of stillness and serenity deep within. Out of that silence may emerge insights that give you answers to immediate problems and guidance about what to do next. See the chapter called "Developing Your Observing Self" (Chapter 9) for more detailed information on meditation.

Finally, the daily practice of inspirational reading is one of the best ways to lift your mind out of worried thinking into a place or "space" of uplifting thoughts. Both motivational and inspirational books can be a powerful form of "cognitive therapy." The positive ideas in such books will immediately help redirect your mind away from worry into an "atmosphere" of optimism and hope. A list of books that I have personally found uplifting can be found in Appendix 4.

Reconnecting with Yourself

Of all the forms of disconnection, separation from self plays the largest role in contributing to anxiety as well as other kinds of emotional difficulties. There may be many origins to a state of division within yourself, but it seems to me that the most important factors are past trauma and cumulative stress.

All of us were traumatized to varying degrees while growing up. Whether the loss or neglect of a parent, physical abuse, family alcoholism, excessive parental criticism, or simply moving too often, a majority of adults in contemporary society have suffered childhood trauma. Many of us responded to trauma by suppressing our true feelings and needs. The pain of what happened is so great that we sealed it off and decided to fit the image our parents and peers held up so we might feel as though we were loved. Thus began an internal split.

The challenges of growing up in modern society, performing in a competitive educational environment, leaving home, finding and maintaining employment, finding a partner, getting married, bearing and raising children—and all the upheaval that can occur at each of these critical points—create a continuous and cumulative source of stress. If you never truly learned as a child how to nurture and care for yourself, you have likely ignored this stress and kept pushing yourself even harder toward external goals, good grades, the best job, the right partner, the best home and lifestyle, continued career achievement, and so on. Society rewards each of us very well for these achievements, but the cost to our physical and emotional beings may often be too great. The cumulative stress of "getting ahead" in society, added to traumas of the past, splits some of us from ourselves to the extent that we become ill. Panic and/or phobias are a common outcome. Major depression is another. Psychosomatic syndromes such as ulcers, hypertension, irritable bowel syndrome, or migraine headaches are yet another.

The most loving response you can make to such illness, whatever form it takes, is to rebuild inner reconnection. This can be done through finding support in the form of therapy, support groups, as well as self-help books and tapes. It is often difficult to do this in isolation. To heal often requires a willingness to seek and receive help from outside. Those who make the choice for inner reconnection and healing, and then commit to that choice over time, tend to recover. A life-defeating and potentially dangerous choice, on the other hand, is to run further from yourself by escaping into addiction. Addiction—whether to substances, habits, or other persons—is often a desperate effort to hide from or ease the pain of a long-standing alienation from self. Tragically, it invariably serves to deepen the split. The eventual consequence of addiction, carried far enough, is illness, serious disease, and/or death. Many people choose to end their addiction at the point of illness—some wait until the stage of serious disease—and some choose death over facing the cumulative pain of a lifetime. Addictions are a most serious departure from self. Fortunately there are a tremendous number of resources available for helping to heal them.

Addiction may lead to the development of anxiety disorders or may be a desperate attempt to assuage anxiety. In either case, the anxiety disorder cannot be healed until the addiction is healed. Once free of attachment to drugs, work, or taking care of another addict, you are free to confront your own inner anxiety and heal the denial of your deepest feelings and needs that contributed to the development of anxiety in the first place.

This book offers a number of ways to reconnect with yourself. The following three chapters, "Simplifying Your Life," "Caring for Your Body: Relaxation, Exercise and Energy Balance," "Caring for Your Body: Nutrition," as well as all of the chapters in Part II are intended to help you establish a closer and more compassionate connection with yourself.

When you reconnect with your innermost being, there is no more need to compulsively search for stimulation or comfort outside yourself. You begin to discover that, by its very nature, *your innermost being is a source of peace, joy, and contentment.* It has always been and always will be the source of what is most fulfilling in life, beyond all of your conditioned perceptions of who you think you might be.

What You Can Do Now

Think over the five areas mentioned in this chapter—family, community, nature, your Higher Power, and yourself. What steps are you willing to take to restore a deeper sense of connection in each area? Write your responses on a separate piece of paper and then keep what you've written to refer back to.

3

Simplifying Your Life

Living more simply is a potent way to give yourself time and space to restore lost connections. To simplify your life is to live more deliberately and with a minimum of needless distractions. It is to establish a more direct and unencumbered relationship with all aspects of your life: work, family, community, nature, the cosmos, and yourself.

Simplifying your life does not mean living in poverty. Poverty is involuntary and disabling, whereas the choice for simplicity is one that is voluntary and empowering. Simplicity is finding the right balance between austerity and excess. It's somewhere between a log cabin in the forest and an estate in the suburbs. Simplicity can even be achieved in an urban environment, if living in the country is unrealistic. Above all, simple living does not mean doing away with modern comforts and conveniences to prove your ability to live apart from twentieth-century technology. Gandhi made an interesting statement about denying the material side of life: "As long as you derive inner help and comfort from anything, you should keep it. If you were to give it up in a mood of self-sacrifice or out of a stern sense of duty, you would continue to want it back, and that unsatisfied want would make trouble for you."

There is no precise formula defining what constitutes living simply. Each individual is likely to discover his or her own ways to reduce complexity and unnecessary encumbrances. One author who has thought a lot about simplicity, Duane Elgin (1994), proposes the following list. Those who choose to simplify their lives:

- Tend to invest the time and energy freed up by simpler living in activities with their partner, children, and friends (walking, making music together, sharing a meal, camping, etc.)

- Tend to work on developing the full spectrum of their potentials: physical (running, biking, hiking, etc.), emotional (learning the skills of intimacy and sharing feelings in important relationships), mental (engaging in lifelong learning by reading, taking classes, etc.), and spiritual (learning to move through life with a quiet mind and compassionate heart)

- Tend to feel an intimate connection with the earth and a reverential concern for nature

- Tend to feel a compassionate concern for the world's poor

- Tend to lower their overall level of personal consumption—buy less clothing, for example (with more attention to what is functional, durable, aesthetic, and less concern with passing fads, fashions, and seasonal styles)

- Tend to alter their patterns of consumption in favor of products that are durable, easy to repair, nonpolluting in their manufacture and use, energy-efficient, functional, and aesthetic

- Tend to shift their diet away from highly processed foods, meat, and sugar toward foods that are more natural, healthy, and simple

- Tend to reduce undue clutter and complexity in their personal lives by giving away or selling those possessions that are seldom used and could be used productively by others (clothing, books, furniture, appliances, tools, etc.)

- Tend to recycle metal, glass, and paper and to cut back on consumption of items that are wasteful of nonrenewable resources

- Tend to develop personal skills that contribute to greater self-reliance and reduce dependence upon experts to handle life's ordinary demands (basic carpentry, plumbing, appliance repair, etc.)

- Tend to prefer smaller-scale, more human-sized living and working environments that foster a sense of community, face-to-face contact, and mutual caring

- Tend to participate in holistic health-care practices that emphasize preventive medicine and the healing powers of the body when assisted by the mind

- Tend to change transportation modes in favor of public transit, car pooling, smaller and more fuel-efficient autos, living closer to work, riding a bike, and walking

Notice how these shifts in lifestyle might serve to heal the sources of disconnection and alienation mentioned in the preceding chapter. If anything, a simpler life gives you more *time* to foster connections with your family, community, nature, Higher Power, as well as yourself. Nothing in nature is isolated—it's only the abstract, conceptual mind that creates distinctions and separations. When you allow yourself to experience the various levels of relatedness that are natural or "indigenous" to life, you begin to overcome separation and heal the problem of anxiety at its roots.

There have been indications in recent years that an increasing number of persons have favored simplifying their lives. After thirty years of economic expansion and material growth, the decade of the nineties was, for many, a time of downsizing. According to a survey conducted in 1991 and quoted by Duane Elgin in *Voluntary Simplicity*:

- 69 percent of the people surveyed said they would like to "slow down and live a more relaxed life," in contrast to only 19 percent who said they would like to "live a more exciting, faster-paced life."

- 61 percent agreed that "earning a living today requires so much effort that it's difficult to find time to enjoy life."

- When asked about their priorities, 89 percent said it was more important these days to spend time with their families.

- Only 13 percent saw importance in keeping up with fashion trends and just 7 percent thought it was worth bothering to shop for status-symbol products.

A poll published in June 1997 in *USA Today* illustrated the fact that by mid-decade (1995) 28 percent of Americans reported they had deliberately made life changes during the preceding five years that resulted in less income, with 87 percent of them reporting satisfaction with the change.

How I Simplified My Life

The trend toward simplification is one in which I've participated. In the midst of my own personal crisis with anxiety, I realized that making my life as simple as possible would be an important part of the healing. A good deal of the stress in my life had resulted from buying into the complexity of life in modern society. There was much that I thought I needed that I actually didn't. Over a period of a year, I made a number of changes—both large and small—that served to reduce the unnecessary complications in my life. I will offer you my personal life-simplification program as an inspiration to create your own, realizing that not all of the items on my list may be feasible or even desirable for you.

Moving to a Small Town

After almost twenty-five years of living in large, urban metropolitan areas, I decided to move to a small town of fewer than ten thousand people. I found that I felt a greater sense of ease in an area where there were no freeways and only rare episodes of traffic congestion. Everything I needed was within easy driving distance, and it took only five minutes to drive out of town to open countryside. Just having a lower population density in itself made a significant difference in the ambiance of the surrounding environment.

I realize that the opportunity to move to a smaller town may not be available or desirable for you. Perhaps your problem with anxiety requires that you confront driving on freeways or dealing with traffic congestion. If so, my sympathies are with you and I hope you may benefit from some of the other strategies to follow.

Downsizing Your Living Situation

Presently, I'm living in a small condominium, a considerable downsizing from the house where I once lived. It's simply not possible for me to accumulate a large number of possessions because there's no room for them. While it was an adjustment at first, I find I'm quite comfortable in smaller quarters. It takes less than an hour to clean and is a whole lot less expensive to maintain.

Letting Go of Things You Don't Need

When I chose to move to a smaller home, I realized much of what I'd previously owned would have to go. Since I wanted to make a fresh start in my life, I decided to let go of everything, including about 95 percent of the furniture, clothes, and books I'd accumulated for three decades. I felt a tremendous sense of freedom and exhilaration in letting go of so many things that I didn't really use or need. In letting go of so much of what was associated with my past, I allowed myself a wide-open space to recreate my life—something that was necessary for my healing.

As a general rule, if you want to reduce clutter, I suggest you consider letting go of everything you haven't used in more than a year, except, of course, items that have sentimental value.

Doing What You Want for a Living

For many years I thought I needed to see twenty to twenty-five clients per week in order to support my lifestyle. The energy expenditure required for such a practice exceeded my personal resources (twenty-five clients equals at least fifty hours' work when you include case preparation, letter writing, telephone calls, insurance billing, and so on). I didn't leave myself enough time for rest and recreation, and, over time, I paid an increasing price. Besides, there was little time left to write, which is what I enjoyed doing most.

Now I've reduced my expenditures to the point where I only do eight to ten phone consultations per week out of my home and have plenty of time for rest, recreation, and writing. The difference in the way I feel—the sense of ease in my life—is enormous.

Doing what you truly want may require time, risk, and effort. It may take one to two years to gain the retraining or retooling you need to begin a new career. Then you may have to endure some time at an entry level before your new line of work meets your financial needs. In my estimation—and those of others who have done it—the time, effort, and disruption involved are worth it.

Reducing Your Commute

Reducing or eliminating your commute to work is one of the most significant changes you can make in simplifying your life. It doesn't take much reflection to see the extent to which negotiating rush hour traffic on a daily basis can add to stress. Moving closer to where you work or choosing to live in a smaller town can help reduce your commute. At the very least, if you have to commute over a long distance, you can try to arrange for flexible hours (to avoid rush hour) or have a comfortable car with a tape deck. At this time, nearly 15 percent of Americans work out of their homes, and the number is rising. If you can figure out a consulting service or computer-based job you can do out of your home, you can join them.

Reducing Exposure to TV

How much time during the day do you spend in front of a screen? When I was a child there were three channels on the TV, and I had to get up out of my chair and walk over to the TV to switch from one to another. In the nineties, the average household had two to three TVs, each with an average of forty to sixty channels. As if this were not enough, forty million American households have computers offering an endless array of child and adult games as well as Internet access to thousands of topics and virtually millions of web sites. Granted, there are many good programs on TV, and the Internet is a wonderful tool for communicating information. My concern is with the sheer complexity of having so many options, all of which involve a passive stance of either witnessing entertainment or absorbing information. While life in front of the screen can be a distraction from anxiety, I wonder how it can contribute to rebuilding a deeper connection with nature, others, or oneself. If anxiety arises from too much stimulation and an experience of disconnection on multiple levels, then it seems to me that time in front of the screen might be done in moderation. Personally, I rarely watch TV and use the Internet in moderation. I prefer the simplicity of spending my time in nature, reading a good book, or developing my creative outlets in writing and music.

Living Close to Nature

Anxiety states are often associated with feelings of disembodiment. Being ungrounded and out of touch with your feelings and physical body is especially evident in the sensations of depersonalization or derealization that can accompany acute anxiety or panic. This disconnection can be aggravated in situations that involve being literally disconnected from the earth, such as riding in a car, being high up in a tall building, or flying. It may also be aggravated in situations where you are bombarded with so many stimuli that your awareness is scattered or dispersed, such as a grocery store, shopping mall, or social gathering.

Taking a walk in the woods or a park is a simple act that can help reverse the tendency to feel disembodied. Being in close proximity to the earth—its sights, sounds, smells and energies—can help you to remain more easily connected with yourself. Choosing to live in such a setting, if possible, allows you to reestablish a connection with earth—that much of modern civilization seems to have lost—on an ongoing basis.

Taming the Telephone

It surprises me to learn that there are people who feel they "should" answer the phone virtually every time it rings, regardless of the time of day or the mood they're in at the time. Whether it's a creditor, a sales solicitation, or a cantankerous relative, some people feel it is an almost sacred obligation to answer every call. For me personally, I have found that life is more simple, peaceful, and easy when I don't have to listen to the phone ring. If I'm in the middle of a meal, a writing project, or meditating, I don't have to worry who might be calling. I used to have an answering machine, but its clicking was only a small improvement over a phone. Now my voice mail faithfully collects all of my messages without my having to hear anything. Then I'm free to respond to them at my leisure. While some readers may feel that I'm not appropriately responsive to my callers, I would rather call them when I'm in the mood to offer them my full and best attention.

Delegating Menial Chores

How many menial chores would you delegate to someone else if money were not an issue? In my own situation, I've been able to simplify my life by delegating most house cleaning, typing, billing, and tax preparation, among other things. Even delegating one activity you don't like to do can make a difference in the sense of ease you bring to your day-to-day life. If money is an issue, is there something your children could learn to do just about as well as you? Can you allow other family members to help with the cooking, yard upkeep, or housecleaning?

Learning to Say "No"

Learning to say no was a major issue in my own case. For many years friends, family, and clients pretty much could rely on me to be available to them on demand, and I prided myself for being so consistently "helpful." The end result of many years of this co-dependent lifestyle was serious burnout and exhaustion. Presently I've learned to carefully evaluate each request I receive as to whether it is serving both my highest interest and the other person's highest interest to respond. Life has definitely been simpler and easier as I've learned to set limits that are consistent with my available energies and capabilities. I feel I can offer my best to others when I am not overextending myself to do so.

There are many other ways you might choose to simplify your life. For example, you can reduce the amount of junk mail you receive by writing to an organization called Stop The Mail at P.O. Box 9008, Farmingdale, NY 11735. Request that your name not be sold to mailing list companies, and you will likely reduce your junk mail by up to 75 percent. Or you can eliminate all of your credit cards except for one, as I did. Having one card comes in handy for making telephone purchases or renting a car. Apart from that, you will save yourself a lot of monthly bills as well as annual fees by reducing your number of credit cards.

About one hundred other ways to simplify your life are clearly described in an excellent book entitled *Simplify Your Life* by Elaine St. James (1994). The author offers a wide range of life-simplification strategies in the areas of work, relationship, finances, health, household, and leisure time. If you're serious about making your lifestyle more simple and easy, the book is an invaluable remedy for the frenzied pace and high complexity of modern life.

Now it's your turn. Take some time to think about ways in which you might simplify your life. Use the following questionnaire to assist your deliberation.

SIMPLIFYING YOUR LIFE QUESTIONNAIRE

1. On a 1 to 10 scale, with "1" representing a high degree of simplicity and "10" representing a high degree of complexity, where would you rate your own lifestyle at present?

2. Have you made any changes in your living arrangements in the past year toward simplicity? If so, what changes?

3. What changes toward simplifying your life would you like to make in general?

4. What changes toward simplifying your life are you *willing* to make in the next year?

5. Check off any of the following simplification strategies you would be willing to try or initiate in the next two months:

_____ Reduce the clutter in your home

_____ Move to a smaller house

_____ Move to a smaller town

_____ Move close to shopping resources so you can do all of your errands quickly

_____ Buy less clothing, with attention to what is functional, durable, and aesthetic—rather than fashionable

_____ Drive a simple, fuel-efficient car

_____ Reduce dependence on your TV

_____ Reduce dependence on outside entertainment (movies, plays, theater, concerts, nightclubs, etc.)

_____ Reduce (or eliminate) magazine subscriptions

_____ Stop newspaper delivery

_____ Stop junk mail

_____ Stop answering the phone whenever it rings

_____ Reduce your commute (if possible, walk or ride your bike to work)

_____ Work where you live

_____ Tell your family and friends you no longer do Christmas gifts (or cards, for that matter)

_____ Take one suitcase if you vacation and only pack essential clothes

_____ Take your vacation near or at home

_____ Reduce your consumption to avoid luxury or designer items; favor products that are durable, easy to repair, and nonpolluting

_____ Take steps to get out of debt

_____ Keep only one credit card

_____ Consolidate your bank accounts

_____ Delegate busywork (e.g., yard work, house cleaning, tax preparation)

_____ Simplify your eating habits to include whole, unprocessed foods

_____ Buy groceries less often, in bulk

_____ Make water your drink of choice

_____ Pack your own lunch

_____ Learn to say no

_____ Stop trying to change people

_____ Stop trying to please people—be yourself

_____ Dispose of all personal possessions you don't really need

_____ Do what you truly want for a living

Some of these changes can be done quickly; others involve a process. It may take a year or two, for example, to arrange your life so that you're doing something you truly enjoy for a living. To dispose of unnecessary possessions, put aside things you think you won't need for a year in a locked closet or storage compartment. At the end of the year, if you've not given them any thought throughout the entire time, let them go. Learning to say no or to stop always trying to please other people requires that you develop assertiveness skills, which you can acquire through classes, workshops, counseling, and books. Getting out of debt is a process that may be helped by consulting the book by Jerry Mundis, _How to Get Out of Debt, Stay Out of Debt, and Live Prosperously_ (see the list of references at the end of this chapter).

I hope this chapter may have given you some ideas about how to reduce the complexity in your life. Living more simply was an important part of my own recovery and may be important for you as well. Greater simplicity in your life will give you more time and ease to build the kinds of connections described in the preceding chapter. It will help you to make healing your problem with anxiety your first priority.

References and Further Reading

Elgin, Duane. 1993. _Voluntary Simplicity_. New York: William Morrow.

Mundis, Jerold. 1990. _How to Get Out of Debt, Stay Out of Debt, and Live Prosperously_. New York: Bantam Books.

St. James, Elaine. 1994. _Simplify Your Life_. New York: Hyperion.

4

Caring for Your Body: Relaxation, Exercise, and Energy Balance

A relaxed and healthy body is less prone to fearful thoughts and feelings. It's that simple: If you take good care of your physical body, you are likely to experience less anxiety.

Most contemporary treatment approaches to anxiety disorders emphasize cognitive therapy—retraining the mind toward constructive thinking. The guiding assumption of cognitive therapy is that replacing fearful, "what-if" thoughts (and underlying mistaken beliefs) with constructive, realistic thinking will promote more adaptive behavior in the face of panic symptoms or phobic avoidance. Anxiety is seen foremost as a result of irrational, catastrophic thinking. Yet the question remains: From where does catastrophic thinking arise? In part from force of habit, to be sure. And certainly from your entire history of previous experience dealing with threatening or fearful situations. Yet self-observation also leads to the conclusion that under conditions of stress, tension, illness, or fatigue, you're likely to be prone to more negative, irrational thinking than when you're feeling well, healthy, and exuberant. While negative thoughts certainly lead to negative moods and feelings, it's also apparent that negative somatic (physical) states arising from stress, muscle tension, underbreathing, overbreathing, or neurotransmitter imbalances help instigate negative thinking. Causal relationships between thoughts and emotional states go both ways. There is no good answer to the question: "Which came first?" Feelings and thoughts are so thoroughly intertwined that it's difficult to detect where a particular depressed mood or anxious state had its origin.

What's important is that it's possible to break the loop between negative thoughts and negative somatic states at either the cognitive or the somatic end. While cognitive therapy is an important strategy for confronting and changing unhelpful thoughts, the cultivation of feeling physically well and vital is equally important since a well body can promote "well" thinking. The most efficient route to healing fear is to cultivate both a positive mind-set and a healthy body.

You don't have to look far to observe how people overly stress and fail to care for their physical bodies. It's ironic that we live in a society where many people take better care of their homes or cars than they do their own health. The dominant messages of modern life tell us to do more, have more, achieve more, and withstand more rather than to live in harmony with ourselves and nature. It may not be until you become quite ill that you reevaluate your attitude and make a commitment to care for and nurture your physical well-being.

Guideposts to better health and wellness are plainly visible. In the past twenty years literally hundreds of self-help books have been written on subjects such as stress management, nutrition, exercise, how to lose weight, how to sleep better, and so on. The holistic health movement has encouraged many persons to rely less on the medical establishment and take more responsibility for their health through changes in lifestyle and daily habits. In my previous book, *The Anxiety & Phobia Workbook*, I outlined in some detail guidelines for incorporating relaxation, exercise, and better nutrition into your life. In this chapter and the next, I want to reiterate the importance of relaxation, exercise, and nutrition for healing anxiety and fear. Some of the guidelines presented will be familiar to those of your who have read *The Anxiety & Phobia Workbook*, although many others are new.

The key issue is not just a particular set of guidelines but your own personal priorities. As you read through the following sections addressing relaxation, exercise, and energy balance (as well as the following chapter on nutrition), it's important to ask yourself: *"How willing am I to make real changes in any of these areas?"*

Part 1: Relaxation

You cannot be relaxed and anxious at the same time. Your ability to relax is at the very foundation of all the skills, strategies, and attitudes you need to heal fear and anxiety. You know when you are relaxed by the way you feel. There are four characteristic signs of being relaxed:

- You are able to breathe easily and deeply, filling both your chest cavity and abdominal area.

- The muscles throughout your body feel soft, loose, flexible and unconstrained.

- Your heart beats calmly and regularly, easily circulating your blood throughout your body so that your hands and feet are usually warm.

- Your mind is clear and calm; you are undistracted and can concentrate easily.

When you are relaxed, a distinct part of your autonomic nervous system—the *parasympathetic nervous system*—is activated. The parasympathetic nervous system is responsible for maintaining normal function of your internal organ systems in times of rest and quiescence. It exactly reverses the effects of the *sympathetic nervous system*, whose function is to activate your body for fight or flight in response to any perceived threat. The sympathetic nervous system increases your heart rate, respiration, blood pressure, and metabolism, tells your muscles to contract, and signals the release of adrenaline. It plays a major role in precipitating stress as well as panic attacks. The parasympathetic nervous system signals all of the organs in your body to slow down and for your muscles to stop contracting. Its function is to return your body to rest after a period of exertion or stress.

People who are anxious or under stress tend to experience high levels of sympathetic nervous system activation much of the time. To use popular expressions, they are "worked up" or "uptight." Even during the times when they begin to calm down, any minor circumstance can "set them off" once again. After you have been in a state of hyperarousal for a long period of time, the sympathetic nervous system "learns" to be triggered at the slightest provocation. At this point, panic disorder may develop.

Cultivating relaxation, at the most basic physiological level, means to strengthen your predisposition to parasympathetic nervous system activation and to decrease your tendency toward "hair trigger" sympathetic nervous system activation. A preference for parasympathetic nervous system arousal is sometimes called "parasympathetic dominance." The good news is that parasympathetic dominance can be *learned*.

There are three keys to cultivating relaxation in your life. If you are serious about becoming more relaxed, you will benefit most by practicing all three:

- Giving relaxation a high priority in your life

- Practicing some form of deep relaxation (such as abdominal breathing or meditation) on a daily basis

- Pacing your life so that you have breaks and periods of downtime alternating with work and exertion

Giving Priority to Relaxation

After years of addressing my own anxiety issues and working with hundreds of clients, I believe that the most important key to relaxation is simply making it a priority. Relaxation is not hard to learn, nor is it hard to practice. What's difficult for many people is to give it much time or energy. It often seems that work, household responsibilities, entertainment, and stimulation are more important. Going to the mall or watching sports on TV is more compelling than meditating or listening to a relaxation tape. This is not surprising in our modern society. The messages we receive from childhood on have to do with achieving, accomplishing, performing, "getting it done." So our days are filled with a hundred things to do both at work and at home. The pace at which most of us work, travel, and live is considerably faster than it has been at any previous time in human history. So, it's no surprise that many people find it difficult to make time to stop and do nothing other than relax. Relaxation is often thought of as doing something distracting, such as watching TV or going to a movie. Yet true relaxation is more than mere distraction. It's slowing down to a full stop, something many persons are just not accustomed to doing. It is an act of will that runs counter to both the values and rhythm of our advanced, technological world.

The issue, then, is not just learning the "right" relaxation technique but making the time and commitment on a consistent basis to practice relaxation in your daily life.

In deciding whether you are willing to make relaxation a priority in your life, it may be helpful to consider the following checklist of attitudes that interfere with a relaxed lifestyle. Do any of them apply in your case? What gets in the way of giving yourself time to relax?

Common attitudes that interfere with relaxation

1. **"I have too much to do—there's no time."**

"I have too much to do," is simply to say relaxation has low priority. What you give your time to is what you give priority. If relaxation has importance in your life, you'll find the time for it.

2. **"Relaxation is too boring."**

    If you feel relaxation is too boring, you may have limited acquaintance with how refreshing and revitalizing a truly relaxed state feels. You may not have learned yet to relax deeply. Keep practicing relaxation techniques until you can experience the true benefit of deep relaxation.

3. **"I watch TV—isn't that relaxation?" "I read the newspaper—isn't that relaxation?"**

    If watching TV or reading the newspaper are what you think of as relaxation, again, you may not yet be familiar with the intrinsic pleasure of being deeply relaxed.

4. **"I have to take care of others."**

    Taking time out from caretaking to relax is again a question of priorities. Although it may be challenging at first to make the time, those you care for will benefit when you care for yourself.

5. **"I just don't have the discipline."**

    If you feel you don't have the discipline to practice regular periods of relaxation, apply the "three-week rule." If you can get yourself to practice deep relaxation every day for three weeks, it will likely become a habit (just like brushing your teeth).

6. **"I'm just too tense to unwind."**

    Being too tense to relax may be a problem. One solution is to exercise first, especially to the point of exertion. After you discharge excess adrenaline and energy, it may be easier to relax. Another alternative is to have someone give you a good back rub, which is likely to help no matter how tense you feel.

7. **"It won't help, anyway."**

    If you believe "it won't help anyway," you might ask yourself whether you have truly given relaxation a fair chance. If your belief "it won't help" is based on prior experience attempting to relax, perhaps you did not stay with it long enough.

8. **"I'm afraid to relax—I might lose control."**

    If this applies to you, start off gently in practicing the relaxation techniques described in the following section. Try abdominal breathing or progressive muscle relaxation only for two or three minutes at first and work up gradually to longer time periods. Should you start to feel anxious at any time, simply open your eyes and stop whatever procedure you're practicing until you feel better. Time and practice are the keys to increasing your tolerance for deeper states of relaxation. If your tolerance doesn't improve, it would be helpful to consult a therapist skilled in treating anxiety disorders to assist you in desensitizing yourself to the anxiety you feel about relaxation.

Ultimately, it's up to you to decide how much of a priority you want to make relaxation. Making time to "just be" and to cultivate inner peace can become the foundation of your life if you want it to. But it requires that you give relaxation a place along with household responsibilities, work, entertainment, and the pursuit of your other personal goals. Who you believe you are and who you want to be is reflected in where you put your time and energy. *When you decide in your innermost self that personal peace is truly important, you'll spend the necessary time to cultivate it.*

Practicing Deep Relaxation on a Daily Basis

In 1975 Herbert Benson first described the body's ability to enter into a deep state of relaxation. In his classic book, *The Relaxation Response* (1975), he enumerated a distinctive set of physiological changes associated with deep relaxation:

- Decrease in heart rate

- Decrease in respiration rate

- Decrease in blood pressure

- Decrease in skeletal muscle tension

- Decrease in metabolic rate and oxygen consumption

- Decrease in analytical thinking

- Increase in skin resistance

- Increase in alpha wave activity in the brain

The most significant thing about Benson's relaxation response is that it can be *trained*. If you're unaccustomed to allowing yourself to deeply relax, you can learn how. Once you've learned, regular practice of deep relaxation for twenty to thirty minutes per day can produce, over time, a general sense of relaxation in the rest of your life. In short, you will find that you feel more relaxed all of the time if you make a commitment to enter into a deeply relaxed state for twenty to thirty minutes each day. This "generalization effect" holds up independent of the quantity and quality of your sleep. Giving yourself time to relax deeply each day will make it easier to let go and relax at other times, as well as prevent the stresses of daily life from becoming cumulative. In fact, people who relax deeply on a daily basis experience a number of long-term benefits in addition to this generalized relaxation. Such benefits include a reduction of generalized anxiety, an increase in energy level, improved concentration and memory, reduced insomnia, relief from a variety of psychosomatic ailments (such as hypertension, ulcers, migraines, asthma, etc.), and increased self-confidence.

How do you enter into a deep state of relaxation or elicit the "relaxation response"? Four common techniques are described below, each of which is often used in the standard treatment of anxiety disorders.

Abdominal Breathing

Abdominal breathing is the most direct and effective somatic technique for reducing anxiety. A few minutes of practice can "turn off" your sympathetic nervous system and activate your parasympathetic system. Practiced regularly over time, abdominal breathing will help you to feel more relaxed in general; practiced in the moment you feel anxious, it will work to offset that anxiety immediately.

Research shows that people who are anxious tend to breathe shallowly and from their chest, while those who are more relaxed breathe more slowly, deeply, and from their abdomens. Shallow, chest-level breathing can aggravate anxiety in either of two ways. If you are underbreathing and not getting enough oxygen to your brain, you may be prone to develop a "closed-in" feeling that becomes progressively more uncomfortable. The "trapped" sensation that prompts many phobic persons to want to flee situations like elevators, waiting in line, or driving in traffic may in part be due to oxygen starvation from underbreathing (along with the restriction of their ability to move). The other type of problem caused by chest-level breathing is breathing rapidly to the point where you exhale too much carbon dioxide. This happens especially if you are breathing through your mouth. Often referred to as *hyperventilation*, this form of overbreathing leads to a cluster of uncomfortable symptoms including jitteriness, tingling in your extremities or face, dizziness, disorientation, and even a sense of unreality or depersonalization. If you interpret hyperventilation symptoms as threatening or dangerous (which they aren't), you may well trigger a panic attack.

The remedy for underbreathing or overbreathing (hyperventilation) is the same: to learn to breathe more deeply, from your abdomen instead of your chest.

Practicing abdominal breathing is the most rapid and direct technique you can use to offset anxiety and relax. A few minutes of breathing from your abdomen can "switch off" the arousal of the sympathetic nervous system associated with anxiety and activate your parasympathetic nervous system. Abdominal breathing is always the first technique I teach my clients to help them cope better with anxiety.

Regular daily practice of abdominal breathing will retrain you to breathe more from your diaphragm and less from your chest. The result is that you will feel more relaxed in general. The abdominal breathing techniques described below can also be used to offset anxiety in the moment it arises. The first technique is presented again in Chapter 6 as a specific technique for coping with panic attacks. For purposes of this chapter, either of the following two breathing techniques can be used as a method for eliciting a state of deep relaxation. Either technique will promote a state of relaxation quickly—generally in about five to ten minutes.

The way you know you are doing abdominal breathing is simple: If you place your hand on your stomach, your hand should rise as you inhale and fall as you exhale. Your chest, however, should move very little or not at all. It's best to sit or lie down while practicing abdominal breathing, as indicated in the following exercise:

ABDOMINAL BREATHING EXERCISE

1. Place one hand on your abdomen, right beneath your rib cage—preferably while sitting or lying down.

2. Inhale slowly and deeply through your nose into the bottom of your lungs (the deepest point in your lungs that you can reach). Your chest should move only slightly, while your stomach rises, pushing your hand up.

3. When you've inhaled fully, pause for a moment and then exhale fully through your nose or your mouth. Be sure to exhale fully. As you exhale, allow yourself to let go and imagine your entire body going loose and limp.

In order to fully relax, take and release ten abdominal breaths. (When you've completed ten breaths, keep practicing abdominal breathing for five to ten minutes more.) Try to keep your breathing *smooth* and *regular* throughout, without gulping in air or exhaling suddenly. It will help to slow down your breathing if you slowly count to four ("one . . . two . . . three . . . four") on the inhale and then slowly count to four again on the exhale. Use the one to four count for at least the first two or three days of practicing abdominal breathing.

After you've become proficient in slowing down your breathing, you can drop the one to four count if you wish. At this point, try counting backward from twenty down to one, one count after each exhale. That is, after the first exhale count "twenty," after the next "nineteen," and so on, down to zero. Remember to keep your breath slow and regular throughout, inhaling through your nose and exhaling through your nose or mouth.

Continue to practice abdominal breathing for at least five minutes. After counting down twenty breaths, start over again. If you start to feel light-headed at any time, stop for thirty seconds and then start up again.

CALMING BREATH EXERCISE

The Calming Breath Exercise was adapted from the ancient discipline of yoga. It is a very efficient technique for achieving a deep state of relaxation quickly.

1. Breathing from your abdomen, inhale through your nose slowly to a count of five (count slowly "one . . . two . . . three . . . four . . . five" as you inhale).

2. Pause and hold your breath to a slow count of five.

3. Exhale slowly, through your nose or mouth, to a slow count of five (or more if it takes you longer). Be sure to exhale fully.

4. When you've exhaled completely, take two breaths in your normal rhythm, then repeat the first three steps in the cycle above.

Keep up the exercise for at least three to five minutes. This should involve going through at least ten cycles of breathe in—count five, hold—count five, breathe out—count five. As you continue the exercise, you may notice that you can count higher than five, or count higher when you exhale than when you inhale. If these variations in your counting do occur, simply allow them to, continuing with the exercise for up to five minutes. Remember to take two normal breaths between each cycle. If you start to feel light-headed while practicing this exercise, stop for thirty seconds and then start again.

Throughout the exercise, keep your breathing *smooth* and *regular*, without gulping in breaths or breathing out suddenly.

Optional: Each time you exhale, you may wish to say "relax," "calm," "let go," or any other relaxing word or phrase silently to yourself. Allow your whole body to let go as you do this. If you keep this up each time you practice, eventually just saying your relaxing word by itself will bring on a mild state of relaxation.

The calming breath exercise can be a potent technique for halting the momentum of a panic reaction when the first signs of anxiety come on. It is also useful in reducing symptoms of hyperventilation.

I recommend you try both of these techniques, but work on mastering the basic abdominal breathing technique first. Practice for at least *five minutes at a time, three times per day, for at least three weeks*. If possible, find regular times each day to do this so that your breathing exercise becomes a habit. With practice you can learn in a short period of time to slow down the physiological reactions underlying anxiety.

When you become proficient with both techniques, choose the one you prefer to practice on a regular basis.

Progressive Muscle Relaxation

After abdominal breathing, progressive muscle relaxation (PMR) is the most common relaxation technique taught by therapists who work with clients who are anxious or stressed. PMR is especially helpful for persons who experience significant muscle tension associated with their anxiety. If you have a tendency to carry high levels of tension in your neck, shoulders, and upper back, I recommend that you learn and practice PMR on a regular basis.

Progressive muscle relaxation was developed in the 1930s by Dr. Edmund Jacobson, who found it was very effective in reducing high blood pressure. Dr. Jacobson discovered that a muscle could be relaxed by first tensing it for a few seconds and then releasing it. Tensing and relaxing various muscle groups throughout the body in sequence produces a deep state of relaxation. Again, this technique is particularly helpful for relieving tight muscles. Other symptoms that respond well to PMR include tension headaches, backaches, tightness in the jaw or around the eyes, high blood pressure, and insomnia. If you are troubled with racing thoughts, you may find that PMR helps you to slow down your mind. Dr. Jacobson himself once said: "An anxious mind cannot exist in a relaxed body."

There are no contraindications for progressive muscle relaxation unless the muscle groups to be tensed and relaxed have been injured. If you take tranquilizers, you may find that regular practice of progressive muscle relaxation will enable you to lower your dosage.

Detailed instructions for practicing progressive muscle relaxation are presented in Appendix 3.

Guided Visualizations

Guided visualizations for relaxation provide an alternative way to achieve a deeply relaxed state without having to tense and relax muscle groups—or do anything at all, apart from listening to a tape. Such visualizations may not release deep-seated muscle tension quite like PMR, and they may not have quite the distraction value of more active techniques. Yet, if you are able to follow and immerse yourself in the particular visualization, you will find it to be deeply relaxing. Many of my clients use guided visualizations on a regular basis to relax.

Scripts and detailed guidelines for practicing guided visualizations can be found in Chapter 12 of *The Anxiety & Phobia Workbook*. Also see the book *Visualization for Change* by Patrick Fanning (1994). Audio cassettes with relaxing visualizations are commonly available at your local bookstore.

Meditation

Meditation is the oldest and most universal relaxation technique. It has been practiced in the Far East for over five thousand years. Traditionally, the purposes and benefits of meditation have been spiritual in nature: becoming one with a deity, attaining enlightenment, achieving selflessness. While many people still practice meditation today for spiritual purposes, just as many do so apart from any religious framework for personal growth or for the simple purpose of relaxing.

Meditation was popularized in the United States in the midsixties as transcendental meditation or TM. In transcendental meditation, an instructor selects a Sanskrit mantra (a word or sound) for you, such as "Om Shanti" or "So Hum." You are then instructed to repeat the sound mentally while sitting in a quiet place. You learn to concentrate completely—without forcing it—on the mantra while letting any distractions just pass through your mind.

In the 1970s, Herbert Benson did research on transcendental meditation, which he published in his book, *The Relaxation Response*. Benson developed his own version of meditation, which involved mentally repeating the word "one" with each exhalation of breath. He documented a number of physiological effects of meditation, including a decrease in heart rate, blood pressure, oxygen consumption, metabolic rate, and lactic acid in the blood.

Benson also established that the positive benefits of meditation are not exclusive to TM, and that an individually selected mantra is unnecessary. His own "respiratory-one" method achieved the same physiological effects as transcendental meditation.

Meditation has repeatedly been found to reduce chronic anxiety. Regular practice of meditation has many benefits including: 1) sharpened alertness, 2) increased energy level and productivity, 3) decreased self-criticism, 4) increased objectivity (the capacity to view situations without judging them), 5) decreased dependence on alcohol or recreational drugs, 6) increased accessibility of emotions, and 7) heightened self-esteem and sense of identity.

Meditation can be used simply as a relaxation technique or as a method for increasing your ability to observe rather than react to ongoing thoughts and feelings. Chapter 9 of this book, "Developing Your Observing Self," explores the latter function of meditation in depth. Specific exercises for practicing meditation are offered. I have personally found the regular practice of meditation to be a very important component of my own recovery from anxiety difficulties.

Guidelines for Practicing Any Relaxation Technique

The following guidelines will help you to make the most of any deep relaxation technique you choose to practice. You may want to photocopy these guidelines and keep them handy when you're first learning a relaxation technique:

1. Practice at least *twenty minutes per day* (except for abdominal breathing, which you should do for five to ten minutes, three times per day). Two twenty-minute periods are preferable. Once a day is mandatory if you want to make a difference in the quality of your life. (You may want to begin your practice with thirty-minute periods. As you gain skill in relaxation techniques, you will find that the amount of time you need to experience deep relaxation will decrease.)

2. Find a *quiet location* to practice where you won't be distracted. Don't permit the phone to ring while you're practicing. Use a fan or air conditioner to blot out background noise if necessary.

3. Practice at *regular times*. On awakening, before retiring, or before meals are generally the best times. A consistent daily routine will increase the likelihood of generalization effects.

4. Practice on an *empty stomach*. Food digestion after meals will tend to disrupt deep relaxation.

5. Assume a *comfortable position*. Your entire body, including your head, should be supported. Lying down on a sofa or bed or sitting in a reclining chair are two ways of supporting your body most completely. (When lying down, you may want to place a pillow beneath your knees for further support.) Sitting up is preferable to lying down if you are feeling tired or sleepy. It's advantageous to experience the full depth of the relaxation consciously without going to sleep.

6. *Loosen any tight garments* and take off shoes, watch, glasses, contact lenses, jewelry, and so on.

7. Make a decision not to worry about anything. Give yourself permission to put aside the concerns of the day. Allow taking care of yourself and having peace of mind to take precedence over any of your worries. (Remember that success with relaxation depends on giving peace of mind high priority in your overall scheme of values.)

8. Assume a *passive, detached attitude*. This is probably the most important element. You want to adopt a "let it happen" attitude and be free of any worry about how well you are performing the technique. Do not try to relax. Do not try to control your body. Do not judge your performance. The point is to let go.

Pacing and Downtime

Cultivating a more relaxed way of life requires more than simply practicing a formal relaxation technique. The techniques just described *can* and *will* enhance your overall feeling of relaxation if you practice them regularly. Yet if you overextend or demand too much of yourself the rest of the time, you may still find yourself prone to stress and anxiety.

Self-image and personal ideals frequently do not harmonize with the needs of the body. Self-imposed standards regarding work, success, achievement, or how well you take care of others can lead you to betray the natural rhythms of your body. The degree of stress you experience today is a direct measure of how far you've gotten ahead of your body's needs in the past. Pacing yourself and giving yourself ample downtime are two ways to begin reversing unhealthy trends and living more in harmony with your bodily self.

Pacing means to live your life at an optimal rate. Too much activity packed into each day, without breaks, leads to exhaustion, stress, and eventual illness. Not enough activity leads to boredom and self-absorption. Many persons with anxiety disorders tend to pace themselves too fast, following the lead of a society in which we're all told to do more, achieve more, and excel no matter what the cost. It took me many years myself to learn that I couldn't do as much as I wanted on any given day and still live in harmony with myself. If I truly wanted more relaxation in my life, I needed to give myself breaks throughout the day rather than rushing from one activity to another. For example, I used to schedule clients on the hour back to back, like most therapists. If I wanted to give a particular client a full hour, I would not leave myself any time to transition to the next client. After five or six sessions like this, I would feel exhausted. While I realized that some therapists could handle such a schedule, I had to let go of comparing myself with others and realize that five or six sessions in a row was too much. Now I see fewer clients and schedule them ninety minutes apart so that I have ample time between sessions. It makes a difference, both in the way I feel throughout the day and in the quality of my work.

If you tend to rush through the activities of your day, experiment with slowing down and giving yourself a five to ten minute "minibreak" every hour or at least every two hours. *Minibreaks can be especially helpful at times when you transition from one activity to another.* For example, after commuting in the morning, take a short break before going into work. Or after cooking a meal, take a short break before sitting down to eat. During your break, you might practice abdominal breathing, meditate, get up and take a short walk, do a few yoga stretches (see the section called "Energy Balance" later in the chapter), or do anything else that helps you to reenergize, relax, and clear your mind. By pacing yourself to allow for short breaks through the day, you'll notice a significant difference in the way you feel. You may also be surprised to find that you get just as much or even more done, because you bring more energy and clarity to your activities. Giving yourself short breaks to regroup through the day is simple in principle, though it will require a commitment on your part to practice. You are likely to find it well worth the effort.

Downtime implies giving yourself more extended periods of time to rest and replenish your energy. While minibreaks will help you to get through your day more calmly, you still need periods of time out away from work and other responsibilities. Without such periods, the stress you experience in dealing with work or other responsibilities tends to become *cumulative*. It keeps building without remission. Sleep at night doesn't really count as downtime. If you go to bed feeling stressed, you may sleep for eight hours and yet wake up still feeling tense, tired, and stressed. Downtime needs to be scheduled apart from sleep during the day. Its primary purpose is to allow a break in the stress cycle—to prevent stress you're experiencing from becoming cumulative. I recommend to my clients that they give themselves the following periods of downtime:

- One hour per day

- One day per week

- One week out of every twelve to sixteen weeks

If you don't have the option to take four weeks off from work in a year, try to obtain at least a few days' break every three or four months (even if your time off is unpaid). During these periods of downtime, you disengage from any task you consider work, put aside all responsibilities, and don't answer the phone unless it's someone you would enjoy hearing from.

There are three kinds of downtime, each of which has an important place in developing a more relaxed lifestyle: 1) rest time, 2) recreation time, and 3) relationship time. It's important that you provide yourself enough downtime so that you have time for all three. Often recreation and relationship time can be combined. However, it's important to use rest time for just that—and nothing else.

Rest time is time when you set aside all activities and just allow yourself to be. You stop action and let yourself fully rest. Rest time might involve lying on the couch and doing nothing, quietly meditating, sitting in your recliner and listening to peaceful music, soaking in a Jacuzzi, or taking a catnap in the middle of the workday. The key to rest time is that it's fundamentally passive—you allow yourself to stop doing and accomplishing and just be. Contemporary society encourages each of us to be productive and always accomplish more and more every moment of the waking day. Rest time is a necessary counterpoint. When you're under stress, one hour of rest time per day, separate from the time you sleep, is optimal.

Recreation time involves engaging in activities that help to "re-create" and replenish your energy. Recreation time brightens and uplifts your spirits. In essence, it's doing anything that you experience as fun or play. Examples of such activities might include puttering in the garden, reading a novel, seeing a special movie, going on a hike, playing volleyball, taking a short trip, baking a loaf of bread, or fishing. Recreation time can be done during the work week, but is most important to have on your days off from work. Such time can be spent either alone or with someone else.

Relationship time is time when you put aside your private goals and responsibilities in order to enjoy being with another person—or, in some cases, with several people. The focus of relationship time is to honor your relationship with your partner, children, extended family members, friends, pets, and so on, and forget about your individual pursuits for a while. If you have a family, relationship time needs to be allocated equitably between time alone with your spouse, time alone with your children, and time when the entire family gets together. If you're single with a partner, time needs to be judiciously allocated between time with your partner and time with friends.

When you slow down and make time to be with others, you're not as likely to neglect your own basic needs for intimacy, touching, affection, validation, and support. Meeting these basic needs is absolutely vital to your well-being. Without sufficient time devoted to important relationships, you will likely suffer—and the people you most care about are bound to as well.

How can you allow for more downtime (all three kinds) in your life? It requires a genuine commitment to leading a more relaxed and easy lifestyle, apart from what the neighbors and the rest of the world may be doing. Deliberately making time for rest, recreation, and relationships may be challenging at first, but tends to become easier and more rewarding as time goes on. For some people, it translates into a fundamental decision to make earning money less important and a simpler, more balanced lifestyle more important. Before you think about leaving your present job, however, consider how you can shift your values toward placing more emphasis on the *process* of life ("how" you live) as opposed to accomplishments and productivity ("what" you actually do) within your current life situation.

DOWNTIME EXERCISE

Take some time to reflect on how you might allocate more time for each of the three types of downtime discussed. Write your answers in the space provided below or on a separate page.

Rest time:

Recreation time:

Relationship time:

Part 2: Exercise

Up until the twentieth century, the idea of making time for daily exercise would have seemed strange indeed. For a majority of people, basic survival depended on frequent physical activity. In times past (and in developing countries to this day) people usually walked long distances to obtain supplies and exerted themselves to provide for basic needs such as food, warmth, and clothing. Not so in modern technologically advanced countries, where we sit while we work, sit while we travel, and sit during much of our leisure time. Overweight is not a problem in some parts of the world but affects more than 50 percent of adult Americans. Along with our sedentary lifestyle comes a variety of chronic, stress-related diseases, especially cardiovascular diseases but also, to a certain extent, anxiety and mood disorders. The human body evolved over the past million years in a physically demanding environment. It functions best when it is frequently used.

Regular physical activity counteracts a predisposition to anxiety. Anxiety arises from a state of physiological activation that prepares the body for "fight or flight." The increased sympathetic nervous system arousal and adrenaline that give rise to anxiety *naturally seek an outlet in physical activity*. When you do nothing in response to this state of activation, the energy implodes (i.e., is turned in on yourself) and tends to push up the level of internal physiological activation—both in your sympathetic nervous system and the limbic system of your brain—to very intense levels. The result is that you feel an overwhelming, "out of control" state of internal activation, including racing heart, sweating, muscle spasms, and a closed-in feeling most likely due to pervasive muscle contraction. If your mind happens to interpret this activation as dangerous or catastrophic, you can escalate quickly to a state of panic. One way to curtail such a reaction is to become physically active the moment you begin to feel physical symptoms of anxiety coming on. You are, in fact, "prewired" to do just this. If you find yourself in a situation where you ordinarily wouldn't move (such as standing in line at the grocery store, eating in a restaurant, or driving on the freeway), give yourself permission to do so as soon as you can. Channel the activation in your body into outward activity rather than absorbing it.

People who exercise regularly tend to have less frequent and severe episodes of anxiety or panic. My conjecture is that regular, vigorous exercise conditions their bodies to *externalize* rather than implode heightened levels of physiological activation. Exercise itself involves a heightened state of physiological arousal, but the energy is always discharged through the activity itself. Although exercise may not "cure" panic disorder, it does tend to help people become less vulnerable to panic attacks. Regular exercise also tends to reduce generalized and/or anticipatory anxiety, thus reducing the tendency to worry or dwell on negative, fear-based scenarios. Many of my clients report that they can offset anxiety or worry by taking time out for vigorous exercise. In addition, regular exercise helps relieve depression.

Exercise has a direct impact on several physiological factors that underlie anxiety. It brings about:

- *Reduced skeletal muscle tension*, which is largely responsible for your feelings of being tense or "uptight"

- *More rapid metabolism of excess adrenaline and thyroxin* in the bloodstream, the presence of which tends to keep you in a state of arousal and vigilance

- A *discharge of pent-up frustration*, which can aggravate phobic or panic reactions

Exercise also has a clearly established ability to raise serotonin levels. It increases not only the level of serotonin but also its activity in the cerebral cortex. Increased serotonin is associated with amelioration of all of the anxiety disorders, which is the reason why many people tend to improve after taking SSRI (selective serotonin reuptake inhibitor) medications (see Chapter 7).

Beyond its specific anxiety-reducing effects, exercise has numerous other physiological benefits, including:

- Enhanced oxygenation of the blood and brain, which increases alertness and concentration

- Stimulation of the production of endorphins, natural substances that resemble morphine both chemically and in their effects; endorphins increase your sense of well-being

- Improved circulation

- Improved digestion and utilization of food

- Improved elimination (from skin, lungs, and bowels)

- Decreased cholesterol levels

- Decreased blood pressure

- Weight loss as well as appetite suppression, in many cases

- Improved blood sugar regulation (in the case of hypoglycemia)

Several psychological benefits accompany these physical improvements, including:

- Increased subjective feelings of well-being

- Reduced dependence on alcohol and drugs

- Reduced insomnia

- Improved concentration and memory

- Reduced depression

- Increased self-esteem

- Greater sense of control over stress and anxiety

Evaluating Your Fitness Level

Do you feel you would like to get more exercise? The following worksheet can help you assess your present level of fitness. Consider the most strenuous physical activity you practice in an average week. When you have completed the questions below, determine your fitness score and evaluate your fitness level.

FITNESS WORKSHEET

Intensity	Frequency	Duration
How strenuous is your exercise?	How many times do you exercise per week?	How long do you exercise each time?
Heavy = 5 points (fast cycling, running, aerobic dancing)	3 or more times = 5 points	21 minutes to 1 hour = 5 points
Moderate = 3 points (jogging, swimming, very fast walking)	1-2 times = 2 points	11 to 20 minutes = 3 points
Light = 1 point (golf, strolling, most housework)	not at all = 0 points	10 minutes or less = 1 point

Add your score: _____   +   _____   +   _____

= _____ Total

Total Score	Fitness Level	Recommended Action
13 to 15	Very good	Congratulations! Maintain your present level of activity
8 to 12	Average	You are moderately sedentary and should increase your level of activity
7 or less	Poor	Begin planning an exercise program now!

An alternative way to assess your level of fitness is to measure your resting pulse rate, the average number of heartbeats per minute when you're at rest. As a rule of thumb, a resting pulse of eighty or above suggests that you could definitely improve your fitness. A resting pulse of seventy to eighty heartbeats per minute suggests that you may need to obtain more exercise. If you are in a fitness program and have an average resting pulse below seventy, you're likely to be in good shape. To measure your pulse, allow yourself to get relaxed, then take the number of pulse beats in twenty seconds and multiply by three.

If you've decided you would like to get more exercise, you need to ask yourself whether you are fully ready to do so. There are certain physical conditions that limit the amount and intensity of exercise you should undertake. If your answer to any of the questions below is "yes," be sure to consult with your physician before beginning any exercise program. He or she may recommend a program of restricted or supervised exercise appropriate to your needs.

Yes   No

_____   _____   Has your physician ever said you have heart trouble?

_____   _____   Do you frequently have pains in your heart or chest?

_____   _____   Do you often feel faint or have spells of dizziness?

_____   _____   Has your physician ever told you that you have a bone or joint problem (such as arthritis) that has been or might be aggravated by exercise?

_____   _____   Has a physician ever said that your blood pressure was too high?

_____   _____   Do you have diabetes?

_____   _____   Are you over 40 years old and unaccustomed to vigorous exercise?

_____   _____   Is there a physical reason, not mentioned here, why you should not undertake an exercise program?

If you answered "no" to all of the above questions, you can be reasonably assured that you are ready to start an exercise program. *Begin slowly and increase your activity gradually over a period of three weeks.* If you are over forty and unaccustomed to exercise, plan to see your doctor for a physical before undertaking an exercise program.

Some individuals are reluctant to take up exercise because the state of physiological arousal accompanying vigorous exercise reminds them too much of the symptoms of panic. If this applies to you, you might want to start out doing thirty to forty-five minutes of walking on a daily basis.

Or you can very gradually build up to a more vigorous level of exercise. You might try just two to three minutes of jogging or cycling and then gradually increase the duration of your daily exercise a minute at a time, remembering to stop and rest for a minute every time you feel even the slightest association with panic. It might also be helpful to have a support person exercise with you initially. If you feel phobic about exercise, a program of gradual exposure will help you desensitize to it in the same way you would to any other phobia. (See Chapter 6.)

Choosing an Exercise Program

There are many types of exercise to choose from. Check off below which types you feel you might be interested in. If you are already exercising, consider whether there are any other forms you would like to try.

ACTIVITY CHECKLIST

____ running/jogging	____ downhill skiing	____ baseball
____ vigorous cycling	____ weight lifting	____ basketball
____ brisk walking	____ tennis	____ bowling
____ jumping rope	____ racquetball	____ golf
____ rowing	____ volleyball	____ gardening
____ stationary cycling	____ isometrics	____ football
____ cross-country skiing	____ handball	____ soccer
____ swimming	____ calisthenics	____ roller skating
____ aerobic dancing	____ ping pong	____ yoga
____ ice skating	____ mini-trampoline	____ ballroom or square dancing

Which forms of exercise you select depends upon your objectives. *For reducing anxiety and/or a proneness to panic, aerobic exercise is the most effective for many individuals.* The activities listed in the first column of the "Activity Checklist" are aerobic. Aerobic exercise requires sustained activity of your larger muscles. It reduces skeletal muscle tension and increases cardiovascular conditioning—the capacity of your circulatory system to deliver oxygen to your tissues and cells with greater efficiency. Regular aerobic exercise will reduce stress and increase your stamina.

Beyond aerobic fitness, you may have other objectives in taking up exercise. If increased muscle *strength* is important, you may want to include weight lifting or isometric exercise in your program (if you have a heart condition or angina, you should probably not engage in weight lifting or bodybuilding). If *socializing* is important, then tennis, racquetball, golf, or team sports such as baseball, basketball, or volleyball might be what you're looking for. Exercise that involves stretching, such as dancing or yoga, is ideal for developing muscular *flexibility*. If you want to *lose weight*, jogging or cycling are probably most effective. *If discharging aggression and frustration* are important, you might try competitive sports. Finally, if you just want to get out into nature, then hiking or gardening would be appropriate. Rigorous hiking (as done by the Sierra Club, for example) can increase both strength and endurance.

Many people find it helpful to *vary* the type of exercise they do. Doing two or more different forms of exercise on alternate days is sometimes referred to as "cross-training." This gives you the opportunity to develop a more balanced state of fitness by exercising different muscle groups. Popular combinations involve doing an aerobic type of exercise such as jogging or cycling three to four times a week and a socializing exercise (such as golf), or a bodybuilding exercise, twice a week. Maintaining a program with two distinct types of exercise prevents either from becoming too boring.

Exercise should be interesting and fun; it's important that you make it interesting early on so that you keep it up. There are several ways to do this. If you're not limited to being indoors, try to get outside, preferably in an attractive natural setting such as a park or, even better, the countryside. If you're doing a solo-type exercise such as swimming, cycling, or jogging, see if you can find a companion to go with you at least sometimes. If you need to exercise indoors because of personal limitations or climate, play music or watch a video while you're on your stationary bike or treadmill. Or you might take a Walkman with you when running or cycling outside. Some people actually learn foreign languages while exercising!

What follows are brief descriptions of some of the more common types of aerobic exercise. Each type has its advantages and possible drawbacks. If you would like more detailed descriptions of various forms of exercise, I recommend the book *Health and Fitness Excellence: The Scientific Action Plan* by Robert K. Cooper, Ph.D. (1989).

Running

For many years jogging or running has been the most popular form of aerobic exercise, perhaps because of its convenience. The only equipment you need is running shoes, and in many cases you need only step out your door to begin. Running is one of the best forms of exercise for losing weight, as it burns calories quickly. Numerous studies have shown its benefits for depression, as it raises both endorphin and serotonin levels in the brain. As mentioned above, running decreases anxiety by metabolizing excess adrenaline and releasing skeletal muscle tension. A three-mile jog (approximately thirty minutes) four or five times per week can go a long way toward diminishing your vulnerability to anxiety. Work up to a pace of one mile every ten minutes.

The downside to running is that, over a period of time, it can increase your risk for injury. In particular, if you run on hard surfaces, the constant shock to your joints can lead to foot, knee, or back problems. You can minimize your risk of injury by:

- Getting proper shoes—those which minimize shock to your joints.

- Running on soft surfaces—preferably grass, dirt, a track, or a hardened beach. Avoid concrete if possible; asphalt is okay if you have good shoes and don't run every day.

- Warm up to running before you begin. Try doing a minute or two of very slow jogging.

- Avoid jogging every day—alternate it with other forms of exercise.

If running outdoors is a problem because of weather, lack of a soft surface, smog, or traffic, you may want to invest in an automatic treadmill. To make this less boring, put it in front of your TV or VCR.

Swimming

Swimming is my personal favorite form of exercise. It's an especially good exercise because it uses so many different muscles throughout the body. Doctors usually recommend swimming to people with musculoskeletal problems, injuries, or arthritis, because it minimizes shock to their joints. It does not promote weight loss to the same degree as running, but it will help firm up your body.

For aerobic-level conditioning, it's best to swim freestyle for twenty to thirty minutes, preferably four or five times per week. For moderate, relaxing exercise, breaststroke is an enjoyable alternative. As a rule, it's best to work out in a heated pool where the water temperature is seventy-five to eighty degrees Fahrenheit.

The major downside with swimming is that many pools are heavily chlorinated. This may be quite irritating to your eyes, skin, or hair—as well as the membranes in your upper respiratory passages. You can counter some of this by wearing goggles and/or nose plugs. If you're fortunate, you may be able to find a pool that uses hydrogen peroxide or bubbled-in ozone as a disinfectant. Either of these is preferable to chlorine.

Cycling

Cycling has become a very popular form of aerobic exercise in recent years. While having many of the same benefits as jogging, it's less shocking to your joints. To achieve aerobic conditioning, cycling needs to be done vigorously—approximately fifteen miles per hour or more on a flat surface. When the weather is good, cycling can be quite enjoyable—especially if you have beautiful surroundings with little traffic or a designated bike trail. If weather precludes cycling, you need a stationary bike indoors, preferably in front of your TV or VCR.

If you want to take up outdoor cycling, you'll need to make an initial investment in a good bike. You may want to borrow someone else's bike until you feel ready to spend several hundred dollars. In purchasing a bike, I'd suggest avoiding racing bikes unless you decide you want to race. You'll probably find sitting upright when you bike to be more enjoyable and less stressful than sitting hunched over. Make sure the bike you purchase is designed and sized correctly for your body—or it may cause you problems. A well-cushioned seat is a good investment.

When you undertake cycling, give yourself a few months to work up to a fifteen miles per hour cruising speed—i.e., a mile every four minutes. One hour of cycling three to four times per week is sufficient. Be sure to wear a helmet and try to avoid riding at night.

Aerobics classes

Most aerobics classes consist of warm-up stretches and aerobic exercises led by an instructor. These are usually done to music. Classes are generally offered by health clubs, with various levels for beginning, intermediate, and advanced participants. Since certain of the exercises can be traumatic to joints, try to find a "low-impact" aerobics class. The structured format of an aerobics class may be an excellent way to motivate you to exercise. If you are self-motivated and prefer to stay at home, there are many good aerobics videos available.

If you decide to do aerobic exercises, be sure to obtain good shoes that stabilize your feet, absorb shock, and minimize twisting. It's best to do these exercises on a wooden surface and to avoid thick carpets, if possible. About forty-five minutes to an hour of exercise (including warm-up) three to four times per week is sufficient.

Walking

Walking has advantages over all other forms of exercise. First, it does not require training—you already know how to do it. Second, it requires no equipment other than a pair of shoes and can be done virtually anywhere—even in a shopping mall if necessary. The chances of injury are less than for any other type of exercise. Finally, it's the most natural form of activity. All of us are naturally inclined to walk. Up until society became sedentary, it was a natural part of life.

Walking for relaxation and distraction is one thing; doing it for aerobic conditioning is another. To make walking aerobic, aim for doing it about one hour at a brisk enough pace to cover three miles. A twenty or thirty minute walk is generally not enough to obtain aerobic-level conditioning. If you make walking your regular form of exercise, do it four to five times per week, preferably outdoors. If you feel an hour of brisk walking is not enough of a workout, try adding hand weights or finding an area with hills.

To get the most benefit out of walking, good posture is important. If it feels natural to allow your arms to swing opposite to the stride of your legs, you'll be getting "cross-lateral conditioning," which helps to integrate the left and right hemispheres of your brain. Good walking shoes are also important. Look for padded insoles, a good arch, and firm support of the heel.

Once you can comfortably walk three or four miles without stopping, consider taking hiking trips—day or overnight—in county, state, or national parks. Hiking outdoors can revitalize your soul as much as it does your body.

Guidelines for Starting an Exercise Program

If you haven't been exercising, it's important not to start off too fast or hard. Doing so often results in prematurely "burning out" on the idea of maintaining a regular exercise program. The following guidelines are recommended for beginning an exercise program:

- Approach exercise gradually. Set limited goals at the outset, such as exerting for only ten minutes (or to the point of being winded) every other day for the first week. Add five minutes to your workout time each successive week until you reach thirty minutes.

- Expect exercise to be difficult at first. Aches and pains are normal if you're out of shape; they will pass. You will come to like exercise more after some practice than you do when you first start. An important principle to keep in mind is that "exercise creates energy." Often when you think you're too tired to exercise, doing so will give you added energy that you didn't think you had.

- Give yourself a one-month trial period. Make a commitment to stay with your program for one month despite aches and pains, inertia, or other resistance to exercise. By the end of the first month you may be starting to experience sufficient benefits to make the exercise self-motivating. Be aware that achieving a high level of fitness after being out of shape takes three to four months.

- Keep a record of your daily exercise practice. Use the *Daily Record of Exercise* on page 67 to keep track of the date, time, duration, and type of exercise you engage in on a daily basis for one month. (You may want to make copies of the *Daily Record* to track your exercise program beyond the first month.) If you're doing aerobic exercise, record your pulse immediately after completing your workout and enter it under "Pulse Rate." Also, be sure to rate your level of satisfaction, using a one to ten scale, where 1 equals no satisfaction at all and 10 equals total satisfaction with your exercise experience. As you begin to get into shape, the ratings should increase. Finally, if you fail to exercise when you intended to, indicate your reason for not doing so. Later on it may be useful to reevaluate these reasons to see if they are truly valid or merely excuses.

- Try to focus on the *process* of exercise rather than the product. See if you can get into the inherently enjoyable aspects of the exercise itself. If jogging or cycling is what you like, it helps to have a scenic environment. Focusing on competition with others or yourself may tend to increase rather than reduce anxiety and stress.

- Reward yourself for maintaining a commitment to your exercise program. Give yourself dinner out, a weekend trip, or new athletic clothes or equipment in exchange for sticking to your program during the first weeks and months.

- *Warm up.* Just as your car needs to warm up before you begin driving, your body needs a gradual warm-up before engaging in vigorous exercise. This is especially important if you are over forty. Stretching is probably not the best way to do a warm-up. Stretching cold muscles is difficult and can result in injury. A better way is to do a slow-motion, low-intensity form of the exercise itself for a few minutes at the outset.

- After vigorous exercise, it's important to give yourself a few minutes to cool down. Walking around for two or three minutes will help bring blood back from peripheral muscles to the rest of your body. Avoid stopping exercise suddenly.

- Avoid exercising within ninety minutes of a meal and don't eat until one hour after exercising, if possible.

- Replenish body fluids. It's a good idea to have an eight-ounce glass of water before exercising. If you work up a good sweat, have another glass of water or juice afterward.

- Avoid exercising when you feel ill or overstressed (try a deep relaxation technique instead). Trust what your body tells you regarding the pace and intensity of your exercise.

- Stop exercising if you experience any sudden, unexplainable bodily symptoms.

- If you find yourself feeling bored with exercising solo, find a partner to go with you or a form of exercise that requires a partner.

Optimizing the Anxiety-Reducing Effects of Exercise

Exercise needs to be of sufficient regularity, intensity, and duration to have a significant impact on anxiety. The following standards can be viewed as goals to aim for:

- Ideally, exercise should be *aerobic*.
- Optimal frequency is *four to five times per week*.
- Optimal duration is *twenty to thirty minutes* or more per session.
- Optimal intensity for aerobic exercise is a heart rate of (220 minus your age) x .65 for at least ten to twenty minutes.
- You can still achieve aerobic conditioning at lower heart rates by exercising for longer periods—i.e., thirty to forty minutes at a time.
- *Avoid exercising only once per week.* Engaging in infrequent spurts of vigorous exercise is stressful to your body and generally does more harm than good (brisk walking is an exception).

Daily Record of Exercise* for _____

(month)

Date	Time	Type of Exercise	Duration	Pulse Rate	Satisfaction Level	Reason for Not Exercising

* Based on a maximum frequency of six days of exercise per week.

Common Excuses for Not Exercising

Below is an annotated list of common excuses people make for avoiding exercise.

- "I don't have enough time."
  What you're really saying is that you're not willing to make time. You aren't assigning enough importance to the increased fitness, well-being, and improved control over anxiety you could gain from exercise. The problem is not a matter of time but one of priorities.

- "I feel too tired to exercise."
  One solution is to exercise before going to work—or on your lunch break—rather than at the end of the day. If this is not possible, don't give up. What many nonexercisers fail to realize is that moderate exercise can actually *overcome* fatigue. Many people exercise in spite of feeling tired and find that they feel rejuvenated and reenergized afterwards. It gets easier once you get past the beginning inertia of starting to exercise.

- "Exercise is boring—it's no fun."
  Is it really true that all the activities listed earlier are boring to you? Have you tried out all of them? It may be that you need to find someone to exercise with in order to have more fun. Or perhaps you need to go back and forth between two different types of exercise to stimulate your interest. Exercise can begin to feel wonderful after a few months, when it becomes inherently rewarding, even if it initially bored you.

- "It's too inconvenient to go out somewhere to exercise."
  This is really no problem, as there are several ways to obtain vigorous exercise in the comfort of your home. Stationary bicycles and treadmills have become very popular, and twenty minutes per day on one will give you a good workout. If this seems boring, try listening to a Walkman or place your stationary bike in front of the TV set. Aerobic exercise at home can be convenient and fun if you have a VCR. There are many good low-impact aerobics videos available. Other indoor activities include jumping on a rebounder (mini-trampoline), using a rowing machine, and/or using a universal gym with adjustable weights. There are also early morning exercise programs on TV. If you can't afford exercise equipment or a VCR, just put on some wild music and dance for twenty minutes. In short, it's quite possible to maintain an adequate exercise program without leaving your home.

- "I'm afraid I'll have a panic attack."
Brisk walking every day for forty-five minutes is an excellent form of exercise that is very unlikely to produce symptoms you might associate with panic. If you would prefer doing something more vigorous, start off with a very short period of two or three minutes and gradually add a minute at a time. Anytime you start to feel uneasy, simply stop, wait until you fully recover, and then try completing your designated period of exercise for that day. The principles of graded exposure described in Chapter 6 can be applied effectively to a phobia about exercise.

- "Exercise causes a buildup of lactic acid, which can cause panic attacks."
It's true that exercise increases the production of lactic acid, and that lactic acid can promote panic attacks in some people who are already prone to them. However, regular exercise also increases *oxygen turnover* in your body—that is, the capacity of your body to oxidize substances it doesn't need, including lactic acid. Any increase in lactic acid produced by exercise will likely be offset by your body's increased capacity to remove it. The net effect of regular exercise is an overall *reduction* in your body's tendency to accumulate lactic acid.

- "I'm over forty—and that's too old to start exercising."
When clients over forty tell me "it's too late" to take up exercise, I remind them that many of the people chosen to be astronauts are in their forties. I also tell them about marathon runners who began running in their fifties and sixties after having not exercised at all. Unless your doctor gives you a clear medical reason for not exercising, age is never a valid excuse. With patience and persistence, it's possible to get into excellent physical shape at almost any age.

- "I'm too overweight and out of shape," or "I'm afraid I'll have a heart attack if I stress my body by exercising vigorously."
If you have physical reasons to worry about stressing your heart, be sure to design your exercise program with the help of your physician. Vigorous walking is a safe exercise for virtually everyone and is considered by some physicians to be the ideal exercise, as it rarely causes muscle or bone injuries. Swimming is also safe if you're out of shape or overweight. Be sensible and realistic in the exercise program you choose. The important thing is to be consistent and committed, whether your program involves walking for one hour every day or training for a marathon.

- "I've tried exercise once and it didn't work."
  The question to ask here is *why* didn't it work. Did you start off too hard and fast? Did you get bored? Did you balk at the initial aches and pains? Perhaps it's time for you to give yourself another chance to discover all the physical and psychological benefits of a regular exercise program.

Regular exercise is an essential component in a total program for overcoming anxiety. If you combine exercise with some form of regular, deep relaxation, you are undoubtedly going to experience a substantial reduction in anxiety and an increase in your resistance to panic attacks (if this is a problem) as well. Exercise and deep relaxation are the two methods *most* effective for altering a hereditary-biochemical predisposition to anxiety, present in about 25 percent of the population. I cannot think of two better ways to spend your time if you wish to live with less anxiety and a greater overall sense of well-being.

Part 3: Energy Balance

The idea of energy balance has its basis in the medical systems and paradigms that have been utilized in the Far East for thousands of years. All of these systems assume that there is a subtle (nonphysical) energy that permeates and circulates throughout the body. Traditional Chinese medicine calls this "chi," eastern Indian medicine (Ayurveda) calls it "prana," and Japanese healing traditions refer to it as "ki." The terms that best describe this energy in English would be "life force" or "vital energy." The difference in energy you feel when you have the flu versus when you are healthy and well is an example of fluctuations in this type of energy.

In Chinese medicine, subtle energy is understood to be distributed throughout the body along channels called "meridians." In the Indian tradition, these invisible channels—and the centers where the energy is concentrated—are called "nadi" and "chakras."

One of the most important functions of all of the energy-balance disciplines, in addition to mind-body integration, is to harmonize and optimize the "flow" of subtle energy by releasing blocks to that flow. Blocked energy leads to tension, stress, and ultimately illness. In fact, Chinese and East Indian medicine trace all disease back to various types and degrees of blockage in the flow of life force and vital energy. Regular practice of energy balance disciplines such as yoga or Tai Chi helps to release blocks to the natural flow of vitality. So does receiving treatments from healing arts which free up obstructions to subtle energy. This is particularly true for acupuncture, but also applies to various forms of massage as well as chiropractic.

The invisible "energy body" (sometimes called "subtle body") which is the focus of Eastern medicine is, as you might expect, intimately related to the physical body. (It's thought, in fact, to provide an energetic matrix or "template" for the physical body.) On a strictly physical level, energy-balance practices help to relieve muscle tension, promote increased oxygenation of tissues and the brain, improve arterial circulation, promote elimination by the kidneys and colon, and stimulate increased production of hormones and neurotransmitters.

However, the fundamental purpose of the energy balance disciplines is to promote mind-body integration—a harmonious interdependence and balance among the spiritual, mental, emotional, and physical aspects of your total being. "Wholeness" is equated with wellness. To the extent you function in an integrated, "whole" manner, you can experience the fullness of your being and genuine health and wellness. To the extent that you are out of touch with the wholeness of your being, you remain out of harmony with yourself and are subject to stress and "dis-ease."

Each of the modalities described below provides a pathway back to inner wholeness and integration. Any one of them can help promote inner peace and freedom from fear, as well as better health and well-being in general.

Yoga

The word *yoga* means to "yoke" or "unify." By definition, yoga is involved with promoting unity of mind, body, and spirit. Although in the West yoga is usually thought of as a series of stretch exercises, it actually embraces a broad philosophy of life and an elaborate system for personal transformation. This system includes ethical precepts, a vegetarian diet, the familiar stretches or postures, specific practices for directing and controlling the breath, concentration practices, and deep meditation. It was originally laid out by the philosopher Pantanjali in the second century BC and is still practiced throughout the world today.

Yoga postures, by themselves, provide a very effective means to increase fitness, flexibility, and relaxation. They can be practiced alone or with a group. Many people, myself included, find that yoga simultaneously increases energy and vitality while calming the mind. Yoga may be compared to progressive muscle relaxation, in that it involves holding the body in certain flexed positions for a few moments and then relaxing. Both yoga and PMR lead to relaxation. However, I personally find yoga to be more effective than progressive muscle relaxation in freeing up blocked energy. It seems to get energy moving up and down the spine and throughout the body in a way that doesn't happen as readily with PMR. Like vigorous exercise, yoga directly promotes mind-body integration. However, in many ways it is more specific. Each yoga posture reflects a mental attitude, whether that attitude is one of surrender, as in certain forward-bending poses, or of strengthening the will, as in a backward-bending pose. By emphasizing certain yoga postures and movements, you may be able to cultivate certain positive qualities or move through other negative, restrictive personality patterns. There is an entire school of "yoga therapy" which uses yoga as a methodology for addressing and working through personality issues.

If you are interested in learning yoga, the best place to start is with a class at a local health club or community college. If such classes are unavailable in your area, try working with a yoga video at home. The popular magazine *Yoga Journal* offers many excellent yoga videos. To supplement your practice, you may want to look at books such as *Yoga for Health* by Richard Hittleman (1983) and *Light on Yoga* by B. Iyengar (1987).

Tai Chi

Tai Chi is an ancient form of movement and exercise intended to unite body and mind. It is said to have originated when a thirteenth-century Taoist monk in China watched a serpent and a crane in battle. As the crane attacked the snake, the snake would smoothly move its position—never allowing the crane to touch it. From this scene the monk developed thirteen moves which have been augmented down through the centuries. Presently, Tai Chi is practiced by millions of people in China and is popular throughout the rest of the world.

Tai Chi can best be described as a form of moving meditation. It consists of a series of movements that proceed slowly and gracefully, flowing one into another. These movements strengthen and ground the body while promoting the flow of *chi* or life force. Students of Tai Chi say that it teaches qualities of fluidity and grace—qualities that can extend to the way you live your entire life. Because the movements are done slowly, Tai Chi also teaches you how to slow down, both in body and mind. Like meditation, it helps you to achieve serenity, clarity, and concentration. Unlike meditation, however, it instills an ability to carry poise and concentration into movement.

Like yoga, Tai Chi helps you to work through blocks to the flow of your life energy, along with promoting physical benefits such as opening the joints (especially the knees), strengthening the spine and lower back, and massaging the internal organs. Because it's practiced with your entire body and with full presence of mind, Tai Chi is a very practical and effective way to foster mind-body integration.

You can find Tai Chi classes offered at some health clubs as well as some martial arts schools (though Tai Chi is generally not used as a form of self-defense). If classes are not available in your area, there are several excellent videos that teach the basic movements. Because it promotes the flow of chi, Tai Chi is sometimes prescribed as an adjunct to acupuncture treatments.

Acupuncture

Acupuncture originated as a healing modality in China about three thousand years ago. Currently, it's practiced in most advanced countries throughout the world. As with Tai Chi, it is based on the assumption that health is determined by the free and proper flow of chi, the vital or subtle energy that pervades all living things. Chi flows along channels in the body called meridians, each of which is linked to a specific organ. When the flow of energy is neither restricted nor excessive, the individual enjoys good health. If the energy flow is unbalanced in either direction, both physical and mental symptoms of distress or disease may result. For example, fear is understood to be due to blocked or excessive energy flow along the kidney meridian. Acupuncture treatments that aim to balance the kidney meridian (and other supporting meridians) can help to relieve fearfulness.

In an acupuncture treatment, the acupuncturist inserts thin needles at specific points in the body. Most people (myself included) feel only a slight prick or no pain at all from the procedure. Typically, the needles are left in place for twenty to thirty minutes, after which it's common to feel very relaxed and rejuvenated. Repeated treatments (twice a week for a few weeks) are often needed to correct an ailment such as migraine headaches, allergies, or back pain. If you wish to utilize acupuncture to help anxiety, regular treatments on a weekly or biweekly basis for several months are advised. Often the acupuncturist will provide herbs in the form of teas or capsules to use at home to enhance the effects of the treatments. A few of my clients report that they have especially benefited from the use of Chinese herbs and continued to rely on them after finishing the acupuncture treatments.

For people who are uncomfortable with the use of needles, acupressure may be a viable alternative. Acupressure (and its cousin, Shiatsu) relies on the same principles as acupuncture; however, energy flow and balance along the meridians is promoted by manual pressure rather than needles. Acupressure is a simple and inexpensive form of energy balance practiced by many massage therapists. You can, in fact, utilize acupressure on your own. A number of self-acupressure books provide instructions for utilizing acupressure yourself.

Chiropractic

Most people think of chiropractic as a healing art that aims to relieve back pain induced by stress or injury. At a more basic level, though, chiropractic strives to promote health by optimizing the flow of nerve impulses up and down the spine and to other parts of the body. Because of the various stresses to which the spine is subject, individual vertebrae can move out of alignment. These misaligned vertebrae block the flow of nerve impulses between brain and body as well as between the spinal cord and various bodily organs. When nerve transmission to a specific organ is reduced or limited, that organ is likely to dysfunction, producing symptoms ranging from mild discomfort to illness. Misalignments of the spine may be caused by injury, but most frequently they are caused by stress. Muscles tightened under chronic stress tend to pull the vertebrae out of alignment. Even if the muscle tension is relieved through exercise or massage, the spinal vertebrae may not easily resume their normal configuration. Thus, a chiropractor seeks to identify and correct vertebral misalignments in order to promote optimal nervous system function and thereby functional integrity of the body as a whole.

Chiropractic can be a helpful strategy for relieving chronic tension, whether or not it's accompanied by pain. An occasional visit to a chiropractor is likely to improve your overall experience of well-being. In locating a qualified chiropractor in your area, try to get a referral from a friend or relative. If you prefer not to receive direct manipulations of the spine, there are some chiropractors that practice a non-manipulative form of adjustment sometimes referred to as "gentle chiropractic."

Massage

Therapeutic massage is a healing art designed to promote deep relaxation through skillful manipulation of muscles and soft body tissues. Professional massage therapists usually obtain five hundred to a thousand hours of formal training in anatomy, physiology, and various forms of bodywork including Swedish massage, deep tissue work, reflexology, acupressure, and Shiatsu.

Receiving a one-hour massage every week—or even twice per month—can promote deep relaxation by relieving chronic muscle tension that you may have been holding in your body for a long time. Massage can enhance and deepen the benefits you obtain from practicing progressive muscle relaxation (PMR). PMR tends to release acute, superficial tension in the outer muscles of your arms, legs, neck, and torso. Massage, particularly "deep tissue" massage, can undo chronic, long-standing tension held in the deeper muscles of the body. In addition to releasing muscle tension, massage can help cleanse your body of toxic accumulations by promoting lymphatic circulation and mobilizing a sluggish colon.

On a more psychological level, receiving a massage is a wonderful way to nurture yourself if you feel stressed. Massage can also provide a corrective emotional experience for survivors of abuse. If you grew up in a dysfunctional family where you either weren't touched or were touched inappropriately, massage can help you work through any painful feelings or resistance around being touched, increasing your ease with what is an innate need for all human beings.

There are several types of massage to choose from. Swedish massage, developed by Peter Ling in the 1800s, uses kneading, stroking, and shaking to induce the body to relax. This is the most common type of massage practiced. Deep tissue massage involves greater pressure on deeper muscles than Swedish massage and generally focuses on specific problem areas. Neuromuscular massage is a form of deep tissue massage that works with specific "trigger points" to release chronically tight muscles. Acupressure, while certainly relaxing, intentionally seeks to promote enhanced energy balance. Through firm pressure applied to specific points for three to ten seconds each, acupressure strives to release blocks to the flow of subtle energy through the acupuncture meridians.

If you'd like to read more about massage, I recommend *The Massage Book* by George Downing (1972).

This chapter has emphasized some very important strategies for reducing anxiety and fear. Making time on a daily basis for abdominal breathing, relaxation, and exercise will go a long way toward reducing your susceptibility to anxiety on a purely physical level. Balancing your life-force energy through a practice such as yoga—or receiving massage, acupressure, or other forms of bodywork on a regular basis—will further improve your sense of physical well-being and equanimity. If you adopt only those strategies suggested in this one chapter, you'll take a significant step in the direction of a more peaceful life.

What You Can Do Now

Relaxation

1. Reread the section on abdominal breathing and decide which breathing exercise you prefer to work with. Practice the exercise you prefer for *five minutes at a time, three times per day, for at least three*

weeks. Practice for one month or longer if you wish to change your breathing pattern from your chest downward toward your abdomen.

2. Practice progressive muscle relaxation for *twenty to thirty minutes per day* (two practice periods per day is optimal) *for at least two weeks.* For the first few times, have someone read you the instructions or record them on tape so that you can follow them effortlessly. Eventually, you'll learn the sequence so well that you can dispense with a tape.

3. After practicing progressive muscle relaxation for at least two weeks, you may enjoy its benefits so much that you decide to adopt it as your preferred deep relaxation technique. Alternatively, you may want to use one of the guided visualizations in Appendix 3 or learn to meditate (see Chapter 9). *The type of relaxation technique you use is less important than your willingness and commitment to practice some method of deep relaxation on a daily basis.*

4. Review the section "Pacing and Downtime." Do you need to allocate more time in your life for rest, relaxation, and personal relationships? What changes would you need to make in your daily schedule to achieve this? Think about at least one change you could make, starting this week. Are you willing to commit to it?

Exercise

5. Determine your level of fitness, using the Fitness Worksheet in the section "Evaluating Your Fitness Level."

6. Determine whether you are ready to begin a fitness program by answering the list of questions on page 59.

7. Choose one or more types of exercise you would prefer to do. If you're out of shape, begin with walking for periods of at least twenty to thirty minutes, or with a more vigorous form of exercise for ten to fifteen minutes. Increase the duration and intensity of your exercise gradually. Exercise at least four times per week.

8. Observe all the guidelines for maintaining a regular exercise program listed in the section "Guidelines for Starting an Exercise Program." It's particularly important to give yourself time to warm up and cool down before and after engaging in vigorous exercise.

9. Monitor your exercise program, using the *Daily Record of Exercise*, for at least one month.

10. If you encounter resistance to exercise—or lose your motivation to keep exercising after the first week or so—reread the section "Common Excuses for Not Exercising." Try to identify what you're telling yourself about exercise that creates your resistance or lack of motivation. Work on countering your negative self-talk by giving yourself positive reasons to exercise the next time you have an opportunity.

Energy Balance

11. Reread the section "Energy Balance." If you decide you'd like to learn yoga or Tai Chi, look for a class in your local area (often available through health clubs). If there are no classes, purchase an instructional video. (Good videos for yoga or Tai Chi can be found in the magazine *Yoga Journal*, available at 1-800-600-YOGA.)

12. If you would like to explore acupuncture, acupressure, therapeutic massage, or chiropractic, ask family or friends to recommend a qualified practitioner. If you need to go through the phone directory, ask practitioners you contact about their education, training, and how many years they've been in practice. Only work with someone with whom you feel a good rapport.

References and Further Reading

Relaxation

Benson, Herbert. 1975. *The Relaxation Response*. New York: Morrow.

———. 1985. *Beyond the Relaxation Response*. New York: Berkeley Books.

Davis, Martha, Elizabeth Robbins Eshelman, and Matthew McKay. 1988. *The Relaxation and Stress Reduction Workbook*. 3d ed. Oakland, California: New Harbinger Publications.

Harp, David. 1990. *The New Three-Minute Meditator*. Oakland, California: New Harbinger Publications.

Jacobson, Edmund. 1974. *Progressive Relaxation*. Midway Reprint. Chicago: The University of Chicago Press.

Lakein, Alan. 1973. *How to Get Control of Your Time and Your Life*. New York: Signet.

LeShan, Lawrence. 1974. *How to Meditate*. New York: Bantam Books.

Mason, John. 1985. *Guide to Stress Reduction*. Berkeley, California: Celestial Arts. (This book is particularly recommended as a good resource for relaxation scripts you can record for yourself.)

Trickett, Shirley. 1996. *Panic Attacks: A Natural Approach*.

Exercise

Bailey, Covert. 1977. *Fit or Fat?* Boston: Houghton Mifflin.

Cooper, Robert K. 1989. *Health and Fitness Excellence: The Scientific Action Plan*. Boston: Houghton Mifflin.

Fixx, J. F. 1980. *Jim Fixx's Second Book of Running*. New York: Random House.

Gale, B. 1979. *The Wonderful World of Walking*. New York: William Morrow.

Smith, D. L. and E. A. Gaston. 1979. *Get Fit with Bicycling*. Emmaus, Pennsylvania: Rodale Press.

Sorenson, J. 1979. *Aerobic Dancing*. New York: Rawson Wade.

Weil, Andrew. 1995. *Natural Health, Natural Medicine*. New York: Houghton Mifflin.

Wiener, H. S. 1980. *Total Swimming*. New York: Simon and Schuster.

Energy Balance

Downing, George. 1972. *The Massage Book*. New York: Random House

Hittleman, R. 1969. *Richard Hittleman's Yoga 28-Day Exercise Plan*. New York: Workman Publishing Co.

———. 1983. *Yoga for Health*. New York: Ballantine.

Iyengar, B. 1987. *Light on Yoga*. New York: Schocken Books.

Mumford, Susan. 1995. *The Complete Guide to Massage*. New York: Plume/Penguin Books.

Vishnudevananda, Swami. 1980. *The Complete Illustrated Book of Yoga*. New York: Harmony Books.

Yoshiro, Manaka, and Ian Urquhart. 1995. *The Layman's Guide to Acupuncture*. New York: Weatherhill.

For an excellent and encyclopedic reference on alternative approaches to healing, see: *Alternative Medicine: The Definitive Guide*. 1995. Edited by the Burton-Goldberg Group. Fife, Washington: Future Medicine Publishing.

5

Caring for Your Body: Nutrition

Over the past twenty years the relationship between diet and mood has been well established. It is known that certain foods and substances tend to create additional stress and anxiety, while others promote a calmer and steadier mood. Certain natural substances have a directly calming effect while others are known to have an antidepressant effect. Many of you reading this book may not yet recognize connections between how you feel and what you eat. You may simply not perceive that the amount of coffee or cola you drink aggravates your anxiety level. You may be unaware that eating insufficient amounts of protein can aggravate your anxiety and depression. Or you may not recognize the connection between your consumption of white sugar and anxiety, depression, or premenstrual symptoms. I hope this chapter will clarify some of these connections and help you to make positive changes in the way you feel.

Your body depends on both an optimal quantity as well as quality of food. As for quantity, you need to balance the number of calories you consume with your level of energy expenditure. Sixty percent of adults in the United States are overweight due to a high caloric diet combined with a sedentary lifestyle. Most weight problems are resolved not by fad diets but simply by eating healthy foods in combination with sufficient exercise. Just as important as quantity is the quality of what you eat. Taking care of your body means being willing to eat whole foods that are free of toxic, artificial substances. Your body also needs food that has sufficient energy to sustain and enhance its intrinsic vitality rather than deplete it. The nutrient content of food is important, but so is its closeness to nature—the less processed, the better. Fresh raw vegetables and fruits are more compatible with health than their cooked, frozen, or canned counterparts. You will derive more energy from an apple than a bag of buttered popcorn. Finally, taking care of yourself means eating food of sufficient variety to meet the full range of your body's needs. This includes complex carbohydrates such as vegetables and whole grains; fats such as oils and nuts; and proteins such as poultry, fish or soy products.

This chapter is divided into three sections. The first offers a series of guidelines for upgrading your diet. My suggestion is that you familiarize yourself with these guidelines but do not try to implement them all at once. Most people find it's easiest to modify their diets gradually, making one or two basic changes at a time. (It took me about ten years to adopt all of the changes suggested in this chapter.)

The second section of the chapter considers vitamins and supplements. It explains why you are unlikely to obtain adequate vitamins from food alone without relying on supplements. Also mentioned are a number of special supplements—amino acids, herbs, glandulars, and hormones that can be used specifically to reduce anxiety and/or depression—or to increase your overall energy level and sense of vitality.

The final section of the chapter addresses the important subject of detoxification. Many people feel unwell because they are toxic—having absorbed toxins from processed foods, from environmental pollutants, or from their own physiological stress response for too many years. The good news is that it is relatively easy to relieve the body of excessive toxicity. The "short" method is to fast for a few days, while the "long" method is simply to eat a wholesome diet consisting of fresh, whole, unprocessed foods. Guidelines for both approaches to detoxification are suggested.

Part 1: Guidelines for Improving Your Nutrition

As you read through these guidelines, be aware that the first three are most directly relevant to reducing your susceptibility to anxiety. The remaining guidelines are important, though, in enhancing your overall health and sense of well-being.

Minimize or Eliminate Caffeine

Of all the dietary factors that can aggravate anxiety and trigger panic attacks, caffeine is the most notorious. Several of my clients can trace their first panic attack to an excessive intake of caffeine. Many people find that they feel calmer and sleep better after they've reduced their caffeine consumption. Caffeine has a directly stimulating effect on several different systems in your body. It increases the level of the neurotransmitter norepinephrine in your brain, causing you to feel alert and awake. It also produces the very same physiological arousal response that is triggered when you are subjected to stress—increased sympathetic nervous system activity and a release of adrenaline.

In short, too much caffeine can keep you in a chronically tense, aroused condition, leaving you more vulnerable to generalized anxiety as well as panic attacks. Caffeine further contributes to your stress by depleting vitamin B1 (thiamine), which is one of the so-called "antistress" vitamins.

Caffeine is contained not only in coffee but also in many types of tea, cola beverages, chocolate candy, cocoa, and over-the-counter drugs.

If you are prone to generalized anxiety, phobias, or panic attacks, I suggest that you reduce your total caffeine consumption to *less than 50 mg per day*. For example, one cup of percolated coffee or one diet cola beverage a day would be a maximum. For coffee lovers this may seem like a major sacrifice, but you may be surprised to find how much better you feel if you can wean yourself down to a single cup in the morning. The sacrifice may well be worth having fewer panic attacks or other anxiety symptoms. For those people who are very sensitive to caffeine, I would recommend eliminating it altogether.

Please note that there are tremendous individual differences in sensitivity to caffeine. As with any addictive drug, chronic caffeine consumption leads to increased tolerance and a potential for withdrawal symptoms. If you have been drinking five cups of coffee a day and abruptly cut down to one a day, you may have withdrawal reactions including fatigue, depression, and headaches. It's better to taper off gradually over a period of a month or two. Some people like to substitute decaffeinated coffee, which has about 4 mg of caffeine per cup, while others substitute herbal teas. At the opposite extreme of the sensitivity continuum are people who are made jittery by a single cola or cup of tea. Some of my clients have found that even small amounts of caffeine predispose them to panic or a sleepless night. So it's important that you experiment to find out what your own *optimal* daily caffeine intake might be. For most people prone to anxiety or panic, this turns out to be less that 50 mg per day. Please refer to the Caffeine Chart on the next page to determine your own level of caffeine intake.

A well-known holistic physician, Andrew Weil (1995), recommends avoiding caffeine if you have any of the following: panic/anxiety, insomnia, migraine, cardiac arrhythmia, hypertension, gastrointestinal disorders, premenstrual syndrome, tension headaches, prostate trouble, or urinary disorder.

In addition to eliminating caffeine, it's important to eliminate stimulants that mimic the effects of caffeine. Ephedrine and pseudoephedrine, found in many over-the-counter cold remedies, can aggravate anxiety in sensitive persons.

Caffeine Chart

Caffeine content of coffee, tea, and cocoa (milligrams per 6 oz. cup)

Coffee, instant	60–70 mg
Coffee, percolated	90–110 mg
Coffee, drip	120–150 mg
Tea bag—5 minute brew	50–60 mg
Tea bag—1 minute brew	30–40 mg
Loose tea—5 minute brew	40–50 mg
Cocoa	10–20 mg
Chocolate (dry, 1 oz.)	5–10 mg
Decaffeinated Coffee	3–10 mg

Caffeine content of cola beverages (milligrams per 12-ounce can)

Coca-Cola	65 mg
Pepsi-Cola	43 mg
Dr Pepper	61 mg
Mountain Dew	50 mg

(Note: This table does not include caffeine present in over-the-counter medications such as NoDoz, Dexatrim, Anacin, Excedrin, or Midol.)

Reduce or Eliminate All Forms of Sugar

Our bodies are not equipped to process large amounts of sugar and, in fact, it was not until the twentieth century that most people (other than the very wealthy) consumed large amounts of refined sugar. Today, the standard American diet includes white sugar in most beverages (coffee, tea, cola), sugar in cereal, sugar in salad dressings, sugar in processed meat, along with one or two desserts per day and perhaps a donut or a cookie on coffee breaks. This sugar may be disguised under a variety of names, including dextrose, sucrose, maltose, raw sugar, brown sugar, corn syrup, corn sweeteners, and high fructose. The average American consumes about *120 pounds* of sugar per year! The result of continually bombarding the body with this much sugar is the creation of a chronic dysfunction in sugar metabolism. For some people this dysfunction can lead to excessively high levels of blood sugar, or diabetes (whose prevalence has increased dramatically in this century). For an even larger number of individuals, the problem is just the opposite—periodic drops in blood sugar level below normal, a condition that is termed *hypoglycemia*.

The symptoms of hypoglycemia tend to appear when your blood sugar drops below 50 to 60 milligrams per milliliter—or when it drops very rapidly from a higher to a lower level. Typically this occurs about two to three hours after eating a meal. *It can also occur simply in response to stress*, since your body utilizes sugar very rapidly under stress. The most common subjective symptoms of hypoglycemia are:

- Light-headedness

- Anxiety

- Trembling

- Feelings of unsteadiness or weakness

- Irritability

- Heart palpitations

These symptoms probably look familiar. All of them are symptoms that can accompany a panic attack. In fact, *for some people panic reactions may actually be caused by hypoglycemia*. Generally, such people recover from panic simply by having something to eat. Their blood sugar rises and they feel better. (In fact, an informal, nonclinical way to diagnose hypoglycemia is to determine whether you have any of the above symptoms three or four hours after a meal, and whether they then go away as soon as you have something to eat.)

The majority of people with anxiety problems find that their panic or anxiety reactions do *not* necessarily correlate with bouts of low blood sugar. Yet hypoglycemia can *aggravate* both generalized anxiety and panic attacks that have been caused for other reasons.

Hypoglycemia can be formally diagnosed through a clinical test called *the six-hour glucose tolerance test*. After a twelve-hour fast, you drink a highly concentrated sugar solution. Your blood sugar is then measured at half-hour intervals over a six-hour period. You will likely get a positive result on this test if you have a moderate to severe problem with hypoglycemia. Unfortunately, many *milder* cases of hypoglycemia are missed by the test. It's quite possible to have subjective symptoms of low blood sugar and test negative on a glucose tolerance test. Any of the following subjective symptoms are suggestive of hypoglycemia:

- You feel anxious, light-headed, weak, or irritable three or four hours after a meal (or in the middle of the night); these symptoms disappear within a few minutes of eating.

- You get a "high" feeling from consuming sugar and this changes to a depressed, irritable, or "spacey" feeling twenty to thirty minutes later.

- You experience anxiety, restlessness, or even palpitations and panic in the early morning hours, between 4:00 and 7:00 A.M. (Your blood sugar is lowest in the early morning because you have fasted all night.)

How do you deal with hypoglycemia? Fortunately, it's quite possible to overcome problems with low blood sugar by 1) making several important dietary changes, and 2) taking certain supplements. If you suspect that you have hypoglycemia or have had it formally diagnosed, you may want to implement the following guidelines:

- Eliminate as much as possible all types of simple sugar from your diet. This includes foods that obviously contain white sugar or sucrose such as candy, ice cream, desserts, and soft drinks. It also includes subtler forms of sugar, such as honey, brown sugar, corn syrup, corn sweeteners, molasses, maltose, dextrose, and "high fructose." Be sure to read labels on any and all processed foods to detect these various forms of sugar.

- Substitute fruits (other than dried fruits, which are too concentrated in sugar) for sweets. Avoid fruit juices or dilute them one to one with water.

- Reduce or eliminate simple starches such as pasta, refined cereals, potato or corn chips, and white bread. Substitute instead complex carbohydrates such as whole grain breads and cereals, vegetables, and brown rice or other whole grains.

- Have a complex carbohydrate and protein snack (such as cheese and whole grain crackers or whole grain toast and tuna, for example) half-way between meals—around ten-thirty or eleven o'clock in the morning and especially around four or five in the afternoon. If you awaken early in the morning, you may also find that a small snack will help you to get back to sleep for a couple of hours. As an alternative to snacks between meals, you can try having four or five small meals per day no more than two to three hours apart. The point of either of these alternatives is to maintain a steadier blood sugar level.

Take the following supplements:

- Vitamin B-complex: 50–100 mg of all 11 B vitamins once per day with meals (under stress, take two per day)

- Vitamin C: 1,000 mg twice per day with meals

- Organic trivalent chromium (often called glucose tolerance factor): 200 mcg per day. This is available at your local health-food store.

Vitamin B-complex as well as vitamin C helps to increase your resiliency to stress, which can aggravate blood sugar swings. The B vitamins also help regulate the metabolic processes that convert carbohydrates to sugar in your body.

Trivalent chromium has a direct, stabilizing effect on your blood sugar level by facilitating the process by which insulin carries sugar to your cells.

If you're interested in exploring the subject of hypoglycemia in greater depth, you might want to read the following books (complete publication information is available in the references list at the end of the chapter): *Sugar Blues* by William Dufty, *Hypoglycemia: A Better Approach* by Paavo Airola, and *Low Blood Sugar and You* by Carlton Fredricks.

Minimize Eating Foods to Which You Are Allergic

An allergic reaction occurs when your body attempts to resist the intrusion of a foreign substance. For some people, certain foods affect the body like a foreign substance, not only causing classic allergic symptoms such as runny nose, mucus, and sneezing but a host of psychological or psychosomatic symptoms, including any of the following:

- Anxiety or panic

- Depression or mood swings

- Dizziness

- Irritability

- Insomnia

- Headaches

- Confusion and disorientation

- Fatigue

Such reactions occur in many individuals only when they eat an excessive amount of a particular food, a combination of offending foods, or have excessively low resistance due to a cold or infection. Other people are so highly sensitive that only a small amount of the wrong food can cause debilitating symptoms. Often the subtler, psychological symptoms have a delayed onset, making it difficult to connect them with the offending foods.

In our culture the two most common foods causing allergic reactions are milk or dairy products and wheat. It is *casein* in milk and *gluten* in wheat (both are types of proteins) that tend to cause problems. Other foods that can be a source of allergic response include alcohol, chocolate, citrus fruits, corn, eggs, garlic, peanuts, yeast, shellfish, soy products, or tomatoes. One of the most telling signs of food allergy is addiction. You tend to crave and are addicted to the very foods to which you are allergic. While chocolate is the most flagrant example of this, you might also take pause if you find yourself tending to crave bread (wheat), corn chips (corn), dairy products, or another specific type of food. Many people go for years without recognizing that the very foods they crave the most have a subtle but toxic effect on their mood and well-being.

How can you find out whether food allergies are aggravating your problems with anxiety? As in the case of hypoglycemia, there are both formal tests you can obtain from a nutritionally oriented doctor as well as informal tests you can conduct on your own.

Among formal clinical tests for food allergies, the RAST test (Radio Allergo Sorbent Test) and the ELISA test (Enzyme-Linked Immunosorbent Assay) are probably the most reliable. These are blood tests that measure the number of antibodies you produce in reaction to a wide range of foods. Elevated numbers of antibodies in your blood after you've been exposed to a specific food indicate that you are allergic to that food. Although expensive, such tests provide a detailed profile of all of the foods to which you're allergic, and can be a very helpful diagnostic tool.

A less formal and expensive way to assess food allergies is to conduct your own "elimination" test. If you want to determine whether you are allergic to wheat, simply eliminate all products containing wheat from your diet for two weeks and notice whether you feel better. Then, at the end of the two weeks, suddenly eat a large amount of wheat and carefully monitor any symptoms that appear over the next twenty-four hours. After testing wheat, you might want to test milk and milk products. It's important to experiment with only one potentially allergic type of food at a time so that you don't confound your results.

Another way to test food allergies is to take your pulse after eating a meal. If it's elevated by more than ten beats per minute above your normal rate, it's likely that you ate something you're allergic to.

The good news is that you probably do not have to permanently abstain from a food to which you are allergic. After a period of several months away from a food, it may be possible to eat it again occasionally without adverse effects. For example, instead of having bread at almost every meal, you'll find that you feel better having it only a couple times per week.

Food allergies can definitely be a contributing factor to excessive anxiety and mood swings for certain people. If you suspect this to be a problem, try experimenting with the elimination method and/or consult a qualified physician, nutritionist, or naturopathic doctor.

Reduce Saturated Animal Fats and Increase Vegetable-Based Fats

Over the past fifty years it has been consistently documented that diets high in saturated fats lead to increased risk of heart disease and stroke. Saturated fats are the fats that come from animal sources: beef, poultry, bacon, butter, eggs, whole milk, and cheese. High amounts of these fats consumed tend to end up as plaque deposits in your arteries, which over time accumulate to produce atherosclerosis. (*Atherosclerosis* is a hardening and thickening of artery walls due to deposits of fatty substances. If, over time, the arteries become blocked, a heart attack or stroke can result.) In fact, you may be surprised to know that saturated-fat consumption correlates more highly with heart disease than even cholesterol intake. Beware of claims about low cholesterol in foods that are still high in saturated fats.

Still it's important to obtain about 20 percent of your calories in fat (unless, because of age or family history, you are susceptible to heart disease. If so, consider lowering fat intake to 10 to 15 percent). Up to half of this should be in the form of polyunsaturated or monounsaturated oils, which are derived from seeds, nuts, and vegetable sources. Be careful that vegetable oils such as sesame and safflower oil are fresh and not rancid. Rancid oils (and nuts) are full of oxidized molecules called "free radicals," which can damage DNA (potentially leading to cancer) or the interior walls of your arteries, leading to atherosclerosis. Deep-fried foods are also a potent source of free radicals. (Antioxidant vitamins such as vitamin C, vitamin E, and selenium can help offset the effects of free radicals.)

Monounsaturated oils such as olive oil and canola oil are probably the safest to use. They tend to lower the "bad" type of cholesterol (LDL) without lowering the "good" kind (HDL). Buy them as "extra virgin" or cold-pressed at your health food store, since brands available at the grocery store are often heated, which changes their molecular structure in unhealthy ways.

I would recommend that, in addition to vegetable-based oils, you obtain the remainder of your fat either from organic poultry or fresh seafood. Salmon contains a fat (omega-3 fatty acid) that has an especially beneficial impact on the body.

Eat Whole, Unprocessed Foods

Try to eat foods that are fresh and as close to their natural state as possible. As one person put it, "If it grows, eat it; otherwise don't." Whole foods include fresh fruits, fresh vegetables, whole grains, unrefined cereals, beans, nuts, seeds, sea vegetables, fresh fish, and free-range, organic poultry. Food processing diminishes or destroys nutritional value in two ways. First, the food is fragmented at a cellular level. For example, in white flour the bran and germ of the wheat has been split off; what's left is only the pulp. In the process twenty different nutrients are removed. When the flour is subsequently "enriched," only four are put back in. Second, *additives and preservatives* are added to foods that are already partial or fragmented. These further reduce the value of the food and can be potentially toxic. Artificial colors and dyes, for example, can interact with and damage DNA. Some have been found to be toxic. Nitrites, added to many canned meats, are not themselves carcinogenic but may easily react with protein breakdown by-products in the digestive tract to form highly carcinogenic compounds known as *nitrosamines*. Among artificial sweeteners, saccharin is known to be carcinogenic and aspartame (Nutrasweet) may be. There is some evidence that high amounts of aspartame may be linked to brain tumors in laboratory animals. People sensitive to aspartame may also experience symptoms such as headaches, nausea, dizziness, insomnia, or depression. Other additives to avoid include monosodium glutamate (MSG), BHA and BHT, and sulfites.

In short, you can do much to enhance your sense of well-being, as well as avoid potential hazards, by replacing processed foods with whole foods whenever possible.

Reduce Consumption of Commercial Beef, Pork, and Poultry

Red meat poses a number of health hazards. It's no accident that countries low in red meat consumption have lower rates of cardiovascular disease and cancer. As mentioned in the previous section, red meats are high in saturated fats. Frequent consumption of beef increases your risk of atherosclerosis, the main cause of heart attacks and strokes. Red meat, pork, and most commercially available forms of poultry are derived from animals that have been fed hormones to promote weight gain and growth. There is good evidence that these hormones stress the animals, and there is reason to believe that they may aggravate stress levels in meat consumers as well. One of the effects of feeding cows, pigs, and chickens hormones is that these hormones suppress the animal's immune systems, making them more susceptible to infectious disease. To solve this problem, the animals are given antibiotics. When you eat commercial beef, pork, or poultry, you may be ingesting antibiotic residues along with hormones. Finally, the conditions in which animals live prior to slaughter are often akin to torture. Is it any wonder that commercial beef and poultry don't taste as good as they did thirty or forty years ago? If you're interested in reading further about abuses of the meat industry and their impact on both your health and society at large, I recommend the book *Diet for a New America* by John Robbins (1987).

Use Organic Foods When Possible

Organic foods are those fruits, vegetables, and grains that are grown with natural fertilizers and are free of being sprayed with pesticides or fungicides. Residues of these substances may be present in any fruit or vegetable not labeled organic. Meat and poultry in most stores is likely to contain steroid and antibiotic residues unless it's labeled organic or, in the case of chicken, is "free range." In response to consumer demand, some supermarkets have been offering produce guaranteed to be low or free of pesticide residues. Most health food stores also offer organic produce. I recommend you try to buy organic vegetables and fruits whenever possible. If they are unavailable in your area, you can minimize your exposure to harmful chemicals by observing the following guidelines:

- Wash all fruits and vegetables thoroughly before eating them.

- Remove the outer layers of head lettuce, cabbage, and other greens.

- If produce such as apples, cucumbers, or peppers have been waxed, peel them first (although this doesn't work well for peppers if you eat them raw).

- Avoid cooking with orange, lemon, or lime rind unless you obtain it from pesticide-free fruit.

Eat More Vegetables

Vegetables provide an excellent source of vitamins, minerals, and fiber. In an era where the standard diet is replete with sweets, soda pop, and snack foods, vegetables have become unpopular for many people. Yet this dislike is likely to have been acquired (most babies like vegetable baby foods) and can be unlearned. As you start to remove unhealthful foods from your diet, you may discover how tasty vegetables can be when they are fresh and properly prepared. Their natural flavors seem to come out best when they are lightly steamed.

It's a good idea to eat both raw and cooked vegetables on a daily basis. A salad consisting of different kinds of lettuce, cucumbers, radishes, carrots, onions, and tomatoes is a good accompaniment to lunch or dinner. Cooked broccoli, spinach, asparagus, string beans, or greens such as kale, chard, or bok choy go well with fish and rice for dinner. Cruciferous vegetables (cabbage, broccoli, kale, collards, mustard greens, brussels sprouts) are better eaten cooked. These vegetables have several benefits, including protection against colon cancer. My personal favorite is a mixture of carrots, potatoes, spinach, and broccoli with onions and ginger added for flavoring. If your energy is low, you will likely feel better after having such a mixture of lightly steamed vegetables, along with rice and tofu for balance.

Increase Fiber in Your Diet

Fiber consists of the indigestible parts of plants you eat. A certain amount in the diet is necessary for the proper functioning of your intestinal tract. If you're lacking fiber, you're likely to be prone to either digestive problems or constipation. Fiber can be found in grains, bran, fresh vegetables, and fruits. To increase your amount of fiber, you can try bran cereals or add bran to your favorite cereal. In general, try to eat ample amounts of fresh, raw vegetables and fruits. I suggest that you have some raw vegetables or a salad to accompany both lunch and dinner. Raw fruits are preferable between meals, since for many people it is difficult to digest fruit and proteins together. A certain amount of fiber is necessary, but too much (for example, a diet consisting solely of raw vegetables and whole grains) can stress the intestinal tract and cause bloating.

Chew Your Food

Apart from what you eat, the way you eat has an impact on the quality of your nutrition. If you eat too fast, or do not adequately chew your food, you'll miss a lot of the nutrient content as well as causing yourself indigestion. Digestion begins when you chew your food. If your food is not properly predigested in your mouth, much of it will not get adequately digested in your stomach. When this partially digested food passes on through your intestines, it's likely to putrefy and ferment—causing bloating, cramps, and gas. Moreover, you will get only a limited amount of the nutrition potentially available from your food, leading to the possibility of subtle forms of undernourishment.

To assure you get the full value of your food, give yourself time to eat and chew each mouthful of solid food at least fifteen to twenty times. If, after doing this, you still feel bloated or have problems with indigestion, I suggest you take digestive enzymes (available at all health food stores) with or after each meal. If you properly digest your food, you should feel satisfied and comfortable after a meal rather than dull or lethargic.

Drink Six to Eight Glasses of Purified Water Per Day

Why should you drink this amount of water? A primary reason is that water helps your kidneys. The main function of your kidneys is to filter out all kinds of toxic waste products of bodily metabolism as well as chemical and environmental pollutants from the outside. For your kidneys to operate properly, you need to drink plentiful amounts of water to help wash away waste. You especially need to drink ample water if you live in a hot environment, eat a lot of protein, drink alcohol or coffee, take medications, are running a fever, or have urinary problems.

The purity of the water you drink is important. Most water purification plants focus primarily on disinfection, largely ignoring chemical contamination from industrial or agricultural wastes that find their way into ground water. Disinfection is often accomplished through chlorination, which poses additional hazards. Chlorine is a poisonous gas that can cause toxic by-products, *trihalomethanes*, which are known to cause cancer and birth defects. For all of these reasons, I strongly recommend you *avoid drinking tap water*.

You can instead buy bottled water or attach a water purification system to your tap. If you buy bottled water, demand a detailed analysis of its contents. Some bottled spring waters may come from sources that have been affected by contaminated ground water. The two types of water purification systems most in use are activated carbon filters and reverse osmosis systems. Both filter out chlorine and toxic organic molecules; however, reverse osmosis systems will also filter out toxic metals. The downside of reverse osmosis systems is that they waste a lot of water. Activated carbon filter systems require that you replace the filter periodically. Either system is a vast improvement over plain tap water and certainly more convenient and cost-effective than continually purchasing bottled water.

Reduce Consumption of Milk and Milk Products

The dairy industry would like you to believe that milk is the healthiest and most nutritious of all drinks. Here are the facts:

- Lactose is part of the carbohydrate component of milk. Like many people, you may be *lactose intolerant*. Your stomach may not make the digestive enzyme *lactase*, which is needed to digest milk sugar (lactose). As a result, when you drink milk, you may experience bloating, excessive gas, and general intestinal distress.

- The butterfat in milk is the worst kind for your heart; it has a very high proportion of saturated fatty acids. Cheeses made from milk also have 50–70 percent butterfat content. If you must have milk or cheese, be sure to get the lowfat or nonfat variety.

- The protein in milk (casein) can produce an allergic response—most frequently in the form of mucus. It is common for milk and dairy products to aggravate chronic allergic conditions such as asthma, bronchitis, and sinusitis. Milk is also known to aggravate autoimmune conditions, such as rheumatoid arthritis and lupus.

- Much of the commercial milk you drink contains residues of drugs and hormones used by the dairy industry to increase the productivity of cows. Homogenization of milk removes bacteria but not the hormone residues. Raw milk from a certified dairy is likely to lack hormones, but it may contain bacteria.

In sum, I suggest you reduce your consumption of cow milk and milk-based products to a minimum. Cow milk is an ideal food for baby cows, but it wasn't intended for adult humans. Learn to enjoy (as I have) soy milk or rice milk, both of which are available in most health food stores.

Increase the Amount of Protein Relative to Carbohydrate You Eat

Until recently most nutritionists advocated eating a high amount of complex carbohydrates (e.g., whole grains, pastas, bread)—as much as 70 percent of total calories. The prevailing idea was that too much fat promoted cardiovascular disease and too much protein led to excessive acidity and toxicity in the body (see the section on detoxification below). The ideal diet was thought to consist of 15–20 percent fat, 15–20 percent protein, and the rest carbohydrates. These, in fact, were the percentages I advocated in the chapter on nutrition in *The Anxiety & Phobia Workbook*.

In the past few years, however, evidence has mounted against the idea of eating high quantities of carbohydrates, especially by themselves. Carbohydrates are used by the body to produce *glucose*, the form of sugar the body and brain use for fuel. In order to transport glucose to the cells, your pancreas secretes insulin. Eating high levels of carbohydrates means your body produces higher levels of insulin, and too much insulin has an adverse effect on some of the body's most basic hormonal and neuroendocrine systems, especially prostaglandins and serotonin.

In short, eating high amounts of cereals, breads, pastas, or even grains such as rice or vegetables such as carrots, corn, and potatoes can raise your insulin levels to the point that other basic systems are thrown out of balance. The answer is not to eliminate complex carbohydrates but to reduce them *proportionately* to the amounts of protein and fat you consume, *without increasing the total number of calories in your diet*. By doing this, you'll not end up eating a diet that is too high in fat or protein. Instead, you'll continue to eat fats and protein in moderation *while decreasing the amount of carbohydrate you have at each meal relative to the amount of fat and protein*. The optimal ratio may be 30 percent protein, 30 percent fat, and 40 percent carbohydrate, with vegetable sources of protein and fat preferable to animal.

Dr. Barry Sears, in his book *The Zone* (1995), presents considerable research supporting the value of reducing the proportion of carbohydrate relative to protein and fat. Personally, after having eaten a mostly vegetarian diet, I've found that I have a higher level of energy and a greater sense of well-being since introducing more protein relative to carbohydrate in my diet. Other clients of mine have said that increasing protein relative to carbohydrate at each meal has had a favorable effect on both anxiety and depression. This isn't surprising because anxiety and mood disorders often involve deficiencies in neuro-transmitters, especially serotonin. The body has no way to make neuro-transmitters (and serotonin in particular) without a steady supply of amino acids, which are derived from protein. Whether or not you agree with Dr. Sears' approach or choose to adopt a 40:30:30 diet, I highly recommend you have some protein (preferably in the form of fish, organic poultry, tofu, tempeh, or beans and grains) at every meal. On the other hand, aim not to exceed 30 percent protein—especially in the form of meat, chicken, or fish—as this may tend to make your body overly acidic.

What to Do When You Eat Out

The pressures and constraints of modern life require that many of us eat lunch or dinner out. The problem is that most restaurant food, even at its best, provides too many calories, too much saturated fat, too much salt, and often food that has been cooked in stale or rancid oils. Much restaurant food is less fresh than what you can obtain on your own. For the most part, eating in restaurants is not optimal for taking care of your health.

If you need to eat in restaurants often, I suggest the following guidelines:

- Avoid all fast food or "junk food" concessions.

- Whenever possible, eat out at natural food or health food restaurants that use whole, preferably organic foods.

- If natural food restaurants are unavailable, go to high quality seafood restaurants and order fresh fish, preferably broiled without butter or oil. Accompany the fish with fresh vegetables, potatoes or rice, and a green salad. On the salad, avoid creamy or dairy-based dressings.

- As a third choice, try a high-quality Chinese or Japanese restaurant, and have a meal consisting of rice, vegetables, and fresh fish or tofu (bean curd). In Chinese restaurants, be sure to ask the waitress to leave off MSG (monosodium glutamate), a flavor enhancer to which many people are allergic.

- As a general rule, when eating out have no more than one roll, one pat of butter, and minimize ordering cream-based soups such as clam chowder (this one has been challenging for me, personally). Get your salad dressings on the side, using oil and vinegar or a low-fat Italian dressing. Stick with simple entrees such as chicken or whitefish without elaborate sauces or toppings. If possible, try to avoid high-fat desserts. Don't hesitate to ask your waitress for assistance in having food prepared according to your needs. Learn to enjoy the subtle tastes of simple foods. This becomes easy and desirable after a while when you omit rich, high-fat, and sugary foods.

As you think back over all of the guidelines for improving your nutrition, keep in mind that it's unnecessary to try to adopt them all at once. I recommend that you begin by decreasing your caffeine and sugar consumption, which will have the most direct impact on reducing your vulnerability to stress and anxiety. Beyond these suggestions, go at your own pace in upgrading your diet. You're more likely to *maintain* a dietary change that you've decided you truly *want* to make—instead of pressuring yourself.

Part 2: Vitamins and Other Supplements

Vitamins play a critical role in regulating thousands of metabolic reactions that occur every moment in your body. There has been controversy over the past two decades, however, regarding the need for taking vitamin supplements in addition to the vitamins naturally obtained in food. Even among nutritionists who generally advocate supplements, there is disagreement over what constitutes appropriate doses. The position offered here reflects both my personal experience as well as the experience of many of my clients.

Fifty years ago, the U.S. Food and Nutrition Board set up the RDA—the "recommended daily allowance"—as the standard amounts of specific vitamins needed by a healthy person. The amounts decided upon were the *minimum* amount of each vitamin needed to ward off diseases such as beriberi, rickets, scurvy, and night blindness. RDAs do not specify *optimal* amounts of vitamins needed to enhance and maximize health. Yet many physicians to this day argue that if you take a multivitamin at all, all you need is one containing the RDAs of vitamins A, B-complex, C, and E.

Such a recommendation underestimates the average person's supplementation needs for several reasons. First, the standard diet eaten by a majority of persons in America consists of large amounts of processed foods that are deficient or devoid of vitamins. Few persons eat the nutrient-rich, farm-fresh foods that our great grandparents enjoyed. Second, even those who are able to eat fresh whole grains, fruits, and vegetables may not get sufficient amounts of minerals. This is due to the widespread depletion of minerals in soils that have been rigorously farmed for many decades. Third, the average person in modern society faces numerous special circumstances where the body's normal store of certain vitamins is rapidly depleted. If you're under stress, for example, you will rapidly deplete B vitamins, vitamin C, calcium, and magnesium. Smoking and drinking deplete certain B vitamins. Living in a polluted area will increase your need for antioxidant vitamins such as vitamin C, vitamin E, and selenium. Special conditions such as pregnancy, old age, or chronic degenerative diseases such as arteriosclerosis, arthritis, or osteoporosis can be benefited by high doses of certain vitamins.

For these reasons in particular, I recommend that you consider taking higher doses of supplements than provided by the RDAs. Some nutritionists have relabeled such doses ODAs—or "optimal daily allowance."

The following regimen of vitamin supplements is recommended for all anxiety disorders as well as any condition or illness accompanied by high stress.

1. Vitamin B-complex: 50 mg one or two times per day. B vitamins are necessary to maintain proper functioning of the nervous system. Taking all eleven of the B vitamins in a B-complex at the suggested dose will increase your resilience to stress.

2. Vitamin C (preferably with bioflavonoids): 2,000–4,000 mg per day. Vitamin C is well known for its ability to strengthen the immune system and promote healing from infection, disease, and injury. It is also important for the adrenal glands, whose proper functioning is necessary for your ability to cope with stress. (If taking vitamin C at these doses bothers your stomach, consider taking it in the form of calcium ascorbate.)

3. Calcium and magnesium in combination: 1,000–1,500 mg calcium to 500–1,000 mg magnesium (preferably chelated forms). Calcium is involved in the process of nerve transmission. Its depletion can cause nerve cell overactivity, which may be one of the underlying causes of anxiety. Magnesium also plays an important role in nerve and muscle activity. Supplements with magnesium can help depression, dizziness, heart arrhythmias, muscle weakness, and PMS. Both calcium and magnesium work as natural tranquilizers when taken in the doses suggested above. It's good to take them together, as they work in tandem and balance each other.

4. Zinc: 30 mg per day. Zinc can have a calming effect on the nervous system. It also contributes to maintaining a healthy immune and reproductive system.

5. Chromium: 200 mcg per day. Chromium is necessary for proper utilization of blood glucose. It is especially important in stabilizing blood sugar levels in hypoglycemia.

In taking vitamin supplements, please observe the following guidelines:

- Always take vitamins with meals. Digestive enzymes secreted in response to food will help digest vitamins.

- Taking B-complex or vitamin C in two or three doses throughout the day is preferable to a single large dose. The body can absorb only so much of a vitamin at a given time; it excretes what it doesn't use.

- Vitamins in capsule form are preferable to tablets, since they are easier to digest.

- Supplements obtained at health food stores are less likely to contain inferior quality fillers or binders, which can cause indigestion or allergic responses in some people.

Amino Acids

Amino acids are natural constituents of protein. For many years they have been used to treat both anxiety and mood disorders. Certain amino acids can have a similar effect as prescription antidepressants since they increase the amounts of particular neurotransmitters in the brain. While these amino acids may not be quite as potent as the prescription medications, they have the advantage of having fewer side effects. You may wish to talk to a qualified health practitioner or see the book *The Way Up From Down* (1987) by Priscilla Slagle to expand on the information below.

Tryptophan

Tryptophan is a chemical precursor of serotonin. Taking supplemental tryptophan will increase serotonin levels in your brain, much as Prozac and other SSRI antidepressants do. However, tryptophan increases serotonin naturally by being directly converted into serotonin after it enters the brain. SSRI medications increase serotonin by blocking its reabsorption at the synapse. Tryptophan is available in two forms, 5-hydroxy tryptophan (5-HT) and L-tryptophan. Both forms help depression and anxiety by raising serotonin levels; however, L-tryptophan has a somewhat more sedative effect and works well as a sleep aid. L-tryptophan was recently reintroduced in the U.S. after a seven-year absence. A tainted batch of tryptophan caused a serious illness, eosinophilia myalgia, in 1989, and so the FDA banned it from over-the-counter sales. The L-tryptophan available today is safe and beneficial, although to my knowledge it's only available by prescription. As of this writing, 5-hydroxy tryptophan is available over the counter in health food stores. Consult your naturopathic or holistic physician if you wish to use tryptophan.

The recommended dose of L-tryptophan is 500–2,000 mg per day; 500 mg is effective as a mild relaxant, whereas 1,000 to 2,000 mg works as a sedative. For 5-HT, the recommended dose is 100 to 500 mg per day. The effect of tryptophan can be enhanced by taking it together with 1) a carbohydrate snack, 2) 50 mg vitamin B6, and 3) the amino acid taurine (500 mg). Avoid taking tryptophan with protein foods, as this causes other amino acids to compete with tryptophan to get into the brain. Please do *not* take tryptophan if you are already taking a prescription SSRI antidepressant medication (Prozac, Paxil, Zoloft, Luvox, or Serzone).

Gamma-Amino Butyric Acid

Gamma-amino butyric acid (GABA) is actually a neurotransmitter that serves to reduce excessive nerve transmission in the brain. Supplemental GABA would be a potent tranquilizer except for the fact that only a very small percentage of what you take actually ever gets to the brain. Many people report they experience a mildly relaxing effect from doses of GABA in the 300 to 1,000 mg range. Various products containing GABA, alone or in combination with relaxing herbs, are available at your health food store. GABA is best taken on an empty stomach or in combination with a carbohydrate snack.

DL-phenylalanine and Tyrosine

Used in the treatment of depression, DL-phenylalanine (DLPA) and tyrosine are chemical precursors of norepinephrine, an important neurotransmitter. Thus they work like tricyclic antidepressants such as imipramine (Tofranil), desipramine (Norpramin), or nortriptyline (Pamelor). They are less potent than prescription antidepressants but also have very few side effects. Therapeutic doses range from 1,000 to 3,000 mg per day. Generally it's good to start with 500 mg and gradually increase the dose over a week. Try DLPA first and, if it has no effect, try tyrosine. Please do not use DLPA or tyrosine if you are pregnant, have PKU (a disease requiring a phenylalanine-free diet), or are taking a MAO-inhibitor medication such as Nardil or Parnate. If you have high blood pressure, have a physician monitor your use of these amino acids. (See *The Way Up From Down* for more detailed information.)

Herbs

Herbs have been used for hundreds of years to induce a relaxing effect. Although not as potent as prescription tranquilizers such as Xanax, Ativan, or Klonopin, they have few side effects and are nonaddictive. Many people obtain benefit in using herbs for mild to moderate states of anxiety. The following herbs have been most helpful to my clients.

Natural tranquilizers

Kava kava: Several of my clients have found kava to be the most potent and useful of herbal tranquilizers. Some have even found it helpful in diminishing their reliance on Xanax. Kava is available in 300 mg capsules and also in liquid extract and sublingual forms. Take one to four capsules to help reduce mild to moderate anxiety. (Do not exceed 12 capsules per day.) If kava causes you to feel drowsy when you need to be awake, reduce the dose.

Valerian root: Valerian has a long history of popularity as a natural relaxant and is widely used in Europe. Use it as directed on the bottle. You may find the liquid extract form or bulk tea to have more potent effects than the capsules.

Passionflower: Passionflower is a popular herb available from several different companies in 300 mg capsules or liquid extracts. Take one to three capsules for a mildly relaxing effect. (Do not exceed 12 capsules per day.)

Gotu kola: Gotu kola has been popular for thousands of years in India. It has a mildly relaxing effect and helps to revitalize a weakened nervous system. It also decreases fatigue and depression while increasing memory and intelligence. It's available from various companies, typically in 300–435 mg capsules or liquid extracts. Take two capsules two or three times per day. I personally use gotu kola and find it to be quite beneficial.

Ginkgo biloba: Research shows that ginko biloba improves brain function by increasing cerebral blood flow and oxygenation. It helps depression, anxiety, headaches, memory loss, and tinnitus. Take three to four 60 mg capsules per day.

St. John's Wort: A number of well-controlled studies have found St. John's Wort to be equally effective as prescription medications in alleviating mild to moderate depression. Results with anxiety disorders are inconclusive to date. This herb may function in a way similar to SSRI medication (see Chapter 7), i.e., blocking the reuptake of serotonin. It is widely used in Germany and is catching on in the United States. Take three 300-mg capsules each day (make sure that you obtain a standardized extract containing 0.3 percent hypericin), and continue for a month before evaluating results. Avoid taking St. John's Wort if you are already taking an SSRI medication. For further information, see the book *Hypericum & Depression*, by Bloomfield, Nordfors, and McWilliams (1996).

Most herbs can be taken in one of three different forms: 1) capsules, 2) liquid extracts or tinctures, or 3) teas. Many people prefer capsules because of their convenience. Others report they get the most potent effects from extracts or teas. You might want to experiment to see which form you prefer. In using herbs, it's best to take them in divided doses two or three times per day, since they tend to be short-acting (one or two hours following dose). A good reference for further information on herbs is the book *Healing Anxiety with Herbs* by Harold Bloomfield (1998).

Glandulars

Glandulars—concentrated forms of various animal glands—are frequently used to enhance the health of certain endocrine glands. For example, raw adrenal glandular extract is helpful in restoring optimal functioning of the adrenal glands, whose activity can be suppressed or exhausted in people who have been exposed to extreme or long-term stress. A number of my clients have found it to be useful. Symptoms of adrenal exhaustion include: 1) dizziness upon standing from a seated or prone position; 2) low stress-tolerance; 3) frequent fatigue or lethargy, 4) high allergic sensitivity, and/or 5) hypoglycemia. Other glandular supplements may be used to enhance the functioning of the thyroid, pituitary, thymus, or sex glands. I suggest you work with glandulars under the supervision of a nutritionally oriented physician or naturopath.

Hormones

Several types of hormones are now available at health food stores to supplement presumed deficiencies. Recently the two most popular entries to this category have been melatonin and dehydroepiandosterone (DHEA).

Melatonin is a hormone secreted at night by the pineal gland to signal the brain that it is time to go to sleep. Supplemental melatonin, in doses of 3 mg, has helped many people to get to sleep. However, some persons report they get no benefit from melatonin and/or experience grogginess in the morning.

DHEA is a hormone manufactured by the adrenal cortex and is used in the synthesis of several other hormones in the body, including the sex hormones estrogen and testosterone. Many people report increased energy and sense of well-being, an improved capacity to cope with stress, and improved mood and sleep after taking DHEA for a few weeks. I have personally found DHEA to be helpful. The standard recommended dose is 25 to 50 mg per day. Avoid taking higher doses, as some physicians believe that high doses can suppress the body's natural ability to make DHEA.

Part 3: Detoxification

Over a period of time, your body tends to accumulate toxins as a result of 1) chemicals and additives in the food you eat, 2) environmental pollutants (in the air, the water you drink, as well as "indoor pollution"), 3) drugs—both prescription and recreational—as well as 4) the waste products of your own metabolism. If you have reached a high level of toxicity, you may experience any of the following symptoms on a chronic basis:

- Excess mucus (coughing and wheezing)

- Allergies

- Digestive problems

- Fatigue and low energy

- Joint pains

- Headaches

- Insomnia

- Constipation

- Sensitivity to chemicals in the environment

Excessive toxicity may not directly increase anxiety. Yet, it adds to the physical stress level of your body, thus indirectly aggravating tension and anxiety as well as affecting your mood.

There are two ways to remedy an overly toxic condition—one short-term and the other long-term. The long-term approach is to adopt changes in your diet and lifestyle that tend to minimize exposure to toxins. The short-term approach is fasting. Let's consider each approach.

Diet and Lifestyle Modifications

You can gradually free yourself of toxic overload through a variety of measures. Some of the most important are as follows:

- Avoid preservatives or additives in foods you consume. Try to eat unprocessed, whole foods as much as possible.

- Eliminate caffeine, nicotine, sugar, and alcohol from your diet—all of which leave toxic waste products in your body.

- Minimize your use of drugs, taking only necessary prescription medications at the minimum dose you need. Recreational drugs are particularly toxic to the body over time.

- Reduce animal proteins (especially meat, poultry, eggs, and dairy) and increase vegetable protein sources (i.e., tofu, tempeh, and beans). When metabolized, animal protein can produce toxic byproducts, especially if it is not properly digested.

- Drink more water (purified if possible). Approximately eight glasses per day will assist your kidneys in their natural process of elimination.

- Move away from acid-forming, congestive foods toward more alkaline-forming, detoxifying foods. Reduce your consumption of red meat, sweets, fried foods, fatty foods, milk, cheese, eggs, refined flour, salty foods, as well as any foods you know you're allergic to such as wheat or dairy. Increase your consumption of fresh vegetables, fruits, whole grains, beans, nuts and seeds, and the proportion of raw to cooked foods that you eat. (Be aware that the degree to which you move from acid to alkaline-forming foods should be tailored to your individual constitution and needs. If you've been highly toxic in your eating habits, make the change gradually.)

- Begin using the antioxidant supplements that aid in detoxifiction—vitamin C, vitamin E, beta-carotene, selenium, zinc, and the amino acids L-cysteine and L-methionine.

- Investigate using the various herbs that can help cleanse your body of toxicity, including garlic, dandelion root, cayenne, ginger, licorice, burdock, echinacea, and goldenseal. Consult a qualified nutritionist or herbologist before using these herbs on your own to support detoxification.

- Regular physical exercise is a particularly important means of clearing your body of toxins through sweating as well as aiding the digestive, renal, and lymphatic systems.

- Colon cleansing can be achieved naturally by increasing fiber in your diet (see above). For a stronger cleanse, use psyllium seed husks, available in most health food stores, to cleanse mucus along the small intestine and pull toxins from both the small and large intestines. Natural laxatives containing bentonite, senna, and/or cascara sagrada can also be helpful.

Having one day per week when you lighten your diet can assist detoxification. Personally, I like to simplify my diet every Sunday—eating one or two meals instead of three and having only vegetables, light grains, and/or fruits. A single two or three day period of light eating each month will provide an even deeper level of cleansing.

Fasting

Fasting is a safe and effective method for detoxifying your body over a relatively short time period. It can be defined as the avoidance of solid foods and taking in liquids only for at least one day. By relieving the body of the work of digesting foods, fasting gives the digestive system a deep rest and allows the body to give its full energy over to elimination of toxins.

Although traditionally fasting meant drinking water alone, I recommend that you do not do this. Fasting on water tends to be hard on most people, especially if you are prone to episodes of low blood sugar (hypoglycemia). The best way to fast is to limit your consumption to only vegetable and fruit juices, as well as herbal teas.

When you stop eating solid foods and allow your stomach to remain empty, your body goes into a natural elimination cycle. The energy you ordinarily use for digestion is redirected toward enhancing elimination as well as immune function. A three-day fast is often sufficient to allow the body to rid itself of excessive toxins, which are released especially from the liver, kidneys, and colon. During this time the blood and lymph (a clear liquid that bathes the tissues of the body) also have an opportunity to detoxify. A five-day fast permits an even deeper process of healing and rebuilding of the immune system. Toxins, including drug and medication residues stored in body fats, are eliminated. During the first two days of a fast, you may experience some withdrawal symptoms, including headaches, weakness, fatigue, irritability, and emotional sensitivity. These symptoms usually diminish by the third day.

If you decide to try fasting, please observe the following guidelines:

- To prepare for the fast, eat only raw vegetables and fruits for one or two days prior to beginning juices alone. If you've been eating a particularly toxic diet, I recommend eating whole grains, vegetables, and tofu for two days before going to raw vegetables and fruit.

- During the fast, drink raw vegetable juices (one or two 8-ounce glasses) three times per day when you would ordinarily have a meal. It's best to prepare these juices from raw vegetables such as fresh carrots, beets, tomatoes, celery, cabbage, and/or green leafy vegetables such as spinach or kale, using a juicer. A juicing machine is a good investment if you intend to do juice fasting. If you do not have a juicer, gently boil the vegetables until you obtain a broth, adding no seasoning. Make the broth each day and use it instead of raw juice. Do not use tomato juice, V-8 juice, or any juice made with additives. If you prefer, you can substitute a blend of fresh fruit juices for one of the three "meals," though this is not recommended if you are hypoglycemic. Dilute all juices with purified water, 1 part water to 3 parts juice.

- If you are hypoglycemic, add a protein supplement (not protein powder) to the fast. Spirulina is a good choice. If you are using tablets, take five tablets three times daily. During your fast, omit vitamin supplements, except for vitamin C.

- While on your fast, consume three cups of herbal tea per day between "meals." The best herbs to use for detoxification are dandelion root, milk thistle, red clover, and/or rose hips (a combination of these is best). If you want a milder, more soothing herb tea, try peppermint or licorice tea, either boiling the bulk tea or using tea bags.

- Be generous in drinking water while fasting. Up to eight 8-ounce glasses of purified water per day will enhance elimination.

- If you want to fast for more than three days, please do so only under the supervision of a qualified health professional who has experience with fasting.

- Colon cleansing is an essential part of fasting. Because you are not eating solid food, your body doesn't eliminate wastes in the normal way. Most fasting programs recommend doing a water enema each day of the fast to flush the colon of toxins. Kits with instructions can be obtained from your local drugstore. If you prefer not using enemas, an alternative is to use powdered psyllium or to take herbal laxatives such as senna or cascara sagrada each day.

- During your fast, try to get plenty of rest. It's preferable not to schedule a fast while working; try it on a three-day weekend or while on vacation, if possible. Mild exercise, particularly walking, is a good idea.

- If you have diabetes, severe hypoglycemia, or any other severe, chronic health issue, please consult with your doctor before fasting. If you are pregnant or lactating, do not fast.

- If you must eat during a fast, have a piece of watermelon, preferably alone (without juice or herb tea).

- After finishing your fast, do not resume your normal diet immediately, as this will undermine the benefits you've just achieved. Phase in your normal diet after a day or two of raw vegetables and fruits, followed by a day or two of cooked vegetables, whole grains, and tofu or tempeh.

For more detailed information on fasting, I would recommend the following books: *Mind-Body Purification System* by Leon Chaitow (1990) and *Staying Healthy with Nutrition* (1992) by Elson Haas (especially Chapter 18).

This chapter has examined a variety of strategies for improving what you eat. I hope it has enabled you to begin making some connections between what you eat and the way you feel, if you haven't done so already. Following even a few (particularly the first three) of the guidelines suggested in Part 1 of the chapter will help to reduce your susceptibility to anxiety. So will making an effort to reduce excess toxicity, whether you choose the more gradual method or decide to fast. In working with this chapter, be willing to experiment at your own pace. What you eat does make a substantial difference in how you feel, yet each of us is unique. Only you can determine for yourself which of the numerous guidelines and supplements suggested in this chapter will be most beneficial in your particular case. Seek help from a holistic doctor, naturopath, or other qualified health professional if you need further guidance.

What You Can Do Now

1. Evaluate the amount of caffeine in your diet, using the Caffeine Chart in this chapter, and attempt to gradually reduce your intake to less than 50 mg per day. If you are especially sensitive, you may want to eliminate caffeine altogether, substituting decaffeinated coffee (or herb teas) for regular coffee.

2. Reduce or stop smoking. In addition to significantly lessening your risk for cardiovascular disease and cancer, you will lower your susceptibility to panic attacks and anxiety.

3. Evaluate whether you experience the subjective symptoms of hypoglycemia—light-headedness, anxiety, depression, weakness, or shakiness—three or four hours after a meal (or in the early morning hours before rising) and whether they are quickly relieved by eating. You may want to follow this up with a formal six-hour glucose tolerance test. If you suspect that hypoglycemia is contributing to your problem with anxiety, strive to eliminate from your diet all forms of white sugar as well as brown sugar, honey, corn syrup, corn sweeteners, molasses, and high fructose. (Be careful also about aspartame or Nutrasweet. There is some evidence of a link between this substance and panic disorder for certain people.) Most fresh, whole fruits (not dried) are fine if you're hypoglycemic, although fruit juices should be diluted with water. Observe the guidelines listed for dealing with

hypoglycemia and consider taking the recommended supplements suggested in this chapter. You may want to consult a nutritionally oriented physician, naturopath, or qualified health practitioner to assist you in setting up an appropriate dietary and supplement regime.

4. Evaluate your susceptibility to food allergies. Take note of any types of food that you crave (paying attention particularly to wheat and dairy products) and try eliminating that food from your diet for two weeks. Then reintroduce the food and notice if you have any symptoms. If you suspect you have a problem with food allergies, consider getting a blood test from a holistic physician or naturopath.

5. Work with the remaining guidelines for improving your nutrition. Instituting even one or two of these guidelines is likely to increase your sense of well-being and resilience to anxiety and stress. In my experience, the guidelines recommending that you eat whole foods, chew your food well, and increase your intake of protein relative to carbohydrate are particularly important if you feel you are under considerable stress. *Avoid pushing yourself to radically change your diet all at once*, or you may end up rebelling against the idea of making any changes. Introduce one small change each week (or perhaps even each month) so that you gradually modify your dietary habits.

6. Take the supplements recommended for anxiety and stress, especially B-complex, vitamin C, and calcium-magnesium.

7. You may want to explore whether amino acids can be helpful, specifically GABA and L-tryptophan for anxiety and 5-hydroxy tryptophan, tyrosine, or DL-phenylalanine for depression. Consult the book by Priscilla Slagle (listed below) or a physician experienced in the use of amino acid therapy for further information.

8. You may want to experiment with relaxing herbs such as kava, valerian, or passionflower to help relieve mild to moderate levels of anxiety. These herbs are available at most health food stores; be willing to try various forms (teas, capsules, tinctures) to see which you prefer.

9. Consult with a holistic physician, naturopath, or qualified nutritionist before using glandulars or hormones (such as DHEA) on your own.

10. Review the section on detoxification. You can relieve yourself of excessive toxicity gradually by following the suggested diet and lifestyle modifications. If you wish to detoxify more quickly via fasting,

please do so only under the supervision of a holistic physician, naturo-path, or qualified health professional (unless you have experience with fasting).

References and Further Reading

Airola, Paavo. 1977. *Hypoglycemia: A Better Approach.* Phoenix, Arizona: Health Plus Publishers.

Balch, James, and Phyllis Balch. 1997. *Prescription for Nutritional Healing* 2d ed. Garden City Park, New York: Avery Publishing Group. (A comprehensive reference book.)

Ballentine, Rudolph. 1982. *Diet and Nutrition: A Holistic Approach.* Honesdale, Pennsylvania: The Himalayan International Institute.

Bender, Stephanie. 1989. *PMS: Questions and Answers.* Los Angeles: Price Sloan.

Bloomfield, Harold H., Mikael Nordfors, and Peter McWilliams, 1996. *Hypericum & Depression.* Santa Monica, California: Prelude Press. (A good reference on St. John's Wort.)

Bloomfield, Harold. 1998. *Healing Anxiety with Herbs.* New York: Harper-Collins.

Chaitow, Leon. 1990. *Body-Mind Purification Program.* New York: Simon & Schuster. (A good reference on fasting.)

Colbin, Annemarie. 1986. *Food and Healing.* New York: Ballantine Books. (Excellent introductory book on nutrition.)

Colimore, Benjamin, and Sarah Steward Colimore. 1974. *Nutrition and Your Body.* Los Angeles: Light Wave Press. (Excellent basic textbook on nutrition.)

Dufty, William. 1974. *Sugar Blues.* New York: Warner Books. (Classic popular book on hypoglycemia.)

Fredericks, Carlton. 1969. *Low Blood Sugar and You.* New York: Grosset and Dunlap.

Haas, Elson M. 1992. *Staying Healthy with Nutrition.* Berkeley, California: Celestial Arts. (A very thorough and comprehensive layperson's text on nutrition.)

Lesser, Michael. 1980. *Nutrition and Vitamin Therapy.* New York: Grove Press. (Good basic introduction to vitamins and vitamin therapy.)

Ley, Beth M. 1996. *DHEA: Unlocking the Secrets to the Fountain of Youth.* Newport Beach: BML Publications.

Mindell, Earl. 1979. *Vitamin Bible.* New York: Warner Books.

Robbins, John. 1987. *Diet for a New America.* Walpole, New Hampshire: Stillpoint Publishing.

Sahelian, Ray, M.D. 1995. *Melatonin—Nature's Sleeping Pill.* Marina Del Rey, California: Be Happier Press.

Sears, Barry. 1995. *The Zone.* New York: HarperCollins.

Shelton, Herbert M. 1971. *The Hygiene System,* vol. 3. Chicago: Natural Hygiene Press.

Slagle, Priscilla. 1987. *The Way Up From Down.* New York: Random House.

Tessler, Gordon. *The Lazy Person's Guide to Better Nutrition.* (Available from Better Health Publications, 90 Madison Ave., Ste. 507, Denver, Colorado 80206—a quick and easy-to-read primer on nutrition.)

Tierra, Michael. 1990. *The Way of Herbs.* New York: Pocket Books. (Excellent reference on herbs.)

Weil, Andrew. 1995. *Natural Health, Natural Medicine.* New York: Houghton Mifflin.

———. 1995. *Spontaneous Healing.* New York: Fawcett Columbine. (Weil's informative and well-written books have spoken to great numbers of people exploring alternative approaches to health and wellness.)

Wurtman, Judith. 1988. *Managing Your Mind and Mood Through Food.* New York: Perennial Library.

6

Tools That Work: Help for Overcoming Panic and Phobias

Many readers of this book probably experience fear in the form of panic attacks, phobias, or other specific anxiety disorders. A wide range of concepts and strategies for overcoming anxiety in these forms are described in my first book, *The Anxiety & Phobia Workbook* (1995). They are also described in a dozen or so other books, written to help persons with anxiety disorders, that have appeared in the past ten years (see the list of references at the end of this chapter). These strategies all fall under the broad approach called "cognitive behavioral therapy." In brief, they include:

- Abdominal breathing
- Relaxation training
- Identifying and eliminating catastrophic thoughts that can cause panic
- Coping strategies to limit panic attacks
- Systematic desensitization for phobias
- Incremental exposure for phobias
- Reducing worry by countering mistaken or distorted thinking
- Assertiveness training

- Exposure and response prevention for obsessive-compulsive disorder

All of these strategies work. In fact, they work well enough that cognitive behavioral therapy has become the dominant approach to treating anxiety disorders by nearly all specialists in the field. Cognitive behavioral therapy will probably remain the dominant and most effective form of treatment for many years to come.

As you no doubt have gathered, the purpose of this book is to explore some perspectives and approaches to overcoming fear that lie beyond the mainstream, cognitive behavioral approach. However, I don't want anything I've written here to detract from the importance and potential effectiveness of cognitive behavioral methods. I strongly believe in the cognitive behavioral approach and use it in my therapy practice every day. The process of healing fear—particularly in the form of panic attacks and phobias—cannot be well served without including cognitive behavioral strategies. In this chapter, I've attempted to summarize what I believe is the very best that cognitive behavioral therapy has to offer. The material presented under the following five headings presents ideas and strategies I've found most helpful in my practice:

1. Panic Attacks Are Unpleasant but Not Dangerous

2. Coping Strategies for Managing Panic or Anxiety

3. How to Change Self-Talk

4. Brief Strategies for Coping with Anxiety

5. How to Face What You Fear

Feel free to read these various topics in whatever order suits you best. For quick and simple techniques to counter panic, anxiety, or worry, see Part 4 first. Parts 2 and 3 cover cognitive therapy for panic and phobias in more depth.

It's impossible to cover in one chapter all of the aspects and ramifications of cognitive behavioral therapy. For a more in-depth discussion of the above topics, please see *The Anxiety & Phobia Workbook*, especially Chapters 4–10.

Part 1: Panic Attacks Are Unpleasant but Not Dangerous

The Panic Cycle

A panic attack is a surge of mounting physiological arousal that can occur spontaneously or in response to encountering a phobic situation. Common physical symptoms of panic include: heart palpitations, tightening in the chest, chest pain, shortness of breath, dizziness, faintness, sweating, nausea, trembling, shaking, and/or tingling in the hands and feet. Psychological reactions that accompany these bodily changes include: an intense desire to run away, feelings of unreality, and fears of having a heart attack, going crazy, dying, or doing something uncontrollable.

Anyone who has had a full-fledged panic attack knows that it is one of the most intensely uncomfortable states human beings are capable of experiencing. Your very first panic attack can have a traumatic impact, leaving you feeling terrified and helpless, with strong anxiety about the possibility of a recurrence of your panic symptoms. Unfortunately, in some cases, panic does come back and occurs repeatedly. Why some people have a panic attack only once—or perhaps once every few years—while others develop a chronic condition with several attacks per week, is still not well understood by researchers in the field.

The good news is that you can learn to cope with panic attacks so well that they will no longer have the power to frighten you. There are two types of interventions that can help you diminish the intensity and frequency of panic attacks: long-term and short-term. Long-term interventions include changes in your lifestyle described elsewhere in this book. Particularly important are:

- Regular practice of deep relaxation (see Chapter 4)

- A regular program of exercise (see Chapter 4)

- Use of medication, if needed (see Chapter 7)

- Simplifying your life (see Chapter 3)

- Addressing personality issues that predispose you to anxiety (see Chapter 8)

Short-term strategies are the subject of this chapter. Such techniques are described in detail in *The Anxiety & Phobia Workbook* (especially Chapter 6) and other books on coping with panic attacks such as *An End to Panic* (1995) by Elke Zeurcher-White, *Don't Panic* (1996), by Reid Wilson, and *Coping with Panic Attacks* (1990) by George Clum. Short-term strategies include reeducation about panic attacks, specifically, that panic is a natural body response that is not dangerous. They also include specific techniques to stop anxiety from getting out of control when it first arises: using the Anxiety Scale, abdominal breathing, coping statements, and other diversion techniques. Revising catastrophic thoughts that contribute to panic is also critical.

A panic attack is the result of a sequence of events involving unpleasant body symptoms and catastrophic thoughts. *People who are prone to panic tend to interpret body symptoms such as heart palpitations or dizziness as dangerous or potentially catastrophic*; most other people do not. The panic sequence is illustrated below:

THE PANIC SEQUENCE

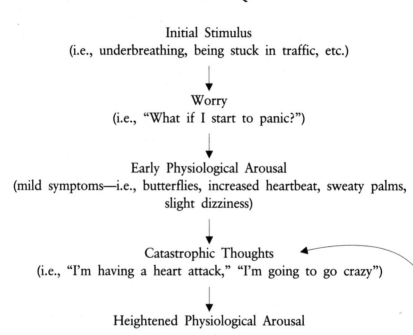

Initial Stimulus
(i.e., underbreathing, being stuck in traffic, etc.)

Worry
(i.e., "What if I start to panic?")

Early Physiological Arousal
(mild symptoms—i.e., butterflies, increased heartbeat, sweaty palms, slight dizziness)

Catastrophic Thoughts
(i.e., "I'm having a heart attack," "I'm going to go crazy")

Heightened Physiological Arousal

This cycle spirals up to full-blown panic

A panic attack begins with an *initial stimulus*—an event that may or may not be apparent to the person who subsequently panics. This initial stimulus can be external, such as encountering a situation where you panicked before, or internal, such as rapid heartbeat or reduced oxygen from underbreathing. Whether or not you're aware of the initial stimulus, you start to worry. Worry thoughts might include:

- "What if I panic here again?"

- "I'm starting to get dizzy—am I going to lose it again?"

- "Something feels off—I need to get out of here."

- "Uh oh—here it comes."

Your worry thoughts may occur so quickly that you don't even notice them. However, they set the stage for the next step in the panic sequence: *physiological arousal.* Your body is programmed to interpret any potential danger as a threat that you need to fight or flee. Within a second or two you respond to worried thoughts with physiological symptoms such as increasing heart beat, increased respiration, muscle tension, and perspiration. Psychologically you feel increasingly uneasy. *You've reached the critical point in the panic sequence.* If you interpret these early physiological symptoms as *dangerous,* you will automatically trigger an *alarm reaction* in your body that's likely to lead to panic. If you ride through the state of physiological arousal without adding catastrophic thoughts, you are less likely to panic. All mammals have a built-in alarm reaction so that they can be mobilized to fight or flee predators. The alarm reaction includes the following components:

- Your heart rate quickly increases to provide blood to the large muscles so that you can run or do battle.

- Your rate of breathing increases to provide energy for sudden, rapid movement (what you may feel is tightness in your chest).

- The blood supply to your brain is slightly decreased and redirected toward your large muscles (what you may feel is sensations of dizziness, confusion, or unreality).

- The blood flow to your extremities is diminished to reduce bleeding if you're injured (what you may feel is cold hands or feet while simultaneously feeling flushed).

- Sweating is triggered so that your skin will be hard for a predator to grasp.

- Digestion is slowed (what you may feel is cramping and nausea).

All of these symptoms are entirely harmless. If you respond to them with catastrophic thoughts, however, you signal your body to accelerate preparations for danger. Examples of catastrophic thoughts might include:

- "I'm going to have a heart attack if I don't get out of here."

- "I'll pass out before I can get off the freeway (or through the stoplight)."

- "I'll start to stammer and make a fool of myself."

- "Oh no—I'm going to go crazy!"

- "This is the end—I'm dying!"

By telling yourself that you're in imminent danger (even though you're actually not), you signal your body to release massive amounts of adrenaline. This instantly ups the level of physiological arousal dramatically, triggering further catastrophic thoughts until the entire sequence spirals upward to a full-blown panic attack.

This sequence does not have to happen. The key is to recognize that the early symptoms of physiological arousal are not dangerous. The following concepts are very useful for learning to cope with panic attacks.

Panic Attacks Are Not Dangerous

Recognize that a panic attack is nothing more than the well-known "fight-or-flight" response *occurring out of context.* This is a natural bodily response that enables you (and all other mammals) to be alerted to and quickly flee a life-threatening situation. What makes a panic attack hard to cope with is that this intense reaction occurs in a situation that poses no obvious or life-threatening danger, such as sitting quietly at home, driving in a car, or attending a social event. Because there is no obvious, external danger, *your mind tends to invent or create danger* to match the intense bodily symptoms you're going through. Your mind can very quickly go through the process: "If I *feel* this bad, I must *be* in some danger." And so it's very common when experiencing panic to invent any or all of the following "dangers":

- *In response to heart palpitations:* "I'm going to have a heart attack" or "I'm going to die."

- *In response to choking sensations:* "I'm going to stop breathing and suffocate."

- *In response to dizzy sensations:* "I'm going to pass out."

- *In response to sensations of disorientation or feeling "not all there":* "I'm going crazy."

- *In response to "rubbery legs":* "I won't be able to walk" or "I'm going to fall."

- *In response to the overall intensity of your body's reactions:* "I'm going to completely lose control over myself" or "I'm going crazy."

The moment you tell yourself that you're feeling any of these dangers, you multiply the intensity of your fear. The idea that what's happening might be dangerous increases your fear greatly. This intense fear makes your bodily symptoms of anxiety even worse, which in turn creates still more fear, and you get caught in an upward spiral of mounting panic.

This upward spiral can be avoided if you fully understand that what your body is going through is not dangerous. All of the above dangers are illusory, a product of your imagination when you're undergoing the intense reactions which constitute panic. There is simply no basis for any of them in reality. Let's examine them one by one.

A Panic Attack Cannot Cause Heart Failure or Cardiac Arrest

Rapid heartbeat and palpitations during a panic attack can be frightening sensations, but they're not dangerous. Your heart is made up of very strong and dense muscle fibers and can withstand a lot more than you might think. A healthy heart can beat two hundred beats per minute for days without sustaining any damage. So, if your heart begins to race, just allow it to do so, trusting that no harm can come of it and that your heart will eventually calm down.

There's a substantial difference between what goes on with your heart during a panic attack and what happens in a heart attack. During a panic attack, your heart may race, pound, and at times miss or have extra beats. Some people even report chest pains, which pass fairly quickly, in the left-upper portion of their chest. None of these symptoms is aggravated by movement or increased physical activity. During a true heart attack, the most common symptom is continuous pain and a pressured, even crushing sensation in the center of your chest. Racing or pounding of the heart may occur but this is secondary to the pain. Moreover, the pain and pressure get worse upon exertion and may tend to diminish with rest. This is quite different from a panic attack, where racing and pounding may get worse if you stand still and lessen if you move around.

In the case of heart disease, distinct abnormalities in heart rhythm show up on an electrocardiogram (EKG) reading. It has been demonstrated that during a panic attack there are no EKG abnormalities—only rapid heartbeat. (If you want to gain additional reassurance about the health of your heart, consider having your doctor perform an EKG.)

In sum, there is simply no basis for the connection between heart attacks and panic. Panic attacks are not hazardous to your heart.

A Panic Attack Will Not Cause You to Stop Breathing or Suffocate

It is common during panic to feel your chest close down and your breathing become restricted. This might lead you to suddenly fear that you're going to suffocate. Under stress your neck and chest muscles are tightening and reducing your respiratory capacity. Be assured that there is nothing wrong with your breathing passage or lungs, and that the tightening sensations will pass. Your brain has a built-in reflex mechanism that will eventually force you to breathe if you're not getting enough oxygen. If you don't believe this, try holding your breath for up to a minute and observe what happens. At a certain point you'll feel a strong reflex to take in more air. The same thing will happen in a panic attack if you're not getting enough oxygen. You'll automatically gasp and take a deep breath long before reaching the point where you could pass out from a lack of oxygen. (And even if you did pass out, you would immediately start breathing!) In sum, choking and sensations of constriction during panic, however unpleasant, are not dangerous.

A Panic Attack Cannot Cause You to Faint

The sensation of light-headedness you may feel with the onset of panic can evoke a fear of fainting. What is happening is that the blood circulation to your brain is slightly reduced, most likely because you are breathing more rapidly. This is not dangerous and can be relieved by breathing slowly and regularly from your abdomen, preferably through you nose. This feeling can also be helped by taking the first opportunity you have to walk around a bit. Let the feelings of light-headedness rise and subside without fighting them. Because your heart is pumping harder and actually increasing your circulation, you are very unlikely to faint (except in rare instances if you have a blood phobia and happen to be exposed to the sight of blood).

A Panic Attack Cannot Cause You to Lose Your Balance

Sometimes you may feel quite dizzy when panic comes on. It may be that tension is affecting the semicircular canal system in your inner ear, which regulates your balance. For a few moments you may feel dizzy or it may even seem that things around you are spinning. Invariably this sensation will pass. It isn't dangerous and very unlikely to be so strong that you'll actually lose your balance. If sensations of pronounced dizziness persist for more than a few seconds, you may want to consult a doctor (preferably an otolaryngologist—an ear, nose, and throat doctor) to check if infection, allergies, or other disturbances might be affecting your inner ear.

You Won't Fall When You Feel "Weak in the Knees" During a Panic Attack

The adrenaline released during a panic attack can dilate the blood vessels in your legs, causing blood to accumulate in your leg muscles and not fully circulate. This can produce a sensation of weakness or "jelly legs," to which you may respond with the fear that you won't be able to walk. Be assured that this sensation is just that—a sensation—and that your legs are as strong and able to carry you as ever. They won't give way! Just allow these trembling, weak sensations to pass and give your legs the chance to carry you where you need to go.

You Can't "Go Crazy" During a Panic Attack.

Reduced blood flow to your brain during a panic attack is due to arterial constriction, a normal consequence of rapid breathing. This can result in sensations of disorientation and a feeling of unreality that can be frightening. If this sensation comes on, remind yourself that it's simply due to a slight and temporary reduction of arterial circulation in your brain and does not have anything to do with "going crazy," no matter how eerie or strange it may feel. No one has ever gone crazy from a panic attack, even though the fear of doing so is common. As bad as they feel, sensations of unreality will eventually pass and are completely harmless.

It may be helpful to know that people do not "go crazy" in a sudden or spontaneous way. Mental disorders involving behaviors that are labeled "crazy" (such as schizophrenia or manic-depressive psychosis) develop very gradually over a period of years and do not arise from panic attacks. No one has ever started to hallucinate or hear voices during a panic attack (except in rare instances where panic was induced by an overdose of a recreational drug such as LSD or cocaine). In short, a panic attack cannot result in your "going crazy," no matter how disturbing or unpleasant your symptoms feel.

A Panic Attack Cannot Cause You to "Lose Control of Yourself"

Because of the intense reactions your body goes through during panic, it's easy to imagine that you could "completely lose it." But what does completely losing it mean? Becoming completely paralyzed? Acting out uncontrollably or running amok? I am aware of no reported instances of this happening. If anything, during panic your senses and awareness are heightened with respect to a single goal: escape. Running away or trying to run away are the only ways in which you would be likely to "act out" while panicking. Complete loss of control during panic attacks is simply a myth.

In sum, the first step in learning to cope with panic reactions is to recognize that they are not dangerous. Because the bodily reactions accompanying panic feel so intense, it's easy to imagine them being dangerous. Yet in reality no danger exists. The physiological reactions underlying panic are *natural* and *protective.* In fact, *your body is designed to panic* so that you can quickly mobilize to flee situations that genuinely threaten your survival. The problem occurs when this natural, life-preserving response occurs outside the context of any immediate or apparent danger. When this happens, you can make headway in mastering panic by learning not to imagine danger where it doesn't exist.

Don't Fight Panic

Resisting or fighting initial panic symptoms is likely to make them worse. It's important to avoid tensing up in reaction to panic symptoms or trying to "make" them go away by suppressing them or gritting your teeth. Although it's important to act rather than be passive, you still shouldn't fight your panic symptoms. Claire Weekes, in her popular books *Hope and Help for Your Nerves* and *Peace from Nervous Suffering* (1978), describes a four-step approach for coping with panic:

Face the symptoms—don't run from them. Attempting to suppress or run away from the early symptoms of panic is a way of telling yourself that you can't handle a particular situation. In most cases, this will only create more panic. A more constructive attitude to cultivate is one that says, "Okay, here it is again. I can allow my body to go through its reactions and handle this. I've done it before."

*Accept what your body is doing—*don't fight against it. When you try to fight panic, you simply tense up against it, which only makes you more anxious. Adopting just the opposite attitude, one of *letting go and allowing* your body to have its reactions (such as heart palpitations, chest constriction, sweaty palms, dizziness, and so on) will enable you to move through panic much more quickly and easily. The key is to be able to *watch or observe* your body's state of physiological arousal—no matter how unusual or uncomfortable it feels—without reacting to it with further fear or anxiety.

Float with the "wave" of a panic attack rather than forcing your way through it. Claire Weekes makes a distinction between *first fear* and *second fear*. First fear consists of the physiological reactions underlying panic; second fear is making yourself afraid of these reactions by saying scary things to yourself like, "I can't handle this!" "I've got to get out of here right now!" "What if other people see this happening to me!" While you can't do much about first fear, you can eliminate second fear by learning to "flow with" the rising and falling of your body's state of arousal rather than fighting or reacting fear- fully to it. Instead of scaring yourself about your body's reactions, you can move with them and make reassuring statements to yourself like: "This too will pass," "I'll let my body do its thing and move through this," "I've handled this before and I can handle it now."

Allow time to pass. Panic is caused by a sudden surge of adrenaline. If you can allow, and float with, the bodily reactions caused by this surge, much of this adrenaline will metabolize and be reabsorbed in three to five minutes. As soon as this happens, you'll start to feel better. *Panic attacks are time limited.* In most cases, panic will peak and begin to subside within only a few minutes. It is most likely to pass quickly if you don't aggravate it by fighting against it or reacting to it with even more fear (causing "second fear") by saying scary things to yourself.

Part 2: Coping Strategies for Managing Panic or Anxiety

Using the Anxiety Scale

With practice you can learn to identify the preliminary signs that a panic attack may be imminent. For some individuals this might be a sudden quickening of heartbeat. For others it might be a tightening in the chest, sweaty hands, or queasiness. Still others might experience a slight dizziness or disorientation. Most people experience some preliminary warning symptoms before reaching the "point of no return," when a full-blown panic attack is inevitable.

It's possible to distinguish among different levels or degrees of anxiety by imagining a ten-point scale.

ANXIETY SCALE

7–10	*Major Panic Attack*	All of the symptoms in Level 6 exaggerated; terror; fear of going crazy or dying; compulsion to escape
6	*Moderate Panic Attack*	Palpitations; difficulty breathing; feeling disoriented or detached (feeling of unreality); panic in response to perceived loss of control
5	*Early Panic*	Heart pounding or beating irregularly; constricted breathing; spaciness or dizziness; definite fear of losing control; compulsion to escape
4	*Marked Anxiety*	Feeling uncomfortable or "spacey"; heart beating fast; muscles tight; beginning to wonder about maintaining control
3	*Moderate Anxiety*	Feeling uncomfortable but still in control; heart starting to beat faster; more rapid breathing; muscles tightening; sweaty palms
2	*Mild Anxiety*	Butterflies in stomach; muscle tension; definitely nervous
1	*Slight Anxiety*	Passing twinge of anxiety, feeling slightly nervous
0	*Relaxation*	Calm, a feeling of being undistracted and at peace

The symptoms at various levels of this scale are typical, although they may not correspond exactly to your own symptoms. The important thing is to *identify what constitutes a Level 4 for you*. This is the point at which—whatever symptoms you're experiencing—*you feel your control over your reaction beginning to diminish*. Up to and through Level 3, you may be feeling anxious and uncomfortable, but you still feel that you're coping. Starting at Level 4, you begin to wonder whether you can manage what's happening, which can lead you to escalate your anxiety further. With practice you can learn to "catch yourself" and limit your reaction *before* it reaches this point of no return. The more adept you become at recognizing slight to moderate levels of anxiety up through Level 4 on the scale, the more control you'll gain over your anxiety.

Abdominal Breathing

Your breathing directly reflects the level of tension you carry in your body. Under tension, your breathing usually becomes shallow and rapid, and occurs high in the chest. When relaxed, you breathe more fully, more deeply, and from your abdomen. It's difficult to be tense and to breathe from your abdomen at the same time.

Some of the benefits of abdominal breathing include:

- Increased oxygen supply to the brain and musculature.

- Stimulation of the parasympathetic nervous system. This branch of your autonomic nervous system promotes a state of calmness and quiescence. It works in a fashion exactly opposite to the sympathetic branch of your nervous system, which stimulates a state of emotional arousal and the very physiological reactions underlying panic and anxiety.

- Greater feelings of connectedness between mind and body. Anxiety and worry tend to keep you "up in your head." A few minutes of deep abdominal breathing will help bring you down into your whole body.

- Improved concentration. If your mind is racing, it's difficult to focus your attention. Abdominal breathing will help to quiet your mind.

- Abdominal breathing by itself can trigger a deep state of relaxation.

Abdominal breathing means breathing fully from your abdomen or from the bottom of your lungs. It's exactly the reverse of the way you breathe when you're anxious or tense, which is typically shallow and high in your chest. If you're breathing from your abdomen, you can place your hand on your stomach and see it actually rise each time you inhale. To practice abdominal breathing, observe the following steps:

1. Place one hand on your abdomen right beneath your rib cage, preferably while sitting or lying down.

2. Inhale slowly and deeply through your nose into the bottom of your lungs (the lowest point into your lungs you can reach). Your chest should move only slightly, while your stomach rises, pushing your hand up.

3. When you've inhaled fully, pause for a moment and then exhale fully through your nose or your mouth. Be sure to exhale fully. As you exhale, allow yourself to let go and imagine your entire body going loose and limp.

4. In order to fully relax, take and release ten abdominal breaths. Try to keep your breathing *smooth* and *regular* throughout, without gulping in air or exhaling suddenly. It will help to slow down your breathing if you slowly count to four ("one-two-three-four") on the inhale and then slowly count to four again on the exhale. Use the one to four count for at least the first week of practicing abdominal breathing.

5. After you have become proficient in slowing down your breathing, you can drop the one to four count if you wish. At this point, try counting backward from twenty down to one, one count after each exhale. That is, after the first exhale count "twenty," after the next "nineteen," and so on down to zero. Remember to keep your breathing slow and regular throughout, inhaling through your nose, and exhaling through your nose or mouth.

6. Continue to practice abdominal breathing for five minutes. If you start to feel light-headed at any time, stop for thirty seconds and then start up again.

7. Practice abdominal breathing for *five minutes at a time, three times per day, for at least three weeks.* If possible, find regular times each day to do this so that your breathing exercise becomes a habit. With practice you can learn in a short period of time to slow down the physiological reactions underlying anxiety.

Once you feel you've gained some mastery in the use of this technique, apply it whenever you feel anxiety beginning to arise. With continued practice, you'll be able to use abdominal breathing to diminish anxiety that occurs spontaneously or in anticipation of facing something you fear. *Abdominal breathing is a most powerful technique for handling all forms of anxiety in the very moment it begins to arise.*

Coping Statements

While the physical symptoms associated with panic (first fear) may come out of the blue, your emotional reaction to these bodily symptoms (second fear) does not. It is based on *what you tell yourself* about these symptoms. If you tell yourself that your physiological symptoms are horrible and very threatening, that you can't stand them, that you're going to lose control, or that you might die, you'll scare yourself into a very high state of anxiety. On the other hand, if you learn to accept what's happening and can make calming, reassuring statements to yourself, such as, "It's only anxiety—I'm not going to let it get to me," "I've been through this before and it's not dangerous," or "I can handle this until it passes," you can minimize or eliminate the escalation of your symptoms.

Practice using any of the following coping statements to help you cultivate an attitude of *accepting* the body symptoms that occur during a panic attack. You may find it helpful to repeat a particular statement over and over the first minute or two, when you feel panic symptoms coming on. You may also want to do deep abdominal breathing in conjunction with repeating a coping statement. If one statement gets tiresome or seems to stop working, try another.

- "This feeling isn't comfortable or pleasant, but I can accept it."

- "I can be anxious and still deal with this situation."

- "I can handle these symptoms or sensations."

- "This isn't an emergency. It's okay to think slowly about what I need to do."

- "This isn't the worst thing that could happen."

- "I'm going to go with this and wait for my anxiety to decrease."

- "This is an opportunity for me to learn to cope with my fears."

- "I'll just let my body do its thing. This will pass."

- "I'll ride this through—I don't need to let this get to me."

- "I deserve to feel okay right now."

- "I can take all the time I need in order to let go and relax."

- "There's no need to push myself. I can take as small a step forward as I choose."

- "I've survived this before and I'll survive this time, too."

- "I can do my coping strategies and allow this to pass."

- "This anxiety won't hurt me—even if it doesn't feel good."

- "This is just anxiety—I'm not going to let it get to me."

- "Nothing serious is going to happen to me."

- "Fighting and resisting this isn't going to help—so I'll just ride it through."

- "These are just thoughts—not reality."

- "I don't need these thoughts—I can choose to think differently."

- "This isn't dangerous."

- "So what."

- "These sensations (feelings) are just a reminder to use my coping skills."

- "These feelings will pass and I'll be okay."

- "This is just adrenaline—it will pass in a few minutes."

- "Nothing about these sensations or feelings is dangerous."

- "Don't worry—be happy." (Use this, if you like, to inject an element of lightness or humor.)

If you have frequent panic attacks, I suggest you write your favorite coping statements on a three-by-five card and carry it in your purse or wallet. Bring the card out and read it when you feel panic symptoms first coming on. Remember to combine the use of coping statements with abdominal breathing. Many of my clients have found this combination particularly helpful.

Other Diversion Techniques

Any technique that helps you to *redirect your attention away from anxiety symptoms as well as fear-provoking thoughts* can be helpful when you're experiencing the onset of a potential panic attack. While abdominal breathing and coping statements should be your first line of defense, any of the following strategies can be useful, especially at levels of anxiety up to and including Level 4 on the Anxiety Scale.

- Talk to another person (this could be someone with you or someone you call on a cellular phone).

- Move around or engage in physical activity.

- Engage in a simple, repetitive activity (count the money in your purse while waiting in line; sing a song during a long elevator ride, for example).

- Express angry feelings (get angry at your anxiety—just don't vent anger on other people).

- Anchor yourself in your immediate environment. Focus on concrete objects in your surroundings—even touch them if that helps.

- Practice thought stopping. Shout the word "Stop" once or twice—or snap a rubber band against your wrist. This will help disrupt a chain of negative thoughts. Follow this with abdominal breathing or by repeating a coping statement.

Putting It All Together

In general, when anxiety symptoms start to come on, use the following three-step technique to manage them. (You may want to think of this as the "ABC technique" to help remember the steps.)

1. **Accept** your symptoms—don't fight or resist them. Resisting or fleeing symptoms of anxiety tends to make them worse. The more you can adopt an attitude of acceptance, no matter how unpleasant the symptoms may be, the better will be your ability to cope. Acceptance prepares you to do something proactive about your anxiety rather than getting caught up in reactions to it.

2. **Breathe**—practice abdominal breathing. When anxiety first comes up, always go to abdominal breathing first. If you've been practicing abdominal breathing regularly, merely initiating it provides a cue to your body to relax and disengage from a potential "fight or flight" response.

3. **Cope**—use a coping strategy. After you begin to feel centered in abdominal breathing, use a coping statement or a diversion technique (for example, talking to another person) to continue to manage your feelings. Any coping strategy will reinforce the basic stance of not giving attention or energy to negative thoughts and/or uncomfortable body sensations. By regularly practicing coping techniques, you reinforce an attitude of mastery—instead of passive submission and victimization—in the face of your anxiety. Be aware that abdominal breathing is itself a coping strategy and sometimes it alone will be enough.

What to Do If Anxiety Exceeds Level 4

If you are unable to arrest an anxiety reaction before it goes beyond your personal "point of no return," observe the following guidelines:

- Leave the situation if possible. Try to return to it later the same day if you can.

- Don't try to control or fight your symptoms—accept them and "ride them out"; remind yourself that your reaction is not dangerous and will pass.

- Talk to someone, if available—express your feelings to them (if in a car or aboard a plane alone, you might use a cellular phone).

- Move around or engage in physical activity.

- Focus on simple objects around you.

- Touch the floor and/or the physical objects around you.

- Breathe slowly and regularly through your nose to reduce possible symptoms of hyperventilation.

- As a last resort, take an extra dose of a minor tranquilizer (with the general approval of your doctor).

If you have a panic attack, you may feel temporarily very confused and disoriented. Try asking yourself the following questions to increase your objectivity (you may want to write these out on a three-by-five card which you carry with you).

- Are these symptoms I'm feeling truly dangerous? (Answer: No.)

- What is the absolute worst thing that could happen? (Usual answer: I might have to leave this situation quickly or I might have to ask for assistance.)

- Am I telling myself anything that is making this worse?

- What is the most supportive thing I could do for myself right now?

Revising Catastrophic Thoughts That Contribute to Panic

It's important for you to identify—and then modify—any catastrophic thoughts that are contributing to your problem with panic. A list of common catastrophic thoughts follows:

1. I'm going to die.

2. I'm going insane.

3. I'm losing control.

4. This will never end.

5. I'm really scared.

6. I'm having a heart attack.

7. I'm going to pass out.

8. I'm going to make a scene.

9. I've got to get out of here.

10. I'm going to act foolish.

11. People will think I'm crazy.

12. I'll always be this way.

13. I don't understand what's happening to me.

14. Something is really physically wrong with me.

15. I'm losing my mind.

16. I'll choke to death.

17. I don't know what people will think.

18. I'm going blind.

19. I'll hurt someone.

20. I'm going to have a stroke.

21. I'm going to scream.

22. I'm going to babble or talk funny.

23. I'm going to throw up.

24. I won't be able to breathe.

25. Something terrible will happen.

You may recognize some of the thoughts on the list as your own. Most likely some of your catastrophic thoughts are not on the list, however, and it's important that you identify these thoughts as well. Follow these steps:

Step 1: Think about what goes through your mind, what kind of thoughts make the most trouble for you, when you have a severe anxiety or panic episode. If you're not clear about this, monitor yourself over the next two weeks, watching for the catastrophic thoughts that precede times when you feel anxious or panicky. Take time after your anxiety subsides to reflect on fearful thoughts that went through your mind. Write them down on the worksheet on page 129, under the column "Catastrophic Thoughts."

Step 2: As you focus on your catastrophic thoughts, ask yourself how strongly you believe in them. On a scale of 1–100, how likely are they to actually come true? Write your estimate on the worksheet under the column "Odds of Coming True."

Step 3: Examine the validity of your catastrophic thoughts. If you look at them objectively, are they actually true? Use the following questions to assist you:

1. How many times in the past did the catastrophe I imagine occur?

2. What has *usually* happened under similar circumstances in the past?

3. What are the objective medical facts (if your catastrophic thought relates to some bodily danger, such as a heart attack or suffocation)? Refer back to the previous section, "Panic Attacks Are Unpleasant but Not Dangerous."

Step 4: Develop a coping plan. After examining the validity of your catastrophic thoughts, you'll usually find that they are not very realistic. Think about the situation that is causing you anxiety and imagine how you can cope. If you discovered that your catastrophic thought was unrealistic (for example, the belief that panic could cause a heart attack or suffocation), then it will be easier to cope—there is no real danger in a situation you once believed was dangerous. If after questioning the validity of your catastrophic thought, you still have *some* belief in it, then imagine how you would cope if the worst case scenario happened. For example, if people did laugh at you as a result of stumbling through your speech, what could you do to cope? Making a joke about the circumstances or telling a personal story about your anxiety would likely help diffuse the situation. Nearly any outcome, no matter how difficult, can be handled if you have a plan to cope. In developing your coping plan, think about coping strategies such as abdominal breathing, temporarily leaving the situation, or specific coping statements. Consider what support you have available from relatives or friends. How have you coped with similar difficult situations in the past? How might someone else cope with such a situation? When you've developed your coping plan, write it down in the column "Coping Plan."

Step 5: After writing down your coping plan, re-estimate your degree of belief in your original catastrophic thought. Write down your estimate under the column "Revised Odds of Catastrophe."

Catastrophic Thoughts Worksheet

Catastrophic Thoughts	Odds of Coming True (0-100%)	Coping Plan	Revised Odds of Catastrophe (0–100%)

For three weeks, fill out your Catastrophic Thoughts Worksheet following any episode where you feel anxious or panicky. Wait until your anxiety subsides, then work through the five steps above. Make fifty copies of the worksheet and use a separate sheet for each and every occasion when you are anxious. The practice of countering catastrophic thoughts in writing will require some effort on your part. However, the effort is worth it; after two or three weeks of filling out the worksheets you will have *internalized* the process of defusing your catastrophic thoughts. As you learn to invest less belief and energy in your catastrophic thinking, you will gain increased confidence in your ability to handle fear.

Part 3: How to Change Self-Talk

The preceding section addressed changing catastrophic thoughts that trigger panic attacks. The present section examines how to identify and change fearful self-talk that perpetuates chronic worry and/or phobias. While the methodology in both cases is similar, this section is especially relevant to people who have anxiety disorders *other than* panic disorder, for example social phobia, specific phobia, generalized anxiety disorder, or obsessive-compulsive disorder (see Appendix 1).

Three factors tend to perpetuate fears and phobias: 1) *sensitization*, 2) *avoidance*, and 3) *negative, erroneous self-talk*. A phobia develops when you become sensitized to a particular situation, object, or event—that is, when anxiety becomes conditioned or associated with that situation, object, or event. If panic suddenly arises one day when you happen to be flying or riding an elevator, you may start feeling anxious every time you subsequently enter either of these situations. Becoming *sensitized* means that the mere presence of—or even thinking about—a situation may be enough to trigger anxiety automatically.

After sensitization occurs, you may start to *avoid* the situation. Repeated avoidance is very rewarding, because it saves you from having to feel any anxiety. Avoidance is the most powerful way to hold on to a phobia, because it prevents you from ever learning that you can handle the situation.

The third factor that perpetuates fears and phobias is erroneous, exaggerated self-talk. The more *worry* you experience about something you fear, the more likely you are to be involved in erroneous self-talk connected with that fear. You may also have negative images about what could happen if you had to face what you fear, or about your worst fears coming true. Both the negative self-talk and negative images serve to perpetuate your fear, guaranteeing that you remain afraid. They also undermine your confidence that you could ever get over your fear. By getting past your mistaken self-talk and negative images, you will be more likely to overcome your avoidance and confront your phobia.

Phobias come in many forms, but the nature of fearful self-talk is always the same. Whether you are afraid of crossing bridges, heights, speaking up in groups, or getting a shot, the types of erroneous thinking that perpetuate these fears are the same. *There are two basic errors in fearful thinking:*

1. *Overestimating a Negative Outcome*—overestimating the odds of something bad happening. Most of the time your worries consist of "what-if" statements that overestimate a particular negative outcome. For example, "What if I panic and completely lose control of myself?" "What if the plane crashes?" "What if I flunk the exam and have to drop out of school?"

2. *Underestimating Your Ability to Cope*—not recognizing or acknowledging your ability to cope with the situation, even if a negative outcome did, in fact, occur. This underestimation of your ability to cope is usually implicit in your overestimating thoughts.

If you take any fear and examine the negative thinking that contributes to maintaining it, you'll probably find these two distortions. To the extent that you can overcome these distortions with more reality-based thinking, the fear will tend to diminish. In essence, you can define fear as *the unreasonable overestimation of some threat, coupled with an underestimation of your ability to cope.*

Here are some examples of how the two types of distortions operate with various fears. In each example, both types of erroneous thoughts are identified. Then the distortions are challenged in each case and modified with more appropriate, reality-based thinking.

Example 1: Fear of Driving on a Freeway

Overestimating Thoughts: "What if I can't handle the car? What if my attention wanders and I lose control of the car? What if I cause an accident and kill someone?"

Challenging Your Overestimating Thoughts: With overestimating thoughts, it's always good to ask: *"Realistically, what are the odds that the negative outcome I imagine will actually happen?"* In the case of this example, you may ask, "If I did panic while driving, what are the actual odds that I would lose control of the car?"

Here is an example of a realistic answer (or "counterstatement") that you might use to respond to the challenging question: "It's unlikely that having a panic attack would actually cause me to lose complete control of the car. The moment I felt my anxiety getting severe, I could pull over to the shoulder on the side of the road and stop. If there weren't any shoulders, I could slow down in the right lane, perhaps to 45 mph, put my flashers on, and keep a grip on myself until I reached the nearest exit. Once I got off the freeway, my panic would begin to subside."

Thoughts Underestimating Your Ability to Cope: "I couldn't cope if I lost control of the car, especially if I got into an accident. What would I say to a policeman—that I'm phobic? I wouldn't be able to start driving again if I got stopped for a ticket. I couldn't live with myself if I caused physical injury to another person—and I know I couldn't face life if I myself ended up in a wheelchair."

Challenging Your Underestimating Thoughts: Countering the idea that you couldn't cope often takes place when you answer overestimating thoughts with a more objective appraisal. However, the process isn't complete until you actually *identify and list specific ways in which you would cope*. Here, it's important to ask yourself the question: *What would I actually do to cope?* In the above example, some possible coping strategies might include:

- "If I did have a panic attack on the freeway, I would cope by getting off the highway immediately or driving slowly to the nearest exit and getting off."

- "In the very unlikely case that I actually caused an accident, I would still cope. I would exchange names and addresses with other parties involved. If my car were wrecked, the police would likely drive me to a place where I would call to have the car towed. It would be a very unpleasant experience, to say the least; but, realistically, I would continue to function. I've functioned in emergencies in the past, and I could function in this case, if I weren't injured."

- "Even given the unlikely possibility that I were injured, I wouldn't 'go crazy' or 'totally lose it.' I would simply wait until the paramedics came and took charge of the situation."

Example 2: Fear of Flying

Overestimating Thoughts: (Suppose you have two separate fears) 1) "With my luck, the plane might get into bad weather. What if it *did* go down?" 2) "Even if the plane makes it, what if I get claustrophobic sitting there for two hours? What if I panic?"

Challenging: 1) "What are the realistic odds that I'll be in a plane crash?" 2) "What is the actual likelihood that I'll panic while aboard the plane? If I do panic, what are the realistic odds I'll feel horribly or irreparably trapped?"

Counterstatements: 1) "The realistic odds of my plane crashing, no matter what the weather or turbulence encountered, is 1 in 7,000,000." (This is actually the case.) 2) "I'm less likely to panic during the flight if I have a support person with me, and I get up several times from my seat to walk in the aisle. The perception of being trapped is an illusion based on the fact that I have a lot of nervous energy without the ability to release it through activity."

Underestimating Ability to Cope: (Imagining the very worst) 1) "There is no way I could cope if the plane went down." 2) "I don't see how I could cope with panicking and the feeling of being trapped. I'd lose control and freak out."

Challenging: "If the worst happened, what could I actually do to cope?"

Coping Strategies: 1) "Probably no one would cope very well if the plane went down. However, there would be very little time to think about it—it would all be over before I had time to react for very long. Also, I would feel no pain because I would be unconscious before I had any time to perceive physical pain. I can resist the temptation to imagine this scenario by reminding myself of the odds of being in a plane crash. I would have to fly every single day for nineteen-thousand years before my 'number would be up.'" 2) "Suppose I did panic midflight. It wouldn't be the end of the world. I could use any of several anxiety management strategies to handle it—i.e., abdominal breathing, walking up and down the aisle, coping statements, talking to my support person (or calling someone on a cellular phone, if available). I could even take medication, if necessary. I'm confident that something would help me to feel better after a few minutes."

Example 3: Fear of Contracting a Serious Illness

Overestimating Thoughts: "I have no energy and feel tired all the time. Maybe I'm developing cancer and don't know it!"

Challenging: "What are the realistic odds that symptoms of low energy and fatigue mean that I'm developing cancer?"

Counterstatements: "Symptoms of fatigue and low energy can be indicative of all kinds of physical and psychological conditions, including a low-grade virus, anemia, adrenal exhaustion or hypothyroidism, depression, and food allergies, to name a few. There are many possible explanations of my condition, and I don't have any specific symptoms that would indicate cancer. So the odds of my fatigue and low energy indicating cancer are very low."

Underestimating Ability to Cope: "If I were diagnosed with cancer, that would be the end. I couldn't take it. I'd be better off ending things quickly and killing myself."

Challenging: "If the unlikely happened and I really were diagnosed with cancer, what could I actually do to cope?"

Coping Strategies: "As bad as a cancer diagnosis would be, it's unlikely that I would totally go to pieces. After an initial difficult adjustment to the fact—which might takes days to weeks—I would most likely begin to think about what I needed to do to deal with the situation. It would certainly be difficult, yet it wouldn't be a situation that I was less equipped to handle than anyone else. My doctor and I would plan the most effective possible treatment strategies. I would join a local cancer support group and get lots of support from my friends and immediate family. I might try alternative methods, such as visualization and dietary changes that could help. In short, I would try everything possible to attempt to heal the condition."

Restructuring Unhelpful Self-Talk

The above three examples illustrate how overestimating thoughts can be challenged and then countered by more realistic, less anxiety-provoking thinking. During the next week, attempt to monitor those times when you feel anxious or panicky. Each time you do, use the following five steps to work with negative self-talk.

1. If you're feeling anxious or upset, do something to relax, such as abdominal breathing, progressive muscle relaxation, or meditation. It's easier to notice your internal dialogue when you take time to slow down and relax.

2. After you get somewhat relaxed, ask yourself, "What was I telling myself that made me anxious?" or "What was going through my mind?" Make an effort to separate thoughts from feelings. For example, "I felt terrified" describes a feeling, while "I will lose control of myself" is an overestimating thought which might lead you to feel

terrified. Sometimes feelings and thoughts occur together in one statement: "I am scared I'll lose control." The negative thought here is still "I will lose control."

3. Identify the two basic types of distortions or errors within your anxious self-talk. Sort out *overestimating thoughts*, and then *thoughts that underestimate your ability to cope*. Note that overestimating thoughts frequently begin with "What if . . ." Thoughts that underestimate your ability to cope might begin with "I can't . . ." or "I won't be able . . ."

4. When you've identified your anxious, distorted thoughts, *challenge* them with appropriate questions.
   For overestimating thoughts: "What are the realistic odds that this feared outcome will actually happen?" "Has this outcome ever happened to me before?"
   For thoughts underestimating your ability to cope: "What coping skills can I bring to bear to handle anxiety?" "If the worst outcome I fear *does* occur, what could I actually *do* to cope?"

5. Write counterstatements to each of your overestimating thoughts. These counterstatements should contain language and logic that reflect more balanced, realistic thinking. Then make a list of ways you might cope with your phobic situation, including what you would do if your most feared outcome actually occurred.

Use The Worry Worksheet on the following page to write down your anxious thoughts and corresponding counterstatements for your specific fear or phobia. In the section at the bottom, list ways in which you would cope if the negative (but unlikely) outcome(s) you fear actually occurred.

Part 4: Brief Strategies for Coping with Anxiety

The preceding two sections provided methods for changing the irrational beliefs that underlie and perpetuate panic, worry, and phobias. Changing fearful self-statements takes time and practice, yet it will result in your being able to handle all the various forms of anxiety more easily.

In this section are two lists of strategies for handling anxiety, panic, or worry *on the spur of the moment*. These are rapid, strategic techniques that do not require you to identify and counter negative self-talk. You simply implement them immediately the moment you experience panic coming on—or the

The Worry Worksheet

Specific Fear or Phobia _____

Anxious Self-Talk	Counterstatements
Overestimating thoughts (or images):	**Your arguments against overestimating thoughts**
"What if . . ."	"Realistically . . ."

Coping Strategies: List ways in which you would cope if a negative (but un-likely) outcome did occur. Use the other side of the sheet if needed. Change "What if" to "*What I would do if* (one of your negative predictions actually did come about) . . ."

1.

2.

3.

Make 30 copies of this worksheet before you start, and use a separate sheet each time you practice disputing your negative self-talk.

moment you find yourself stuck in unnecessary worry. The first list, Active Strategies for Coping with Panic, Anxiety, or Worry, is divided into two parts. The first seven techniques are specifically designed to diffuse the early symptoms of panic. Try using any one of them to stop a panic reaction before it gets going. If these techniques don't work as well as you would like at first, keep trying. Practicing them repeatedly will increase your proficiency.

The remaining seven techniques on the list are distraction strategies for diverting your attention and energy away from worry. Use any of them the moment you feel yourself getting "stuck" in worry. Again, practice makes perfect with any of these techniques.

The second list, Cognitive Strategies for Changing Your Perspective on a Problem, provides what I like to think of as "instant cognitive therapy." All of these techniques involve a quick *reframing* of the way you perceive a worrisome situation. They allow you to shift your perspective on a problem without taking the time to analyze and counter negative self-talk. That's not to say that examining your self-talk around a fear or worry isn't quite useful. However, these brief cognitive strategies may help you to change your perspective on the spur of the moment before you take the time to work through an analysis of your self-talk. Not all of these strategies will be equally helpful; pick the ones that are most effective for you.

ACTIVE STRATEGIES FOR COPING WITH PANIC, ANXIETY, OR WORRY

Coping with Panic

- Engage in abdominal breathing for three to five minutes.

- Talk to a supportive person nearby or by phone.

- Get up and move around. Walk outdoors. Engage in your favorite type of exercise. Do household chores.

- Repeat your favorite coping statement for a minute or two (see the list on p. 123). Try combining repetition of a coping statement with abdominal breathing. If you get bored with a particular statement, switch to another (alternatively, read down a prepared list of coping statements).

- Stay in the present moment. Allow yourself to accept—not resist—what's happening. Abdominal breathing and focusing on your body (particularly your arms and legs) may help.

- Get angry at your anxiety. Shout at it with statements like "Get out of my way—I have things to do!" "You're not going to run my life!" Pound a pillow with both fists if necessary.

- Experience something immediately pleasurable. Have a significant other or friend hold you. Take a hot shower. Sing a favorite song.

Distraction Techniques for Worry
(These techniques work primarily for low levels of anxiety or obsessive worry.)

- Do physical exercise, outdoors if possible.

- Do progressive muscle relaxation (see Appendix 3 for instructions).

- Talk to someone about something other than the worry, unless you want to express your feelings about it.

- Use visual distractions, i.e., TV, videos, your computer, or board games.

- Do something physical with your hands, i.e., arts and crafts, repairing something, or gardening.

- Divert your obsessiveness to a jigsaw puzzle, crossword, or any type of puzzle you prefer.

- Take action on the issue that causes you worry. If you're afraid of flying, read a book or listen to a tape on overcoming that fear. If you're afraid of public speaking, practice giving your talk to a tape recorder.

COGNITIVE STRATEGIES FOR CHANGING YOUR PERSPECTIVE ON A PROBLEM

The following ideas may help you to shift from a negative to more positive context for thinking about your problem.

- Surrender to the fact that the situation is the way it is whether you like it or not.

- Acknowledge that it would be okay to lighten up about it.

- Expand your compassion for all people who experience similar things—you're not alone.

- Cultivate a sense of fascination with it—notice that it's at least interesting or novel.

- Be open to the problem making a contribution to you somehow. There may be something it's teaching you.

- Turn everything over to God.

- Imagine that working with the problem might strengthen your character.

- Feel the tingle of aliveness within the pattern of energy you've got going around the problem. Focus on just the energy itself. After a while it may shift.

- Trust that you are strong enough to handle even the worst of this.

- Realize that it's very likely not as bad as your worst thoughts about it.

- Be very gentle, patient, and caring with yourself in the presence of your feelings.

- Consider whether some part of you might actually rather have the problem than change.

- Acknowledge that you've struggled with this about long enough and that trying to control it may not be your best strategy.

- Welcome this as an opportunity to let go of ego.

- See the problem possibly as a metaphor for your entire life.

- Trust that since other people have made it through this, you can, too.

- Acknowledge that what's bothering you is not what really matters the most in life anyway.

- Notice that, if you're doing your best, that's the best you can do anyway.

- Trust in the inevitability of this passing. Affirm: "This too will pass."

- Breathe more deeply and just be with it. Trust that in a while, it will shift.

Part 5: How to Face What You Fear

As was mentioned earlier, three factors contribute to establishing and maintaining a phobia or fear: sensitization, avoidance, and fearful self-talk. The third factor was addressed in some detail in the previous section on changing negative self-talk. This next section addresses how to overcome sensitization and avoidance. But first, what are sensitization and avoidance, and how do they cause phobias?

Sensitization is a process of conditioning where you become "sensitized" to a particular object or situation. Perhaps you once panicked or experienced high anxiety while flying, giving a talk, driving on the freeway, or being home alone. If your anxiety level was high enough, it's likely that you acquired a strong association between being in that particular situation and being anxious. Thereafter, being in, near, or perhaps just thinking about the situation automatically triggered your anxiety: a connection between the situation and a strong anxiety response was established. Because this connection was automatic and seemingly beyond your control, you probably did all you could to *avoid* putting yourself in the situation again. Your *avoidance* was rewarded because it saved you from re-experiencing your anxiety. At the point where you began to *always* avoid the situation, you developed a full-fledged phobia.

Desensitization is the process of *unlearning* the connection between anxiety and a particular situation. For desensitization to occur, you need to approach and enter your phobic situation while you're in a relaxed or close-to-relaxed state. To do this, *you need to gradually face your phobia through a series of small, incremental steps*. For example, if you're fearful of flying, you would first look at pictures or videos of planes in flight; then you might drive to the airport and watch real planes take off; then you might board a grounded plane; and finally, you would take a short flight, having someone go with you. By gradually facing the situation in small increments, keeping your anxiety level low, you accomplish two things: 1) you unlearn the association you've made between a particular situation and an automatic anxiety response, and 2) you reassociate feelings of relaxation and calmness with the particular situation. *Repeatedly facing* a phobic situation at low levels of anxiety will eventually enable you to overcome your tendency to respond to it with high anxiety or panic. While desensitization is the result you seek, the process of facing a phobia in small, incremental steps is usually called *exposure*.

Exposure (sometimes called "exposure therapy") is the most effective available treatment for phobias. Nothing works better in overcoming a fear than simply to face it. Exposure is made feasible through a process of gradually confronting a fearful situation through a series of small, manageable steps. Exposure is simple in principle, but it's not always particularly easy or comfortable in practice. The following guidelines can help make exposure achievable.

Break Down the Process of Facing Your Fear into Manageable Steps

The best way to face what you fear is to break it down into a series of small, incremental steps. This is accomplished by creating what is called a *hier-*

archy—a progressive sequence of exposures to your feared situation. These exposures vary in their anxiety-provoking potential from mild to intense. For example, if you're afraid of public speaking, you would undertake a progressive sequence of exposures to this task as follows:

1. Preparing a talk which you don't give

2. Preparing a talk and delivering it in front of one friend

3. Preparing a talk and delivering it in front of three friends

4. Giving a brief presentation to three or four people at work who you know well

5. Same as Step 4 but a longer presentation

6. Giving a brief presentation to 10–15 acquaintances at work

7. Same as Step 6 but a longer presentation

8. Giving a brief presentation to three or four strangers

9. Same as Step 8 but a longer presentation

10. Giving a brief presentation to 10–15 strangers

11. Giving a brief presentation to 50 strangers

Or, if you were afraid of flying, you would break the process of confronting your fear down into many steps, such as:

1. Approaching the airport with a support person and driving around it

2. Parking at the airport with your support person for five minutes

3. Entering the terminal with your support person and walking around for five minutes

4. Going to a departure gate with your support person and watching planes take off and land

5. Repeating Steps 1–4 alone

6. Arranging to visit a grounded plane and spending one minute on board with your support person

7. Same as 6 but staying on board for five minutes; try buckling into a seat

8. Repeating Steps 6 and 7 alone

9. Scheduling a short flight (15–30 minutes) and going with your support person

10. Scheduling a longer flight and going with your support person

11. Repeating Steps 9 and 10 alone

See Chapters 7 and 8 of *The Anxiety & Phobia Workbook* for detailed instructions about how to construct hierarchies for facing phobias.

Rely on a Support Person—at First

For many people, facing a phobia or fearful situation is made easier by having someone accompany them. This "support person" can provide: 1) reassurance and a sense of safety, 2) distraction (by talking to you), 3) encouragement to persist with confronting the various steps in your hierarchy, and 4) praise for your incremental successes.

While a support person goes with you to provide encouragement, they shouldn't push you to do more than you're ready or willing to do. It's up to you to decide how far to go each time you undertake facing your phobia. At any point when it feels as though you're anxiety might get excessive or out of control, it's important to back off from exposure and then return to the situation when you have given yourself time to recover. Your support person needs to support you in doing just that.

A support person can help give you the confidence to face a situation you've long avoided. However, to fully master that situation, you need eventually to wean yourself away from your support person. The latter stages of exposure usually involve negotiating those steps you previously did with your support person on your own. You have the best chance of preventing a return of your fear (and avoidance) in the future if you can face your phobic situation fully alone.

Use Anxiety Coping Strategies

By breaking the process of exposure into incremental steps and relying on a support person, you can make facing any phobia a lot easier than you might think. The process is helped even further by using the anxiety coping strategies described earlier in this chapter, particularly: 1) abdominal breathing, 2) coping statements, and 3) diversion techniques such as talking to your support person.

It's important to gain proficiency with these techniques before you utilize them during the process of exposure. Work on practicing abdominal breathing or coping statements to manage everyday episodes of anxiety first. Then such techniques will serve you well when you need them in the course of exposure to a phobia.

See Chapter 6 of *The Anxiety & Phobia Workbook* for a more complete description of a variety of coping techniques to handle anxiety.

Avoid Flooding

"Flooding" refers to the situation where your anxiety gets out of control—rising to a panic level—during the course of exposure. Although some therapists advocate flooding as a method of overcoming phobias, my own experience indicates that flooding often makes exposure more difficult and protracted.

Flooding can be avoided if you learn to back off or "retreat" from exposure at the very first sign that your anxiety might get out of control. You want to stay in a difficult situation as long as you can if you are moderately anxious. However, if your anxiety approaches a point where you question your ability to control it (Level 4 on the Anxiety Scale—see page 119 of this chapter) it's time to back off. *Retreat is not the same as escape or leaving the situation.* If you *leave* the process of facing a difficult situation and go home, you are very likely to reinforce your need to keep avoiding it. Retreat means you back off from a phobic situation temporarily and then *return* to it (within the same hour, if possible) after your anxiety has diminished. This minimizes the risk of flooding.

For example, if you are overcoming a fear of driving on freeways, retreat means you pull over to the shoulder of the highway temporarily if your anxiety reaches Level 4 on the Anxiety Scale. (If there is no shoulder, you would pull off at the nearest exit.) Or, if you're afraid of being in social situations (e.g., staff meetings, classrooms, parties), retreat means you excuse yourself to go to the bathroom for ten minutes and then return to the situation when your anxiety has diminished.

Practice Regularly

Going out to face your phobia repeatedly is simply the best way to overcome it. In twenty years of helping people overcome phobias, what I've noticed that differentiates those who succeed from those who don't is a willingness to keep practicing exposure day after day. In general, I recommend practicing exposure *three to five times per week* while progressing up a phobia hierarchy. Longer practice sessions, with several trials of exposure to your phobic situation, tend to be more effective than briefer sessions. As long as you retreat when appropriate, it's impossible to undergo too much exposure in a given practice session (the worst that can happen is that you'll end up feeling tired or exhausted). Perseverance and patience are the traits you will need if you want to succeed in overcoming phobias or fears.

Accept Setbacks and Go On

Overcoming a phobia does not proceed in a linear fashion—there are plateaus and regressions as well as times of moving forward.

For example, suppose you're working on overcoming a phobia of driving freeways. Your exposure practice sessions over a four-week period might go like this:

Week 1: During three out of five practice sessions you can drive the distance of one exit on the freeway.

Week 2: For five out of five practice sessions you can't get on the freeway at all. (This degree of regression is not at all uncommon.)

Week 3: For two out of five practice sessions you are able to drive the distance of one exit. During two other sessions you're able to drive the distance of two exits. One day you can't get on the freeway at all.

Week 4: Due to illness you only get in two practice sessions. On one of those days you're able to manage three exits, on the other day you go one exit.

There is nothing wrong with setbacks—*they're a normal and expected part of exposure*. The important thing is to know how to handle them. Keep three things in mind:

- First, setbacks happen to everyone. Practically no one is able to overcome a phobia without periods of regression. All kinds of circumstances related to exposure—or apart from it—can come up to interfere with forward progress. The saying, "Life is what happens to you while you're making other plans" is applicable. If you expect to have setbacks, you'll be less surprised or discouraged by them.

- Second, setbacks are always temporary, provided you resolve to go forward. You don't lose the ground you've gained prior to the setback—it may just seem like that temporarily. When the setback passes, you will resume from where you left off in a short time if you keep practicing.

- Third, it's important to view any setback not as a defeat but as an opportunity to learn. When you understand the circumstances that caused the setback, you may be able to avoid repeating those circumstances in the future. The greatest opportunity afforded by a setback is the chance to build confidence in mastering your fear. Nothing builds confidence like being able to pass through a setback and continue on your way toward your goal. However discouraging a setback may seem initially, it's always an opportunity to gain strength and confidence in your eventual success. (This is true of life in general, not just the mastery of phobias.)

Follow Through to Completion with Exposure

Overcoming a phobia (or fear) means you no longer avoid the situation and you can handle being in the situation with a minimum of anxiety. In short, you are able to negotiate the situation as if you had never been afraid of it in the first place.

To reach this level of mastery, it's usually necessary to expose yourself to the situation many times, without any of the supports you might have relied on to help you face it at the outset. If you initially had a support person accompany you, you need to let them go and face the situation on your own. If you relied on other supports such as medications, lucky charms, or a cellular phone, you need to relinquish such devices and gain confidence in your ability to handle the situation without them.

It's okay not to let go of supports—but in so doing, you set up a situation in which you'll probably continue to rely on them indefinitely. In this instance, you're coping with your phobia but not fully mastering it. If you only face the situation occasionally (for example, long-distance flights), coping may certainly be sufficient. If you need to face the situation frequently (for example, being home alone), you may want to follow through with exposure practice until you reach the level of mastery. Not having to reach for a pill or another person to get you through will likely increase your sense of confidence.

Maintaining the Right Attitude

In my experience as a therapist, I've learned that approaching fearful situations with the *right attitude* is as important (if not more important) as learning specific strategies for exposure. If you begin with the right attitude, then utilizing appropriate techniques becomes much easier. The following seven attitudes are particularly important in increasing your ability to effectively face and overcome your fears.

Accept Body Symptoms of Anxiety

Recall Claire Weekes' four points, stated in the beginning of this chapter: 1) *face* your symptoms, 2) *accept* your body's reaction, 3) *"float"* with the "wave" of anxiety, and 4) *allow time to pass*. Struggling with body symptoms of anxiety that arise while facing something difficult will make them worse. Trying to deny or run away from them will also make them worse. *Acceptance* of the body symptoms of anxiety is the first thing you need to do when anxiety comes up. It's an attitude you can learn and cultivate. One of the best ways of doing so is to gain proficiency with abdominal breathing. Since breathing directly reduces the physical symptoms of anxiety, it's a powerful strategy for cultivating your ability to accept or "stay with" body symptoms until they subside and pass. Abdominal breathing will help you change your initial response to anxiety symptoms from "Oh no" to "So here it is again; I know what to do to cope."

The process of accepting anxiety symptoms can be further deepened by developing your "observing self," which is described in detail in Chapter 9.

Stay Grounded in the Present Moment

Anxiety begins as a physical reaction and is aggravated further by "What-if" or catastrophic thoughts. The more you can stay grounded in your body in the present moment, the less you'll be carried away by such thoughts. Again, abdominal breathing is an excellent way to stay focused in your body. Breathing is a process that is centered in your body rather than your mind. Another helpful strategy is to focus on your arms and legs while you breathe. The more attention you can bring down to your arms and legs, the less involved you're likely to be in your thoughts.

Focus on Anything Other Than Your Anxious Thoughts

Abdominal breathing and grounding in the present moment are the first and probably most effective strategies for avoiding becoming stuck in catastrophic "What-if" thoughts. However, any other object of focus will do. The "top three" reported by my clients are coping statements (see the section earlier in this chapter), talking to another person, and physical movement. The latter two strategies work because, like abdominal breathing, they move you away from your mind and anxious thoughts. While repeating coping statements is a more mental process, doing so will directly replace scary thoughts or images with calming, self-supporting ideas. It's helpful to have a list of coping statements written down on a card that you take with you when you face a situation that you've previously avoided. Some people prefer to listen to a recorded script of coping statements (see Chapter 12 of the book *Thoughts & Feelings* [1997] for instructions on how to do this).

Know That Fear Always Passes

No state of anxiety is permanent—it always passes. This attitude, first proposed by Claire Weekes, is based on the idea that the highest levels of anxiety (panic) are caused by an outpouring of adrenaline. The body metabolizes excess adrenaline in five to ten minutes, so the worst degree of panic you might ever experience is not likely to last beyond this. Lesser degrees of anxiety may persist longer than a few minutes, but they, too, will eventually pass. *Sooner or later, whatever you have constructed in your mind as threatening disappears because your mind stops focusing on it and moves on to something else.*

The worst case scenario is that you'll exhaust yourself with anxiety. At that point exhaustion will overtake your fear and induce you to let go of your scary thoughts (at least long enough to rest!).

Be Willing to Take Risks

The willingness to take a risk is the best definition of "courage" I know of. Courage is not fearlessness, but the ability to *risk* facing something you've been avoiding in spite of the inevitable anxiety that comes up. There is probably no risk-free way to overcome whatever it is you fear. Facing it requires an act of courage—a willingness to step into the unknown. How you acquire that courage is the subject of this book. Virtually all of the perspectives and strategies covered in the various chapters of this book can help to strengthen your courage to take risks. See the final chapter "Conclusion: Acquiring Courage" for an overview.

If You're Anxious About Something, You're Already Desensitizing to It

When you face something you fear, you almost inevitably experience some anxiety. Rather than magnifying the anxiety with further anxious thoughts, reframe it with the attitude: "This anxiety means I'm already beginning to desensitize." You cannot desensitize to anxiety without at first feeling it to some extent. The path out of anxiety starts with walking directly into it. If you know this, facing what you fear becomes easier. Every time your anxiety recurs, you can confidently remind yourself you are a step closer to being done with it.

Desensitization Always Works—with Practice

It's my observation—and personal experience—that there is no fear that cannot be overcome by repeated exposure or desensitization. Habituation always defeats fear, if you're willing to persevere with facing what you fear again and again. Anxiety is based on the projection of frightening outcomes in the face of something not fully known. Once that "something" becomes fully known and familiar, it invariably loses its ability to evoke fear. Desensitization always works. Truly knowing that will help give you courage to persist in facing your fear, no matter how challenging it appears at the outset.

What You Can Do Now

1. Reread the section "Panic Attacks Are Unpleasant but Not Dangerous" several times to reinforce the idea that the various symptoms of a panic attack are not dangerous.

2. Work on learning to recognize your own early symptoms of panic. Identify what symptoms constitute a Level 4 for you on the Anxiety Scale (the point at which you feel like you're beginning to lose control).

3. Experiment with different coping strategies when you feel anxiety symptoms progressing up to or through Level 4. Which strategies work best for you?

   • Practice abdominal breathing for five minutes per day until you've mastered the technique. Then use it to reduce arousal when you feel the initial physical symptoms of panic coming on.

   • Choose one or more coping statements and practice using them at the moment you notice that you're starting to scare yourself into more anxiety or panic with negative self-talk. Repeat your coping statements for two minutes or until you're able to overcome any negative self-talk going on in your head.

   • Try out other diversion techniques such as talking to someone, moving around, or getting angry at your anxiety when you feel symptoms first beginning to come on. Try abdominal breathing first before you go to these strategies.

4. Make a list of all your phobias and other specific fears, then rank them from the most to least bothersome. Complete The Worry Worksheet for each of your most difficult phobias or fears. For each one, write down overestimating thoughts that keep the fear going. Then refute these negative thoughts with more reasonable and positive counterstatements. Finally, write down ways in which you would cope if what you feared were actually to come about.

5. Review the section "How to Face What You Fear" for an understanding of guidelines and attitudes that are appropriate for overcoming phobias (or any type of fear). If you decide you want to master a specific phobia, such as fear of walking or driving far from home, fear of flying, or fear of public speaking, you may want to consult a therapist skilled in cognitive behavioral therapy. Otherwise, see the two chapters on "Help for Phobias" (Chapters 7 and 8) in *The Anxiety & Phobia Workbook*.

References and Further Reading

Barlow, David, and Michelle Craske. 1989. *Mastery of Your Anxiety and Panic*. Albany, New York: Graywind Publications. (Presents a scientifically validated treatment program for panic disorder.)

Beckfield, D. 1994. *Master Your Panic and Take Back Your Life*. San Luis Obispo, Calif.: Impact Publishers. (A very thorough and useful self-help guide for overcoming panic attacks.)

Bourne, Edmund J. 1995. *The Anxiety & Phobia Workbook*. 2d ed. Oakland, Calif.: New Harbinger Publications.

Clum, George. 1990. *Coping with Panic*. Pacific Grove, Calif.: Brooks/Cole.

Helmstetter, Shad. 1982. *What to Say When You Talk to Yourself*. New York: Pocket Books.

McKay, Matthew, Martha Davis, and Patrick Fanning. 1997. *Thoughts and Feelings: The Art of Cognitive Stress Intervention*. 2d ed. Oakland, Calif.: New Harbinger Publications.

Peurifoy, R. 1995. *Anxiety, Phobias and Panic*. New York: Warner Books.

Ross, Jerilyn. 1994. *Triumph Over Fear*. New York: Bantam Books. (An inspiring and valuable guide for both clients and professionals.)

Weekes, Claire. 1978. *Hope and Help for Your Nerves*. New York: Bantam Books. (A classic in the field which is still helpful to many persons.)

———. 1978. *Peace from Nervous Suffering*. New York: Bantam Books.

Wilson, Reid. 1996. *Don't Panic*. 2d ed. New York: HarperCollins. (A thorough and state-of-the-art guide for overcoming panic attacks and agoraphobia.)

Zeurcher-White, Elke. 1995. *An End to Panic*. Oakland, Calif.: New Harbinger Publications. (A concise and well-thought-out presentation of the cognitive behavioral treatment approach to overcoming panic attacks.)

7

Medication: Healing Your Brain When Anxiety Is Severe

The use of medication remains a central issue among professionals treating anxiety disorders as well as among those who struggle with these disorders on a daily basis. For many people, medication is a major and positive turning point along the path to recovery. For others, medication can confuse and complicate the recovery process, when a degree of freedom from anxiety is purchased at the cost of long-term addiction. For still other people—those who are either phobic or philosophically opposed to all types of drugs—medication may seem not to be an option. One thing is clear: The pros and cons of relying on medication are unique and variable in each individual case.

My own position on medication has changed some since the publication of my first book, *The Anxiety & Phobia Workbook*. One major reason for the shift has been the appearance in the nineties of a new class of medications, the selective serotonin reuptake inhibitors or SSRIs (for example, Prozac, Paxil, Zoloft, Luvox, and Serzone). These new medications have proven helpful in the treatment of all types of anxiety disorders, apart from specific phobias (i.e., single phobias of snakes, heights, blood, etc., without panic attacks). Evidence of epidemic levels of serotonin deficiency in contemporary society argues for the utility of this class of medications as an *adjunct* to—not a replacement for—cognitive, behavioral, and other methods of overcoming anxiety. Moreover, there are occasions where the use of medication seems critical to stem the rising tide of anxiety, which, left unchecked, might lead to a more severe and chronic disability than is necessary. If timely use of medication can forestall the development of a chronic anxiety disorder, I, for one, am certainly in favor of it. For such reasons, which I'll detail below, I've come to take a more favorable view of medication than I did nearly a decade ago.

This does not mean I am in any way less supportive of natural methods of recovery. We're living in a time when people are looking for natural and alternative ways to heal disease and disability. The natural way is always to be preferred if a realistic assessment of the situation indicates that is *all* that is needed. Yet the reality is that there are many situations where a *combination* of natural (or alternative) and standard medical approaches provides the most helpful, effective, and compassionate approach to recovery. I feel strongly that holistic and conventional (allopathic) methods of healing should collaborate in the treatment of any disorder, medical or psychiatric, that is likely to respond best to an integration of both approaches. Thus, for me, there is no conflict between the use of medication along with holistic and spiritually based approaches such as are described in this book. I believe God does not play favorites between alternative and conventional strategies to achieve health and well-being. Inspired practitioners and treatment modalities are available in both directions. It's your own deepest intuition that will inform you of the "right" combination of approaches in your own case. I chose to include a chapter on medication in this book because I feel medication is often a viable and helpful approach to healing problems with anxiety—especially in severe cases. The following two sections make a case for the usefulness of medication.

Serotonin Deficiency—an Epidemic?

Serotonin is one of several critical neurotransmitters in the brain. In his recent book, *Beyond Prozac* (1995), psychiatrist Michael Norden cites research in support of the notion that a vast proportion of the population suffers from behavior disorders related to serotonin deficiency. For example, one such study, published in the 1994 *Archives of General Psychiatry*, found that *nearly 50 percent* of persons between the ages of eighteen and fifty-four met formal diagnostic criteria for at least one of fourteen psychiatric illnesses that can be related to serotonin deficiency. These illnesses include, among others:

- Alcoholism (drug dependency)

- Anorexia nervosa (refusal to eat)

- Body-dysmorphic disorder (imagined ugliness)

- Bulimia (binge eating/purging)

- Depersonalization disorder (chronic sense of unreality)

- Dysthymia (chronic low-grade depression)

- Major depression (at least one episode of severe depression)

- Obsessive-compulsive disorder

- Panic disorder—with or without agoraphobia

- Post-traumatic stress disorder

- Seasonal affective disorder

- Social phobia

- Insomnia

- Impulsive aggression

While broad-scale studies actually measuring levels of serotonin in the brain have not been done, it appears that all of these conditions are at least in part related to a stress-induced deficiency in serotonin. Such a deficiency is pervasive because high stress is so pervasive in modern society. Apart from anxiety, the following common conditions are particularly indicative of a serotonin deficiency: 1) irritability and proneness to anger, 2) craving for sweets (especially in the winter months), 3) insomnia, 4) poor tolerance for heat, 5) mood swings, 6) severe PMS, and 7) depression that's worst in the morning and improves as the day goes on.

If you are among the 50 percent of adults that have some degree of serotonin deficiency, what can you do about it? Taking an SSRI medication for a period of at least six months is one powerful and effective option; these medications very directly increase brain serotonin levels by blocking their reuptake at the synapse. (Synapses are tiny spaces between nerve cells. Transmission of nerve impulses from one cell to another takes place by the release of chemical neurotransmitters such as serotonin into the synapse.) If you elect to take an SSRI you will not be alone—approximately 10 percent of the adults in the United States do so. Perhaps the widespread use of SSRIs in the population is further indication of a serotonin deficiency epidemic as proposed above.

It should be pointed out that while SSRIs help overcome anxiety (and depression) by raising brain serotonin levels, the way they actually work is a bit more complicated. It usually takes SSRIs about four weeks to take effect. While they raise levels of serotonin in the brain immediately, what's happening during the four-week period of time is that the number of synaptic receptor sites available to take up serotonin is *decreasing*. When serotonin levels are low, the brain creates more receptor sites to utilize the reduced amounts available. Having a large number of sites *increases the sensitivity* of the serotonin network of nerve cells in the brain, which is thought to be associated with increased susceptibility to anxiety and depression. After a month of raising serotonin levels in the brain, the number of serotonin receptor sites decreases. Thus the serotonin network in the brain becomes less sensitive (the technical word is "down-regulated"), resulting in less vulnerability of the brain to anxiety and/or depression.

If you're opposed in principle to taking medications—or if you don't like the side effects of the SSRI medications that you've tried—there are natural alternatives. While the alternatives may not be as potent in raising brain serotonin levels as the SSRIs, they can be helpful in ameliorating some of the conditions associated with low serotonin—in particular, depression.

A brief enumeration of natural methods for enhancing serotonin follows.

Tryptophan

As was previously discussed in the chapter on nutrition, the amino acid tryptophan is a natural precursor to serotonin. Your body makes serotonin (and also melatonin) out of tryptophan. So, taking supplemental tryptophan can increase brain serotonin levels, although not as powerfully as prescription SSRI antidepressants, which actually block the reuptake of serotonin at synapse in the brain. Tryptophan is available in two forms: 5-hydroxy tryptophan and L-tryptophan. The former is available in health food stores; the latter, at the time of this writing, is available by prescription. Both supplements have produced moderate improvements in anxiety and depression in several studies; L-tryptophan seems to be especially helpful for sleep. Standard doses are 1,000–2,000 mg per day for L-tryptophan and 300–1000 mg per day for 5-HT (either should be taken with a carbohydrate snack and no protein to optimize utilization by the brain). Please do not take tryptophan if you are already taking an SSRI medication.

St. John's Wort

St. John's Wort (*hypericum*) is an herb that has recently become popular in the United States after years of use in Europe. Several controlled studies have found that it's effective in ameliorating symptoms of depression, sleep disturbances, and anorexia. It appears to increase serotonin levels in the brain by blocking reuptake of serotonin at the synapse, much like prescription SSRI antidepressants. To be effective, St. John's Wort should be taken in a standardized extract containing 0.3 percent hypericin. The therapeutic dose is 300 mg three times daily; it takes four to six weeks to achieve its full therapeutic benefit. Avoid taking St. John's Wort if you are already taking an SSRI medication. See the section on herbs in the chapter "Caring for Your Body: Nutrition" for further information.

Exercise

Brain serotonin levels rise in response to exercise. One study found that ninety minutes on a treadmill *doubled* brain serotonin levels. It appears exercise not only increases the amount of serotonin but also the activity of serotonin in the cerebral cortex (the "higher" brain responsible for thinking and problem solving). Vigorous exercise also leads to a release of endorphins in the brain—natural opium-like substances that the brain releases when you feel pleasure or a sense of well-being. The so-called "runner's high" is attributed to endorphin release. It's likely that the combination of enhanced serotonin and endorphin release accounts for the beneficial effects of regular exercise on depression, a result that has been confirmed by numerous studies.

Light

Systematic research has found that exposure to bright light relieves seasonal affective disorder (SAD), a seasonal depression that many people experience during winter months in northern latitudes where light is diminished. It used to be thought that SAD was primarily due to insufficient suppression of the hormone melatonin, which is secreted by the brain to induce sleep during evening and at night. Results of studies attempting to establish a connection between SAD and melatonin have been mixed, however. The hypothesis that's currently receiving the most attention is that light insufficiency can cause a reduction in brain serotonin levels. Norman Rosenthal, one of the leading researchers in this field, writes that when susceptible individuals are exposed to too little environmental light—such as during winter—they produce too little serotonin. Rosenthal and others believe that low serotonin levels are responsible for the symptoms of SAD.

Light therapy is used to alleviate the symptoms of SAD. There are several different devices available designed to increase your exposure to light indoors. Information on about a dozen companies that manufacture light therapy devices is available from the National Organization for Seasonal Affective Disorder (NOSAD), P.O. Box 40133, Washington, DC 20016.

Diet: Higher Protein Relative to Carbohydrate

The standard of a high-carbohydrate/low-fat diet, which has been popular for over two decades (largely because of its benefits in preventing heart disease), has come under question recently. Research conducted by dietary endocrinologist Barry Sears (author of the book, *The Zone*) leads to the conclusion that for most people, each meal should contain proportionately more protein relative to starch than has been conventionally recommended. Sears favors a ratio of 30 percent protein, 30 percent fat, and 40 percent carbohydrate at each meal. While many nutritionists feel this is too much protein, Sears' approach advocates reducing the total number of calories you consume. Thus, you end up eating about the same amount of protein you have all along, but in better *proportion* relative to amounts of fat and carbohydrate. Research shows that eating less starch relative to protein has a very favorable effect on the hormonal system, particularly the balance of insulin to *glucagon*. (Glucagon releases sugar into your bloodstream from its stored form in the liver.) This improved balance of insulin and glucagon favorably affects the prostaglandin system, which then favorably affects serotonin. The complex interactions between hormones, prostaglandins, and serotonin are detailed in Sears' book, but the upshot is that eating protein to carbohydrate in a 30:40 ratio will help your body work better in a number of ways, including stabilizing blood sugar levels and enhancing serotonin production. (Vegetable-based proteins, such as soy, tofu, and beans with grains are preferable to animal-based proteins such as meat and cheese.)

Support—Meeting Basic Needs for Intimacy and Affiliation

It's well known that isolation aggravates anxiety and depression, while supportive interpersonal contact diminishes both. To my knowledge, there is no systematic research confirming the association between serotonin and interpersonal support. However, common observation and experience would suggest that one exists. The fact that love is a great healer will be explored in detail in Chapter 14. In my opinion, *part* of the beneficial effects of love and support are likely mediated at a neurochemical level. How else can a single hug affect our mood so quickly?

The Use of Medication to Stop Escalating Anxiety

The kinds and degrees of stress that precipitate anxiety disorders frequently upset the neuroendocrine regulatory systems in the brain. Once an anxiety disorder develops, these systems are further stressed and disrupted. Such disruption can easily become severe enough that natural methods alone are insufficient to abate it. At this point, medication (tranquilizers or, preferably, SSRI antidepressants) can be very helpful in breaking the spiral of mounting anxiety. Not to introduce medication at this critical point can result in traumatization that, sadly, may lead to a long-term, chronic anxiety disorder. The traumatization that occurs when severe anxiety continues unchecked is, in my observation, most likely to occur on *both* emotional and neurophysiological levels. (The term "kindling" is often used among psychiatrists to refer to this phenomenon where acute anxiety, left untreated, spirals up into a severe and chronic condition—as if a fire had started.) In short, timely and appropriate use of medication is, in many cases, the best way to reduce the risk of developing a more severe, chronic problem with anxiety. Taking medication under such circumstances does not conflict with holistic values any more than reliance on allopathic methods in a medical emergency.

Other Situations Where the Use of Medication Is Appropriate

The following are common types of situations where the addition of medication to cognitive behavioral treatment can be particularly helpful:

- Where panic or anxiety is so severe or distressing as to interfere with the ability to complete homework assignments associated with cognitive behavioral therapy.

- Where a person with agoraphobia has a difficult time undertaking graded exposure. Low doses of a benzodiazepine tranquilizer (i.e., Xanax or Klonopin, .25–.5 mg) or an SSRI antidepressant medication (Paxil or Zoloft) at therapeutic dose levels may enable such a person to negotiate exposure. After exposure hierarchies have been completed with medication, it's important to eventually rework them without medication to ensure lasting recovery.

- Severe situational stress (i.e., death of a close relative, a significant health crisis, trauma such as rape or natural disasters) may be mitigated by medication. Short-term use of a benzodiazepine tranquilizer can be helpful because of its immediate effects.

- Moderate to severe depression accompanying an anxiety disorder will usually benefit from antidepressant medication. Such medication should also help relieve anxiety. Mild to moderate depression may respond to trytophan or St. John's Wort.

- Severe social phobia or social anxiety can be helped by SSRI antidepressants, benzodiazepines, or MAOI antidepressants (see below) in conjunction with individual, or preferably group, cognitive behavioral therapy.

- Approximately 70 percent of cases of obsessive-compulsive disorders can be helped by the SSRIs (particularly Prozac, Effexor, and Luvox) or the cyclic antidepressant Anafranil.

Types of Medication Used to Treat Anxiety Disorders

What follows is a description of the major classes of prescription medications used in the treatment of anxiety disorders. Potential advantages and drawbacks of each type of medication are considered.

SSRI Antidepressant Medications

The SSRI (Selective Serotonin Reuptake Inhibitor) antidepressant medications include Prozac (fluoxetine), Zoloft (sertraline), Paxil (paroxetine), Luvox (fluvoxamine), and Serzone (nefazodone). (Technically, serzone is both a serotonin receptor antagonist as well as a reuptake inhibitor.) In the past few years they have become the first choice for most psychiatrists among the various types of medications used to treat anxiety disorders. The SSRIs all increase levels of the neurotransmitter serotonin in the brain by preventing the reabsorption of serotonin at synapses. With increased serotonin, the number of serotonin receptors on nerve cells in the brain can decrease (not as many are needed), a process sometimes called "down-regulation." Thus all of the millions of nerve cells in the serotonin receptor system, particularly those in parts of the brain responsible for anxiety (particularly within the limbic system), become less sensitive or volatile to changes in the neurochemical environment of the brain created by stress. That means less precipitous shifts in mood and less vulnerability to anxiety.

The SSRIs tend to be as effective—and sometimes more effective—than the older cyclic antidepressants that have been used to treat panic (e.g., imipramine, desipramine, nortriptyline). They also have the distinct advantage of causing fewer side effects for most people than the older antidepressants. SSRIs are used most often to treat panic, panic with agoraphobia, or obsessive-compulsive disorder. (See appendix 1 for descriptions of the various anxiety disorders.) They have also found use with social phobia, particularly generalized social phobia, where a person is phobic of most types of social situations and encounters. Sometimes they are used to treat post-traumatic stress disorder or generalized anxiety disorder, especially when these difficulties are accompanied by depression. People differ quite a lot in their response to the SSRIs. If you try one and experience no benefit, be willing to try another. To gain full benefit from an SSRI, you may need to take it for one to two years. Typical effective daily doses for SSRIs are: Prozac, 20–40 mg; Paxil, 20–40 mg; Zoloft, 50–100 mg; Luvox, 50–100 mg; and Serzone, 150–300 mg. Effective doses of these medications for OCD are somewhat higher. Some clients find, however, that they obtain good results from somewhat lower doses.

Advantages: The SSRIs can be helpful for any of the anxiety disorders or depression. They have been particularly helpful for persons with severe panic disorder, agoraphobia, or obsessive-compulsive disorder. SSRIs are easily tolerated and safe for medically ill or elderly persons. They have no likelihood of causing addiction. In most cases they do not lead to weight gain.

Drawbacks: Although SSRIs have fewer side effects than the older cyclic medications, they can cause side effects in some people, including: jitteriness, agitation, restlessness, dizziness, drowsiness, headaches, nausea, gastrointestinal distress, and sexual dysfunction. These side effects tend to go away after two weeks, so it's important to try to ride them out during the early phase of treatment. *All of these side effects can be minimized by starting off with a very low dose of the medication and increasing it, over time, to therapeutic levels.* For example, doses might start at 5 mg per day for Prozac or Paxil and 10 mg for Zoloft or Luvox. To achieve such doses you need to start with a quarter of a tablet per day, in most cases, then gradually increase up to a tablet per day over a period of several weeks.

The one side effect that can be problematic over time is reduced sexual motivation and/or sexual dysfunction (for example, absent or delayed orgasm). This can be upsetting to many people and in some cases leads individuals to discontinue the medication. For a certain percentage of people who take SSRIs, normal sexual functioning will resume after two or three months on the medication, so it's a good idea to stay with an SSRI even if at first you experience diminished sex drive. If the problem doesn't get better, it can be mitigated in one of four ways, under the supervision of your doctor: 1) reducing the dose of the SSRI 50 percent the day you choose to be sexually active, 2) augmenting the use of the SSRI with 5–10 mg/day of Buspar, 3) supplementing with the medications amantidine or cyproheptidine, 4) trying the supplement DHEA 25–50 mg/day available at most health food stores (see the chapter "Caring For Your Body: Nutrition"). Many persons find that one or two of these interventions can help them restore more normal sexual activity while continuing to take an SSRI.

A third disadvantage is that SSRIs, while often effective, take four to five weeks to produce significant therapeutic benefit. Sometimes the full therapeutic potential is not achieved until twelve weeks or longer. (There is some evidence that even further benefits occur over the course of one year.) If you are suffering from severe and disabling panic, your doctor may recommend you take a tranquilizer (most likely a high-potency benzodiazepine—see below) while waiting for the SSRI to take effect.

Abrupt discontinuation of an SSRI medication can cause withdrawal symptoms, including low mood, lethargy, dizziness, irritability, and what have been described as "flu-like" symptoms. These symptoms can be minimized or eliminated by tapering down the dose gradually over a period of one month.

A final drawback of SSRIs is their expense. Without insurance, you can pay upwards of two hundred dollars per month out-of-pocket for some SSRIs. The optimal duration for taking an SSRI medication is one to two years. You increase your risk of a return of symptoms if you take the medication for a shorter time period.

High-Potency Benzodiazepines

The high-potency benzodiazepine tranquilizers (BZs) Xanax (alprazolam), Ativan (lorazepam), and Klonopin (clonazepam) are commonly used to treat anxiety disorders. Older benzodiazepine drugs such as Valium, Librium, or Tranxene are occasionally tried when a person is sensitive to the side effects of the newer BZs. The benzodiazepines are often used in conjunction with SSRI antidepressants (or older cyclic antidepressants) to treat severe cases of panic disorder. Frequently it's possible to withdraw from use of the BZ after the antidepressant medication has achieved its full anti-anxiety benefit (i.e., four to six weeks).

Benzodiazepine drugs generally depress the activity of the central nervous system and thus directly and efficiently decrease anxiety. They do so by binding with receptors in the brain that function to tone down or suppress activity in those parts of the brain responsible for anxiety—the locus ceruleus and limbic system. In higher doses, BZ tranquilizers act like sedatives and may promote sleep. Lower doses tend to simply reduce anxiety without sedation. The main difference between various benzodiazepines is their "half-life," or length of time their chemical metabolites tend to stay in your body (for example, Xanax has a half-life of 8 hours, Klonopin 18–24 hours, and Valium 48–72 hours).

At present, the most common tranquilizer used to treat anxiety disorders is Xanax (alprazolam). Alprazolam differs from other BZs in that it has an additional antidepressant effect as well as the ability to relieve anxiety. It also tends to have a less sedating effect than other tranquilizers. Because Xanax has a short half-life, two or three doses per day are usually prescribed. If you take only one dose per day, you may experience *rebound* anxiety—the tendency to experience heightened levels of anxiety as the medication wears off. BZs with longer half-lives such as Klonopin tend to cause less rebound anxiety and can often be taken in a single dose per day. Research indicates that high doses of Xanax, 2–9 mg per day, are necessary to fully suppress panic attacks. In clinical practice, however, it's common to administer low doses: in the range of .25–1 mg two or three times per day. (Daily doses of Xanax tend to be higher than for Klonopin.) Such doses can significantly diminish the symptoms of panic attacks with less sedating side effects.

Advantages: BZs work very quickly, reducing symptoms of anxiety within 15–20 minutes. Unlike antidepressants, which need to be taken regularly, BZs can be taken on an "as needed" basis only. That is, you can use a small dose of Xanax, Ativan, or Klonopin only when you have to confront a challenging situation, such as a graded exposure task, going to a job interview, or making a flight.

The BZs tend to have less bothersome side effects for many people than the antidepressant medications (especially the cyclic antidepressants). Sometimes they are the only medication that can provide relief when a person is unable to take any of the antidepressant medications. Generic forms of BZs are available, reducing their cost.

Drawbacks: BZs, unlike antidepressant medications, tend to be addictive. The higher the dose (i.e., more than 1 mg per day for high-potency BZs) and the longer you take them (i.e., more than one month), the more likely you will become physically dependent. Physical dependency means that if you stop taking the medication abruptly, severe anxiety symptoms are likely to occur. Many people who have taken Xanax (or other BZs) in high doses for a month or low doses for several months report that it's very difficult getting off the medication. (There is some evidence that withdrawal from Klonopin, because of its longer half-life, may be slightly easier and less protracted than withdrawal from Xanax.) *Abrupt* withdrawal from these medications is *dangerous* and may produce panic attacks, severe anxiety, confusion, muscle tension, irritability, insomnia, and even seizures. A more gradual tapering of the dose, stretched out over many weeks or even months, is what makes withdrawal possible. People vary in the ease with which they can withdraw from Xanax, but as a general rule it's best to taper off very gradually over a period of one to six months under medical supervision. During this withdrawal period you may suffer a recurrence of panic attacks or other anxiety symptoms for which the drug was originally prescribed.

If a BZ medication is tapered off too quickly, you can experience *rebound* anxiety. Rebound is the occurrence of anxiety symptoms equal to or *greater* than those you experienced prior to ever taking the drug in the first place. Rebound may lead to *relapse*, a return of your anxiety disorder at equal or greater severity than what you experienced before taking the medication. To minimize the risk of rebound, it is critical to withdraw from your dose of a BZ very gradually, preferably over several months. (For example, if you have been taking 1.5 mg of Xanax per day for six months, reduce your dose by .25 mg every two or three weeks.)

Another drawback of BZs is that they only are effective as long as you take them. When you stop taking them, your anxiety disorder has virtually a 100 percent chance of returning unless you've learned coping skills (i.e., breathing, relaxation, exercise, stress management, working with self-talk, assertiveness, etc.) and made lifestyle changes that will result in long-term anxiety relief. Taking a BZ only, without doing anything else, amounts to merely suppressing your symptoms without getting at the cause of your difficulty.

A final problem with benzodiazepines is that they tend to have a blunting effect not only on anxiety but also on feelings in general. Many people report that their affective response is lower while they are taking these drugs (for example, they may have trouble crying or getting angry even at times when these reactions are appropriate). Thus, to the extent that anxiety is related to suppressed and unresolved feelings, taking these drugs will tend only to alleviate symptoms rather than relieve the cause of the problem. (Some people have a paradoxical reaction to benzodiazepines where they actually become *more* emotional or impulsive, although this tends to be the exception rather than the rule.) Emotional blunting is less likely with antidepressant medications, although it may occur.

Long-term use of BZs (more than two years) is sometimes necessary in those cases of severe panic and anxiety that do not respond to any other type of medication. While enabling many people to function, long-term BZ use has several problems. Many long-term BZ users report that they feel depressed and/or less vital and energetic than they would like. It's as though the medication tends to sap them of a certain degree of energy. Often, if they are able to switch to an antidepressant medication to help manage their anxiety, they regain a sense of vitality and more enthusiasm for life. In my experience, the BZs are most appropriate for treating short-term acute anxiety and stress rather than longer-lasting conditions such as agoraphobia, PTSD, or OCD. Wherever possible, chronic, long-term anxiety disorders are most appropriately treated with SSRI antidepressants. There are, however, certain individuals who seem to need to take a low-dose of a BZ long-term in order to function. They accept the physical dependence and other side effects in exchange for protection from anxiety that they've been unable to manage using solely natural techniques or other types of medication. If they are over fifty and have been taking a BZ medication for more than two years, such persons should periodically receive medical checkups, including an evaluation of liver function.

Cyclic Antidepressants

Cyclic antidepressants include Tofranil (imipramine), Pamelor (nortriptyline), Norpramin (desipramine), Anafranil (clomipramine), Elavil (amitriptyline), Desyrel (trazadone), and Sinequan (doxepin), among others. These medications (especially imipramine) are frequently used to treat panic attacks, whether such attacks occur by themselves or in conjunction with agoraphobia. Cyclic antidepressants seem to reduce both the frequency and intensity of panic reactions for many people. They are also effective in reducing depression that often accompanies panic disorder and agoraphobia. While it used to be believed that Tofranil (imipramine) was the most effective antidepressant for treating panic, more recent evidence indicates that any of the cyclic antidepressant medications can be helpful, depending on the individual. Anafranil (clomipramine) tends to be specifically helpful in treating OCD.

The cyclic antidepressants are used somewhat less these days than SSRI antidepressants because they tend to have more troublesome side effects. For example, in studies of imipramine, about one-third of the subjects dropped out because they couldn't tolerate side effects (only about 10 percent of subjects have dropped out in studies using SSRIs). On the other hand, cyclic antidepressants are sometimes a better choice than SSRIs for certain people because most of them (other than Desyrel and Anafranil) modify a different receptor system in the brain (the noradrenergic system instead of the serotonin system). As with SSRIs, cyclic antidepressants are best tolerated by starting with a very low dose (e.g., 5 mg per day of imipramine) and gradually working up to a therapeutic dose level (approximately 100–200 mg per day).

Advantages: Cyclic antidepressants, like the SSRIs, do not lead to physical dependence. They have a beneficial effect on depression as well as on panic and anxiety. They block panic attacks even if you are not depressed. Because generic forms are available, they are inexpensive.

Drawbacks: Cyclic antidepressants (unlike SSRIs) tend to produce *anticholinergic* side effects (they block the neurotransmitter acetylcholine). These side effects include dry mouth, blurred vision, dizziness or disorientation, constipation, and postural hypotension (causing dizziness). Weight gain and sexual dysfunction can also occur. With imipramine in particular, anxiety may *increase* during the first few days of administration. With clomipramine (effective for OCD), side effects can be particularly bothersome.

Although these side effects tend to diminish after one or two weeks, they can still be uncomfortable for 25 to 30 percent of people who take cyclic antidepressants after the initial adjustment period.

Like the SSRIs, cyclic antidepressants take about three to four weeks to offer therapeutic benefits. While able to block panic attacks, these medications may not be as effective as SSRIs and benzodiazepine tranquilizers in reducing anticipatory anxiety about potentially having a panic attack or having to face a phobic situation. Finally, about 30 to 50 percent of people will relapse (i.e., experience the return of panic or anxiety symptoms) after discontinuing cyclic antidepressant medications. Clearly, this is a much lower rate than occurs with benzodiazepines. Without learning cognitive and behavioral strategies to manage panic and anxiety, relapse after discontinuing BZs approaches 100 percent. Relapse with SSRI medications appears to be low when the medication is taken at least eighteen months; however, reliable data on the exact percentage of relapse is not in at the time of this writing.

MAO Inhibitor Antidepressants

If you have given SSRIs and cyclic antidepressants a fair trial and still obtain no benefit, your doctor may try the oldest class of antidepressant medications—the MAO-inhibitors (MAOIs). Nardil (phenelzine) is the MAOI most commonly used to treat panic, although Parnate (tranylcypromine) is sometimes used. While MAOIs are potent medications, they are frequently last in line to be tried because they can cause serious or even fatal rises in blood pressure when combined with: 1) foods that contain the amino acid tyramine, such as wine, aged cheeses, and certain meats; and 2) certain medications, including some over-the-counter analgesics. If you are taking a MAOI, you should be under close supervision by your doctor.

Advantages: MAOIs have a potent panic-blocking effect and are sometimes effective when other types of antidepressants have failed. There is also some research indicating they are helpful in treating social phobia, especially generalized social phobia (a tendency to be phobic toward a wide range of interpersonal situations or encounters). They may also help severe depression that has been unresponsive to other classes of antidepressants.

Drawbacks: Side effects include weight gain, hypotension (low blood pressure), sexual dysfunction, headache, fatigue, and insomnia. These side effects may be most pronounced during the third and fourth weeks of treatment and then are likely to diminish.

Dietary restrictions are critical. When taking an MAOI, you need to avoid foods containing tyramine, including most cheeses, homemade yogurt, most alcoholic beverages, aged meats and fish, liver, ripe bananas, and certain vegetables. Over-the-counter cold medicines, diet pills, and certain antihistamines need to be avoided. Also, prescription amphetamines and SSRI or cyclic antidepressants should be avoided.

Other Antidepressants

Other antidepressant medications sometimes used with anxiety disorders include Effexor (venlafaxine) and Wellbutrin (bupropion). Effexor combines a cyclic antidepressant with an SSRI in one pill. It can be particularly helpful for OCD and depression. Wellbutrin may be helpful for depression, but can be difficult for people with anxiety disorders to tolerate, since its side effects include anxiety and insomnia.

Beta-Blockers

Although there are several different beta-adrenergic blocking drugs (popularly called *beta-blockers*), the two most commonly used with anxiety disorders are Inderal (propranolol) and Tenormin (atenolol). These medications can be helpful for anxiety conditions with marked bodily symptoms, especially heart palpitations (rapid or irregular heartbeat) and sweating. Beta-blockers are quite effective in blocking these peripheral manifestations of anxiety, but are less effective in reducing the internal experience of anxiety mediated by the central nervous system. Inderal or Tenormin may be used in conjunction with a benzodiazepine tranquilizer, such as Xanax, in treating panic disorder when heart palpitations are prominent. By themselves, beta-blockers are often given in a single dose (for example, 20–40 mg Inderal) to relieve severe bodily symptoms of anxiety (rapid heartbeat, shaking, or blushing) prior to a high-performance situation, such as public speaking, a job interview, final examinations, or a musical recital. Beta-blockers are also often used to treat mitral valve prolapse, a benign heart arrhythmia that sometimes accompanies panic disorder.

Although these medications are relatively safe, they can produce side effects, such as excessive lowering of blood pressure (causing dizziness or light-headedness), fatigue, and drowsiness. In some people they can also cause depression. Unlike tranquilizers, these medications do not tend to be physically addictive. Still, if you've been taking them for a while, it's preferable to taper your dose gradually to avoid rebound elevations of blood pressure. Beta-blockers are not recommended for persons with asthma or other respiratory illnesses that cause wheezing, or for persons with diabetes.

Buspar

Researchers do not yet fully understand how Buspar (buspirone) works, but it's frequently used in the treatment of anxiety. To date it has been found useful in diminishing generalized anxiety, but is ineffective in reducing the frequency or intensity of panic attacks. There is some research that indicates Buspar can be helpful in treating social phobia or in augmenting the effects of SSRI medications used to treat OCD. Many practitioners prefer it to Xanax (and other benzodiazepines) for treating generalized anxiety because it is less prone to cause drowsiness and is nonaddictive. There is relatively little risk of your becoming physically dependent on Buspar or requiring a protracted period of time to withdraw from it.

An ordinary starting dose for Buspar is 5 mg two or three times per day. It takes from two to three weeks before the full anti-anxiety effect of this medication is achieved. Some individuals with generalized anxiety respond well to Buspar, while others report side effects (lethargy, nausea, dizziness, or paradoxical anxiety).

The Choice to Use Medication: What to Consider

The decision to include medication in your program for recovery from anxiety involves many considerations. First and foremost, it's always a decision made in consultation with your treating physician. Your doctor should be knowledgeable and experienced in treating anxiety disorders and should work with you in a collaborative (not authoritarian) way. Second, your decision depends on a number of personal factors, including 1) the severity of your problem with anxiety, 2) your personal outlook and values regarding medication, and 3) your patience, in those situations where several medications need to be tried before the "right" one for you can be found.

Be wary of pat answers and simple generalizations when you consider undertaking a course of medication. The following twelve vignettes illustrate the complex range of situations that might lead a person to decide for or against taking medication.

- A busy physician has numerous duties at work, home, and in his community. He takes time to meditate, jog, express feelings, and work with self-talk, but still has debilitating panic attacks. He finds that an SSRI antidepressant helps him to sleep better and carry out his round of daily responsibilities with less anxiety.

- A mother who has been housebound with agoraphobia for a long time has a difficult time beginning exposure therapy. She finds taking an SSRI medication helps her to get started. After six months of exposure she is confident enough to continue without medication.

- A secretary who has been taking medication for mixed anxiety and depression for a year discovers she is pregnant. She stops her medication and puts up with intensified symptoms until after her baby is born.

- A husband going through a divorce has a major heart attack followed by mixed anxiety and depression. Although he has been opposed to taking medication up to this time, he decides to rely on a benzodiazepine medication to help him negotiate a severe crisis.

- A woman who has just been promoted to a more demanding job learns her mother has died. She elects to take medication for a period of several months to handle her stressful life circumstances.

- A chiropractor who teaches classes in nutrition and is heavily involved in alternative health practices has obsessive-compulsive disorder. He finds that he needs to take an SSRI antidepressant in order to handle his work.

- A student who decides to enroll in a certificate program to be an acupuncturist has a strong desire, despite her panic attacks, to embrace only natural methods (such as herbs, nutrition, Tai Chi, and meditation) to handle her anxiety. She decides not to use medication.

- A man who has been taking various SSRI antidepressants for panic disorder over five years wants to evaluate how he might do without medication. He discontinues it, over a period of two months, and does well.

- A long-term user of benzodiazepines feels they are causing her to be depressed and decides she would rather have some anxiety and emotional intensity in her life than feel numbed or de-energized by a tranquilizer.

- A minister with panic disorder is unable to tolerate any antidepressant medication. He finds he is best able to work taking a very low dose of a tranquilizer every day, long-term.

- A woman who belongs to a religious affiliation that believes prayer and right living is the answer to life's difficulties has a strong philosophical belief that medications are unnecessary for her recovery. She elects not to use medication for her panic attacks.

- A recovering alcoholic with two years' sobriety begins taking Xanax to manage his anxiety. Within two months he starts escalating the dose. Both his doctor and his twelve-step program friends advise him to discontinue the medication. In the interest of maintaining a commitment to a substance-free lifestyle, he does so.

Whether you're considering starting medication, or thinking about stopping medication you've been taking for a while, the two most important factors to look at in making a decision for yourself about medication are *severity of your condition* and your own *values*. Each of these is considered below.

Personal Values

The first consideration in your decision whether to take medication is your own personal values. Are you open to including medication as a part of your recovery program, or do you feel strongly about adhering to natural methods alone? While your symptoms may warrant trying medication, and while your doctor might encourage you to do so, the decision is ultimately your own. If you happen to be committed to the ideal of natural healing without the aid of medication, that is an admirable option. Many persons can recover from anxiety disorders by natural methods alone, if they have sufficient motivation, persistence, and diligence in practicing natural methods such as are outlined in this book and my first book, *The Anxiety & Phobia Workbook*. At the opposite extreme, there are people who lack sufficient interest or motivation to put in the time and effort involved in practicing relaxation, exercise, desensitization, and cognitive skills on a daily basis. They seek immediate relief of symptoms through taking a drug. In many cases, this is also a viable choice. It's not for anyone to judge a person's decision to seek relief from anxiety disorders through medication. Medications certainly do provide a great deal of symptom relief for many people.

In making a choice whether to rely on medication, it's important to have all the information that you need to make the most informed and enlightened decision possible. Such a decision should not be based solely on impulse, for example, a desire to take a high dose of medication to eliminate all symptoms of anxiety as soon as possible. Nor should it be based upon fear or avoidance of medication because you have a phobia of it. The purpose of this chapter is to give you as much information as possible so that you can make the optimal decision for yourself.

Severity

Apart from your personal values, the next thing to look at in considering medication is the severity of your symptoms. As a general rule, the more severe your problem, the more likely you will benefit from a trial of medication. Severity can be defined in two ways: your ability to function and your level of distress. Use the following questions to evaluate the severity of your own condition.

First, does your problem with anxiety interfere with your ability to function in normal adult roles? Are you having a hard time working or are you unable to work at all? Is your ability to raise your children or be responsive to your spouse impaired by your anxiety? Do you have a hard time organizing your thoughts to complete basic tasks such as cooking or paying bills?

Second, does your problem with anxiety cause you considerable distress to the point where you have two or more hours every day where you feel very uncomfortable? Is it hard for you just to make it through each day? Do you wake up each morning in a state of dread?

Another factor in considering medication is depression. Significant depression accompanies anxiety disorders in about 50 percent of cases. It's especially common with panic disorder, agoraphobia, obsessive-compulsive disorder, and post-traumatic stress disorder. There is also a new syndrome—mixed anxiety and depression—that has received attention recently. Criteria for depression include: lack of energy, continuous low mood or apathy, loss of appetite, disturbed sleep, frequent self-criticism, and possibly suicidal thoughts. If you are depressed, antidepressant medication can be especially helpful because it tends to restore the motivation and energy you need to practice skills such as abdominal breathing, relaxation, exercise, cognitive restructuring, and graded exposure. If you have had suicidal thoughts, your doctor will most certainly recommend medication.

In addition to severity of symptoms, *chronicity*—how long you've had your problem—is another important factor to consider. If your anxiety is of recent origin and a response to stressful circumstances, it may pass when you learn stress-management techniques and work through whatever problem instigated the stress. On the other hand, if you've been suffering for more than a year—and especially if you've tried cognitive behavioral therapy and not yet received the benefit you wanted—a trial medication may well be helpful. To conclude: *the more severe and/or the more chronic (long-standing) your condition, the more likely you may respond favorably to medication.*

How Long to Take Medication

For anyone who is considering trying or is presently taking a prescription medication, this is a very important question. Unfortunately, there is no simple answer. The length of time you take medication depends on at least three different factors:

- What type of medication (e.g., tranquilizer or antidepressant)

- What type of anxiety disorder (e.g., panic, social phobia, obsessive-compulsive disorder)

- Your motivation and commitment to utilize natural approaches (a committed program of nonmedication approaches may enable you to stop relying on medication or else reduce your dose)

What Type of Medication

Some types of medication, such as tranquilizers or beta-blockers, can be used on an "as-needed" basis only. That is, you only use the medication when dealing with an acutely anxiety-provoking situation, such as confronting a phobia. Tranquilizers can also be used over a period of a few weeks to help you get through a particularly difficult situation, such as the death of a loved one or taking the Bar Exam. For a period of one to two years, tranquilizers may be useful if you are unable to take any type of antidepressant medication. Long-term use of tranquilizers (more than two years), while having certain problems, may even be justified in some cases (see the previous section on benzodiazepine tranquilizers).

Antidepressant medications are usually taken on a daily basis for a minimum of six months. In my experience, they are *most effective in treating more severe anxiety disorders when taken for a period of eighteen months to two years*. Risk of relapse once you discontinue the antidepressants is lower if you've taken them for this length of time. For some persons, long-term use (more than two years) of antidepressant medication, at a "maintenance" dose level, offers an optimal quality of life.

What Type of Anxiety

If you have a mild to moderate case of agoraphobia, you may only need to take medication (a tranquilizer or an antidepressant) up to and during the early stages of graded exposure to your phobic situations. Then during later stages you may wean off the medication and work through your exposure hierarchies on your own. Being able to do so without the use of medication will enhance your sense of mastery over your phobias. On the other hand, if you are having frequent panic attacks and/or are housebound, it may be beneficial for you to take medication for a longer time. For SSRI antidepressant medications, the eighteen-month to two-year period mentioned above is optimal. Long-term maintenance on antidepressant medication may be necessary in some cases.

For social phobia, you may take an antidepressant (SSRI antidepressant or MAO-inhibitor) or a benzodiazepine such as Klonopin, especially if you suffer from *generalized social phobia* (see Appendix 1). One to two years on the medication will likely optimize your treatment. Long-term maintenance at a low dose may, as with agoraphobia, be necessary in some cases.

With obsessive-compulsive disorder (OCD), long-term use of an SSRI medication such as Prozac, Luvox, or Paxil at a higher dose is usually the best strategy. After a year you can try lowering the dose to see what is the minimum you need to correct the neurobiological problem associated with OCD. On the other hand, some persons with OCD are able to manage their problem with cognitive behavioral strategies alone—sometimes from the outset and sometimes after a year or two on medication. (See the book *Brain Lock* by Jeffrey Schwartz [1996], cited at the end of this chapter.)

Generalized anxiety disorder will only require medication in moderate to severe cases or in situations where you are unmotivated or unwilling to make the behavioral and lifestyle modifications that can help.

Finally, post-traumatic stress disorder may frequently be helped by antidepressant medication in conjunction with cognitive behavioral therapy; severe cases may need a long-term maintenance dose.

Your Motivation and Commitment to Natural Approaches

In many cases, it's possible to eliminate or at least reduce your need for medication over the long term if you maintain a committed program of natural approaches. *The brain has an inherent ability to heal from stress-induced imbalances that may have led to your original need for medication.* While it may take your brain somewhat longer to recover than would be the case if you had broken a bone or torn a ligament, the brain can, with proper cognitive, behavioral, and lifestyle modifications, restore much or all of its natural integrity over time. Your very belief that you can recover from anxiety and eventually wean yourself off medication will help make that eventuality more likely. The popular idea of "mind over matter" is not an idle notion, as will be discussed in more detail in Chapter 13 "Affirming Your Recovery." Any of the approaches suggested in this book or in *The Anxiety & Phobia Workbook* will help you to heal yourself naturally. The more of these approaches you're able to implement on a regular basis, the sooner and more powerfully you will be able to foster a state of natural health in body and brain.

Discontinuing Medication

If you've decided that you want to stop relying on prescription medications, observe the following guidelines:

1. *Be sure you've gained some level of mastery of the basic strategies for overcoming anxiety and panic presented in this book and* The Anxiety & Phobia Workbook. In particular, it would be a good idea to have established a daily practice of deep relaxation and exercise, along with skills in using abdominal breathing, muscle relaxation, and self-talk to counteract anxiety symptoms. If you plan to withdraw from Xanax or another BZ tranquilizer, these skills will serve you well in dealing with possible recurrences of anxiety during the withdrawal

period as well as over the long run. Be assured that any resurgence of high anxiety during withdrawal from a tranquilizer is temporary and should not persist after you've completed the withdrawal.

2. *Consult with your doctor to set up a program for gradually tapering off the dosage of your medication.* This is especially important if you've been taking a BZ tranquilizer (the tapering-off period is dose-dependent, but may need to be as long as several months). A tapering-off period also needs to be observed if you're curtailing your use of an antidepressant medication such as Paxil or a beta-blocker such as Inderal.

3. *Be prepared to increase your reliance on strategies described in Chapters 4 and 6 of this book during your tapering-off period*—especially abdominal breathing, relaxation, exercise, coping strategies for anxiety, and countering negative self-talk. Your withdrawal from medication is an opportunity to practice and improve your skills at using these strategies. You'll gain increased self-confidence by learning to use self-activated strategies to master anxiety and panic without having to rely on medication.

4. *Don't be disappointed if you need to rely on medication during future periods of acute anxiety or stress.* Stopping regular use of a medication doesn't necessarily mean that you might not benefit from the short-term use of that medication in the future. For example, using a tranquilizer or sleep medication for two weeks during a time of acute stress due to a traumatic experience is appropriate and unlikely to lead to dependence. If you're subject to seasonal affective disorder (pronounced depression during the winter months), you may stand to benefit from taking an antidepressant medication during that time of the year. Don't consider it a sign of weakness or a lack of self-control if you occasionally need to rely on prescription medications for a limited period of time. Given the stress and pressures of modern life, there are quite a few people who occasionally use prescription medications to help them cope.

Working with Your Doctor

The purpose of this chapter has been to provide a balanced view of the role of medications in helping to heal anxiety. There are certainly a variety of situations where the benefits of prescription drugs outweigh their associated risks and drawbacks. It's important, however, that before taking any medication you are fully aware of all of its potential side effects and limitations. It is your doctor's responsibility to 1) obtain a complete history of your symptoms, 2) inform you of the possible side effects and limitations of any particular drug, and 3) obtain your *informed consent* to try out a medication. As added insurance to being fully informed, you might look up the description of a medication you're considering in the *Physician's Desk Reference*, available at your doctor's office or your local library. It's your responsibility not to withhold information your doctor requests in taking your medical history, as well as to let the doctor know, should he or she fail to ask, whether 1) you have allergic reactions to any drugs, 2) you are pregnant, or 3) you're taking any other prescription or over-the-counter medications.

Once this exchange of information has taken place between you and your physician, both of you will be in a position to make a *fully informed and mutual decision* about whether taking a particular prescription medication is in your best interest. If your doctor is unwilling to take a collaborative rather than authoritarian stance or to allow for your informed consent, I strongly recommend that you find another doctor who will. Medications may enable you to "turn the corner" in recovering from your particular problem, but it is essential that they be used with the utmost care and responsibility.

In conclusion, keep in mind that the appropriate use of medication does not conflict with holistic values or a natural lifestyle. There is a time and place for the use of medication in treating anxiety disorders, and not to use them at those times is equivalent to not taking good care of yourself. The real question to ask, in my opinion, is *what is the most compassionate thing you can do for yourself?* In some cases, the answer may be to wean yourself off medication—especially if you have become overly dependent or addicted to a drug for several years without having evaluated how you might do without it. In some cases, the answer may be to use medication for a period of several months up to a year to get through a difficult time or to "jump-start" your motivation to utilize cognitive behavioral and other natural approaches. In other cases, long-term use of medication (particularly the SSRIs), *in conjunction with the full spectrum of cognitive, natural, and lifestyle changes suggested in this book*, may be the most compassionate response you can make to yourself.

There are few set answers when it comes to the subject of medication. Getting all the information you can, working with a competent physician whom you can trust, and then listening to your own intuition is the best you can do.

I hope in this chapter to have provided you with ample information to make the best choice—in conjunction with your doctor—regarding whether and how long to use medication in healing your anxiety. Beyond all the information, the highest court of appeal is to *keep asking what is the most compassionate thing you can do for yourself and to keep listening to your own highest intuition.* If you do these two things, you are unlikely to go astray.

What You Can Do Now

1. Review this chapter to provide yourself with an overview of the various types of medications used to treat anxiety disorders. Be familiar with the benefits and limitations of those medications that may have relevance for your particular issue.

2. If you are not currently taking medication but wonder if you could benefit from doing so, contact a psychiatrist who is knowledgeable about anxiety disorders to discuss your options. *The National Professional Membership Directory*, published by the Anxiety Disorders Association of America (see Appendix 2), lists psychiatrists specializing in anxiety disorders as well as other professionals who would know of such psychiatrists.

3. If you are currently taking a medication and would like to stop, consult your prescribing physician to discuss the appropriateness of doing so. If you and he/she jointly decide that you are ready to discontinue the medication, follow the guidelines in the section "Discontinuing Medication." Remember, it's preferable to discontinue medication only after you've gained some mastery of the skills discussed in Chapters 4 and 6 of this book.

References and Further Reading

Kessler, R.C., et al. 1994. Lifetime and 12-month prevalence of DSM-III-R psychiatric disorders in the United States. Results from the National Comorbidity Survey. *Archives of General Psychiatry* 51:8-19.

Norden, Michael. 1995. *Beyond Prozac.* New York: HarperCollins.

Preston, John, John H. O'Neal, and Mary C. Talaga. 1994. *Handbook of Clinical Psychopharmacology for Therapists.* Oakland: New Harbinger Publications.

Physicians Desk Reference. 1997. Oradell, New Jersey: Medical Economics Co. Inc.

Rosenthal, Norman. 1993. *Winter Blues: Seasonal Affective Disorder and How to Overcome It*. New York: Guilford Press.

Schwartz, Jeffrey. 1996. *Brain Lock*. New York: HarperCollins.

Sears, Barry. 1995. *The Zone*. New York: HarperCollins.

Wilson, Reid. 1996. *Don't Panic*. 2d Ed. New York: HarperCollins. (See Chapter 19.)

8

Addressing Personality Issues

The strategies described in the previous two chapters are critical for overcoming the debilitating effects of panic, phobias, and other anxiety disorders. Cognitive behavioral therapy (CBT) provides the means to manage bodily symptoms of anxiety, change counterproductive thinking, and overcome phobic avoidance. Medication is often essential to reduce severe anxiety symptoms, as well as depression, so that it's possible to utilize and follow through with cognitive behavioral strategies. Together CBT and medication define the state of the art in treating anxiety and anxiety disorders. CBT alone or in combination with medication is more effective than any other form of conventional therapy, and it works over a short time period, typically a few months. At the end of eight to sixteen weeks of CBT/medication therapy, a majority (about 70–80 percent) of persons suffering from diagnosable anxiety problems are doing significantly better. Yet an important question to raise at this point is: *How long will they continue to do better?*

Research indicates that, unfortunately, there can be a trend toward relapse over a period of one to two years following CBT, with or without medication. For some people, anxiety symptoms recur only for periods of a few days or weeks now and then; for others, however, their problem returns in full force, seeming to negate the effects of therapy. Cognitive behavioral therapy and medication appear to have helped them to ameliorate the symptoms of their problem without changing the underlying causes. The short-term gains bestowed by effective treatment did not lead to long-term recovery.

The problem of relapse following what initially appeared to be successful treatment is disappointing to both clients and therapists alike. What accounts for this tendency toward relapse over the long term? How can it be prevented?

In my experience, there are at least four reasons why people relapse after effective treatment with CBT and/or medication:

1. *They do not continue to practice cognitive behavioral strategies,* such as abdominal breathing, deep muscle relaxation, exercise, countering negative self-talk, graded exposure, assertiveness, etc., on a regular basis. In short, they have not incorporated anxiety-management skills into their lifestyle. It requires both time and commitment to spend a half-hour each day practicing relaxation, another half-hour doing aerobic exercise, setting aside frequent times to examine and counter distorted self-talk, or regularly practicing exposure to phobic situations. Keeping up with these practices within the structure of weekly therapy is one thing; doing them on your own long-term is another. There are at least two possible ways to overcome this difficulty. One possibility is to have periodic "booster sessions" with your original therapist to help you stay on track with your recovery program. Another is to attend a support group where people express their feelings about life stressors that interfere with the daily practices and help each other to stay with them. In sum, anxiety disorders have a way of coming back if you do not incorporate the skills learned in therapy into the way you live your life.

2. *People stop taking medication before it has offered its full benefit.* Research indicates, for example, that with antidepressant medications, the most effective period of treatment for panic disorder is eighteen months. Rates of relapse were found to be 70 percent for a group that took these medications six months and only 30 percent for another group that took medication for eighteen months. My speculation is that staying on medication for a longer period enables the brain to recover and regenerate from trauma caused by severe anxiety symptoms. The initial trauma of a severe anxiety disorder actually may have physical effects on the brain (particularly the "inhibitory" neurotransmitter receptors); the longer severe anxiety symptoms persist, the greater the potential trauma (see Chapter 7 for information on medication). Beginning medication sooner rather than later may help mitigate the initial trauma. Then staying on the medication for at least eighteen months allows the brain an opportunity to rest and regenerate. Hopefully there will be more research in the future to evaluate this hypothesis. This observation applies primarily to the use

of SSRIs and cyclic antidepressants. Relapse rates following the use of high-potency tranquilizers such as Xanax tend to be very high, even after taking the medication for several years, if you haven't learned skills or made lifestyle changes to help overcome your problem.

3. *People have core fears and associated personality issues* which have not changed as a result of cognitive behavioral therapy. You may be practicing cognitive behavioral skills and attaining some symptom relief. However, if you remain overly perfectionistic, you may relapse in the face of a sudden increase in life stress. Or if you can't give your own needs at least equal time with those of others, you may not acquire enough confidence in yourself to ensure long-term recovery. If you're fundamentally afraid to take risks, you may progress only so far in your exposure to difficult phobic situations. Addressing core fears and personality issues is the subject of this chapter.

4. Finally, the problem accounting for relapse may lie even deeper than personality. Anxiety may return after therapy and medication because *you experience a sense of meaninglessness or emptiness about your life.* In our present time, with so many conflicting values and a loss of traditional authorities such as the church or social mores, it's easy to feel adrift and confused. What's been called "existential anxiety" does not respond to cognitive behavioral therapy and demands a different kind of approach. You may need to develop your own unique gifts and creativity, finding a way to meaningfully express them in the world. How to do this is taken up in detail in the chapter "Finding Your Unique Purpose." Another possibility is that you're in need of enlarging your view of life—to base your perception of yourself and life on broader, perhaps more spiritual values. Suggestions toward this end can be found in the chapter "Enlarging Your View of Life."

The remainder of this chapter returns to the third reason described above. What kinds of deep-seated fears or persistent personality issues impede long-term recovery, even after cognitive behavioral therapy?

(Please note: This is a lengthy chapter. It would be best to read it in parts, focusing on only one core fear at a time. Feel free to skip ahead to later chapters in the book and return to this chapter at different times.)

Core Fears

There appear to be five basic fears that underlie most of the more specific fears and phobias that affect people. These basic or "core" fears include:

- Fear of Abandonment or Isolation

- Fear of Rejection or Embarrassment

- Fear of Losing Control

- Fear of Death or Injury

- Fear of Confinement

The fear of what is strange or unfamiliar may also be a core fear (see the chapter "Fears from the Past" in *The Anxiety & Phobia Workbook*), but it appears less related to personality issues than the preceding five fears. It can generally be overcome through habituation or desensitization. What is unfamiliar loses its sting, as it becomes familiar. Existential anxiety or the fear of meaninglessness also plays an important role in human problems with anxiety. Again, I believe it isn't, strictly speaking, a personality issue but a question of how you interpret the meaning and purpose of your own life (and human existence in general). Chapters 10 and 11 address this issue in detail.

The present chapter is concerned with the five core fears described above. The first part of the chapter describes each of these fears, how they arise from childhood circumstances, and personality traits that tend to accompany them. The second part of the chapter offers strategies for overcoming each of them. When cognitive behavioral therapy and medication are insufficient to ensure long-term recovery from anxiety, it's important to address and work with these fears on their own terms.

Fear of Abandonment or Isolation

At its root, the fear of abandonment is a fear of being alone, isolated, and without support. It's certainly one of the most pervasive fears known to human beings. We all come into life very dependent on others and remain interdependent to some degree throughout our lives. To be alone and without connections is to most of us a frightening prospect. Solitary confinement is thought of as the worst form of punishment.

A deep-seated fear of abandonment can develop early in childhood as a result of several types of circumstances. Most common is the actual loss of a parent or close relative due to illness or divorce. Many persons with panic disorder who are afraid to venture far from their "safe person" or "safe place" experienced such losses early in life. Fear of abandonment may also be the result of having never bonded closely with one or both parents. Perhaps because they were neglectful, unavailable, or abusive, you made the decision to withdraw into yourself and "go it alone" at an early age. Later on, you may have developed a fear of isolation and loneliness. Finally, even if you had intact and close relationships with your parents, a fear of being alone might have developed as a result of leaving home early (for example, being sent away to school) or losing a significant friend or loved one in adolescence or early adulthood. Persons having an acute fear of abandonment sometimes have a history of several traumatic losses after childhood.

The two personality traits most likely to accompany a strong fear of abandonment are *insecurity* and *dependency*. When these traits are pronounced, you may have difficulty making decisions for yourself without a lot of reassurance or advice from others. You do not want to disagree with others close to you for fear of losing their support. And you may lack confidence in yourself to take initiative to do things on your own apart from your significant other(s). Having a close relationship on which you depend may seem vital to your very survival. You fear that if you were to lose that relationship, you could not function or care for yourself.

If you feel that you identify with some of these characteristics, *your area of growth is to learn to develop greater autonomy and self-sufficiency*—without being afraid of losing support in the process.

Fear of Rejection or Embarrassment

With the fear of rejection, you believe that others will not accept you just the way you are. If they *really* knew you, they would dislike or ridicule you. You may feel inherently flawed or unworthy, believing you need to keep up a front to avoid others' contempt. In social situations especially, you feel vulnerable and try hard to maintain a good impression. You're constantly on guard about saying or doing something embarrassing. Others' approval becomes vital to you. In intimate and family relationships, as well, you may go out of your way to take care of everyone else's needs at the expense of meeting your own. Since your self-esteem comes from pleasing others, you tend to overextend yourself in taking care of their needs.

A sense of shame and fear of rejection often develop from having grown up with overly critical parents. If you were frequently criticized or punished, you probably learned to feel inadequate. As a child you may have also learned to hide and discount your true impulses and needs so that you could match the image your parents wanted. If you were once anxious about being accepted by your mother or father, you may, as an adult, be excessively concerned with getting others' approval. If you believed you had to go out of your way to receive your parents' acceptance, you may still try too hard to please others at the expense or your own feelings and needs. Apart from your parents, shame and a fear of rejection could have started with your experiences at school or with your peer group. If, for any reason, you were singled out by other children as being "different," "weird," "too short," "too smart," or whatever, you may have acquired a tendency to feel vulnerable or ashamed.

There are two basic responses to shame and/or the fear of rejection: *over-accommodating* or *avoiding closeness* with other people. If you were very afraid of losing your parents' favor, you likely grew up with a tendency to be over-accommodating. As an adult you strive very hard to maintain the approval of your significant others to avoid feeling guilty or unworthy. You may tend to become "codependent"—which means deriving your self-worth from rescuing, taking care of, or simply pleasing others. The other type of response to shame is avoidance of close relationships. Instead of trying to please others to avoid criticism and disapproval, you simply withdrew from them. Believing that you couldn't win their acceptance anyway, you decided to distance yourself. As an adult, it may be hard for you to participate in group interaction because you're preoccupied with being criticized or rejected. It's also difficult to risk getting close to someone unless you're certain of being liked. The end result of this pattern of avoidance may be social phobia—either specific social fears or a generalized fear of all kinds of social situations.

If you feel unworthy and fear rejection, *the most important area of growth for you is to develop self-worth and self-respect.* An important corollary trait to develop is *assertiveness*—the ability to stand up and ask for what you want, as well as say no to what you don't want.

Fear of Losing Control

In essence, the fear of losing control involves a difficulty with trust. It's difficult to let go and trust life, because life, by its very nature, is unpredictable and uncertain. Other people can be as well. So your response to this inherent uncertainty is to be ever vigilant, perhaps tending to over-manipulate circumstances (or other people) without giving them time to unfold (respond) in their natural sequence. Closely allied with the fear of losing control is perfectionism: a tendency to set excessively high standards as well as to be overly concerned with small flaws and mistakes.

Often the fear of losing control has its origins in a traumatic personal history. Any traumatic experience that undermined your sense of life being stable and predictable—especially if it left you feeling frightened or powerless—might have instilled a fear of losing control. Having a parent suddenly leave or die during childhood, for example, might leave you feeling not only vulnerable to loss and abandonment, but also fearful of anything that could upset your basic sense of security and stability. Or, if one of your parents abused alcohol, the resulting instability in your early family environment might have led you to respond with an excessive need to control. At the time, over-control might have seemed necessary to your very survival.

Any serious trauma—in childhood or adulthood—can lead you to respond with increased vigilance and distrust toward life. Survivors of severe trauma often develop highly controlled or controlling personalities. This is only natural if it's the only way to maintain a semblance of stability when one's whole world seems to have fallen apart.

There are many pathways to overcoming the fear of losing control (and its associated trait of perfectionism). Some of these are discussed at length in the chapter called "Letting Go" (Chapter 12). Most important is the cultivation of a *basic trust in life and in others*. Such trust can be fostered by learning to accept life on its own terms, by building supportive connections with others, and by faith in a Higher Power or God.

Fear of Death or Injury

Phobias of natural phenomena such as fire, water, heights, or tornadoes may express an underlying fear of death or injury. (Sometimes, of course, they are merely a result of conditioning.) Similarly, fears of flying or driving freeways can result from anxiety about personal injury, although these latter phobias may also express fears of loss of control or confinement. For many people, the fear of death combines with a fear of abandonment in their excessive worry about a loved one being injured or killed in an accident. Fear of dying itself is the sixth most common phobia (fear of public speaking is first). Existentialist philosophers such as Camus and Sartre have argued that a fear of death underlies all other types of fears.

Traumatic experiences in which you have had a close brush with death, or suffered injury or pain, can predispose you to be fearful about any situation that might potentially cause a similar experience. It also happens frequently that the death of someone close to you can lead to increased sensitivity and fearfulness about death—for others or for yourself. Several clients of mine, who have experienced the death of a parent from chronic illness, subsequently developed *hypochondriasis*—the fear that almost any minor ailment could be cancer or something terminal. Perhaps the fear of death can begin as early as birth, if the birth was difficult and there was a question about the newborn's survival.

An unfortunate consequence of excessive anxiety about death or injury is a tendency to be fearful of taking even minor risks. You may perceive the world as a dangerous place and deny yourself access to much of what life can offer. An excessive need for safety can lead to boredom as well as restrict you from developing your full potential.

The lesson for persons fearful of death/injury is *to learn to fully accept the fact of human mortality.* The reality is that there are no guarantees that adversity won't befall us—and the eventuality of our death is certain. Learning to accept these facts and take them in stride fosters your ability to make the most of your life. Attempting to ignore or run from them leaves you feeling vulnerable and unable to take even modest risks.

Fear of Confinement

The fear of confinement runs through a number of different situational fears including: fear of flying, fear of elevators, fear of crowded public places, fear of small enclosed places (claustrophobia), and fear of being "stuck" anywhere (traffic, bridges, tunnels, or riding on public transportation). Of all the core fears, I believe that fear of confinement most frequently disguises an underlying fear of something else (what some psychologists would call a "displaced" fear).

Growing up in a dysfunctional family situation, in which your parents were physically or sexually abusive, or perhaps alcoholic, can instill a fear of being unable to escape or get away. A child has no choice but to endure such mistreatment—it's easy to understand how a fear of being trapped might develop under such circumstances.

It's also evident that a fear of being confined (in traffic, elevators, and so on) may point to a deeper sense of *feeling trapped in your current life situation.* Perhaps you feel trapped by your job, your marriage, a long-standing interpersonal conflict, loneliness, or possibly by a chronic illness. Yet, you haven't fully become aware of your deeper feelings of entrapment; instead your fear is expressed in the form of a specific phobia, such as fear of bridges, tunnels, elevators, or other enclosed places.

Finally, the fear of confinement may arise simply from *feeling trapped in your own body without the ability to easily move.* When you're anxious, your muscles tighten up and your body naturally prepares for "fight or flight." However, if you're in a situation where it's difficult to move, for example, the window seat on an airplane or next in line at a checkout counter, you may suddenly feel very stuck. There you are, in a sense "locked" within the tightening muscles of your abdomen, chest, shoulders, and neck, with no way to actively channel the sympathetic nervous system arousal or adrenaline surging through your bloodstream. Your body is preparing for flight or fight, but you can't move. If the sensation grows strong enough, it may pass from mere "stuckness" to "entrapment"—*especially if you tell yourself you're "trapped."*

At this point you may escalate to a full-blown panic reaction with a strong urgency to run. Had you been able to move more easily in the first place, perhaps the fear of entrapment would have never occurred.

If fear of confinement is a problem, *you need to address the underlying issue.* Is your fear left over from a previous trauma? Is it a metaphor for some current situation in your life? Or is it simply your way of perceiving situations where your mobility is restricted? Perhaps two or three of these possibilities are simultaneously true for you. When you understand the source of your fear, you can then overcome it.

Exploring Your Childhood

What kinds of circumstances in your childhood might have predisposed you to develop one or more of the core fears described above? Your present personality was influenced not only by your genetic makeup but also by the conditions in which you grew up. The way in which your parents responded to you—both their ability to express love and support and their methods of socializing and disciplining you—profoundly shaped your development. So did the values and beliefs of your parents—and later those of the peers and teachers you encountered at school. Significant losses, trauma, or abuse within your family may have set the stage for later problems.

Numerous types of childhood circumstances can predispose you to be fearful. A variety of examples are offered below. These examples are based on my own experience working with clients for over twenty years. As you go through them, reflect on which type(s) of conditions might have affected you.

Overly Critical Parents

Parents who were constantly critical or set impossibly high standards of behavior may have left you feeling guilty; that somehow you could "never be good enough." As an adult, you may continue to strive for perfection to overcome a long-standing sense of inferiority. You may also have a strong tendency toward self-criticism. Perhaps you may feel unworthy in social situations and strive to maintain a pleasing "front." It's hard to believe people will accept you as you are.

Significant Childhood Loss

If you were separated from a parent as a result of death or divorce, you may have been left feeling abandoned. You may have grown up with a sense of emptiness and insecurity that can be restimulated very intensely by losses of significant people in your adult life. As an adult, you may seek to overcome old feelings of abandonment by overdependence on a particular person or other addictions to food, drugs, work, or whatever works to cover the pain. You may feel frightened of venturing far from a safe person or place. Or you may find it difficult to assert yourself for fear of alienating the person you most depend on.

Parental Abuse

Physical and sexual abuse are extreme forms of deprivation. They may leave you with a complex mix of feelings, including insecurity, inadequacy, lack of trust, guilt, and/or rage. Adults who were physically abused as children may become perpetual victims or may themselves develop a hostile posture toward life, victimizing others. Adults—especially men—who were sexually abused as children sometimes express their rage by turning to rape and abuse as adults. Or they may turn that rage inward in deep feelings of self-loathing and inadequacy. Survivors of abusive childhoods often, and understandably, have difficulty with intimate relationships in their adult lives. While less flagrant, constant verbal abuse can have equally damaging effects.

Parental Alcoholism or Drug Abuse

Much has been written in recent years on the effects of parental alcoholism on children. Chronic drinking or substance abuse creates a chaotic, unreliable family atmosphere in which it is difficult for a child to develop a basic sense of security or trust. The attendant denial of the problem (often by both parents) teaches the child to deny his or her own feelings and pain connected with the family situation. Many such children grow up with poor self-esteem or a poor sense of personal identity. They may be over-controlling, have difficulty with feelings and intimacy, and/or abuse substances themselves.

Parental Neglect

Some parents, because they are preoccupied with themselves, their work, or other concerns, simply fail to give their children adequate attention and nurturing. Children left to their own devices often grow up feeling insecure, worthless, and/or lonely. As adults, they may have a tendency to discount or neglect their own needs. It may be difficult to get close to other people because they can't perceive the possibility of intimacy. A deep-seated fear of rejection is a common outcome.

Parental Rejection

Even without physical, sexual, or verbal abuse, some parents impart a feeling to their children that they are unwanted. This profoundly damaging attitude teaches a child to grow up doubting his or her very right to exist. Such a person has a tendency toward self-rejection or self-sabotage. It remains possible for adults with such a past to overcome what their parents didn't give them through learning to love and care for themselves.

Parental Overprotectiveness

The child who is overprotected may never learn to trust the world outside of the immediate family and risk independence. As an adult, such a person may feel very insecure and afraid to venture far from a safe person or place. When you learn that the outside world is threatening, you automatically restrict your exploration and risk-taking. You grow up with a tendency to worry excessively and be overly concerned with safety. Through learning to acknowledge and care for their own needs, overprotected individuals can gain the confidence to make a life of their own and discover that the world is not such a dangerous place.

Parental Denial or Suppression of Feelings

If your parents suppressed their feelings, especially sadness or anger, then you were likely trained to withhold your own feelings. They may have actively told you "Don't cry!", "Shut up!", "Don't talk back to me!", or you may have learned to withhold your emotions simply by following their example. As a result you may have grown up exerting a restrictive, even punitive attitude toward your own expression of feelings. At present you may deny expressing or even acknowledging painful or angry feelings, striving to maintain an image of yourself as "objective," "tough," "cool," or perhaps "nice" and "compliant." If you've withheld your feelings for a long time, their sudden recurrence under stress may instigate anxiety or panic. Frequently, people who have learned to suppress feelings (particularly anger) are more prone to anxiety, depression, and a host of stress-related disorders ranging from migraines to ulcers. They may also have difficulty asserting their needs. Learning to acknowledge and express withheld feelings is an important part of the process of healing anxiety. You will find more information on how to do this in the chapter "Identifying and Expressing Your Feelings" in *The Anxiety & Phobia Workbook* (1995).

Switching Roles with Your Parents

If one of your parents was absent, ill, or emotionally needy, you may have assumed the role of parent within your family. This could involve taking over parental responsibilities such as cooking and child care, or it may have meant actually caring for an ill or alcoholic parent. Children who prematurely assume adult responsibilities often lose the opportunity to have a real childhood. They tend to grow up being overly serious and perfectionistic, denying their own needs, feelings, and innate playfulness. As adults, they may need to learn to reclaim and express their own "inner child."

Parental Overindulgence

The "spoiled" child of overindulgent parents is given insufficient exposure to "deferred gratification" or appropriate limits. As adults, such people tend to be bored, lack persistence, or have difficulty initiating and sustaining individual effort. They tend to expect the world to come to them rather than taking responsibility for creating their own lives. Until they're willing to take personal responsibility, such people feel cheated and very insecure because life does not continue to provide what they learned to expect during childhood.

Evaluating Your Childhood

Which, if any, of these types of childhood circumstances apply to you? Does more than one? You may initially find it difficult to identify problems in your past. Our memory of childhood is often hazy and indistinct—especially when we do not *want* to recall what actually happened. The point of remembering and acknowledging what happened to you as a child is not so that you can blame your parents. Most likely, your parents did the best they could with their available personal resources, which may have been severely limited as a result of deprivations they experienced with *their* parents.

How did your childhood contribute to developing any of the core fears and associated traits described in this chapter? Review the list of basic fears and corresponding traits below. Then use the space which follows to write about how your childhood may have led you to develop one (or more) of them.

CORE FEAR WORKSHEET

Basic Fears	*Personality Traits*
Fear of abandonment (being alone)	Insecurity, dependency
Fear of rejection	Shame or unworthiness, excessive need for approval
Fear of losing control	Perfectionism, excessive need to control
Fear of death or injury	Overcautiousness, difficulty taking risks
Fear of confinement	Prone to feel "trapped," possible rebelliousness

Write your response here
(Use extra sheets of paper if you need):

The remainder of this chapter focuses on ways to overcome these five basic fears. Particular attention is given to the fears of abandonment and rejection, since these are so pervasive among persons struggling with anxiety difficulties.

Overcoming the Fear of Abandonment or Isolation

The fear of abandonment or being left alone is nearly universal—it affects all of us to some degree. It is an especially common fear, however, for people having panic disorder with agoraphobia. For such persons it's difficult to be far from safety, whether in the form of a safe person or place. Fear of abandonment certainly *can* be assuaged by external support from other people, yet ultimately it is best overcome by building a sense of safety within yourself. A sudden turn of events can undermine any of the external sources of security you rely on, whether in the form of loved ones, home, employment, or finances. In a changeable world, it's important to build an *internal* sense of safety and security that is less vulnerable to the vicissitudes of life.

In my experience, there are three ways to do this:

- Developing a loving relationship with yourself (including befriending your "inner child" and making time to nurture yourself on a daily basis)

- Building a support system beyond your immediate family

- Cultivating trust in a Higher Power

I have found these three approaches to be helpful both personally and with clients. Beyond this, the fear of being alone can be diminished by establishing a strong sense of identity—finding meaningful work or a way to express your capacities and talents out in the world. Finding your place or "niche" helps you to feel less dependent on others for your sense of self-worth. I've touched on this in what follows and say more about how to actually do it in a later chapter: "Finding Your Unique Purpose."

Learning to Love Yourself

A loving relationship with yourself is vital to healing fear and other personal ills. Such a relationship begins with the way you speak to yourself. Many of us speak to ourselves like a harsh drill sergeant rather than with kindness.

There are four "characters" or "subpersonalities" within each of us that can interfere with our ability to accept, respect, and care for ourselves:

1. *The Worrier:* the part of you that constantly projects danger or potential catastrophe. The dangers are imagined, not real—yet you believe them. This character's favorite expression is "What if . . ."

2. *The Critic:* the part of you that berates and puts you down for making mistakes or not meeting your highest standards. The critic often represents the internalized voice of a critical parent. Typical expressions are: "That was dumb," "Why can't you be like _____."

3. *The Victim:* this is the part that tells you that you're helpless or powerless to do anything about your situation. It regrets the past and complains about the way things are, often telling you they are hope-

less. Its favorite expressions include: "I can't," "It's hopeless," "What's the use?"

4. *The Perfectionist:* the perfectionist is similar to the critic, but it prefers to push and goad you instead of putting you down. Its favorite word is "should," as it likes to tell you things like: "You should be working harder," "You should have everything under control," "You should be competent," "You shouldn't be angry," and so on.

One way to begin building a more loving relationship with yourself is to recognize each of these voices within. Then you can begin to work on not giving them so much of your attention and energy. It's helpful to identify specific negative self-talk that each subpersonality uses against you. Then you can practice challenging and countering these negative self-statements with more helpful and constructive statements. Detailed guidelines for working with these subpersonalities can be found in Chapter 9 of *The Anxiety & Phobia Workbook*, "Self-Talk."

There are other ways of cultivating a positive relationship with yourself that work on a more emotional level. Two approaches I've found to be helpful with many of my clients include: 1) befriending your "inner child" and 2) making time to nurture yourself on a daily basis. Each approach will help you to create a more accepting and caring relationship with yourself on a feeling level.

Befriending Your Inner Child

The concept of the *inner child*—the childlike part of yourself—has been around for many decades. The eminent psychologist Carl Jung referred to it as the "divine child," while the religious thinker Emmett Fox called it the "wonder child." Some characteristics of the inner child include:

- That part of you that feels like a little girl or boy

- That part of you which feels and expresses your deepest emotional needs for security, trust, nurturing, affection, touching, and so on

- That part of you which is alive, energetic, creative, and playful (much as real children are when left free to play and be themselves)

- Finally, that part of you that still carries the pain and emotional trauma of your childhood. Strong feelings of insecurity, loneliness, fear, anger, shame, or guilt—even if triggered by present circumstances—belong to the inner child. Actually there are very few new feelings. Especially when they are strong, most of our feelings reflect ways we reacted or failed to react a long time ago as a child.

How do you get along with the little child inside? Do you tend to be too busy to give her or him much of your time? Do you regard your inner child as too needy and demanding? Too rebellious or bratty? Do you pay attention to the little girl or boy inside, or do you suppress her/his needs and impulses? If you are inclined to restrict your inner child, you may:

- Find it difficult to be spontaneous, play or have fun

- Tend to be conventional and conforming, while possibly acting out painful patterns of addiction or compulsion

- Find it difficult to be vulnerable and trusting—not allowing yourself to receive others' affection

- Find it hard to be in touch with your own feelings

The way you treat your own inner child likely parallels the way your parents treated you as a child. You simply internalized their patterns and attitudes and have carried them forth into adulthood. If they were overly critical toward you, you likely grew up overly self-critical, especially of your "childish" or less rational, impulsive side. If they neglected you, you likely grew up tending to ignore or neglect the needs of your own inner child. If they were too busy for you as a child, you may be too busy for your inner child as an adult. If they abused you, you may have become self-destructive as an adult or else may be abusive of others. If your parents placed a taboo on acknowledging and expressing your feelings and impulses, you may have grown up denying your feelings. The list goes on. To cultivate a healing, caring relationship with your own inner child—to become a good parent to yourself—you need to overcome any internalized parental attitudes that cause you to criticize, abuse, neglect, or deny the needs and feelings of your child within. Working with your internalized critic and perfectionist, as described above, is one place to begin.

While learning to overcome negative patterns internalized from your parents, you may wish to begin befriending your inner child directly. It's useful to begin this even before you work through all of the limitations you've learned to impose on your child within. There are several ways to go about doing this, including: 1) visualizations, 2) using photos as a reminder, 3) writing a letter to your inner child, and 4) real-life activities that validate and nurture your inner child. You may be surprised to find that caring for your own inner child is a lot less time—and energy—consuming than bringing up a real one!

Visualization

Below is a visualization to help you foster a closer relationship with your own inner child. Put this visualization on tape, pausing for a few moments between each sentence and for ten to twenty seconds when the instructions say "pause." You can do this yourself, or find a friend whose voice you like to prerecord the script for you. Make sure that you give yourself a few minutes to deeply relax before beginning the visualization, since your capacity to remember and see yourself as child will be greatly enhanced by deep relaxation. (You can use progressive muscle relaxation, meditation, or any deep-relaxation technique you wish.)

Healing Your Inner Child

Imagine sitting down in a rocking chair and getting very comfortable. Feel yourself rocking easily, back and forth. As you continue rocking, you might find yourself starting to drift ... drifting more and more. Rocking back and forth, you might find yourself gently drifting back in time. Rocking gently and drifting ... slowly drifting back in time. Year by year you might imagine yourself getting younger and younger. The years are going by ... back through the 1990s ... back through the 1980s ... Gently drifting back ... feeling younger and younger. Back into a time long ago. Drifting back to a time where you were perhaps very young. You're imagining now that you can see the little child you were a long time ago. Very soon you can imagine seeing yourself as a little child. Perhaps you can see her [him] there now. What does she [he] look like? What is she wearing? About how old is she? Can you see where she is? Indoor or outdoors? Can you see what she's doing? Perhaps you can see her face, and, if you look carefully, you can see the expression in her eyes. Can you tell how this little child is feeling right now? (Pause.) As you look at this little person, can you recall anything that was missing in her life? Is there anything that kept her from being fully happy? (Pause.) If there was anyone or anything that got in the way of this little child being completely happy and carefree, perhaps you can imagine seeing that person or situation. (Pause.) If no one is there yet, perhaps you can imagine your dad or your mom or whomever you'd like standing in front of you right now. (Pause.) What does your little child feel toward dad, mom, or whoever is standing in front of you right now? ... Is there anything that your child would like to say to that person right now? If so, it's okay to go ahead and say it right now . . . you can go ahead and say it. (Pause.) If your little child is feeling scared or confused about saying anything, imagine that your present-day, adult self enters the scene right now and goes up and stands next to your little child. (Pause.) Now when you're ready, imagine your adult self, standing next to your little child, speaking up to whomever is there on your little child's behalf. Your adult self can say whatever she wants. Tell your parent—or whoever is there—whatever you need to say . . . whatever it was that never got expressed. (Pause 30 seconds or longer.) If you wish, you might complete the sentence, "How do you think it makes me feel that . . ." (Pause 20 seconds or longer.) Or you might complete the sentence "I wish you had . . ." (Pause 20 seconds or longer.) Tell your parent, or whoever is there, anything you wish they had done, but they didn't. When you speak up, speak loud and clear so you can be sure that whoever is there really hears you. (Pause 20 seconds or longer.) Does the person you're facing have any response? Listen to see if they do. (Pause 20 seconds or longer.) If so, you can respond to what they say. If not, you can just finish what you need to say. (Pause.) When you're finished speaking, you can ask whoever is there to either go away and leave you alone . . . or to go away for a while until you're ready to talk again . . . or you can ask them to stay . . . and, if you choose, you can accept them as they are and give them a hug. (Pause.)

Now go back and see your present-day, adult self standing next to your little child. (Pause.) If you're willing, pick that little child up in your arms this very second and love her. Wrap your arms around her and say that it's okay. Tell her that you know how she feels. Tell her that you understand. You're here and you're going to help her and you love her very much. (Pause.) If you could give a color to the love you feel, what color comes to mind? (Pause.) Surround your little child with a light of that color and let her feel the peace of being in your arms. (Pause.) Tell her that you think she's a great little person. . . that you love the way she talks, walks, laughs . . . and does everything. Tell her that you care and that she's precious . . . (Pause 30 seconds or longer)

Optional: *Now sit your child on your lap and talk to her. She's got a good mind, and if someone would only explain things, she would understand. Tell her that because of the problems mom and* *dad had in their own childhood, they couldn't care for her and love her in the way she deserved to be loved. It wasn't that they didn't want to love her ... it was because of their own difficulties that they couldn't love her the way she wanted. This little child simply needs someone to explain to her ... nobody ever explained to her about the problems her parents had when they were growing up.* (Pause.) *Can your little child understand that because of their problems, mom and dad weren't able to love or take care of her in the way she truly deserved? Is your little child ready to forgive mom and dad for what happened?* (Pause.) *If she's not ready right now, perhaps she'll be ready later. If she is ready now, go ahead and picture mom and dad standing in front of you.* (Pause.) *Now tell them, in whatever way you wish, that you forgive them. You're willing to forgive them for their shortcomings because you know that their own problems interfered with their being the best parents they could. Go ahead and forgive them now ...* (Pause 30 seconds or longer.)

Photographs

Carry a photo of yourself as a child in your purse or wallet and take it out periodically as a reminder of your child within. Reflect on what was going on and how you felt in your life around the time the photo was taken. After a week or so with one photo, pick another from another age and repeat the process.

Write a Letter to Your Inner Child

After having done the preceding visualization, or as a result of looking at photos of yourself as a child, you may wish to write a letter to your inner child. You can tell your child about: 1) how you feel about her or him, 2) how you feel about what happened to her or him as a child, 3) how you would like to get to know her or him better, and 4) what you would like to learn from her or him. When you've completed this letter, open your mind and see if you can take the role of the little child. Then write a child's letter back to your adult self, saying how you feel about your adult self and what you would like from her or him. You might even try using child's handwriting for this letter to help get more in touch with how your little child feels. You will be surprised at how well this works in opening up communication between your adult and inner child "selves." Here is an example of such a letter from an adult to her inner child.

Dear Little Child,

I have long wanted to reach back in time to tell you how much I love you and how much I want to protect you from all the pain and suffering you've been going through. You're much too small and vulnerable to be facing such pain by yourself. I want you to know that you'll have me beside you from now on, and whenever you're frightened you can run to me. I'll be there to hold you and comfort you and protect you.

I know that seeing your daddy lose his temper is very, very frightening. He makes as much noise as he can, and sometimes he hits your mommy or your brother. He doesn't hit you and in a way this just makes you feel guilty. It makes it seem as if you're on his side, and that every time he hits one of them, it's your fault too.

I wish you could tell me more about how you feel, about yourself, your daddy, your mommy, and your brother. I think that a lot of things have happened to you that you just can't remember—either because they didn't make sense at the time or they were just too horrible to remember. It's hard to remember things that don't have any pictures or words attached to them—it's like trying to remember dreams.

As you remember more, I'll be able to understand more about who I am and how I act and what I feel. I know that it's painful trying to remember, and I want you to know how grateful I am to you for trying. Remember that from now on we'll always be there for each other.

Love,
(sign your name)

Real-Life Activities

A number of real-life activities can foster increased awareness of and closeness to your inner child. Spending ten minutes daily doing any of the following may help:

- Hugging a teddy bear or stuffed animal

- Going to a children's playground and using the swings or other playground equipment

- Playing with your own child as if you were a peer rather than an adult

- Having an ice-cream cone

- Going to the zoo

- Climbing a tree

- Engaging in any other activity you enjoyed as a child

Try to get into the spirit of being a child as you do any of the above. Your feelings in doing so will tell you a lot about your attitude toward your own inner child.

Making Time to Nurture Yourself on a Daily Basis

Although life brings ups and downs—even sudden, unexpected challenges—you can build a sense of inner security through small acts of kindness toward yourself on a daily basis. Doing so requires first that you make time to nurture yourself apart from the responsibilities of work and household. Building a loving relationship with yourself is really not much different from developing a close relationship with someone else; both require some time, energy, and commitment. Taking out regular down time, as described in Chapter 4 ("Caring for Your Body: Relaxation, Exercise, and Energy Balance"), is one way to do this. The following list describes a number of other simple activities that involve nurturing yourself. When outer life circumstances seem harsh, it's particularly important to make time for yourself without feeling guilty about being self-indulgent. You have nothing to lose but your sense of insecurity or inadequacy—nothing to gain except increased self-acceptance and self-respect.

SELF-NURTURING ACTIVITIES

1. Take a warm bath

2. Have breakfast in bed

3. Take a sauna

4. Get a massage

5. Buy yourself a bouquet

6. Take a bubble bath

7. Go to a pet store and play with the animals

8. Go for a scenic walk (this may involve driving to a park)

9. Visit a zoo

10. Have a manicure or pedicure

11. Stop and smell some flowers

12. Take time to watch the sunrise or sunset

13. If it's cold outdoors, sit by the fire indoors

14. Relax with a good book, magazine, and/or soothing music

15. Go rent a funny video

16. Play your favorite music and dance to it by yourself

17. Go to bed early

18. Sleep outside under the stars

19. Take a "mental health day off" from work

20. Fix a special dinner just for yourself and eat by candlelight

21. Sit and have a cup of your favorite herb tea

22. Call a good friend—or several good friends

23. Go out to a fine restaurant

24. Go to the beach (or lake, mountains, etc.)

25. Take a scenic drive

26. Meditate

27. Buy some new clothes

28. Browse in a book or record store for as long as you want

29. Buy yourself a cuddly stuffed animal and play with it (your inner child will thank you)

30. Write yourself an upbeat letter and mail it

31. Ask a special person to nurture you (feed, cuddle, and/or read to you)

32. Buy yourself something special that you can afford

33. Go see a good film or show

34. Go to the park and feed the ducks, swing on the swings, and so on

35. Visit a museum or other interesting place

36. Give yourself more time than you need to accomplish whatever you're doing (let yourself dawdle)

37. Work on your favorite puzzle or puzzle book

38. Go into a hot tub or Jacuzzi

39. Record an affirmation tape

40. Write out an ideal scenario concerning a goal, then visualize it

41. Read an inspirational book

42. Write a letter to an old friend

43. Bake or cook something special

44. Go window shopping

45. Play with your pet

46. Listen to a positive, motivational tape

47. Write in a special diary about your accomplishments

48. Apply fragrant lotion all over your body

49. Exercise

50. Sit and hold your favorite stuffed animal

Building a Support System

A deep-seated fear of abandonment may go hand in hand with excessive dependency on your spouse, partner, or some significant other. When you make another person your source of safety, you tend to feel unsafe whenever they go away or when you go far from them. You may be very fearful of the possibility (however remote) of something happening to them. You imagine you couldn't cope in the event of their absence.

A more reliable security can be found in developing a support system in your community beyond your significant other(s). There are many options possible for doing this, including support groups for women, men, persons suffering from anxiety disorders, survivors of various types of abuse or loss, and for persons specifically wanting to address issues of codependency (see the list of resources in Appendix 2). If your town is too small to offer these kinds of groups, you can still build support and community through your local church, service organizations, or other special interest groups. If you are restricted in getting to such groups on your own, ask a family member to take you. Having supportive connections outside your immediate family will not only increase your sense of security but will also enrich your life.

Developing a Stronger Sense of Personal Identity

If you rely on someone else to give you a sense of personal security, you may need to work on finding more of a life of your own. You are less likely to be vulnerable to fears of abandonment or aloneness if you've developed a strong sense of personal identity. An important part of personal identity consists in discovering and expressing your unique purpose(s) in life. To know this purpose means identifying your own particular gifts and talents and then expressing them either in a vocation or avocation. Your unique gift may be to inspire others, create music, provide leadership, counsel, or teach. Or it may simply be to offer hospitality in your home or to beautify your backyard. The scale of what you do is not so important; rather, it's your awareness of what you're here to do and your willingness to do it. In fact, as you get to know yourself, you'll find you need to do it. In many cases you may have to go back to school or obtain specific training to develop your particular skills and talents. Or, you may simply need to find a job where your special capacity to work with or assist others can be fully realized. You know that you're expressing your life purpose when you feel inspiration and enthusiasm in the process of doing it. You are not doing it for some external goal; the process itself is intrinsically rewarding.

Discovering your unique purpose(s) not only heals a fear of aloneness; it can relieve the "existential anxiety" that arises when you experience your life as meaningless or pointless. If you want to further explore the issue of finding your own purpose in life, see the chapter "Finding Your Unique Purpose."

Cultivating Trust in a Higher Power

There is much healing and benefit to be obtained by cultivating your spiritual life. Developing a relationship with a Higher Power (God) may not cure a specific obsession or phobia, but it will provide you with the moral support, courage, and faith to follow through with all of the work involved in re-covering from anxiety difficulties. It will certainly help overcome the fear of abandonment and increase your sense of inner security.

You can define "Higher Power" as a presence or reality that transcends your personal self and the human order of things. This reality has been called "God" in Western society and by many other names elsewhere. It can take the form of a specific being, such as Christ, or be as abstract as the "life force" in all things or the "eternal 'isness'" of the present moment. Each of us defines it in our own way. You may already have a well-developed understanding from your particular religious faith. Or you may not be interested at this time in seeking further understanding. The existence of your Higher Power cannot be rationalized or proved; it's something that is revealed in a personal way within your own experience. Developing a relationship with your Higher Power re-quires effort and commitment. If you're willing to do your part, you will very likely receive the insight and inspiration that you seek.

Further discussion of various ways to approach and cultivate a relation-ship with a Higher Power are offered in three chapters of this book: "Enlarg-ing Your View of Life," "Letting Go" (Part 2), and "Affirming Your Recovery."

Overcoming the Fear of Rejection or Embarrassment

Behind the fear of rejection are usually deep-seated feelings of unworthiness or inferiority. Overcoming such feelings means developing a sense of self-worth and self-respect. Much has been written on the topic of how to develop self-worth—I would especially recommend the writings of Nathaniel Branden and John Bradshaw (see the references at the end of this chapter). Many of the ap-proaches for building self-worth are the same as those for creating an inner sense of safety and security, as described in the previous section on the fear of abandonment. Cultivating a loving relationship toward your own inner child helps to heal critical and rejecting attitudes you may have internalized from your parents. Learning to do small acts of kindness toward yourself on a daily basis accomplishes the same end. Building a support system beyond your im-mediate family provides sources of validation and acceptance that can help. And finding your own niche—a meaningful form of work or a way to fulfill your own creative talents—is particularly critical to a sense of self-worth.

The fear of rejection can lead to two quite different ways of relating to other people, both of which are dysfunctional. On one hand, you may com-promise your own needs in order to please and accommodate other people. Your are excessively concerned about maintaining their approval at whatever cost to yourself. On the other hand, you may withdraw from people because you've concluded there is nothing you can really do to be likable. Your opinion of yourself is so low that you assume people in general are going to find fault, no matter what you do. It's interesting that the first type of behavior seems to be more common among women, while the second is more common among men, although there are plenty of exceptions on both sides. The first type of behavior is associated with personality traits of dependency and what is popularly called "codependency." The second type is associated with social phobia, particularly *generalized* social phobia where you tend to be fearful of most or all types of social situations. Ways to address each type of difficulty are summarized below.

Overcoming the Excessive Need for Approval

Attempting always to please and accommodate others usually means neglecting your own needs. The first step in overcoming such a tendency is to *get more in touch with what your own needs are*. All human beings have a variety of different needs; the following list enumerates some of the more important ones:

1. Physical safety and security

2. Financial security

3. Friendship

4. The attention of others

5. Being listened to

6. Guidance

7. Respect

8. Validation

9. Expressing and sharing your feelings

10. A sense of belonging

11. Nurturing

12. Physically touching and being touched

13. Intimacy

14. Sexual expression

15. Loyalty and trust

16. A sense of accomplishment

17. A sense of progress toward goals

18. Feeling competent or masterful in some area

19. Making a contribution

20. Fun and play

21. A sense of freedom, independence

22. Creativity

23. Spiritual awareness—connection with a "Higher Power"

24. Unconditional love

As you look over this list, ask yourself how many of these needs you're actually fulfilling at this time. Which needs do you tend to neglect? What steps would you be willing to take in the next month or two to take better care of the needs you've neglected? Take time to reflect on your response to these questions and then write it down on a separate sheet of paper.

Identifying your unmet needs is important, yet not enough. Two more attitudes are critical—especially if you tend to be excessively concerned with others' approval:

- *It's okay to take care of your own needs—you're not selfish to do so.*

- *It's okay to ask for what you want*

Many hours of psychotherapy have been devoted to helping people cultivate these two attitudes. Years of parental programming that it's not okay to have needs, to express them, or to ask to have them met may need to be overcome. The first of these two attitudes involves overcoming what has been called "co-dependency." The second attitude is associated with learning to be assertive. Each area of personal growth is discussed in what follows.

LETTING GO OF CODEPENDENCY

Which of the following statements reflects the way you feel? Put a check next to those that apply.

_____ If someone important to me expects me to do something, I should do it.

_____ I should not ever be irritable or unpleasant.

_____ I shouldn't do anything to make others angry at me.

_____ I should keep people I love happy.

_____ It's usually my fault if someone I care about is upset with me.

_____ My self-esteem comes from helping others solve their problems.

_____ I tend to overextend myself in taking care of others.

_____ If necessary, I'll put my own values or needs aside in order to preserve my relationship with my significant other.

_____ Giving is the most important way I have to feel good about myself.

_____ Fear of someone else's anger has a lot of influence on what I say or do.

If you checked three or more statements, you probably need to address your own attitudes of codependency.

Codependency can be defined as the tendency to put others' needs before your own. You accommodate to others to such a degree that you tend to discount or ignore your own feelings, desires, and basic needs. Your self-esteem depends largely on how well you please, take care of, and/or solve problems for someone else (or many others).

The consequence of maintaining a codependent approach to life is a lot of silent resentment, frustration, and unmet personal needs. When these feelings and needs remain unconscious, they often resurface as anxiety—especially chronic, generalized anxiety. The long-term effects of codependency are enduring stress, fatigue, burnout, and eventually serious physical illness.

Recovering from codependency basically involves learning to love and take care of yourself. It means giving at least equal time to your own needs alongside those of others. It means setting limits on how much you will do or tolerate, and learning to say "no" when appropriate. The following list of affirmations constitute a first step toward cultivating a more self-respecting attitude that can help move you beyond codependency:

• I'm learning to take better care of myself.

- I recognize that my own needs are important.

- It's good for me to take time for myself.

- I'm finding a balance between my own needs and my concern for others.

- If I take good care of myself, I have more to offer others.

- It's okay to ask for what I want from others.

- I'm learning to accept myself just the way I am.

- It's okay to say 'no' to others' demands when I need to.

- I don't have to be perfect to be accepted and loved.

- I can change myself, but I accept that I can't make another person change.

- I'm letting go of taking responsibility for other people's problems.

- I respect others enough to know that they can take responsibility for themselves.

- I'm letting go of guilt when I can't fulfill others' expectations.

- Compassion toward others is loving; feeling guilty about their feelings or reactions accomplishes nothing.

- I am learning to love myself more every day.

In order to work with your own codependency issues, you may want to read some of the classic books on the subject, such as *Codependent No More* by Melody Beattie (1987), *Facing Codependence* by Pia Mellody (1989), and *Women Who Love Too Much* by Robin Norwood (1985). Also consider attending a local meeting of Codependents Anonymous, which offers a twelve-step approach to overcoming codependent attitudes. When codependency is deep-seated, working with a skillful psychotherapist may be helpful.

All of the approaches to building self-worth described in previous sections of this chapter will help you to deal with codependency. The bottom line, though, is to *give yourself permission to take care of your own needs*. A principle that I've personally found helpful in this regard is expressed particularly well by one of the affirmations listed above:

"If I take good care of myself, I have more to offer others."

Becoming More Assertive

Becoming assertive begins with an awareness of your own needs—knowing what it is you want. Then you need to learn that it's okay to meet your needs without feeling selfish or fearing disapproval, as described in the previous section. You become assertive, finally, when *you know you have the right to ask for what you want.* You are conscious of your basic rights as a human being *and you're willing to exercise those rights.*

What are those basic rights? A partial list might include:

PERSONAL BILL OF RIGHTS

1. I have the right to ask for what I want.

2. I have the right to say no to requests or demands I can't meet.

3. I have the right to express all of my feelings, positive or negative.

4. I have the right to change my mind.

5. I have the right to make mistakes and not have to be perfect.

6. I have the right to follow my own values and standards.

7. I have the right to say no to anything when I feel I am not ready, it is unsafe, or it violates my values.

8. I have the right to determine my own priorities.

9. I have the right not to be responsible for others' behavior, actions, feelings, or problems.

10. I have the right to expect honesty from others.

11. I have the right to be angry at someone I love.

12. I have the right to be uniquely myself.

13. I have the right to feel scared and say, "I'm afraid."

14. I have the right to say, "I don't know."

15. I have the right not to give excuses or reasons for my behavior.

16. I have the right to make decisions based on my feelings.

17. I have the right to my own needs for personal space and time.

18. I have the right to be playful and frivolous.

19. I have the right to be healthier than those around me.

20. I have the right to be in a nonabusive environment.

21. I have the right to make friends and be comfortable around people.

22. I have the right to change and grow.

23. I have the right to have my needs and wants respected by others.

24. I have the right to be treated with dignity and respect.

25. I have the right to be happy.

I suggest you photocopy this list and post it in a conspicuous place. Take some time to read through it every day for a few weeks.

To act assertively includes two things: you must be willing to ask for what you want and be willing to say "no" to what you don't want. The importance of learning to be assertive can best be appreciated when you consider the consequences of being unassertive, namely:

- People don't know what you want, so they are indifferent to your needs or impose their own agenda.

- People take advantage of you (particularly when you can't set limits or say no).

- You suffer stress from having your own needs going unmet.

- You end up resenting the people you want to love, because they aren't responsive to your unstated needs.

Learning to be assertive means you strike a balance between two extremes: submissiveness and aggressiveness. *Nonassertive* or *submissive* behavior means yielding to someone else's preferences while discounting your own rights and needs. You don't express your feelings or let others know what you want. The result is that they remain ignorant of your feelings or wants (and thus can't be blamed for not responding to them). Submissive behavior also includes feeling guilty—or as if you are imposing—when you do attempt to ask for what you want. If you give others the message that you're not sure you have the right to express your needs, they will tend to discount them. Anxiety-prone people are often submissive because they are overly invested in being "nice" or "pleasing" to everybody. Or they may be afraid that the open expression of their needs will alienate a spouse or partner on whom they feel dependent.

Aggressive behavior, on the other hand, may involve communicating in a demanding, abrasive, or even hostile way with others. Aggressive people typically are insensitive to others' rights and feelings and will attempt to obtain what they want through coercion or intimidation. Aggressiveness succeeds by sheer force, creating enemies and conflict along the way. It often puts others on the defensive, leading them to withdraw or fight back rather than cooperate. For example, an aggressive way of telling someone you want a particular assignment at work would be to say: "That assignment has my name written on it. If you so much as look at the boss when she brings it up during the staff meeting, you're going to regret it."

As an alternative to being openly aggressive, many people are *passive-aggressive*. If this is your style, instead of openly confronting an issue, you express angry, aggressive feelings in a covert fashion through passive resistance. You're angry at your boss, so you're perpetually late to work. You don't want to comply with your spouse's request, so you procrastinate or "forget" about the request altogether. Instead of asking for or doing something about what you really want, you perpetually complain or moan about what is lacking. Passive-aggressive people seldom get what they want because they never get it across. Their behavior tends to leave other people angry, confused, and resentful. A passive-aggressive way of asking for a particular assignment at work might be to point out how inappropriate someone else is for the job, or to say to a coworker, "If I got more interesting assignments, I might be able to get somewhere in this organization."

Assertive behavior, in contrast to the above-described styles, involves asking for what you want (or saying "no") in a simple, direct fashion that does not negate, attack, or manipulate anyone else. You communicate your feelings and needs honestly and directly while maintaining respect and consideration for others. You stand up for yourself and your rights without apologizing or feeling guilty. Others feel comfortable when you're assertive because they know where you stand. They respect you for your honesty and forthrightness. Instead of demanding or commanding, an assertive statement makes a simple, direct request, such as, "I would really like that assignment," or "I hope the boss decides to give that particular assignment to me."

Assertiveness is a skill you can learn. More detailed guidelines for cultivating assertive behavior can be found in the chapter "Asserting Yourself" in *The Anxiety & Phobia Workbook*, as well as in classic books on the subject such as

Your Perfect Right by Robert Alberti and Michael Emmons (1974) or *Asserting Yourself* by Sharon and Gordon Bower (1976). Even better, you may find a class on assertiveness at your local college or adult education center.

Overcoming Social Avoidance

If fear of rejection has led you to distance yourself from people—especially groups—there are several quite specific things you can do. It's still important, of course, to address emotional issues around shame and low self-worth, as described above. In addition to this, cognitive behavioral therapy offers three specific types of interventions:

- Social skills training

- Graded exposure to social situations

- Cognitive behavioral group therapy

Social skills training may be appropriate if you feel at a loss about how to converse with people in small or large groups. You can gain proficiency in starting and maintaining conversations, drawing other people out, listening, maintaining good eye contact, and disclosing your own feelings by role-playing these skills with a family member or a therapist. You can also role-play more specific activities such as interviewing for a job, using "small talk" at a party, or asking someone out on a date. Once you gain confidence in such skills with a supportive friend or therapist, you can begin to try it out in real life.

Graded exposure to social situations involves setting up a series of specific activities that you commit to doing, either with the help of a therapist or on your own. The various activities are arranged in a "hierarchy" from easiest to most difficult. A typical hierarchy might look like this:

Initiating conversations

1. Call two stores to ask if something is in stock.

2. Call a counseling hot line and talk about yourself.

3. Attend a small meeting and say your name.

4. Attend a small meeting and make two comments.

5. Repeat 3 and 4 with a small group of friends.

6. Attend a social gathering and stay for twenty minutes.

7. Same as 6, but stay for an hour, responding when other people talk to you.

8. Same as 7, but you initiate at least two conversations.

9. Initiate conversations while waiting in line with people you don't know.

10. Walk up to someone in a shopping mall and make conversation.

You might also construct a hierarchy for one specific type of behavior, breaking it down into a series of steps. For example, in learning to ask someone out for a date, you might practice with people listed through a dating service before you try walking up to someone at a party. More detailed instructions for doing exposure to social situations can be found in the book *Dying of Embarrassment: Help for Social Anxiety and Social Phobia* (1992). (See references at the end of this chapter.)

Cognitive behavioral group therapy, if available in your area, is perhaps the optimal way to overcome social anxiety and a fear of participating in groups. In such a group you work on challenging and countering socially phobic thinking, i.e., self-statements such as "I'll humiliate myself," "People will think I'm weird because I don't know what to say," or "What if they see me blush." In addition, you practice speaking up, expressing your ideas, maintaining conversations, asking for what you want, responding to criticism, and other types of activities relevant to participating in groups. By continually practicing activities you previously avoided in a supportive group setting, you can learn to desensitize to them and gain confidence in yourself. If cognitive behavioral group therapy is not available in your area, you can still do the cognitive part of the work with an individual therapist experienced in working with social anxiety or social phobia. Then you can try out what you've learned in various group settings, beginning with situations you deem "easy" and progressing to more difficult ones. Learning to speak up or express your ideas, for example, can be practiced first in a class or workshop, then at a twelve-step group, and ultimately at a toastmaster's meeting (or a similar training in public speaking).

Overcoming long-standing shyness or social anxiety takes work and sustained commitment on your part. You may find it somewhat easier under the guidance of a skilled cognitive behavioral therapist who is familiar with social anxiety and social phobia. In some cases, medication can also be helpful. Current treatment strategies for more severe social anxiety or generalized social phobia combine therapy with an SSRI medication such as Paxil (or a benzodiazepine such as Klonopin). This combination of therapy and medication seems to be very effective for many people.

Overcoming the Fear of Losing Control

There are a number of ways to loosen up around an excessive need to control. Three general approaches I've found personally helpful and have used with clients include:

- Letting go of perfectionism

- Learning to live with the inherent unpredictability of life

- Cultivating a spiritual approach to life

Letting Go of Perfectionism

Perfectionism has two aspects. First, you have a tendency to have expectations about yourself, others, and life that are unrealistically high. When anything falls short, you become disappointed and/or critical. Second, you tend to be overly concerned with small flaws and mistakes in yourself or your accomplishments. In focusing on what's wrong, you tend to discount and ignore what's right.

Letting go of perfectionism can be fostered by:

- Not equating your self-worth with your achievements

- Cultivating a sense of humor

- Setting goals that are realistic

- Allowing more pleasure and recreation into your life

- Focusing on the *process* of getting to your goal as much as the goal itself

All of these approaches and others are discussed in Chapter 12, "Letting Go." Please read Part 1 of that chapter carefully to address any problems you have with perfectionism.

Living with the Inherent Unpredictability of Life

The only true constant in life is change. It's inevitable that you'll encounter changes in your environment, in the way others choose to behave, and in your own physical health that you're simply unable to predict or control. You may have resources to cope with these changes, but you are not always going to be prepared for them. There are likely to be times when your personal life circumstances may seem relatively chaotic, disordered, or out of control. Rather than fearing and struggling with situations that don't obey your expectations, you can learn to let go and go with the change. Popular expressions for this are "go with the flow" and "take things in stride." In short, you relinquish your *resistance* to the inevitable ups and downs life presents.

How do you do this? Letting go of perfectionism certainly provides a good start. A willingness to let go of unrealistic expectations can save you a lot of frustration and disappointment. Relaxation is also an important key. The more relaxed you remain, the less likely you are to feel fearful and defensive when circumstances suddenly change and don't go your way. When you're relaxed, you are able to slow down, and it's easier to keep perspective in the face of the unexpected.

A sense of humor toward life can also be very helpful. Humor enables you to step back from those times when everything appears to be in disarray and achieve perspective. If you can stay relaxed and laugh a little at situations that appear out of control, your response begins to change from "Oh my God!" to "Oh well—that's the way it goes."

Affirmations that can help you develop greater acceptance of life on its own terms include:

- "I'm learning to take life as it comes."

- "It's okay to let go and trust that things will work out."

- "I can relax and tolerate a little disorder."

- I'm learning not to take myself or life so seriously."

Choose one of these affirmations and work with it on a daily (or even moment to moment) basis during times when you feel circumstances are "out of control." Again, see the chapter on "Letting Go" for further insight on living with the inevitable unpredictability of life.

Cultivating a Spiritual Approach to Life

Cultivating a spiritual approach to life can mean many things. In essence, it means believing in a Higher Power, Force, or Intelligence that transcends the world as you ordinarily perceive and know it. Very often it also implies having a personal relationship with that Power, Force, or Intelligence.

Developing your spirituality offers at least two ways to assuage the fear of losing control. First, it gives you the option to "turn over" any problem that seems insoluble, overwhelming, or just plain worrisome to the care of your Higher Power, however you choose to define such a Power. This process is expressed in the third step of all twelve-step programs as "[We] made a decision to turn our will and our lives over to the care of a Higher Power as we understood that Power." This does *not* mean that you cease to take responsibility for handling the challenges that come up in life. It does mean believing in a higher resource (higher in the sense of being beyond your own capabilities) that can be of support and assistance when you've reached the point where a problem appears insoluble. Faith in such a resource enables you to let go of the idea that you have to fully control everything. Some of my clients find that they can approach a phobic situation more easily by "turning over" their worry and anxiety to their Higher Power. See the chapter "Letting Go" (Part 2) for further discussion of the process of relinquishing fear to a Higher Power.

The second way in which a spiritual view of life can reduce your need for control is in nurturing the belief *that there is a larger purpose in life beyond the overt appearance of what happens from day to day.* If you believe that there is no spiritual foundation to reality, then the unpredictable and unforeseen events of life can seem both random and capricious. You can feel distressed because there is no explanation for why this bad event happened or that seemingly unfair situation occurred. Most forms of spirituality offer an alternative view that the universe is not random. Events that may appear meaningless and brutal from a human perspective have some meaning or purpose in the broader scheme of things.

A popular phrase that expresses this idea is, "Everything happens for some purpose." Often hindsight provides us with clearer vision. When you reflect deeply on some of the unforeseen mishaps in your life, you may see in retrospect how they served you—either in an obvious way or simply in promoting your growth and development as a human being. See the chapter "Enlarging Your View of Life" if you would like to explore further how spirituality can change your perception of life.

Overcoming the Fear of Death or Injury

The fear of death or injury can often be traced back to a major loss. If such a fear arose in response to the death of a significant other, this loss needs to be fully acknowledged and grieved. Working through unexpressed grief with a counselor or trusted friend will help you to accept what happened and go on. If your fear is related more to the prospect of your own death or potential injury, there are several things you can do. First, work on increasing your internal sense of security along the lines described in the previous section on overcoming the fear of abandonment. You can also cultivate your spirituality and trust in a Higher Power if this seems appropriate. In the context of spirituality, it's important to address and accept the fact of your own mortality. You can do this by talking to others about your feelings regarding death.

Paradoxically, the best way to come to terms with your eventual demise is not to dwell on it—or to deny it. Rather, it's to simply *acknowledge* it and then go about living your life fully. Ultimately, the fear of death is connected with a fear of not having fully lived your life. To die without having taken much advantage of the opportunities your life offers is a dismal prospect. The more life-enhancing activities you engage in today—from small things such as going out to dinner to large things such as developing your creative gifts—the easier it becomes to accept the eventuality of death. Beyond this, you may also choose to assuage the fear of death by holding the view that your soul continues on after physical death (see the chapter "Enlarging Your View of Life"). Whether or not you believe in life after death, enjoying life in the here-and-now will help to make the fact of mortality more acceptable.

People fearful of death or injury may find it difficult to live life to the fullest because of a *low tolerance for taking risks*. In fact, an unwillingness to take risks not only accompanies the fear of death and/or injury but is also one of the biggest stumbling blocks to overcoming all kinds of fears. How can you move out of your comfort zone and be willing to take more risks with your life? Working on overcoming the three fears previously described—abandonment, rejection, and loss of control—will all contribute to increasing your ease with taking moderate risks. It's important also to start off small.

If you want to increase your risk-taking ability in general, make a list of risks you might consider taking in your life and then rank them from least to most difficult. Then proceed step-by-step up your list. If it helps to have a loved one accompany you in taking these risks, by all means include them. You can best increase your risk-taking ability by deliberately committing yourself to do so and then following through, at your own pace, with whatever support you need. As you gain confidence with smaller risks, larger ones become more feasible.

The following examples pertain to physical risk:

1. Bicycling on level roads

2. Bicycling up and down hills

3. Ice-skating

4. Roller skating

5. Riding a motor scooter on back roads

6. Snow skiing—beginner's slope

7. Riding a motor scooter on busy roads

8. Snow skiing—intermediate slope

9. Skydiving with an instructor

10. Skydiving alone

A special problem sometimes associated with the fear of death or injury is *hypochondriasis*. This is a tendency to imagine that you have a serious illness and then persistently seek out medical authorities for reassurance. If you aren't fully satisfied with what one doctor says, you try going to another, obtaining a second, third, and fourth opinion in some cases. Hypochondriasis is a misdirected quest to create a sense of personal safety. The most effective behavioral treatment (the same as is used with OCD) is *response prevention*—simply ceasing all your attempts to get reassurance and letting time pass to allow you to desensitize to the resulting anxiety. Working on building an inner sense of security, as previously described, is also very important. Since hypochondriasis appears to have some relationship with OCD, SSRI medications are often used in the treatment of more severe cases.

Overcoming the Fear of Confinement

The fear of confinement or being trapped often masks a deeper fear. In many cases it's this underlying fear that needs to be addressed.

If the fear of confinement has its origin in a childhood trauma (including birth trauma) where you actually were confined or trapped, you may benefit from seeking the assistance of a therapist skilled in treating post-traumatic stress difficulties. It may be necessary to recall the original incident, fully express any feelings you had at the time, and then make a new decision—a reinterpretation of the meaning of the incident so that you can let it go and be free to continue on with your life. Techniques such as hypnotherapy and EMDR (eye-movement desensitization and reprocessing), as described in the chapter "Fears from the Past" in *The Anxiety & Phobia Workbook*, may help to assist this process.

In my experience with clients, fears of confinement are more frequently related to present circumstances than past. The fear may serve as a metaphor for some way in which you feel confined or trapped in your present life, whether in your job, your relationship with your spouse or partner, economic constraints, health limitations, or even your daily schedule. By addressing and freeing up the problem in your life, you suddenly find you can drive at rush hour or stand in line at the grocery store more easily. This is not to deny the importance of exposure therapy in overcoming situational phobias. *Yet it may be necessary both to do exposure and address issues of interpersonal or existential confinement in your current life to ensure long-term recovery.* If you happen to be dealing with a phobia where you have a problem with feeling trapped, you might ask yourself whether there is any broader sense in which you feel trapped by the circumstances of your present life.

Sometimes the fear of confinement does not have any larger ramifications. It simply doesn't connect with any underlying issue, past or present. It arises from the fact that you can't move in a situation when your physiology predisposes you to "fight or flee." You are standing in line or seated on an airplane with your adrenaline pumping, yet you aren't able to do anything. Instead of perceiving the situation for what it is—an uncomfortable experience of restriction—your mind jumps to danger with self-statements such as "I'm trapped!" "I've got to get out of here right now!" These thoughts can become automatic conditioned responses; you can't seem to reason with yourself that you really aren't in danger—the perception of being trapped persists.

In my experience the most effective way to handle this situation is to go with your body's need to move. If you're standing in line at the checkout counter, move your cart aside and leave the store for a minute, walk around, and then return. If you're stuck in traffic on the expressway, pull over to the shoulder if possible, get out and move about. If you're seated on an airplane, get up and walk to the bathroom and come back, repeating this several times if necessary. If you have to keep your seat belt fastened and can't leave your seat, shake your leg, wring a towel, write in your journal but do something to channel the excess activation in your body. Keep telling yourself, "This restriction will be over in a while and I can get up and move again," or "There's nothing dangerous—I'll be able to move about soon." The better you become at perceiving the situation for what it is—restriction and not entrapment—the less anxiety you are likely to experience.

As you've read through this chapter, I hope you've acquired a better idea of any long-standing fears or personality issues that might be contributing to your problem with anxiety. The latter part of the chapter described a variety of strategies for overcoming these fears/issues. If you are highly self-motivated, you can probably utilize these strategies on your own. Simply making a commitment to do so is a most important first step. For many persons, though, it's easiest to work through personality issues in the context of individual or group psychotherapy. In finding a good therapist, talk to friends who have had therapy or consult the Anxiety Disorders Association of America (at [301] 231-9350) to locate a therapist who treats anxiety difficulties in your area. The ultimate criteria for evaluating therapy is your own gut feeling—do you feel comfortable with the therapy and do you feel you're truly receiving help? If you don't within the first few sessions, look for another therapist (or group). Apart from therapy, you can also address personality issues by participating in twelve-step "anonymous" groups such as Phobics Anonymous, Emotions Anonymous, or Codependents Anonymous. Your local Alcoholics Anonymous group may have a list of these other twelve-step groups. See also *The Self-Help Sourcebook* for a list of several hundred national self-help organizations along with toll-free 800 help lines (available from Self-Help Clearinghouse at 973-625-7101).

What You Can Do Now

1. As you read through this chapter, determine which, if any, of the five core fears and associated personality traits apply to you.

2. If fear of abandonment and being alone is a major issue, give particular attention to the exercises on befriending your inner child. See the books by Bradshaw, Missildine, and Whitfield in the reference list below for further assistance. Also, make time to do nurturing things for yourself on a daily basis, drawing from the Self-Nurturing Activities listed in this chapter. Work on developing a support system in your community if you feel overly dependent on your significant other or family members. Finally, see Chapter 10, "Finding Your Unique Purpose," if you feel you need to give more attention to finding your place or "niche" in the world. If the fear of abandonment is deepseated and based on trauma from your past, consider working with a skilled psychotherapist.

3. If fear of rejection or embarrassment is an issue, you likely need to work on self-esteem. See the chapter on self-esteem in *The Anxiety & Phobia Workbook* as well as the books by Bradshaw and Branden below. If you tend to be too much of a people pleaser at your own expense, you might want to read the books by Beattie, Mellody, and Norwood below. Consider getting involved with a Codependents Anonymous group in your area, if available. If you tend to avoid people, or have a problem with social anxiety, see the books by

Zimbardo and Markway et al. You might also want to consider working with a therapist experienced in treating social phobia.

4. If fear of losing control is an issue for you, see Chapter 12, "Letting Go," for further assistance.

5. Overcoming the fear of death, injury, or illness requires coming to terms with your own mortality and increasing your willingness to take risks. You may want to work with a counselor to assist you with this.

6. When fears are deep-seated, they often have their origin in the past. If you feel you haven't received sufficient help for your anxiety or phobia from cognitive behavioral therapy (including systematic exposure)—and especially if you had a traumatic childhood—you might want to consider working with a therapist who is skilled in addressing emotional issues left over from the past. There are, for example, therapists who specialize in working with people recovering from physical, sexual, or emotional abuse. Sometimes specific techniques such as hypnotherapy or EMDR (eye movement desensitization and reprocessing) can assist this process (see the chapter "Fears from the Past" in *The Anxiety & Phobia Workbook*).

References and Further Reading

Alberti, Robert E., and Michael Emmons. 1974. *Your Perfect Right*. San Luis Obispo, Calif: Impact Press.

Bass, Ellen, and Laura Davis. 1994. *The Courage To Heal*. 3d ed. New York: HarperCollins. (incest, molestation)

Beattie, Melody. 1987. *Codependent No More*. San Francisco: Harper/Hazelden.

Bourne, Edmund J. 1995. *The Anxiety & Phobia Workbook*, 2nd ed. Oakland, Calif: New Harbinger Publications.

Bower, Sharon, and Gordon Bower. 1976. *Asserting Yourself*. Reading, Massachusetts: Addison-Wesley.

Bradshaw, John. 1988. *Healing the Shame That Binds You*. Deerfield Beach, Florida: Health Communications, Inc.

———. 1990. *Homecoming: Reclaiming and Championing Your Inner Child*. New York: Bantam.

Branden, Nathaniel. 1969. *The Psychology of Self-Esteem*. New York: Nash.

Jeffers, Susan. 1987. *Feel the Fear and Do It Anyway.* San Diego: Harcourt, Brace, Jovanovich.

Markway, Barbara, Cheryl Carmin, Alec Pollard, and Teresa Flynn. 1992. *Dying of Embarrassment: Help for Social Anxiety & Phobia.* Oakland, Calif: New Harbinger Publications.

McKay, Matthew, and Patrick Fanning. 1992. *Self-Esteem.* 2d ed. Oakland, Calif: New Harbinger Publications.

Mellody, Pia. 1989. *Facing Codependence.* San Francisco: Harper & Row.

Miller, Alice. 1983. *The Drama of the Gifted Child.* New York: Basic Books. (emotional abuse)

Missildine, Hugh. 1963. *Your Inner Child of the Past.* New York: Simon & Schuster.

Norwood, Robin. 1985. *Women Who Love Too Much.* New York: Pocket Books.

Smith, Manuel J. 1975. *When I Say No, I Feel Guilty.* New York: The Dial Press.

Whitfield, Charles. 1987. *Healing the Child Within.* Pompano Beach, Florida: Health Communications.

Woititz, Janet. 1983. *Adult Children of Alcoholics.* Hollywood, Florida: Health Communications.

Zimbardo, Philip. 1990. *Shyness: What It Is, What to Do About It.* Redding, Massachusetts: Addison-Wesley.

Part II

Beyond the Basics

9

Developing Your Observing Self

Developing your observing self is a potent method for overcoming fear. It allows you to put some distance between your immediate awareness and the fearful reactions and thinking that perpetuate anxiety.

Anxiety encompasses three levels of inner experience: anxious thoughts, emotions of fear or apprehension, and physiological reactions in your body. Your higher brain—the *cerebral cortex*—creates "What if" thoughts such as "What if I lose control?" "What if I make a mistake?" or "What if they see me panic?" Your midbrain or *limbic system*, starting with the hypothalamus, generates fearful emotional reactions, and your autonomic nervous system, particularly the sympathetic branch, stimulates increased physiological arousal (i.e., rapid heartbeat, sweating, muscle contractions, etc.) that accompany anxiety. These three components of anxiety tend to mutually amplify one another. An anxious "what if" thought may trigger an emotional reaction of fear and subsequent bodily reactions of increased heartbeat and sweating. Or underbreathing may reduce the supply of oxygen to your brain to the point that it causes you to feel uncomfortable, "closed-in" sensations, which in turn trigger anxious thoughts, which in turn lead to emotional reactions of fear.

Using constructive self-talk and coping statements (for example, "This is just anxiety—I can handle it"), as described in Chapter 6, can be helpful in turning around fear-provoking thoughts. Practicing abdominal breathing in conjunction with constructive self-talk may work even better, at those times when you feel anxious, because you're addressing both the scary "what if" thoughts as well as the emotional and bodily reactions that all contribute to the total experience of anxiety.

Developing your observing self takes this entire process a step further. It goes beyond simply attempting to control your anxiety states. It's a method that allows you to *stand back and observe*—instead of *react to*—all three components of anxiety, including the what-if thoughts, the fearful feelings, and the bodily reactions. As you learn to stand back and witness with precision these different aspects of anxiety, you become less vulnerable to being caught up or "swept away" by any of them. You are better able to see what's going on in your mind and body without just reacting to the point where you feel out of control. In short, you have more freedom of choice to *respond* to whatever comes up, rather than unconsciously and automatically *react* to it.

There are three stages to the process of developing your observing self: 1) learning to relax, 2) learning to counter negative self-talk, and 3) the practice of meditation. While this chapter primarily focuses on the third stage, it's important to mention the first two.

To become a witness to your experience of anxiety first requires learning to relax. The practice of deep relaxation can help you to *slow down* the stream of fearful thoughts and images in your mind so that they become *less automatic*. The problem with fearful self-talk is not merely that you don't see it. Even when you do, it's usually so automatic that it triggers anxiety almost instantaneously—long before you can take action or counter with a positive thought. Learning to relax deeply can help you slow down the rapid-fire sequence of your mind to the point that you are able to distinguish each link in a chain of thoughts that leads to anxiety. It's difficult to observe what you're thinking otherwise. See Chapter 4 for detailed guidelines on how to relax.

Second, identifying and countering negative self-talk—what you say to yourself—will help you to see the conditioned thinking patterns that generate fear. It's very instructive to *write down* "what-if" or catastrophic self-statements that accompany your anxiety (this is best done after an episode of anxiety when you are relaxed) so that you can observe how they instigate and exaggerate your fear. This is the first step. Then you can develop constructive counterstatements to your fearful self-talk. In so doing you'll begin to break negative habits of mind that have maintained and aggravated your fear (as well as depression, anger, guilt, etc.). Detailed guidelines for identifying and countering negative self-talk may be found in Chapter 6 of this book and Chapter 9 of *The Anxiety & Phobia Workbook*.

Meditation

Once you are able to slow your mind down (relaxation) and identify some of your conditioned thinking patterns (discerning negative self-talk), you're ready to take the process a step further. The practice of meditation is, in my experience, the most useful and powerful method for developing your observing self.

Meditation was conceived in ancient times as a methodology for transcending human suffering and reconnecting with the spiritual dimension of life. For thousands of years Eastern philosophy has taught that the origin of human suffering is in our automatic, conditioned thoughts and reactions (the term "automatic thoughts" used in cognitive therapy is very similar to this notion). Nothing in life is inherently bad except that *we think about it or react to it as such*. If we can step back and simply witness our reactive patterns, we are then able to free ourselves from suffering. According to the Eastern perspective, meditation is the method *par excellence* for achieving a state of freedom or "liberation" from the suffering we create in our minds. (Christian mystics have also practiced meditation down through the centuries.)

How does meditation help to achieve this freedom? In short, you can say that it is by the enlargement or "expansion" of *awareness*. Awareness can be defined as a pure, *unconditioned* state of consciousness that we all can experience. It exists "behind" or prior to the conditioned patterns of thinking and emotional reactivity we've learned over a lifetime. This awareness is always available to us, but much of the time it's clouded by the incessant stream of mental chatter and/or emotional reactions that make up ordinary moment-to-moment experience. Only when we become very quiet and still, *willing to "just be" rather than striving to do anything*, can this uncluttered awareness that precedes our thoughts and feelings reemerge.

To expand or enlarge awareness is simply to allow yourself to settle into greater degrees of it. Awareness lies along a continuum—it's possible to enter into it by degrees. Our language, in fact, contains references to these varying degrees of awareness in the expressions "small-minded" vs. "large-minded." Another way of understanding degrees of awareness is by the concept of "depth." Greater awareness is associated with greater depth. Thinking that is associated with less awareness is called "shallow," that which is associated with greater awareness is called "deep." It's my observation that there is no limit to the potential enlargement or depth of awareness. As your awareness grows, it can continue to enlarge or deepen indefinitely. According to Eastern philosophy, your deepest inner awareness is a link or bridge to the experience of your Higher Power (God), that which has been spoken of in other contexts as "Universal Mind" (Spinoza, Hegel) or "Cosmic Consciousness" (Bucke). At a deep level, your individual awareness joins up—or flows into—a much larger aware-ness that has no limit, much as a drop of the ocean is continuous with the en-tire ocean. As you enlarge or deepen your personal awareness, you can begin to participate to a greater degree in a larger, more universal awareness. Re-member that you don't have to do anything to enlarge your awareness; it is something that emerges naturally when you become still.

Meditation, then, is a very powerful method for enlarging or deepening your awareness. It enables you to set aside conditioned patterns of thinking and feeling long enough so that you can begin to experience the emergence of deeper levels of your own inborn awareness. Your deepest awareness is nothing to be afraid of because it's inherently beyond (or prior to) fear itself.

When you experience expanded awareness, you simply feel a deep sense of peace. Out of this place of inner peace can arise other nonconditioned states such as unconditional love, wisdom, deep insight, and joy. In itself, this state of peace is nothing you need to develop. It's always there, deep inside of you, and you can discover it if you can become still and quiet enough to *allow* it to emerge. The practice of meditation is the most straightforward way to do this.

Meditation practice allows you to expand your awareness to the point where it's *larger* than your fearful thoughts or emotional reactions. As soon as your awareness is larger than your fear, you are no longer swept up by the fear but able to *stand outside* of it—in your mind—and merely *witness* it. It's as though you're identified with a part of your mind that's larger than the part that's constricted by fearful thoughts. As you continue to practice meditation and enlarge your awareness, it becomes easier *on an ongoing basis* to observe the stream of thoughts and feelings that make up your experience. You are less prone to get "stuck" or lost in them.

You might be concerned that increasing your ability to observe your inner thoughts and feelings sounds like becoming internally divided rather than more connected with yourself (the theme of Chapter 2 in this book). In fact, the op-posite is true. It's your reactive thoughts and conditioned emotional patterns that tend to pull you away from your own center—to lead you away from your deeper inner self and into what has been popularly termed "mind trips" or "personal dramas." To practice meditation is to cultivate states of greater wholeness. As you deepen and enlarge your awareness, you begin to be in touch with more of yourself. Your reactive thoughts and feelings still occur, but you're not so strongly claimed by them. You are more free to truly enjoy your life because you don't get as stuck or lost in any particular state of fear, anger, guilt, shame, grief, and so on. Rather, you're able to acknowledge the reaction, allow it to move through, and let it go. Your inner consciousness be-comes spacious enough so that you can observe a worried thought, then take action if it's reasonable or choose to let it go if it's unreasonable. You begin to experience a greater sense of wholeness because you are not as scattered and dispersed by your mind's endless cascade of reactive thoughts and feelings. While these thoughts and feelings still occur, your *relationship* to them is different. You become large enough to witness them rather than be carried away by them. This is the ultimate goal of developing your inner observing self.

A final benefit of meditation practice is the development of compassion toward yourself. Just as you learn to become less reactive to mental, bodily, and circumstantial triggers of fear, you also learn to be less reactive (and thus less judgmental) toward yourself. Feelings of anger, shame and self-reproach may arise if you don't like something you said, did, or what your body or brain is "doing to you." Yet, you don't have to get stuck or lost in these feelings. Instead you can witness them, allow them to pass, and cultivate an attitude of kindness and respect toward yourself. Human beings are actually compassionate by nature when they are able to rise above all the adverse mental/emotional conditioning acquired over a lifetime. Practicing meditation and moving into a stance of witnessing your own mind will help you to access this innate compassion within yourself.

Learning to Meditate

Learning to meditate is a process that involves at least four distinct stages:

- Right attitude
- Right technique
- Developing concentration
- Cultivating awareness

Right attitude is a mind-set or mental stance that you bring to meditation. Such an attitude takes time and commitment to develop. Fortunately, the practice of meditation itself helps you to learn right attitude. *Right technique* involves learning specific methods of sitting and focusing your awareness that facilitate meditation. *Developing concentration* involves practicing additional techniques to reduce the inevitable distractibility that all beginners (and sometimes veterans) of meditation confront. The culmination of these first three stages is "mindfulness"—or what is referred to in this chapter as "awareness." *Cultivating awareness* is the process of making a fundamental shift in your relationship with your own inner experience, as described in the preceding section. It is to develop an "inner observer" within yourself that enables you to bear witness rather than react to the ups and downs of everyday (and even moment to moment) existence.

Right Attitude

The attitude that you bring to the practice of meditation is critical. In fact, cultivating right attitude *is a part of the practice*. Your success and ability to persevere with awareness meditation will in large part be determined by the way you approach it. The following eight aspects of right attitude are based on the writings of a prominent educator in the field of awareness meditation, Jon Kabat-Zinn. Both of his books, *Full Catastrophe Living* (1990) and *Wherever You Go, There You Are* (1994), are highly recommended if you're serious about undertaking a regular meditation practice.

Beginner's Mind

To observe your immediate, ongoing experience without any judgments, preconceptions, or projections is often referred to as "beginner's mind." In essence, it is perceiving something with the freshness you would bring to it if you were seeing it for the very first time. It's seeing—and accepting—things as they actually are in the present moment, without the veil of your own assumptions and judgments about them. For example, next time you're in the presence of someone familiar, consider seeing them as much as possible as they actually are, apart from your feelings, thoughts, projections, or judgments. How would you see them if you were meeting them for the first time?

Nonstriving

Almost everything you do during your day is likely to be goal-directed. Meditation is one thing that is not. Although meditation takes effort to practice, it has no aim other than to "just be." When you sit down to meditate, it's best to clear your mind of any goals. You are not *trying* to relax, blank your mind, relieve stress, or reach enlightenment. You don't evaluate the quality of your meditation according to whether you reach such goals. The only intention you bring to meditation is simply to be—to observe your "here and now" experience as it is, perhaps using the repetition of a mantra or observing your breath to assist your focus. If you are tense, anxious, or in pain, you don't strive to get rid of these sensations; instead you simply observe and be with them as best you can. You let them remain simply as they are. In so doing, you cease resisting or struggling with them.

Acceptance

Acceptance is the opposite of striving. As you learn to simply be with whatever you experience in the moment, you cultivate acceptance. Acceptance does not mean that you have to like whatever comes up (such as tension or pain, for example), it simply means you're willing to be with it without trying to push it away. You may be familiar with the saying, "What you resist persists." As long as you resist or struggle with something, whether in meditation or life in general, you actually energize and magnify it. Acceptance allows the discomfort or problem to just be. While it may not go away, it becomes easier to deal with because you cease to struggle with and/or avoid it.

In life, acceptance does not mean that you resign yourself to the way things are and cease trying to change and grow. On the contrary, acceptance clears a space in your life to reflect clearly and act appropriately, since you remain unfettered by reacting to or struggling with the difficulty. Sometimes, of course, it's necessary to go through a range of emotional reactions first—such as fear, anger, or grief—in order to get to acceptance.

In meditation practice, acceptance develops as you learn to embrace each moment as it comes, without moving away from it. As you learn to do this, you discover that whatever was there for a given moment will soon change. More quickly, in fact, than if you tried to resist it.

Nonjudging

An important prerequisite for acceptance (as well as for beginner's mind) is nonjudging. When you pay attention to your ongoing experience through the day, you'll notice that you frequently judge things—both outer circumstances as well as your own moods and feelings. These judgments are based on your personal values and standards of what is "good" and "bad." If you doubt this, try taking just five minutes to notice how many things you judge during that short time interval. To practice awareness meditation, it's important to learn not so much to stop judging but to gain some distance from the process. You can simply *observe* your inner judgments without reacting to them, least of all judging them! Instead you cultivate a suspension of any judgment, watching whatever comes up, including your own judging thoughts. You allow such thoughts to come and go, while continuing to observe your breathing or any other object you have selected as a focus for meditation.

Patience

Patience is a close cousin to acceptance and nonstriving. It means allowing things to unfold in their own natural time. It is letting your meditation practice be whatever it is without rushing it.

Patience is needed to make time to meditate for a half-hour to an hour every day. Patience is also required to persist with your meditation practice through the days or weeks when nothing particularly interesting happens. To be patient is to stop hurrying. This often means going against the grain of a fast-paced society where rushing from one destination to another is the norm.

The patience you can bring to your meditation practice will help assure its success and permanence. Sitting in meditation regularly will help you develop patience, as it will help you cultivate all of the characteristics described in this section. The attitudes that help you develop a meditation practice are the very same attitudes that are deepened by the practice itself.

Letting Go

In India there is an efficient way to catch monkeys, recounted by Jon Kabat-Zinn. A hole is drilled in a coconut just large enough to accommodate a monkey's hand. The coconut is then secured to a tree by a wire. Then a banana is placed inside the coconut. The monkey comes, puts his hand in the coconut and grabs a hold of the banana. The hole is small enough so the monkey can put his open hand in but cannot pull his closed fist out. All the monkey needs to do to be free is to let go of the banana, yet most monkeys don't let go.

Our minds are often like the monkey. We grab on to a particular thought or emotional state—sometimes one that is actually painful—and then we don't let go. Cultivating the ability to let go is crucial to meditation practice, not to mention a less anxious life. When you hold on to any experience, whether pleasant or painful, you impede your ability to simply be present in the here and now without judgment or striving. Learning to let go of things is assisted by learning to accept them. Letting go is a natural consequence of a willingness to accept things as they are. If you find that, prior to meditation, you have a hard time letting go of some concern, you can actually use your meditation as a means to witness the thoughts and feelings you're creating around the concern—including the thought of "holding on" itself. *The more minutely you observe the specific thoughts and feelings you have created around a problem, the more quickly you'll be able to expand your awareness around that problem and let it go.* When the concern is intensely charged emotionally, it's probably best to release your feelings by talking or writing in a journal about them before you sit down to meditate. Cultivating all of the attitudes described in this section will help with letting go.

A more in-depth discussion of letting go in context of healing fear and life in general may be found in Chapter 12.

Trust

Another important attitude to bring to meditation is a basic trust in yourself. This means you honor your own instincts, reactions, and feelings, regardless of what any authority or other person may think or say. You refrain from judging what comes up in your experience and believe in the inherent goodness of your soul—your essential self. The practice of meditation is about becoming more fully your own self. Practicing awareness means you take responsibility for your own experience on a moment-to-moment basis. It's you who are responsible for your experience and no one else. To fully embrace that experience, you need to trust it. Trusting you own insights and wisdom helps you to develop compassion toward yourself as well as others.

Commitment and Self-Discipline

A strong commitment to work on yourself, along with the discipline to persevere and follow through with the process, is essential to establishing a meditation practice. While awareness meditation is very simple in nature, it's not easy in practice. Learning to value and make time for "just being" on a regular basis requires a commitment in the midst of a society that is strongly oriented toward *doing*. Few of us have grown up with values that cherished nonstriving, and so learning to stop goal-directed activity, even for just thirty minutes per day, requires commitment and discipline. The commitment is similar to that which is required in athletic training. An athlete in training doesn't practice only when he or she just feels like it, when there is time enough to fit it in or other people to keep her company. The training requires the athlete to practice every day, regardless of how she feels or whether there is any immediate sense of accomplishment.

To establish a meditation practice, it's best to sit whether you feel like it or not—whether it's convenient or not—six or seven days per week, for at least two months. (If you find you're unable to sit that often at first, don't chastise yourself—just do your best.) At the end of this time, if you've truly practiced regularly, the process will likely be enough of a habit (and sufficiently self-reinforcing) to continue. The experience of meditation varies from session to session: sometimes it feels good, sometimes it seems ordinary, and other times you will find it difficult to meditate at all. Although the point is not to strive for anything, a long-term commitment to regular meditation practice will transform your life fundamentally. Without changing anything that might happen in your life, meditation will change your relationship to everything you experience, on a deep level. In my personal experience, the hard work involved in establishing and maintaining a meditation practice is worth it. There may be no conscious aim of meditation practice itself, but the benefits that naturally follow from developing your observing self are profound.

Right Technique: Guidelines for Practicing Meditation

There is a technique to proper meditation. Probably the most important aspect is to sit in the right fashion, which means sitting upright with your back straight either on the floor or in a chair. There seems to be a certain energetic alignment within the body that occurs from sitting up straight. It's not likely to happen when you're lying down, although lying down is fine for other forms of relaxation. It's also important to relax tight muscles before you meditate. In historic times, the main purpose of yoga postures was to relax and energetically balance the body prior to meditating. The guidelines that follow are intended to help make your meditation practice easier and more effective.

1. *Find a quiet environment.* Do what you can do to reduce external noises and distractions. If this is not completely possible, play a record or tape of soft, instrumental sounds, or sounds from nature. The sound of ocean waves also makes a good background.

2. *Reduce muscle tension.* If you're feeling tense, take some time (no more than ten minutes) to relax your muscles. Progressive muscle relaxation of the upper portion of the body—your head, neck, and shoulders—is often helpful (see Chapter 4). The following sequence of head and neck exercises may also be helpful (some progressive muscle relaxation in addition to this sequence is probably optimal).

   * Slowly touch your chin to your chest three times.

   * Bend your head back to stretch the back of your neck three times.

   * Bend your head over to your right shoulder three times.

   * Bend your head over to your left shoulder three times.

   * Slowly rotate your head clockwise for three complete rotations.

   * Slowly rotate your head counterclockwise for three complete rotations.

3. *Sit properly.*

   Eastern Style: Sit cross-legged on the floor with a cushion or pillow supporting your buttocks. Rest your hands on your thighs. Lean slightly forward so that some of your weight is supported by your thighs as well as your buttocks.

Western Style (preferred by most Americans): Sit in a comfortable, straight-backed chair, with your feet on the floor and legs uncrossed, hands on your thighs (palms down or up, whichever you prefer).

In either position, keep your back and neck *straight* without straining to do so. Do not assume a tight, inflexible posture. If you need to scratch or move, do so. In general, do not lie down or support your head; this will tend to promote sleep.

4. *Set aside twenty to thirty minutes for meditation* (beginners might wish to start out with ten minutes). You may wish to set a timer (within reach) or run a background tape that is twenty to thirty minutes long so that you'll know when you're done. If having a clock or watch available to look at makes you more comfortable, that's okay. After you have practiced twenty to thirty minutes per day for several weeks, you may wish to try longer periods of meditation up to an hour.

5. *Make it a regular practice to meditate every day.* Even if you meditate for only five minutes, it's important to do it every day. It's ideal if you can find a set time to practice meditating. Twice a day—upon rising in the morning and before retiring for the evening—is optimal; once per day is a minimum.

6. *Don't meditate on a full stomach.* Meditation is easier if you don't practice on a full stomach or when you're tired. If you are unable to meditate prior to a meal, wait at least a half-hour after eating to do so.

7. *Select a focus for your attention.* The most common devices are your own breathing cycle or a mantra. The structured meditation exercises below use both of these techniques. Other common objects of meditation include pictures, repetitive music, or a candle flame.

Developing Concentration

As a preliminary to practicing awareness meditation, it's helpful to work on developing your ability to concentrate or focus your mind. This will enable you to reduce the inevitable distractibility that occurs when you practice. Those forms of meditation that require continuous focus on a particular object are called "structured meditation." The two most common types—mantra and counting breaths—are described below. (See the book *How to Meditate* by

Lawrence LeShan [1974] for more detailed information and exercises on structured meditation.)

Using a Mantra

1. Select a word or short phrase to focus on:

   • A Sanskrit mantra such as "Om Shanti," "Sri Ram," "So-Hum."

   • A word or phrase that has significance within your personal belief system, such as "Let go, let God," or "I am at peace."

2. Silently repeat this word or phrase, ideally on each exhalation.

3. As any thoughts, reactions, or distractions come to mind, just let them pass over and through you and gently bring your attention back to the repetitive word or phrase.

4. Continue this process for at least ten minutes.

Counting Breaths

1. As you sit quietly, focus on the inflow and outflow of your breath. Let yourself breathe slowly and evenly. Each time you breathe out, silently count the breath. You can count up to ten and start over again, or keep counting as high as you like.

2. Each time your focus wanders, bring it back to your breathing and counting. If you get caught in an internal monologue or fantasy, don't worry about it or judge yourself. Just relax and return to the count again.

3. When you lose track of the count, start over at one or at a round number like fifty or one hundred.

4. After practicing breath-counting meditation for a while, you may want to let go of the counting and just focus on the inflow and outflow of your breathing.

5. Continue this process for a minimum of ten minutes.

In doing structured meditation, it's important to concentrate on whatever you've chosen as your object of meditation—but *not to force or strain yourself to do so*. Proper meditation is a state of relaxed concentration. When thoughts, daydreams or external stimuli distract you, attempt neither to hold on to them or to reject them too vigorously. Just allow them to come and go.

Mantra or breath-counting meditation exercises are useful when you first begin to practice meditation because they will help you develop your concentration. Some people, myself included, like to use them at the outset of each meditation session for five to ten minutes as a way to increase focus.

During any form of meditation it's generally helpful to close your eyes in order to reduce outside distractions. Some people, however, find they prefer to keep their eyes slightly open—just enough to see external objects indistinctly. This can reduce the tendency to be distracted by inner thoughts, feelings, and daydreams. Try this if you're having difficulty with distractibility.

You are unlikely to be aware of just how distractible your mind is until you first sit down to meditate. In India it's said that the untrained mind acts like a crazed or drunken monkey. Using structured meditation techniques will build your capacity to concentrate in the beginning. Later you may want to drop these forms and focus more directly on developing your observing self.

Cultivating Awareness

The basic instruction for awareness meditation is simple—to gently pay attention to your breathing. You simply observe your breath as it flows in and out. You give your full attention to the feeling of your breath as it comes in and your full attention to the feeling of your breath as it goes out. You don't try to deepen your breath or do anything with it (unless you are using a breath counting technique initially to help you focus). The idea is simply to observe the process of your breathing without force or effort, experiencing all the sensations, gross and subtle, associated with it.

The process of observing your own breathing cycle is simple, although it's not easy. After two or three minutes you're likely to find that your mind gets bored and wants to go on to do something else. Or your body will have had enough and want to shift your position or get up and do something. It's just at this point that the "work" of meditation begins. Instead of giving in to the impulse to do something else, you simply *observe* the impulse itself and then gently bring your attention back to your breathing, watching your breath from moment to moment.

The tendency to become distracted and stop observing your breath is inevitable. In five minutes it may happen ten or perhaps fifty times. It's *very important not to judge yourself* when you get distracted. Simply notice that you did and then gently bring your attention back to your breathing. If you don't like the fact that you're so distractible, simply notice your not liking it and then bring your focus back to your breath. If you're really enjoying how you feel, simply observe *that* and return to your inhalation and exhalation. Be aware that there is no such thing as a "good" meditation session or a "bad" one. Often you will notice that you feel "good" or "bad" about how a particular session went. Yet keep in mind that the whole point of meditation is to simply witness your experience in the present moment without striving to achieve anything or evaluating how well the experience went.

"Success" in meditation is just doing it. The more often you do it, the more quickly you will train your mind to be less reactive, more stable, and better able to observe. You will be training it to be able to take each moment as it comes, without valuing any one above any other. Working regularly with the resistance of your mind builds inner strength. Regular meditation practice will foster the development of the very attitudes that help facilitate the practice in the beginning: acceptance, patience, nonjudgment, letting go, and trust.

Meditation Exercises

The following five awareness meditation exercises were inspired by Jon Kabat-Zinn, Jack Kornfield, and other teachers of meditation. They derive from basic practices that have been used by students of meditation for thousands of years. The exercises emphasize maintaining a focus on your breathing—continually bringing your attention back to your breath each time you become distracted. It's probably best to do them in sequence, spending a week or two on each exercise. Once you've gained some experience with meditation, you can incorporate aspects of all of the exercises into your daily practice. The walking meditation can be used by itself or as a break in the middle of a long period of sitting meditation.

BASIC MEDITATION ON THE BREATH

1. Sit in a comfortable yet upright position. Focus on your breathing as you breathe slowly from your abdomen for ten minutes. Let the sensations of inhaling and exhaling be the object of your focus. (This process is quite similar to the Abdominal Breathing Exercise in Chapter 4.)

2. If your mind wanders from the focus on your breath, let it do so without judging it. Then gently bring your attention back to your breath. Do this as many times as you need to during the course of your meditation. Attempt to concentrate on your breathing in a relaxed way, without forcing it.

3. If you find yourself getting frequently distracted, use the breath counting technique (counting on each exhale) described in the

previous section of this chapter. When you feel you've relaxed enough to stay relatively well-focused on your breath, try dropping the count.

4. Begin practicing this exercise for ten minutes and gradually work up to thirty minutes. You may find it useful to set a timer or play a thirty-minute tape of meditative music so that you'll know when you're done.

SENSING YOUR BODY DURING MEDITATION

1 Begin this exercise with focusing on your breath. Then extend your attention to include an awareness of your entire body. In particular, focus on your arms and legs along with your breath. When your attention wanders, bring it back to focus on your arms and legs.

2. As in the preceding exercise, don't judge yourself when your mind wanders. Each time you find yourself distracted, gently bring your attention back to the focus on your arms, legs, and breathing. You may need to do this many times at first. With practice, your concentration should improve.

3. Start with practicing this exercise for ten minutes and work up to thirty minutes.

WITNESSING THOUGHTS AND FEELINGS

1. When you've become comfortable with the first two exercises above, let your awareness expand to include your thoughts and feelings.

2. Simply observe your thoughts and feelings as they come and go, just as you would watch cars going by or leaves floating down a river. Let each new thought or feeling be a new object to witness.

3. If you become "stuck" in feelings or reactions during this process, simply observe that and let it pass.

4. Note the impermanence of your thoughts and feelings. They tend to come and go quickly unless you prolong a particular one of them by "holding on" to it.

5. If certain thoughts keep coming back, let them do so. Just keep observing them doing this until they eventually move on.

6. If you notice particular feelings of restlessness, impatience, irritability, or "wanting to get through this," simply observe them without judgment and allow them to pass.

7. If feelings of fear, anxiety, anger, sadness, or depression arise, don't go into them. Just be with them, going back to your focus on breathing, until they pass. You'll find that staying with your breathing helps you to move through such feelings.

8. Any time you feel you're getting stuck in a thought or emotional reaction, just go back to a focus on your breathing and your arms and legs. If you find yourself particularly distracted, try counting your breaths from twenty down to one, one count on each exhale. Repeat this process until you feel more centered.

9. When you first begin to practice witnessing thoughts and feelings, begin with shorter periods of practice and then work up to thirty minutes per day.

OBSERVING WHATEVER COMES INTO AWARENESS

Let yourself observe, without judgment, *whatever* passes through your awareness: thoughts, reactions, physical sensations of discomfort, impatience, restlessness, sleepiness, comfort, relaxation. Let each aspect of your experience arise and move on without giving any one aspect special attention. Whenever you get stuck in a particular thought or reaction, just go back to your breathing. Stay with your breathing as your principal focus. Practice acceptance and nonjudgment toward whatever occurs in your experience while you sit for thirty minutes each day.

WALKING MEDITATION

1. In the privacy of your home, take five minutes to walk *slowly* with awareness. You can walk back and forth or in a loop.

2. Keep in mind as you walk that you're not trying to get any-where; instead, you are being mindful of the process of walk-ing itself.

3. Be fully present with each step that you take. Focus on the sen-sations you feel in your feet, ankles, calves, knees, and thighs as your legs move slowly through each step. Go as slowly as you wish in order to stay focused.

4. If your attention wanders into thoughts, reactions, or other dis-tractions, allow it to do so without judgment. Then bring your focus back to the sensations in your legs and feet as you slowly walk.

5. Start practicing walking meditation for five minutes and work up to fifteen minutes.

Practicing any of these exercises regularly will help you estab-lish a foundation for awareness meditation—the basic method for cultivating your observing self. Starting a meditation practice is straightforward. Maintaining it takes additional commitment, as de-scribed in the following section.

Maintaining a Meditation Practice

The motivation, commitment, and self-discipline necessary to establish a medi-tation practice has already been touched on in the section on right attitude. Learning to meditate can be compared with learning a sport like baseball, rac-quetball, or golf. A considerable amount of time in training is necessary before you become proficient. This involves a commitment to keep sitting on those days when you don't feel like it or find it inconvenient to do. Setting aside a regular time to practice for thirty minutes to one hour each day makes this easier. The best times are generally first thing in the morning upon awakening or in the evening before you go to bed, provided you are not too tired. Other possible times would be before lunch or dinner. By setting aside a regular time, you "build in" a place in your life for meditation.

Besides your own personal commitment and self-discipline, there are several things that can greatly support your practice. Probably most supportive is to find a local class or group that meditates regularly. You may find such a class at a local hospital or college (adult education program) in your area. Or there may be a free-standing meditation group within driving distance. Programs in Transcendental Meditation, or "TM" (a specific form of meditation developed by Maharishi Mahesh Yogi), are offered in many areas. While TM teaches only mantra meditation, it's a good place to begin. Having the support of a group with whom you meditate regularly will assist your motivation at those times when it seems hard to keep up your daily practice.

In some areas you may be fortunate to be close to a teacher thoroughly grounded and skilled in the practice of meditation. If you are interested in finding a group or teacher in your area, you can write to:

Insight Meditation Society
1230 Pleasant Street
Barre, MA 01005-9701

or

Insight Meditation West
P.O. Box 909
Woodacre, CA 94973

The Insight Meditation Society offers meditation retreats in various places throughout the United States. A meditation retreat generally involves sitting in meditation for eight to twelve hours per day (with hourly breaks) for one to ten consecutive days, although a few go even longer. Doing a retreat is a powerful way to deepen your ongoing meditation practice. It is generally not recommended for beginners.

Finally, there are a number of excellent books that can support your practice. The two books mentioned by Jon Kabat-Zinn are a good place to start. Any of the books listed at the end of this chapter can also be helpful.

Meditation and Compassion

An important aspect of developing a capacity to observe your mind is to bring *compassion* into your observation. It may not be enough to learn merely to observe your reactive thoughts and feelings. Without cultivating compassion toward your reactivity, you may remain at war with it. To bring compassion and heart into your self-observation is to begin to make peace with yourself.

Many people, especially if they are perfectionistic, treat themselves as though they were a harsh drill sergeant disciplining a new recruit. If this seems hard to imagine, then watch yourself to see how much time you spend criticizing yourself, putting yourself down, or pushing and driving yourself to do what you don't really want to do. When you're not pushing or criticizing yourself, you may fall into a more passive stance of fear—or of being a victim. Out of fear, your mind constantly scares you with "What if this . . ." "What if that . . ." When you fall into a victim stance, you may depress yourself with "It's no use . . ." "It's hopeless . . ." "It's a lost cause . . ." As soon as you start to feel less depressed, your perfectionism may keep you on a treadmill with "I should . . ." "I must . . ." "I have to . . ." Notice how much you criticize, scare, depress, or push yourself, and you'll learn quite a bit about your own mind. Unfortunately, all of the cognitive therapy in the world is not going to help if you still basically dislike yourself.

Cultivating compassion in self-observation is fundamental to changing your relationship with yourself. Compassion allows you to move away from judgment, criticism, and even contempt toward tolerance, acceptance, and love. Compassion depends on *accepting* yourself—and the rest of the world—*as it is*, an attitude that can be cultivated through meditation practice. Living with your limitations and embracing your humanness is something you can learn. Apart from this chapter, two later chapters in this book, "Letting Go" and "Learning to Love," provide some guidelines that may help you grow in your ability to accept and be more compassionate toward yourself. For a more in-depth statement about the role of compassion in meditation, see Jack Kornfield's book *A Path with Heart* (1993).

Medication and Meditation

Few, if any, books on meditation address the question of how prescription medications affect the experience of meditation. Some formal meditation training programs, such as Transcendental Meditation, request that beginners get off all nonessential prescription drugs before learning to meditate. My own observation, based on personal experience as well as the experience of clients, is that different medications affect different people in different ways.

Two generalizations, however, can be made:

1. Benzodiazepine medications such as Xanax, Ativan, or Klonopin seem to increase distractibility, making it more difficult to focus during meditation. It has been found that the benzodiazepines tend to increase beta wave activity in the brain (rapid, nonsynchronous brain

waves associated with thinking) and reduce the ability to enter into alpha brain-wave states (synchronous brain waves associated with relaxed states as well as meditation). While it's certainly not impossible to meditate while taking a benzodiazepine medication, you may find it more difficult.

2. SSRI antidepressant medications (such as Prozac, Zoloft, Paxil, Luvox) do not seem to impede meditation for most people. There are a few people who report that meditation is more difficult while taking an SSRI medication. On the other hand, I've also heard reports that some people find it easier to meditate after taking SSRIs because they feel calmer and less subject to intrusive thoughts and feelings. In general, it seems the news regarding SSRIs and meditation is good: you can cultivate a meditation practice while taking an SSRI.

Unfortunately, I have no information on the effects of tricyclic antidepressants (such as imipramine or nortriptyline) or MAO-inhibitors on meditation. Nor do I with Buspar. It's possible to evaluate the effects of such medications if you stop the medication for a few days while meditating and then resume taking it. Please consult with your prescribing physician before you try this.

How Your Observing Self Can Help Overcome Fear

Meditation practice helps you to develop your "inner observer." Perhaps the most important application of your inner observing self is learning to *witness in detail* the *internal bodily and/or emotional* sensations that accompany negative feelings, particularly anxiety. Any negative feeling can be analyzed into two components: (1) internal sensations (or emotions) and (2) thoughts.

Unpleasant internal sensations include muscle tension, headache, fatigue, and indigestion, as well as vague aches and pains. Unpleasant emotions include states of fear, sadness, or anger that occur spontaneously without any thought. More complex feelings, including anxiety, consist of these basic sensations or emotions *combined with* mental interpretations or judgments about those sensations/emotions. For example, if you add the thought "What if I have a heart attack?" to the physical sensation of rapid heartbeat, you'll create a strong feeling of anxiety. If you add the thought "What will they think of me?" to a basic emotional state of fear, you create a more complex feeling of anxiety. If you can separate the basic sensations/emotions you experience from subsequent thoughts you have about them, more complex negative feelings simply don't arise. Anxiety will fade the moment you can separate out your immediate bodily sensations/emotions from any accompanying thoughts. As you develop your observing self, you'll become more capable of doing just this.

The nature of fearful thoughts is to move you away from the present moment. When you add the thought "What if . . ." to an unpleasant inner sensation, you immediately begin to focus on future catastrophe rather than your present experience. Fear is a mental "sleight of hand" that quickly takes you out of the immediacy of the present moment. As long as you allow your mind to distract you from the present moment, you may get stuck in what is only a possibility (the "what if" thought), not the concrete reality of what is actually happening here and now. *Fear will dissolve to the extent that you can clearly and simply observe what sensations you're experiencing in the present moment, without jumping ahead in your thoughts.*

So, it's possible to *learn to directly witness just the internal sensations/emotions* that accompany fear in the immediate moment apart from the negative mental interpretations and self-talk that add to it. The pioneer of behavioral approaches to handling anxiety, Claire Weekes (1978), made this distinction long ago. She referred to the internal body sensations as "first fear" and the accompanying fearful thoughts, which aggravate the situation, as "second fear". To the extent that you can learn to distinguish first and second fear as they occur, it becomes possible to eliminate the latter. In short, fear is an interweaving of unpleasant internal sensations and scary thoughts. If you can slow down enough—and stand back enough—to separate the two, fear will lose its grip on you.

Developing your inner observer through awareness meditation is, in my opinion, the most powerful strategy available for distinguishing internal sensations from fearful thoughts. With practice, you can learn to witness your own internal sensations in the present moment so well that you actually see the point at which you begin to add negative thoughts. When you reach this point, your negative thoughts are no longer *automatic*—they no longer happen outside your conscious awareness—and you're in a position to *choose* not to go with them. The final outcome of developing a strong inner observer is that you can actually achieve the goal Claire Weekes described—the ability to observe the sensations of first fear without moving on into the fearful thoughts.

What You Can Do Now

1. To begin a meditation practice, follow the guidelines in the sections "Right Technique" and "Developing Concentration" for two or three weeks. You may want to begin with ten-minute meditation periods

and gradually increase the duration up to thirty minutes. Make a commitment to yourself to practice every day. Review the section on "Right Attitude" to help cultivate the proper attitudinal stance for meditating.

2. After two or three weeks—or when you feel you have gained some ability to maintain concentration—work with the exercises in the section "Cultivating Awareness." Stay with the daily practice of awareness meditation, using your breath as a focus, indefinitely.

3. To support your practice, find a class or group that meditates regularly. If this is unavailable, I recommend you work with audiotapes relevant to meditation, which are available form the Insight Meditation Society (see p. 240 for address). Also see the books on meditation listed in the references, especially those by Kabat-Zinn, Kornfield, and Goldstein.

References and Further Reading

Goldstein, Joseph, and Jack Kornfield. 1987. *Seeking the Heart of Wisdom: The Path of Insight Meditation.* Boston: Shambhala.

Harp, David. 1996. *The Three-Minute Meditator.* 3d ed. Oakland, Calif.: New Harbinger Publications.

LeShan, Lawrence. 1974. *How to Meditate.* New York: Bantam Books.

Levine, Stephen. 1979. *A Gradual Awakening.* Garden City, New York: Anchor/Doubleday.

Kabat-Zinn, Jon. 1990. *Full Catastrophe Living.* New York: Delta.

———. 1994. *Wherever You Go, There You Are.* New York: Hyperion.

Kornfield, Jack. 1993. *A Path with Heart.* New York: Bantam.

Weekes, Claire. 1978. *Hope and Help for Your Nerves.* New York: Bantam.

———. 1978. *Peace from Nervous Suffering.* New York: Bantam.

10

Finding Your Unique Purpose

Among the many possible sources of anxiety, one that's common in contemporary society is a lack of personal meaning. The inability to find meaning in life usually reflects a degree of self-alienation. Such a condition results in a tendency to pursue satisfactions and stimulation on the outside rather than from within. Materialistic goals, concern with appearances, and addictions may all be used to fill an inner emptiness which is often felt as an unsettled feeling or chronic anxiety. External solutions may work, but only temporarily—they provide a quick fix rather than a true healing.

To reestablish meaning in life is to rediscover your soul. An important step in this direction is to find your soul's own innate and natural expression of creativity. Your unique, innate creativity is itself not something you have to create. You came into the world with it, and it likely was evident when you were a child. Unfortunately, education, socialization, and the trauma of entering adulthood may have obscured the natural gifts and talents you brought into the world to express. If you've wandered too far away from your innermost wellspring of creativity, you've probably ended up, like many people, feeling too busy and too anxious. Rediscovering your unique creativity—what I'm referring to here as your unique life purpose—can go a long way toward healing self-alienation and therefore anxiety. Life cannot be as empty or fearful when you experience it as purposeful and creative. Discovering your unique purpose (or purposes) will restore meaning to your life—and an increased willingness to look to yourself rather than the outside for the spark of life itself.

Defining "Life Purpose"

What is meant by the idea of "life purpose"? If you search inside yourself, it's something you need to do in order to feel whole, complete, and fulfilled in your life. It's uniquely your own—something that can't be duplicated. Only you can do it. Your unique life purpose comes from within and has little or nothing to do with what your parents, partner, or friends might want you to do. It's something that expresses a particular talent, gift, skill, or desire that you hold most dear. In fulfilling it, you discover your own unique way to be creative.

Generally, your life purpose is something that reaches beyond the limited needs and concerns of your own ego. It is "other-directed," having an impact on something or someone beyond just yourself. Your life purpose might involve raising a child, contributing to your community, or teaching something you've learned from your personal experience. When you're fulfilling your life purpose, your life takes on a new dimension of meaning beyond self-interest.

From a metaphysical standpoint, your life purpose is an important activity or service your soul came into this world to accomplish. The metaphysical idea of "life purpose" appears in various religious traditions. In Christianity it's referred to as a "calling," while in Hinduism it is spoken of as your "personal dharma." The assumption is that your life purpose, especially the gifts and talents on which it's based, is God-appointed. In some lofty sense, it was decided on and perhaps even planned out before you were born. You came into the world with your unique purpose as a potential. It's your choice and free will that determines whether you fulfill your particular purpose, as well as how you go about doing it. Yet the potential itself remains latent in your soul. As long as your life is focused solely on personal gratification of bodily and ego needs, you may continue to feel something is incomplete or missing. To the extent that you discover and begin to express your unique purpose, you are likely to feel a deep sense of rightness and direction in your life. To be aligned with your life purpose gives life a positive direction—not to may result in a sense of drifting, or keeping busy to avoid feeling empty. There is no longer as great a need to seek pleasure in outer material things, since you begin to feel an increasing inner satisfaction that you are "on course"—doing what you came here to do.

To align with your unique life purpose is an important step in healing yourself and becoming all you can be. It is to live more from the truth of your soul rather than from ego needs and goals. As such, you begin to be more in touch with the creative forces and guidance of Spirit.

It's important to realize that your life purpose may not necessarily be grand in scope. Size of impact is less important than *quality*. Your purpose may be about raising a family, contributing to a social or political cause, or sheltering injured or sick animals. Or, it might involve artistic pursuits, such as painting, playing an instrument, or writing poetry. Perhaps volunteering your services for a youth group or teaching a Sunday school class might fulfill your life purpose.

Often your life purpose does not become clear until you've worked through some of your personality issues, as was discussed in Chapter 8. Resolving unfinished business with your parents, taking care of your financial and security needs, overcoming social fears and learning to be assertive may all be part of the "groundwork" that needs to be done before you can fully express your life purpose. It's difficult for your creativity to fully blossom until you've freed up sufficient energy within yourself from personality and interpersonal conflicts. In fact, confronting and dealing with personality issues is also an important part of what you came here to do, along with expressing your unique creativity. In an important sense, a major part of your life purpose is to do the inner psychological work necessary to handle your personal needs and achieve a sense of identity and self-worth. (That's not to say that you can't begin to express your unique creativity while still addressing your personality issues.)

Discovering Your Own Life Purpose

If you currently feel out of touch with your life purpose, how do you go about discovering what it is? The questionnaire that follows is designed to stimulate your thinking in ways that can help you to formulate your own unique goals. Your answers to the questions may give you some insights into what it is that is most important for you to do with your life. Give yourself at least one full day to reflect on these questions and write out your answers. You may even want to ponder these questions for a week or a month. After you've arrived at the answers for yourself, practice visualizing what your life would look like if you were truly fulfilling your special purpose. I also recommend that you share your answers to these questions with a close personal friend or counselor and get that person's input and feedback. If realizing your purpose involves making a career change, it might be helpful to work with a career counselor. If it involves going back to school, you'll want to talk to an academic guidance counselor at the school you're considering (see the section of this chapter called "Implementing Your Life Purpose").

LIFE PURPOSE QUESTIONNAIRE

1. Does the work I'm presently doing express what I truly want to be doing? If not, how can I begin to take steps toward discovering and doing work that would be more personally fulfilling?

2. Am I satisfied with the education I've obtained? Would I like to go back to school and increase my education and training? If so, how can I begin to move in that direction?

3. If I need to be doing my job for now, are there any hobbies or avocations that I've thought about developing?

4. Do I have creative outlets? Are there any areas of my life where I feel I can be creative? If not, what creative activities could I develop?

5. What kinds of interests or activities spark my enthusiasm? What do I naturally enjoy doing (alone, with friends, family, outdoors or indoors)?

6. What would I like to do with my life if I could do what I truly wanted? (Assume, for the purpose of this question, that money and the responsibilities of your current job and family are not a limitation.)

7. What would I like to accomplish with my life? What would I like to have accomplished by the time I reach seventy in order to feel that my life has been productive and meaningful?

8. In what way(s), however small, do I feel I could make the world a better place?

9. What are my most important values? What values give my life the greatest meaning? Some examples of values include:

Happy family life	Material success
Intimacy	Career achievement
Friendship	Creative expression
Good health	Personal growth
Peace of mind	Spiritual awareness
Serving others	Dedication to a social cause

10. Is there anything that I deeply value and yet feel I haven't fully experienced or realized in my life? What changes do I need to make—or what risks do I need to take—to more fully realize my most important values?

11. Do I have any special talents or skills that I haven't fully developed or expressed? What changes do I need to make—or what risks do I need to take—in order to develop and express my special talents and skills?

12. In the light of the above questions, I feel that my most important life purposes would include (list):

13. What obstacles exist to pursuing and realizing my life purposes?

14. What am I willing to commit to doing in the next month, year, and three years to eliminate the obstacles in Question 13 and move toward realizing my special purpose(s)?

One month:

One year:

Three years:

Guidelines for Reflecting on Your Life Purpose

To assist you in thinking about the questions posed in the Life Purpose Questionnaire, you may find the following guidelines helpful:

1. Listen to what your heart tells you about what you would most love to do or be.

2. Be sure to separate your unique goals and objectives from those of your parents, spouse, friends, or others. Only you can know what your true mission is.

3. Your life purpose may or may not be your actual vocation. It could be a hobby, pastime, or avocation.

4. Notice negative self-talk that puts down the dreams or inner fantasies that your heart offers up. For example:

    "I can't do what I want and still make a living."

    "It's too late to go back and get the training."

    "It's too expensive."

    "It's impractical."

    "They won't approve."

    "I don't have the talent for it."

    "I don't have the time."

    "It's too much work—too difficult."

    "No one's going to be interested, anyway."

    Statements like these are often clues to showing you what your deepest purpose or "personal dream" actually might be.

5. Keep in mind the famous maxim: "God never gives us a vision without also giving us the capacity to make it come true."

6. Ask your own inner wisdom or Higher Power to help you discover and clarify what your life purpose might be. In your deepest self, you already know what your mission or purpose is.

7. Look for synchronicities. When you are moving toward or on the path of your life purpose, amazing coincidences will often happen to give you confirmation that you're on the right course.

8. Realize that fulfilling your life purpose may involve taking risks and giving up certain aspects of your life as you know it right now. Are you up to taking such risks? If not, how might you gain support to do so?

Visualize Your Life Purpose

After you have a good idea about the nature of your life purpose, write a scenario on a separate sheet of paper about what your life would look like if you were to fully realize this purpose (or purposes). You can design separate visualizations for each purpose or incorporate the realization of all of your life purposes into a single description. Be sure to make your scenario sufficiently detailed to include where you're living and working, who you're with, what activities make up your day, and what a typical day would look like. Once you've completed a detailed description, record it on tape, preferably in your own voice. You may want to record it after a few minutes of preliminary instructions to relax. Visualizing the fulfillment of your life purpose on a regular, consistent basis will go a long way toward helping you to actually realize your goal. (See Chapter 13, "Affirming Your Recovery," for further discussion of this point.)

Implementing Your Life Purpose
Do the Necessary Research

If you're thinking about changing your occupation, you may want to work with a career counselor to help delineate new vocational options. If you already know what you want to do, consult the *Occupational Outlook Handbook* (1996) at your local library to find out about entry requirements and job prospects in your field of choice. If you want to take up a hobby in astronomy, gardening, or antique collecting, research existing information on the subject at the library or on the Internet if you have access. Talk to people who are already involved in the vocation or avocation that interests you.

Acquire the Necessary Skills and Training

Entering a new career generally requires retraining or retooling. If formal training is needed, is it available in your area? Can retraining be acquired by correspondence or apprenticing to someone already skilled in the field? Are you willing to make the time for retraining? Learning to do oil painting or play the piano will require a one or two year commitment to taking classes or working with a teacher. Many things you might do as a life purpose do not emerge spontaneously but require an intensive period of learning and/or training.

Persevere

Anything truly worth doing—and few things are likely to be more important to you than fulfilling your life purpose—will take time, effort, and discipline. Whether it's pursuing a new career or hobby, contributing to your larger community, or healing yourself from chronic illness—your unique life mission will require a consistent commitment and energy expenditure over time. The main reason why many noble projects fail is not for lack of inspiration or even skill, but lack of follow through.

Watch for Negative Self-Talk

Continue to monitor yourself for negative attitudes or self-statements that interfere with your progress toward fulfilling your dream. Statements such as those mentioned under number 4 in the previous Guidelines section are notorious for interfering with the pursuit of anyone's creative purpose. Talk back to your inner critic or cynic with affirmative statements such as:

- "I accept and believe in myself."
- "I am a unique and creative person."
- "I have unique gifts that are mine to express."
- "I have the capability to realize my goals (or dream)."

Trust That the Universe Will Support You

Your unique creative purpose is something you came into the world to do. The sources of inspiration for it come from your own inner spiritual source—your Higher Power. So you can trust that, in pursuing your particular purpose, you will receive guidance and support from a place beyond your conscious self or ego. If you feel shaky about what you're doing, it's important to keep asking your Higher Power to assist you. If you are on course with your purpose, and ask with sincerity, help will be forthcoming.

Set Aside Time Each Day

The process of realizing your life purpose requires a time and energy commitment. To move it from the realm of ideas and inspiration into practical form will be helped by setting aside time each day to work on it. If you're at the beginning of the process, you need to make time to discover your purpose or do the necessary research to find out how to realize it. If you're at the stage of learning how to do it, this too requires a daily commitment until you have learned the requisite knowledge and skills.

Finally, actually expressing your purpose requires a regular commitment, time and effort. However, the work you'll be doing at this stage is work that you'll deeply enjoy.

Although this has been one of the shorter chapters in this book, don't underestimate its importance. If you've felt that your life doesn't have the meaning and sense of direction that you would like, spend some time with this chapter and consult the books listed in the references. Finding and expressing your unique creative gifts can go a long way toward healing your personal struggle with anxiety. It can help someone else, too. As Nelson Mandela once said: "You are a child of God; your playing small doesn't serve the world."

What You Can Do Now

1. Do you feel aware of your own unique life purpose or purposes? Use the Life Purpose Questionnaire to assist you in clarifying what you would most like to do with your life.

2. Review the section "Implementing Your Life Purpose." If you feel ready to begin taking action to express your unique purpose, what steps are you willing to take (for example, learning appropriate skills, talking to others involved in a particular vocation or hobby, making time in your schedule to develop a creative pursuit, etc.):

In the next month?

In the next year?

3. If you decide you want to change your line of work, you might do so by following these steps:

Find a career counselor you respect (or take a course in exploring career options at a local college).

Explore different options by:

- Reading about different vocations in books such as *What Color Is Your Parachute?* and *The Occupational Outlook Handbook.*
- Talking to people who hold positions in vocations to which you feel drawn.
- Narrow down vocational options to one particular type of work (obtain whatever help you need to do this)—focus is extremely important in achieving goals.
- Obtain education or training for the line of work you've chosen.
- Find out where training is available in your area (your local library is a good resource for doing your research).
- Apply to appropriate schools or training programs.
- Apply for an educational grant or loan if your education or training will require a full-time commitment.
- Complete your education or training (if possible while maintaining your current job).
- Search for an entry-level position in your new career.
- Obtain resources that tell you where jobs are available (professional or trade newsletters, journals, alumni organizations, newspapers, and job hot lines are all good resources).

- Prepare a professional-looking resume.
- Apply for jobs.
- Go for interviews.
- Begin you new career.

References and Further Reading

Bolles, Richard. 1997. *What Color Is Your Parachute?* Berkeley: Ten Speed Press.

Braham, Barbara J. 1991. *Finding Your Purpose.* Menlo Park, Calif.: Crisp Publications.

LeShan, Lawrence. 1989. *Cancer as a Turning Point.* New York: Dutton. (Although this book is written for persons dealing with cancer, it's relevant to anyone who wants to redesign their life to have greater meaning, purpose, and creativity. Case histories are inspiring and instructive.)

Occupational Outlook Handbook. 1996. Bureau of Labor Statistics. Washington D.C.: U.S. Government Printing Office.

Stephan, Naomi. 1989. *Finding Your Life Mission.* Walpole, New Hampshire: Stillpoint Publishing. (Many practical exercises for getting in touch with your unique purpose.)

11

Enlarging Your View of Life

Each of us has an explicit or implicit philosophy of life. Depending on how much you've thought about it, you may have an undeveloped or a highly elaborate set of ideas about such basic questions as: "What is the meaning and purpose of life?" "Why do innocent people suffer terrible misfortune?" "Is there a Deity?" "What happens after I die?"

Some people are content not to grapple with such questions. They have a pragmatic approach to life and choose to set aside such questions in the interest of "getting on with the business at hand." To contemplate such questions seems impractical or useless. Other people may give passing attention to these questions, but are content to settle for answers given to them by their parents, teachers, or respected authorities, such as their church. Conventional answers to the basic questions of life are enough. Finally, there are people who need to search and explore in order to discover the answers for themselves. Dissatisfied with answers of their parents or the socially sanctioned answers of conventional authority, they seek to find out for themselves what is true.

This chapter was written for those readers who belong to the third group—those of you who are seeking answers to life's basic questions for yourselves. I believe the number of people in this category has increased dramatically in the past fifty years, as the institutions that traditionally provided answers (church, government, and accepted social conventions) have tended to become fragmented and pluralistic. There is no longer a single, dominant view of life in our culture. In fact, I believe much of the stress and uncertainty of our present time is due to the lack of a consistent, agreed-upon set of ideas, norms, and beliefs regarding life's basic questions. Many of us feel we have been left to find our own answers, and the options available—communicated to us by TV, books, films, music, the arts, and the Internet—seem almost limitless. Without a coherent philosophy of life and set of values to follow, it's easy to feel in a state of limbo about who you are and what your life is about. Out of that limbo can come quite a bit of uneasiness, and even outright anxiety.

If there *has* been any dominant worldview in the technologically advanced societies of the twentieth century, it has been "scientific materialism." As the term implies, scientific materialism places an implicit faith in science and a material view of the world. It begins with the assumption that *all* valid knowledge about human beings, nature, and the universe at large can be revealed through scientific investigation. The "materialism" part of this viewpoint assumes that everything in the world, including our own thoughts, motives, feelings and aspirations can be understood in terms of physical processes and events. The entire world, including humanity, should ultimately be described, explained, and predicted according to scientific concepts and laws.

Scientific materialism has influenced (and continues to influence) our lives in many ways, some of them quite favorable. It underlies the tremendous technological progress that has provided countless conveniences and time-saving devices that make life less laborious than it was in the recent past. No one can argue that medical science has not achieved many miracles in our century. And a scientific approach to psychology and human behavior has added immensely to our understanding of human psychological difficulties and how to go about remedying them. One of the most recent, best-known examples to many readers of this book is the cognitive behavioral approach to understanding and treating anxiety disorders and depression. This approach grew out of the marriage of behaviorism and cognitive psychology, both of which were scientific approaches to human behavior that developed over the past eighty years in American universities. Certainly no one can argue with the success of the cognitive behavioral model in providing a viable treatment approach to anxiety disorders and depression. Recently, cognitive behavioral therapy has joined with another scientifically based approach, biological psychiatry, in further improving the quality and effectiveness of treatment that is available.

The scientific-materialistic paradigm has allowed us to gain considerable mastery over countless types of circumstances that lay beyond our grasp not so long ago. In the future, it will doubtless continue to make adaptation to life easier for most of us. For all of their innovations in the way we live, science and technology deserve respect. At the same time, most of us are aware of the serious problems created by our scientific-technological approach to the world. Too often in the twentieth century, mastery over nature has turned into exploitation, leaving us with a range of serious environmental problems such as pollution, deforestation, and nuclear contamination. (Perhaps we should not blame science and technology themselves, but our own *misuse* of them, for the earth's current environmental disasters.) While making life physically easier, our scientific-technological innovations have also made it considerably more complicated. The downside of that complexity was detailed in Chapter 2. There it was pointed out that technologically sophisticated, industrialized society can and often does lead to an increased sense of alienation from nature, community, others, and even ourselves. With increased alienation comes increased anxiety. In fact, it might be asked whether anxiety (as opposed to objective fears of war, famine, plague, disease, oppression, etc., that were prevalent in previous centuries) is a unique creation of our complicated twentieth-century way of life—a lifestyle that has been so powerfully shaped by scientific innovation and technology.

In this chapter I'm not so much concerned with the limitations of science and technology themselves as with the scientific-materialistic worldview which they presuppose. This is the worldview that has dominated our thinking in Western society throughout the twentieth century. Yet it is a view that, in my opinion, is hard put to provide satisfactory answers to basic questions about the meaning and purpose of human life. To review what some of these questions are, consider the following seven:

1. What is the ultimate meaning and purpose of life?

2. Why do innocent people suffer terrible misfortunes?

3. How can we reduce hatred, prejudice, and violence in our families, communities, society, and the planet?

4. Is there a Deity? If so, is "It" concerned about human welfare?

5. What happens after we die?

6. What is human creativity?

7. What is human consciousness? (Not just thoughts and feelings, but the self-awareness that precedes them.)

To my knowledge, not very many of us turn to science for answers to such questions. The scientific-materialistic paradigm either offers no answers to questions like these or, in some cases, rather limited answers. For most of us, such answers don't go far enough. To say, for example, that there is no purpose to life other than biological adaptation or no reason for calamitous misfortune other than "bad luck" leaves many people cold. For me personally, a world based on answers such as these seems pretty bleak. It is sad that there are many people in our society and century who have resigned themselves to such answers.

The world's philosophies and religions have provided more satisfactory answers to these troubling questions. Countless and varied answers to these questions have been offered by the world's philosophical and religious traditions for thousands of years, for the questions themselves have always intrigued people. The types of answers usually offered go well beyond conventional science. For some people this is not a problem. Religious faith and its answers are on one side of the fence; scientific knowledge and investigation on the other—totally separate with no relation to each other. In the twentieth century it has been perceived as necessary to keep science and religion separate. The problem is that there is only one world out there, which bides no radical compartmentalization. *The separation between science and spirituality is a human construction, and not likely to be inherent in the true nature of things.*

A peculiar thing happened in the last three hundred years. Because of the enthusiasm generated by so many innovations and progress made through science, large numbers of people began to believe that scientific knowledge was the only kind of valid knowledge possible. Accordingly to this view, whatever we can possibly know—both about nature and humanity—should be able to be *fully* understood through science. Furthermore, the physical, material world that is the object of scientific investigation must be all there is to reality, *because only that which science can investigate exists.* Even if your inspirations and aspirations don't look like material events, they have to be reducible to physical events (in the brain) because science must be able to explain them like everything else.

This peculiar view constitutes scientific-materialism *taken literally.* It is sometimes referred to simply as "scientism." If you subscribe to such a view, then any insights or answers to life's basic questions offered by philosophy and religion become suspect, because they can't be proven scientifically. Such insights tend to get relegated to the realm of superstition and fantasy, since they are not empirically verifiable. This view was particularly dominant in the first half of the twentieth century and influenced many of Western society's institutions, including government, higher education, medicine, social sciences, and psychology. It even encroached on religion when a large number of theologians in the early sixties espoused the notion "God is dead."

In the last forty years this view has been questioned, and an outright revolution has been staged on many fronts against scientism. People began to vaguely feel that something was amiss. For all its progress and technological innovation, the scientific-materialistic paradigm did not offer a large enough view of the world; in short, it did not adequately provide answers to many of life's most basic questions. In the late sixties, a reemergence of high ideals and spiritual values in opposition to the so-called "military-industrial establishment" (that took its values from scientism) appeared in the antiwar movement as well as in the musical and political expressions of millions of youth.

The idealism and spirituality of the time did *not* develop out of existing religious institutions. It appeared spontaneously as a new force unto itself (although it often sought its philosophical justification from the religions of the Far East). Since the late 1960s this revolution has grown and spread in ways too numerous to enumerate here. Three of its better-known facets—the human potential movement, the holistic health movement, and the new age spirituality movement—served to awaken many people from a purely scientific-materialistic worldview in the seventies and eighties.

In the nineties, this reaction against scientism began to go mainstream. In fact, it began to have major impact on institutions such as education, business, and medicine that were strongly shaped by scientism only thirty years ago. At present, the American public makes more visits to alternative health practitioners than to conventional medical doctors. There are tremendous spiritual revival movements going on within mainstream religions. Outside of the mainstream, there is a whole spectrum of alternative holistic and spiritual perspectives that question or move beyond the scientific-materialistic paradigm.

Spirituality in particular has had increased impact on society, science, and medicine in recent times. Three trends in particular bear witness to this impact: 1) the proliferation of twelve-step programs; 2) the emergence of what has been called a "new physics;" and 3) the rapid growth of alternative or "complementary" medicine.

New Trends in Spirituality
The Growth of Twelve-Step Programs

The first twelve-step program, developed by Bill Wilson and Dr. Bob Smith in the 1930s, was Alcoholics Anonymous. Sixty years later, in the 1990s, the twelve-step model of AA has been extended to over forty different types of human difficulties, including phobias, obsessive-compulsive disorder, and post-traumatic stress disorder.

All of the twelve-step groups follow principles that are fundamentally spiritual in nature, as evidenced particularly in the second and third steps.

2nd Step: Came to believe in a Power greater than ourselves that could restore us to wholeness.

3rd Step: Made a decision to turn our will and our lives over to the care of our Higher Power, as we understood our Higher Power.

(Wording from the steps of Phobics Anonymous.)

Anyone who has been acquainted with twelve-step groups has likely heard stories of "miraculous" recoveries. Leaders and others in such groups recount how deep a "bottom" they succumbed to before finding their way back to wholeness through the assistance of their Higher Power. Without being a formal church, the twelve-step groups demonstrate a major interest and reliance on spiritual methods of healing at the grassroots level.

The New Physics

Physicists such as Fritjof Capra, David Bohm, Fred Wolf, and others have shown that the model of the universe that arises out of twentieth-century quantum mechanics and relativity theory has many similarities to the mystical view of the cosmos espoused by Eastern philosophy and religion for over three thousands years. For example, modern physics views the cosmos not as an orderly machine but more like a sea of energy fluctuations that are indeterminate and unpredictable at their core. The universe also appears to be organized like a hologram. Every part of the universe is intimately linked with every other part through an unseen "implicate order." The holographic paradigm makes the even more radical prediction that every part of the universe implicitly contains the whole. No longer are we living in a universe of separate and discrete objects and events. Current cosmological models talk about a unified field theory, which Einstein sought his entire life, as requiring up to twelve dimensions. In short, there may be much more to the universe than our perceived three-dimensional world. The current state of modern physics is captured by the statement from Shakespeare's Hamlet: "There are more things in heaven and earth, Horatio, than are dreamt of in your philosophy."

Alternative Medicine

Physicians such as Bernie Siegel, Deepak Chopra, Larry Dossey, and Andrew Weil are perhaps best known for incorporating spiritual principles into their views on health, healing, and longevity. However, many doctors are investigating various aspects of spirituality these days.

The Office of Alternative Medicine, a branch of the National Institute of Health, is sponsoring research on the efficacy of prayer as an adjunct to conventional medical treatment. Even psychiatrists are becoming more open-minded. For example, the American Psychiatric Association recently invited Scott Peck, author of *The Road Less Traveled* (1978) and several other books exploring the relationship between spirituality and psychology, to give the keynote address to their National Conference. Peck called upon psychiatrists to take the spiritual motivations and aspirations of their patients seriously. Psychology is embracing this shift as well, and the twenty-year-old field of transpersonal psychology (whose intention is to explore the interface between psychology and spirituality) is gaining increasing recognition. The tight demarcation between psychology and spirituality, which was first established by structuralist psychology as well as psychoanalysis at the end of the nineteenth century, is beginning to be questioned at the end of the twentieth.

These trends and others offer a reframing of our conception of life and the world. They provide, in various ways, answers to life's basic questions, which go well beyond the scientific-materialistic worldview that has dominated thinking in the West for three hundred years. In so doing, they are renewing the more spiritually based conception of the world that has predominated in all societies throughout human history—except the last three hundred years in Western Europe and America. Their intention is not to return to the prerational theologies of the Middle Ages. Instead it is to seek a post-rational, post-scientific worldview that does not deny the significance and role of science but puts scientific knowledge and methodology into proper context. Such a view acknowledges that science has its place—a very important and helpful one—but that it cannot account for or explain the full range of human experience. Nor can it embrace everything that exists. There are realities that lie outside the compass of the physical, space-time universe that conventional science cannot (yet) investigate or comprehend. These realities (at present) are approached experientially rather than empirically—they are perceived and understood through personal insight and discernment rather than direct observation of external processes and events.

Ultimately, it seems likely that scientific and spiritual-philosophical worldviews will be integrated in a single paradigm that we can only vaguely grasp at our present level of understanding. For now and the immediate future, we can expect to see an increasing accommodation of mainstream disciplines, particularly medicine and psychology, to holistic and spiritual concepts, principles, and values.

What does all this have to do with healing fear? The basic point of this chapter is that your feelings, moods, and outlook on life are not only influenced by your self-talk and beliefs about yourself (as described in Chapter 6) *but by your own unique "philosophy of life" or "worldview."* Each of us has one, whether or not it has been expressed explicitly. One way of articulating your own philosophy of life is to examine your answers to some of the basic questions about life, as were described above.

I believe that spirituality can offer much to help enlarge a person's view of life. It certainly has for me personally. Spirituality can suggest answers to questions that may restore your faith in life and renew your optimism about your future, no matter what your current predicament might be. It can help develop the conviction (if you don't already have it) that you have a unique reason for being here—a unique purpose to serve—no matter how you might view yourself now. (See the chapter "Finding Your Unique Purpose.") Even your struggle with anxiety can be understood as having a larger purpose—not simply as an accident of nature with which you have been arbitrarily or unfortunately afflicted.

For the purpose of this chapter, "spirituality" can be understood as distinct from religion. Different world religions have proposed various doctrines and belief systems about the nature of a Higher Power and humanity's relationship with it. Spirituality, on the other hand, refers to the *common experience* behind these various points of view—an experience involving an awareness of and relationship with "something" that transcends your personal self and the human order of things. This something has been referred to by many different names, the most common in our culture being "God." The remainder of this chapter explores a number of dimensions of spirituality. First, I will address the issue of how spirituality can help overcome anxiety and anxiety disorders. This section includes a description of personality and attitude changes—often brought about by an active spiritual involvement—that can help heal anxiety and fear. The section following that, "Exploring Your Own View of Spirituality," offers you the opportunity to explore some of your own ideas and personal experiences with spirituality. It may help you to clarify your ideas about the nature of your Higher Power and your relationship with such a Power. Finally, I will present my own personal understanding of spirituality, in the form of twelve assumptions that I believe are frequently associated with a spiritual view of life. You may find you agree or disagree with some of these ideas. If they help you to enlarge your view of life, however, they will have served their purpose.

How Spirituality Can Help Overcome Anxiety

Taking holistic and spiritual ideas seriously does not imply doing away with cognitive behavioral and biopsychiatric approaches to treating anxiety, panic attacks, and phobias. Cognitive behavioral therapy is, without question, very effective in helping people to change catastrophic thoughts, which aggravate panic attacks and anticipatory anxiety. Exposure is very effective in helping people to confront and overcome many types of phobias. Medication is a critical part of treatment in many cases, helping people who are debilitated by panic attacks, agoraphobia, or OCD to be more responsive to cognitive behavioral interventions. The current paradigm for treating anxiety disorders has provided a tremendous advance over the state of treatment prior to 1980. It will continue to be refined and improved into the foreseeable future.

I would like to suggest that spirituality, *in addition* to cognitive behavioral therapy, has a special role to play in recovery from anxiety:

- It can increase your belief and hope that recovery is possible.

- It can provide a way to handle more severe and chronic anxiety disorders.

- It can lead to distinct changes in personality, attitude, and behavior that increase your ability to cope with an anxiety disorder.

- It can provide a more positive frame of reference for perceiving your difficulties with anxiety (and life in general). Instead of being an arbitrary hardship, your problem, however challenging, can be understood as an opportunity to grow and evolve as a human being.

The first three points are discussed in what follows. The fourth point is elaborated in considerable detail in the final section of this chapter.

Increased Hope in the Possibility of Recovery

Spirituality has always provided people with hope. The word "inspiration" literally means "in-spiriting." To be involved with some form of spirituality is to regularly experience inspiration, a sense of renewal or rejuvenation that can motivate you to persist in your efforts toward self-improvement. Spirituality doesn't take the place of doing the necessary footwork, which typically means learning concepts and skills and practicing them on a regular basis. However, it does provide the impetus to persist even when the journey gets difficult.

As anyone who has dealt with anxiety disorders knows, recovery is often fraught with setbacks. It's my impression and personal experience that working with spiritual practices such as prayer and meditation can be a very powerful way to sustain motivation in the face of these setbacks. Such practices provide ways to "keep the faith"—to keep moving forward toward your goal in spite of periods of discouragement. Sustaining faith in recovery, despite setbacks, is critical to overcoming any long-standing problem with anxiety.

Ways to Handle More Severe and Chronic Problems

Among the various anxiety disorders, some types of problems are easier to change than others. Panic disorder can often be relieved by effective cognitive behavioral therapy, sometimes with and sometimes without medication. Specific phobias can often be remedied by systematic desensitization and graded exposure. Social phobia can be overcome by effective cognitive behavioral group treatment. On the other hand, more severe cases of anxiety may show only moderate improvement in response to cognitive behavioral treatment and/or medication. For example, severe post-traumatic stress disorder or severe OCD may improve only partially in response to the best available treatment. After years of good treatment and making your best effort with cognitive behavioral approaches or medication, what do you do if you're still having some degree of difficulty? It is in this situation that I feel spirituality can have much to offer.

One thing you can do is to follow the path recommended in all of the twelve-step programs—to "turn over" your problem to the care of your Higher Power. This does not mean relinquishing your responsibility for doing what you can to help yourself. It does imply that you're willing to admit that you cannot totally resolve the issue by your own will alone. Instead, you are open to receiving assistance, support, and guidance from a Higher Source. The next chapter, "Letting Go," explores in more detail this approach of turning over a difficult problem to a Higher Power.

Another thing you can do is to visualize or affirm your ultimate recovery, despite any difficulties you currently face. This would seem to be an opposite approach to the one of letting go just described yet, in fact, it's actually complementary. The process of visualizing or affirming your healing can be empowered greatly by relying on a Higher Power to assist with the realization of your goal. The chapter "Affirming Your Recovery" describes how it's possible to create a new experience of your life, no matter how restrictive or limiting your present condition might seem.

What are the possible outcomes of relying on spiritual resources to assist in recovery? From my own experience, I believe there are two possible outcomes—an actual miracle and/or an inner transformation:

1) A miracle may happen. The problem, no matter how resistant to conventional psychotherapeutic, medication, and self-help approaches—simply goes away. It is seemingly lifted, as a result not only of your own efforts but of something more—something beyond your own effort or understanding. This may not be a very frequent phenomenon, but it does sometimes happen. Traditional Judeo-Christian religion views such miracles as "grace" or "deliverance." This kind of thing happens, for example, in spontaneous, inexplicable remissions from terminal illness. It also happens in twelve-step programs to people who felt completely defeated by their addictions prior to making a commitment to work the steps. In my own experience I've seen it happen to a few persons with long-standing anxiety problems that did not respond to any conventional forms of treatment. I also feel my own life has, to a large degree, been affected in this way, as I discussed in Chapter 1.

2) No miracle happens. Anxiety symptoms, whether in the form of panic, generalized anxiety, a particular phobia, an obsessive-compulsive problem—do not go away altogether in spite of good treatment and involvement with spirituality. However, you're able to make substantial *inner changes* in attitude that enable you to live so well with the problem that its intensity is significantly lessened. What once was a painful, seemingly insurmountable problem is now less painful—and thus less of a problem. You have developed sufficient inner peace, strength, and faith in life that you can accept your limitations with equanimity. Acceptance is not the same as resignation or fatalism. It means working with adversity as a way to deepen your relationship with your Higher Power and also to evolve as a human being. If your problem hasn't entirely gone away, despite your best efforts, you may conclude: "The lesson isn't over yet—there's more to learn by working with this limitation, either by way of healing it or accepting and transcending it (or both)." I can say that this type of outcome also applies to my personal experience with anxiety. Although I have largely recovered, there is still more work to be done.

Personality and Behavioral Changes Associated with Spirituality

Certain personality, attitudinal, and behavioral changes frequently occur in persons who have been involved with spirituality for a while. There is a field known as the "psychology of religion" which studies such changes. You would not (and probably cannot) deepen your involvement with spirituality out of a motive to "acquire" such personality changes. However, they are a natural consequence of making a long-term commitment to grow spiritually. I mention those here that I feel are particularly relevant to healing anxiety and anxiety disorders.

A Sense of Security and Safety

An abiding sense of inner security and safety can go a long way toward overcoming needless worry and the tendency to project potential catastrophe. Through developing a connection with your Higher Power, you can gain security through the conviction that you are not all alone in the universe, even at those times when you feel temporarily separated from other people. You feel increasingly safe as you come to believe that there is a source you can always turn to in times of difficulty. There is much security to be gained through the understanding that there is no problem or difficulty, however great, which cannot be resolved through the help of your Higher Power.

Peace of Mind

Peace of mind is the result of feeling a deep, abiding sense of security and safety. The more reliance and trust you develop in your Higher Power, the easier it becomes to deal with the inevitable challenges life brings without worry or fear. It's not that you give up your will to such a power; rather you learn that you can "let go" and turn to your Higher Power when you feel stuck with a problem in living and don't know how to proceed. Learning how to let go when solutions to problems aren't immediately apparent can help significantly to reduce worry and anxiety in your life (see the chapter on "Letting Go"). Peace of mind is what develops in the absence of such worry.

Ability to Gain Distance from Conditioned Emotional Reaction Patterns

Spiritual practices, particularly meditation, can help you to become more in touch with your unconditioned self. This is a deep, inner state of consciousness, beyond ego, that is always still and at peace no matter what melodramas you may be caught up with in your day-to-day life. Moving into your unconditioned self is like reaching a calm oasis beyond anything you might be anxious about. Such a state can be deliberately cultivated if you're willing to make the time for it.

Some ways to do so include meditation, quiet time devoted to inspirational reading, guided visualizations, inspirational music, or physical disciplines such as yoga or Tai Chi. See the chapter called "Developing Your Observing Self" for a more in-depth discussion of meditation.

Relinquishing the Excessive Need to Control

Worry has to do with predicting unfavorable outcomes associated with situations you can't fully control. By worrying, you provide yourself with an illusion of control. If you worry about something enough, then you feel that somehow you're not at a total loss with it—you won't be caught off guard. If you were to stop worrying, you imagine that you would give up control. Spiritual growth, regardless of the tradition or approach you follow, encourages the cultivation of a willingness to surrender control. Without relinquishing self-responsibility, you learn to allow your Higher Power to have some influence in determining the outcome of situations you feel you can't control. I believe this is one of the most important aspects of spiritual growth that can contribute to reducing anxiety. Being able, at times, to turn over your worries to a Higher Power can relieve some of the burden you think you have to carry in order to solve your problems.

Increased Self-Worth

As you develop a relationship with a Higher Power, you come to recall that you did not actually create yourself. You remember that you are a part of the universe of creation as much as the birds, stars, and trees. If this is a benign and supportive universe we live in—and developing a relationship with your Higher Power will help you to believe that it is—then, in essence, you're good, lovable, and worthy of respect just by virtue of the fact that you're here. We treat our pets with respect and love just for being who they are, yet we often fail to do so with ourselves. However you behave—whatever choices you make—you are still inherently good and worthwhile. Your own judgments of yourself, however negative, do not ultimately count if you are a creation of the universe as much as everything else. As one person humorously put it: "God doesn't make junk." (It is, of course, a mistake to assume that this type of reasoning can be used to justify ignorant or unethical behavior. It's important to keep in mind the distinction between how a person behaves and what they are in essence.)

Relaxing Perfectionistic Standards of Achievement

If your essential worth is inborn, then basing self-worth on striving to meet external standards of perfection, standards prescribed by society (i.e., perfect career, perfect house, perfect figure, perfect children, and so on) is misplaced. Socially prescribed standards are relatively superficial, and striving for them does not provide ultimate satisfaction. While it is fine to do your best in life, it's also important to affirm your intrinsic worth—who you are, apart from outer accomplishments. When people are near death, it has been found that there are only two things that they invariably feel were important about their lives: 1) learning how to love others and 2) growing in wisdom. How would your view of yourself change if you evaluated yourself by these two standards?

Increased Capacity to Give and Receive Unconditional Love

A fundamental characteristic of your Higher Power is that it offers you an experience of unconditional love. This is a kind of love that differs from romantic love or even ordinary friendship. It entails an absolute caring for the welfare of another without any conditions. That is, no matter how another person appears or acts, you have compassion and care for them without judgment. As you develop a deeper connection with your Higher Power, you come to experience greater degrees of unconditional love in your life. You feel your heart opening more easily to people and their concerns. You feel freer of judgment toward them or of making comparisons among them. Unconditional love shows up both in your increased capacity to give love to others as well as to experience more of it coming into your life. You begin to experience less fear and more joy in your life as you help to inspire others to experience their own capacity for unconditional love. This kind of love also manifests itself through the experience of having everything you need in your life to get on with what you want to do. See the chapter "Learning to Love" for further discussion of this point.

Exploring Your Own View of Spirituality

The purpose of this section is to help you better understand your own ideas and experience with spirituality. By taking time to think about your answers to the questions posed in the exercises, you may gain clarity about: 1) your own personal concept of a Higher Power or God and 2) what you might want to do, if anything, to deepen your commitment to spirituality.

What Is Your Concept of God?

One thousand years ago the medieval theologian St. Anselm argued that any concept of God is a contradiction, because God is infinite and anything that is truly infinite must be greater than any concept we can grasp. Humans nonetheless have attempted to comprehend the Divine in countless ways for thousands of years. Each of the major world religions proposes its own unique theology, attempting to answer questions both about what God is as well as the nature of our relationship as humans to God. In order to think or converse about a Higher Power at all, it seems necessary to have *some* concept about what God is, even if it's very approximate and incomplete.

A detailed excursion into the subject of theology is beyond the scope of this book. From the standpoint of overcoming fear, merely *having* a belief in a Higher Power is important. To embrace such a belief can give life a new dimension of meaning. You begin to trust that there is something beyond surface appearances—beyond your own little, everyday melodramas. When you have exhausted all your options and feel up against a wall in life, there is a higher resource you can turn to. You feel less alone in the universe. In short, *that* you believe in a Higher Power is more important than how you conceive of such a power.

Nevertheless, I am going to describe briefly some of the polarities that have traditionally influenced discussions about the nature of God. I do so in order to assist you in clarifying your own ideas about your Higher Power. If these distinctions help you to reflect on and clarify your own ideas about deity, they will have served their purpose.

Historically, deity has been conceptualized through four contrasting polarities. (A great deal of religious persecution has occurred and even wars waged around these differing views of God.)

- Theistic vs. Nontheistic

- Personal vs. Impersonal

- Monotheistic vs. Polytheistic

- Immanent vs. Transcendent

Let's consider each one:

Theistic vs. Nontheistic

Theistic views of God use a personal name to refer to Divinity: God, Allah, Yahweh, Brahma, Heavenly Father, Lord, etc. The use of a name doesn't necessarily imply that God is like a person. Yet there is an implication that the Divine is in some respects a being, although perhaps not in any way we can understand the notion "being." If the Divine were equated with a "being" in the usual sense, it would be difficult to see how it could be infinite or without limits. What kind of a being could be infinite?

Perhaps the most important implication of personal names such as God or Allah is the possibility of a personal experience and, in fact, a personal relationship with the Divine. It is the personal aspect of the Divine that permits us to have a personal encounter and intimate connection with a Higher Power. This can provide tremendous support, peace, and guidance in the face of difficult life circumstances. In short, theistic concepts point to the potential of a personal relationship with a Power greater than ourselves—not like a human relationship, but a relationship nonetheless.

In other contexts the words "Spirit," "Cosmic Consciousness," "Ground of Being," "the Absolute," "the Infinite," "Essence," or even "the Void" are used to refer to the Divine. These words seem to speak of a concept of deity having attributes that are nonpersonal, transpersonal, beyond something humans can personally relate to or even comprehend. If the Divine is truly infinite and beyond anything we can conceive, then nontheistic terms would seem very appropriate. Such terms are capable of more fully encompassing everything that the Divine might be. God's personal aspect (which we refer to by a personal name) is probably the most important characteristic of deity to us humans. Yet it's unlikely to fully contain all that Divinity is. Words like "Spirit," "Essence," and "the Absolute" are more open-ended—they leave more room for a deity of infinite proportions.

Personal vs. Impersonal

This polarity echoes the previous one. You can have a personal relationship with your Higher Power, and yet the full compass of Deity likely goes beyond your relationship with it. Deity may reveal itself to you in a highly personal way, and yet Deity itself, in its mysterious and intrinsic nature, may be impersonal or transpersonal.

Monotheistic vs. Polytheistic

Ancient peoples such as the ancient Egyptians, Greeks, Romans, and Celts worshipped a pantheon of deities. There were gods of love, war, the sea, earth, the underworld, knowledge, the bounty of nature, and on and on. Some people even attributed deities to every local mountain, hill, and sacred place. "Sub-deity" beings (for lack of a better word) such as elves, fairies, rock spirits, and tree spirits abounded throughout many traditions. In addition to Jesus and Mary, Catholics have worshipped archangels, angels, and saints. Hindus have worshipped Shiva, Vishnu, and a host of other deities.

All of these polytheistic notions conceive of the Divine as a plurality. Often these pluralistic concepts coexist with a monotheistic one. The Greeks placed Zeus above the other gods; native Americans place the Great Spirit above the spirits of the wind, earth, fire, and directions. Catholics place God and Christ above the archangels and angels. Hindus place Brahma above all other deities.

In recent years there has been a resurgence of interest in polytheistic approaches to the Divine. For example, there has been a revival of interest in the pantheon of Celtic deities among people who want to celebrate the spirituality of the earth and view God as present in all aspects of nature. Other people have sought to revive an interest in angels and archangels. At least a dozen recent books have explored the various types and functions of angels.

Some people give these polytheistic notions precedence; others see them as coexisting with a monotheistic view of Deity. Such popular expressions as "It all goes back to the Source," or "We're all one" convey this idea of relating the many spirits to the One Spirit.

Immanent vs. Transcendent

This polarity is related to the previous one. If you believe somehow that there is a spiritual force in every rock, tree, and mountain (that deity is immanent in nature) then you may perceive the Divine as a multiplicity that "inspires" every physical thing in creation. The philosopher Spinoza conceived of the world in this way. So did most native Americans. A well-known spiritually based community in Scotland, called Findhorn, revived this form of animism in recent times by claiming to actually communicate with the spirits of individual plants, as well as archetypal spirits that oversee an entire plant or animal species, what they called *devas*.

The transcendent view of the Divine, on the other hand, is reflected in the Buddhist notion that the ultimate transcends everything that exists and everything we can conceive that exists. Nirvana, or the Great Formless Reality, lies beyond all manifest creation, and beyond even the potential or archetypal forms of what might exist. Christianity leans toward a transcendent view of God, maintaining that God is totally beyond the natural and human order of things. And yet it allows for the immanence of God in believing that the Holy Spirit is able to enter into human awareness and inspire us.

Where do you stand on these contrasting views of Deity?

In my own attempts to reckon with the nature of the Divine, I've thought a lot about these dichotomies. After some years I've come to two conclusions:

1. In some way, both sides of each polarity are true.

2. The seeming contradictions between the polarities are only seeming. We humans find it hard to conceive of our world except in terms of dualities. However, on the level at which the Divine exists, there are no dualities—the Divine itself is beyond duality.

A useful metaphor that has helped me to resolve some of the seeming contradictions is the notion of a *holographic universe*, intimated by the late physicist David Bohm (1993). According to Bohm, all of the separate things we perceive in the physical world constitute what he calls the "explicate order." However, these various things are all enfolded into one another in a way that renders them "all one." The level on which this happens is beyond our perception and construction of a three-dimensional universe. Bohm refers to this level as the "implicate order." Bohm's ideas are not philosophical speculations but constructs that help to explain the phenomena of modern quantum physics. Though not yet fully substantiated, there is actually some empirical evidence to support Bohm's view that the universe is organized holographically. (Bohm prefers to describe the universe as a "holomovement," since viewing it as a hologram is artificially static. A popular explanation of Bohm's ideas, making them available to the public, can be found in Michael Talbot's book *The Holographic Universe* [1992].)

If everything that exists is organized like a hologram, the implications are remarkable to the point of defying comprehension. One of the most fundamental aspects of a holographic image is that every part contains the information from the whole. If the entire universe is organized holographically, that means everything, including you, me, and the neighbor's cat, implicitly contains the whole. We're all enfolded through the implicate order back into one. In a sense, we're all emanations or permutations of one singular reality.

If you believe this, it doesn't really matter whether you want to emphasize polytheistic vs. monotheistic or immanent vs. transcendent views of the Divine. Such dualities are humanly constructed distinctions. In a holographic universe they don't exist. The many aren't really distinct from the One, because each of the many is simply another permutation of the Whole. Spirit is both immanent and transcendent since, ultimately, the distinction doesn't exist. So you can let go, and enjoy whatever construct of the Divine makes you most comfortable. All of the distinctions can be understood as different facets of the same crystal—different views of the same elephant.

YOUR CONCEPT AND RELATIONSHIP WITH A HIGHER POWER

Reflect on the following questions. Write your responses in the spaces provided or on a separate sheet of paper.

1. What does the idea of God or a Higher Power mean to you personally?

2. Describe the attributes defining your notion of God, Spirit, or a Higher Power. When you think about the nature of God, what ideas and images come to mind?

3. Do you experience a personal, conscious connection with your Higher Power? How have you experienced this connection?

4. What obstacles do you feel interfere with your acceptance and/or experience of a Higher Power?

5. What would you hope to gain by developing and/or deepening your connection with a Higher Power?

What Personal Experiences Speak to You of the Presence of the Divine?

If you feel you already have a personal relationship with your Higher Power or God, how do you experience it? As you think back over your life, perhaps you can recall times when you felt inspired, moved, or uplifted beyond your everyday awareness. These are moments when you felt touched by something larger than yourself or believed there might be more to life than meets the eye.

SPIRITUAL EXPERIENCES

Write your responses to the following questions in the spaces provided or on a separate sheet of paper.

1. What situations, places, persons, activities, or events give you a feeling of inspiration? A feeling of wonder or awe?

2. Which of the following experiences do you consider to be "spiritual"? Write down an example of an inspiring experience you had in each case.

   Natural beauty
   (A place or occasion in nature that filled you with awe or wonder)

   Deep insight
   (A sudden recognition of something you knew to be true)

   Creative inspiration
   (Something creative you felt genuinely inspired to do)

   Expressions of love received or given
   (Indicate when and with whom)

3. The following experiences are commonly thought to be spiritual. Describe any of your own personal experiences that apply.

   Receiving answers to prayers

   Synchronicities (uncanny coincidences)

   Guidance

Miracles

4. Mystical or visionary experiences—describe instances where you experienced any of the following:

Feeling supported by a loving presence

A sudden feeling of peace in the midst of turmoil

A sense of the oneness of everything—or of yourself being one with or part of everything

Experiencing an infusion of light that led to a feeling of peace, bliss, or joy

Witnessing a spiritual being or presence (i.e., angels, Jesus, or other figures within your particular spiritual tradition)

Other (any other experience you consider to be a direct manifestation of your Higher Power)

How Can You Deepen Your Connection with Your Higher Power?

Cultivating a relationship with your Higher Power is in some ways similar to developing a relationship with another person. The more time and energy you give to it, the closer and deeper the relationship becomes. If you're willing to give such a relationship high priority, it will develop into an important part of your everyday life.

Among the many ways to spend time cultivating spirituality, five most common and widely practiced methods include:

Prayer—a way of actively communicating with your Higher Power, usually in the form of a request. Sometimes you may ask for a particular quality such as strength, peace, or clarity. Other times you may ask for your Higher Power simply to be present in a particular situation. Or you may relinquish a problem to God without asking for anything in particular.

Meditation—a practice of becoming quiet to the point that you get in touch with a deeper part of your inner being, one that is nonreactive, beyond conditioning, and ultimately in tune with your Higher Power. Meditation is a way to learn to disidentify with self-limiting emotions and thoughts so that you can witness rather than react to them. For thousands of years, meditation has been a way to "still the mind" and directly access the "kingdom of heaven within." (See the earlier chapter, "Developing Your Observing Self.)

Reading spiritual literature—reading uplifting spiritual books (or listening to tapes) is a wonderful way to move away from worry or a negative mind-set. You can choose from traditional sacred books such as the Bible or a wide range of contemporary books. A list of my personal favorites can be found in Appendix 4.

Spiritual fellowship—remembering the sacred in the presence of others is a common and powerful way to renew your connection with God. This can happen through church attendance, spiritual classes and workshops, or sacred rituals (see below).

Compassionate service—serving others out of a genuine motive to help. This can be volunteer work or just simple acts of kindness to others in day-to-day life.

There are many other ways of cultivating a relationship with your Higher Power that have developed out of specific religious traditions and affiliations. Some of the most common ones include:

- Twelve-step work—attending twelve-step groups and working the steps to overcome specific addictions

- Listening to sacred music—classical or modern

- Sacred singing or chanting (e.g., joining a church choir)

- Sacred dance (e.g., Sufi dancing)

- Guided visualizations

- Working with spiritual affirmations (see the chapter "Affirming Your Recovery")

- Attending classes or workshops on religious topics

All of these activities may contribute to strengthening and deepening your relationship with your Higher Power. If you're ready to make a commitment to cultivating a deeper relationship with your Higher Power, complete the following exercise.

SPIRITUAL PRACTICES

Reflect on the following questions and write your responses in the spaces provided or on a separate sheet of paper.

1. Do you pray? How often? With what effect?

2. Do you meditate? How often? For how long? With what effect?

3. Do you read religious or inspirational teachings? How often? With what effect?

4. Do you engage in any other spiritual practices (e.g., chanting, rituals, singing, dancing, vision quests, etc.)? How often? With what effect?

5. Are you involved with a church, center, or other spiritually based group of people? How often are you in contact with this group? What do you get out of it?

In the space below, write a statement of commitment to yourself. Which of the above activities you would be willing, in the next month, to give more of your time?

Everyday Uplifts

If Spirit is truly everywhere and ever present, it can be found in many ordinary activities of daily life, provided you are open and aware. Any of the following common activities may help you to connect with spirituality. Each provides a way to move into a place larger than your worries and personal dramas.

1. Take a walk outdoors—rain or shine. Experiencing the open space of outdoors, beyond the four walls of work or home, can provide an immediate uplift (especially if away from concrete and cars).

2. Walk near water. Whether waves, ripples, or rapids, there is something quite soothing to the soul in a natural body of water.

3. Get up to watch the sunrise (or wait to watch the sunset). The magnificence of a sky full of colors is well known for its ability to inspire.

4. Visit an art museum. Exploring the inner world of great artists can touch aspects of your soul otherwise unknown.

5. Listen to great classical music. The best-known works of Bach, Mozart, Beethoven, and Brahms are particularly inspiring.

6. Visit historic sites. Looking backward in time may give you an entirely new perspective on the present.

7. Watch a great movie. The best movies have the capacity to move you to a higher plane of consciousness. Many of the greatest films have

won "best picture" Oscars or were nominated for the same. This is a good idea for an uplift during inclement weather.

8. Read a short, inspirational statement. Your local bookstore is full of pocket-sized books that offer daily meditations or affirmations.

9. Play with a pet. The unconditional love of an animal can help you to remember that capacity within yourself.

10. Hug your children. Children remind you to love at those times when you least expect to.

11. Make something with your hands. Creativity is the soul's expression in material form. Whether a model airplane, a garden, a pie, or a painting, a creative project is an excellent way to move into a larger space within yourself.

12. Perform an act of kindness. Helping someone else overcomes self-absorption. When done from the heart, it will inevitably lighten your soul.

Twelve Ideas Regarding Spirituality: A Personal View

The purpose of this chapter is to invite you to enlarge your view of life by exploring your ideas and experiences regarding spirituality. You may, of course, already have a well-defined understanding of spirituality—or you may still be searching to know more. In either case, *by embracing a spiritual view of life, you can reframe the way you perceive your own difficulties with fear or anxiety.* Spirituality can offer insights both into the meaning of your problem with anxiety as well as how to go about healing it.

If you are still exploring what spirituality means, I offer the following twelve ideas to stimulate your thinking. If you've read the chapter on spirituality from *The Anxiety & Phobia Workbook* (1995), you will recognize many of them. These ideas are not taken from any one source, tradition, or creed, but are based on my own personal experience. They have been useful points of departure for discussion with a number of my clients. You may or may not agree with them. As you read through the ideas, give consideration to those that fit or make sense to you and feel free to discard those that do not. Each of us has a basic philosophy about life, which we have to formulate on our own.

Some of these ideas may stimulate questions that you may want to discuss with a significant other, a trusted friend, or even a minister, priest, or rabbi.

All of these ideas can lead to a more optimistic and tolerant view of life. They have done this for me personally. As you adopt any of these ideas that fit for you, you may find your attitude about your condition—as well as life in general—becoming a little more positive and less burdensome.

1. *Life is a school. The primary meaning and purpose of life is that it is a "classroom" for growth in consciousness.*

Most people tend to define their life's meaning in terms of those people, activities, self-images, or objects to which they attach the greatest value. Whatever you value most in life—whether family, another individual, work, a particular role or self-image, your health, or material possessions—these things are probably what define your life's meaning. If you lost what you valued the most, your life might seem to lose its meaning. Think for a moment about what you value most highly in your life and what gives you the greatest satisfaction and comfort. Then imagine what your life would be like if these things were all suddenly taken away.

The truth, of course, is that everything you value most *will* eventually pass away. Nothing that you cherish lasts forever. Yet if everything you value must someday cease to be, what is the *ultimate* meaning of life? And as long as you assume that there is nothing more to existence than your present life—what there is right now—then there doesn't seem to be *any* ultimate meaning. You end up saying (along with Jean-Paul Sartre and other existentialists) that the only meaning life has is what you make of it in the present moment. Apart from this, life appears to have no meaning in and of itself. Since everything, including life itself, eventually passes away, how can there be any ultimate point to any of it?

Most forms of spirituality, traditional and modern, move beyond this existential predicament. Most of them make some kind of assumption that human life is not all there is. Something of us persists beyond human life, and so life comes to be seen as a temporary sojourn—not the final destination. Life comes to be understood as a preparation or training ground for something else that cannot be fully understood or revealed while you're alive.

It is this particular interpretation of life's "ultimate" meaning that I found to be most valid and helpful. If the final meaning of life is that it is a classroom or school for growth in consciousness—for the development of wisdom and the capacity to love—then the fact that everything passes away takes on an entirely new meaning. The tasks and challenges that come up in life, and your response to them, do not have eternal repercussions. Nor do they have no meaning at all. They are more like lessons in a school, lessons to which you apply yourself, and which you try to master as best you can. Each lesson is repeated until it's mastered. As you master old lessons, new ones are put before you. This "earth school" is thus a place where you learn and grow; it's not your final dwelling place. Eventually it's time to leave this classroom and move on.

2. *Adversity and difficult situations are lessons designed for your growth—they are not random, capricious acts of fate. In the larger scheme of things, everything happens for a purpose.*

If you accept the idea that life is a classroom, then the adversity and difficulties that come into your life may be viewed as part of the curriculum—as lessons for growth. This is a very different point of view from one that sees life's misfortunes as random quirks of fate. The latter perspective leads to a sense of victimization. You can end up feeling powerless in a capricious world that appears to be completely inequitable in its treatment of people, some of whom have such good luck, while others have misfortune heaped upon them.

The view proposed here is that the difficulties of life are lessons to promote growth in wisdom, compassion, love, and other positive qualities (some religious traditions refer to "tests," although I prefer the notion of "lessons"). The greater the difficulty, the greater the potential for learning and growth. If you accept this idea, then the next question you may ask is who established the curriculum or "assigns" your life lessons? Many of us may ask this question in one form or another when a given life challenge seems particularly difficult. We tend to protest and even rail against some of the misfortunes and limitations we're faced with. The question arises: "How could a loving God permit this?"

There is no easy answer to this question. None of us can fully understand how our life lessons are administered and assigned, though different spiritual traditions have different views on this matter (Eastern traditions speak of "karma," while Judeo-Christian traditions speak of "tests" and "temptations"). Each of us has to struggle with the challenges life brings without fully understanding why. What does seem apparent is that growth could not occur if the lessons were always easy. If the purpose of life is for us to grow in wisdom, consciousness, and compassion, then at least some of the lessons need to be difficult. This may not be an altogether consoling view, but it at least makes some sense out of the difficult situations that occur in life.

Given this view, you can stop asking, "Why did this happen to me?" and instead ask the more constructive questions: "What is this meant to teach me? How can I learn from this?" You might take whatever worry or concern is bothering you most in your life at this time and try asking the latter two questions instead of the first.

3. *Your personal limitations and flaws are the "grist" you have to work with for your inner growth. Sometimes you can heal and overcome them with modest effort. In other cases, they may stay with you for a long time in order to push you to evolve and develop to your fullest potential. You are not "wrong" or in any way to blame because of your limitations.*

Think for a moment about some of your own personal limitations—the ones you find most difficult to live with. If you're dealing with an anxiety disorder, think about your condition. You may ask why anyone should have to deal with a difficult condition such as panic disorder, agoraphobia, social phobia, or an obsessive-compulsive disorder even for a few months, let alone a longer time. Hopefully you have utilized all of the best treatments—including medication, if necessary—and have experienced a significant and genuine recovery. In many cases, a full recovery from an anxiety disorder is certainly possible. Suppose, however, that you have received all the best treatments, worked very hard for one or two years, and have experienced *some* improvement—yet you're still dealing with your condition to a degree. Is that a reason for you to think of yourself as a failure? A reason to think that you are somehow less skillful or persistent than those people who overcame their condition quickly?

If you've worked hard on overcoming your condition, but are still troubled by it, perhaps there is some significant growth experience to find in the process of having to work with your difficulty for a long time. It all depends upon the lesson you happen to be learning. Having a difficult condition that is easily dispensed within a short time would certainly help develop your confidence in your own self-mastery—an important lesson in itself. Yet it wouldn't necessarily develop qualities of compassion or patience. It often seems that only through having to struggle with our own infirmities for a time can we learn fully how to feel compassion or have patience with others' difficulties.

As a second example, suppose that your lesson is to learn how to let go of the excessive need for control—even more, to learn how to let go and allow your Higher Power or God to have an impact on your life. One way (not the only way) this might be learned is to have to deal with a difficult situation in which all your efforts to control just don't work. The ability to let go of control is often fostered by those very difficulties in life that are most challenging. Some conditions and situations are so challenging that they *compel* us to let go. There is no other alternative. To struggle or fight against the condition only creates more distress and suffering. It is often at the exact moment when you fully let go of your worry or stop struggling that you may experience some kind of response or relief from your Higher Power. To let go and trust in your Higher Power should not be thought of as foregoing responsibility for your life. Rather, it involves doing all you can to help yourself first, while at the same time turning things over to another source of assistance.

In sum, it's a mistake to fault yourself for having any intractable condition, no matter how disabling or how long you've had it. It is there to foster and deepen certain qualities of your inner self. *How you respond to it and what you learn from it is what's important—not the condition itself.*

4. *Your life has a creative purpose and mission. There is something creative that is yours to develop and offer.*

Your life is not a random sequence of accidental events—it follows a plan. This plan is created from a level that none of us can fully understand. Part of this plan consists of the lessons for growth in consciousness that were described in the preceding three sections.

Another very important aspect of the plan is your creative endowments, talents, or "gifts." Each of us has at least one personal form of creativity that can give our life meaning and purpose. The development and full expression of your creative talents and gifts is your "life purpose" or "life mission" spoken of in Chapter 10 of this book.

Your life purpose is something that you feel you *need* to do in order to feel whole, complete, and fulfilled in your life. It's uniquely your own—something that can't be duplicated. Only you can do it. It comes from within, and has nothing to do with what your parents, partner, or friends might want you to do. Generally it moves you beyond yourself and has an impact on something or someone else.

Your purpose or mission can be a vocation or avocation—its scope can extend to the entire world or to just one other person. Examples would include: raising a family, mastering a musical instrument, volunteering your services to help youth or the elderly, writing poems, speaking eloquently before groups, or tending the garden in your backyard.

Until you develop and express your creative gifts, your life will seem incomplete. You will feel more anxiety because you're not making time to do what you truly want to do, what you were in fact born to do. See the chapter "Finding Your Unique Purpose" for further discussion of these ideas and guidelines for discovering your own special purpose.

5. *A Higher Source of support and guidance is always available.*

This idea is at the basis of much of this chapter. Fear and anxiety are based on the perception that you are separate and alone—or else on the anticipation of rejection or loss that might eventually result in being separate and alone. The truth is that you're not alone. Even at those times when you might find it difficult to turn to other human beings for support, there remains another source of support that can always be called on. Your Higher Power is not merely an abstract entity that created and sustains the universe. It is a force, power, or presence with which you can enter into a personal relationship. This relationship is as personal as any you could have with another human being.

In this personal relationship, you can experience both *support* and *guidance*. Support often appears in the form of inspiration or enthusiasm that can help lift and sustain you at times of low motivation and discouragement. Guidance can come in the form of clear insights and intuitions that provide discrimination and direction about what you need to do. Frequently this type of inspired insight or realization is wiser than anything you might have figured out with your rational mind.

You may experience a dilemma about this. If you think of inspiration and intuition originating in your own subconscious mind, how do they come then from a Higher Power—from something seemingly separate from you? Certainly from the perspective of the conscious mind, everything does seem separate—you perceive yourself as separate from others, the world, and most likely from a Higher Power. There is another level, though, that the conscious mind can't comprehend, where all things are joined. Eastern philosophy refers to this as "the One in which all things reside." The modern physicist David Bohm speaks of the "implicate order" in which everything is connected. In the Bible (New Testament) this idea is expressed in the statement: "The Kingdom of Heaven is within you."

To receive support and guidance from your Higher Power, you simply need to ask. Nothing more is necessary. While this might seem easy enough, it may not be in practice if you believe that you're supposed to figure out and handle everything entirely on your own. Or it may not be easy if you feel that it's irrational, weak, or in some other way beneath your dignity to rely on an invisible power for support. To trust and rely on your Higher Power, it takes a certain willingness to let go of control as well as a certain humility (it's often humbling to come to the realization that you can't handle something completely on your own). The ability to let go and trust is something that can be learned. Often the life lessons that are the hardest—the ones that push you to your absolute limit—tend to be the ones that have the most to teach about letting go.

As you increasingly learn to allow your Higher Power (Spirit) to assist in your life, you can grow in trusting that it is sometimes appropriate to relinquish control. Chapter 12, "Letting Go," explores this point further.

6. *Contact with your Higher Power is directly available within your personal experience.*

You can discover a personal relationship with your Higher Power within your own immediate experience. It is a two-way relationship—you can receive support, guidance, inspiration, peace of mind, inner strength, hope, and many other gifts from your Higher Power; you can also communicate your needs to Spirit through prayer, and directly communicate feelings of gratitude and reverence. Such a relationship can deepen and grow to the extent that you choose to give it attention and time.

There are numerous ways in which your Higher Power can manifest itself in your personal experience. Feelings of awe in the presence of nature, a deep insight that seems to come out of nowhere, synchronicities (uncanny coincidences), a sudden feeling of support in times of turmoil, and small miracles are some of the more common types of spiritual experience. See the exercise called "Spiritual Experiences" earlier in this chapter to explore your own experiences with spirituality.

7. *Questions sincerely asked of your Higher Power are answered.*

This idea is really an extension of the previous point about your Higher Power being a source of support and guidance. The point is emphasized to underscore the fact that your Higher Power's support and guidance is not only bestowed on you—you can deliberately ask for it. The famous quote of Jesus, "Ask and you shall receive," is true regardless of the particular spiritual tradition or orientation you follow.

It is the assumption of all religious approaches that incorporate prayer that prayer will be answered. Perhaps you have had experiences of your prayers being answered. It often seems that the degree of earnestness of your request has something to do with how readily the prayer receives a response. A common example is when you feel overwhelmed with some situation and you almost literally cry out for help to your Higher Power. In many cases, something about the situation improves or shifts, often within a short time.

There is actually scientific research that confirms the efficacy of prayer. Several well-controlled empirical studies of prayer are reported in the book *Recovering the Soul: A Scientific and Spiritual Search* by Larry Dossey (1989).

In sum, there is both anecdotal and research support for the idea that prayer is effective. This doesn't mean that whatever you pray for will come true. There are some qualifications that, I've discovered in my experience, need to be kept in mind: 1) the request needs to be made with genuine earnestness and sincerity, 2) the "answer" or response to prayer may not come immediately—it may take days, weeks, or months, 3) the answer may not come all at once—instead, only a step in the direction of the answer may come (for example, if you're praying for healing from chronic pain, the answer may come in the form of a strong intuition to visit a particular doctor or healing practitioner). Prayer can be answered in many ways, and sometimes the answer may not be what you expected. It's not possible to know in advance how a particular prayer will be answered (that is where faith comes in). What can be trusted is that there will be an answer, and that the answer will serve your highest good.

8. *What you truly ask for or intend from the deepest level of yourself—from your heart—will tend to come to you.*

One of the most powerful things that can foster positive change and healing is a sincerely held intention. With clients, and in my own experience, I have observed how the power of intention can promote miraculous consequences. What you believe in and commit to with your whole heart tends to come true. When the intention is for your own highest good—and when it doesn't conflict with anyone else's highest good—it is most likely to become manifest.

A deeply held intention shifts and focuses your own consciousness. It also appears to have ramifications on events in the world apart from you. Events in the outer world will tend to align with your most deeply held intention. Goethe summed this up in his famous remark:

Concerning all acts of initiative or creation,
there is one elementary truth;
the ignorance of which kills countless ideas and splendid plans.

The moment one definitely commits oneself,
then Providence moves too.

All sorts of things occur to help one
that would never otherwise have occurred.

A whole stream of events issue from the decision,
raising in one's favor
all manner of unforeseen incidents and assistance,
which no person could have dreamt
would have come their way.

A positive belief in your ability to recover from anxiety will not only help your mood and perception of your situation—it will actually help draw to you the healing you seek. The idea that you can actually create a positive reality in accord with your beliefs is explored in detail in the chapter "Affirming Your Recovery."

9. *Each of us is an individualized expression of Spirit.*

There is an aspect of your innermost being that is connected with and is an extension of All Being. This aspect has been referred to as the "Self" (or "Atman") in Eastern philosophy. Many people in the West have called it the "soul." Transpersonal psychology refers to it as the "Higher Self." The Higher Self is understood as an individualized or personalized aspect of Universal Spirit that is at the very center of your being. In short, each of us, at our core, is an individualized expression of the One Spirit that exists in all things. Each of us is a drop in the ocean that is God.

It's important to add that your conscious, ego self or personality is not a direct extension of God. It can be disturbing to hear people say they are "ultimately one with God" and then imagine they are talking about their personal ego. (Many would call that blasphemous.) Your *conscious self* (personality) is instead a complex series of concepts, memories, habits, and images that you have created over a lifetime. *Who you think you are* is something you've learned and created—it's not who you *essentially* are. The part of you that is connected with God is mostly unconscious and tends to emerge only in moments of heightened awareness or deep meditation. The "I" that can observe "me" or reflect on "who I am" lies closer to that inner core of being that is a part of Spirit.

10. *Evil is not a separate force but a misuse of one's creative power.*

When you're separated or alienated from your innermost being, what you create—in your mind as well as in your physical reality—is not likely to be in complete harmony or to completely fulfill you. Such creations are out of step with your essence and therefore the essence of all things. To the extent that you are out of alignment with your true self, you may create self-limiting situations in your life. Since no one is perfect, this happens, to varying degrees, to everyone. Life for everyone is a mix of affirmation and restriction, light and dark, or what we label "good" and "evil." Without these polarities, life would not allow for learning. There is no way to learn what light really is without darkness—or what love and beauty truly are without fear and ugliness. A life without polarities or contrasts would not offer much opportunity to grow. If life truly is a school, polarities are likely to be a necessary part of it.

"Evil" is not an inherent force separate from and against God. (If this were so, God could not be infinite, as something else would exist outside of and independent of God.) It is instead a misuse of our creative power when we make choices that are not in step with our innermost self—our soul. This leads to outcomes that are contrary to our highest good, which is the same as our well-being, happiness, and fulfillment. If we choose to do our *highest* good, we are naturally fulfilled—there can be no disappointment in the outcome. All other choices outside of this may bring relative degrees of satisfaction and/or suffering, either of which lasts only for a while. We are not punished by an angry God for our mistakes; instead, we reap negative consequences—sooner or later—as a result of our own actions that are out of step with our Higher Self (and thus the universe). To err is simply not to be true to your own deepest self.

"Evil" is a relative term—it is a matter of degree. Eating food that is not healthful may be out of alignment with your true self, but would not usually be called evil. Neither would unintentionally causing an accident that hurts someone else. Actions labeled evil (for example, serious crimes) are usually deliberate and grossly out of alignment with the perpetrator's innermost being or soul. If, as has been said, "we are all one," or "joined at the highest level," to willfully do harm to another is to harm oneself, and all of Being. In the

Bible, Christ says: "Even as you do it unto the least of them, you do it unto Me." In time one will eventually reap the fruits of one's actions. In Eastern philosophy this is spoken of as "karma." In the Bible it is said, "As you sow, so shall you reap." Although God is not wrathful or punitive, there is a law of conservation in the universe whereby each of us will, sooner or later, absorb the effects of our actions, for better or for worse.

We "should" therefore want to do what is our highest good—what we can intuitively discern to be our highest good—*not* because we should do it in any *moral* sense, but because our highest good is always what we truly *want* in our deepest, innermost self anyway. If there is any ethical imperative, it is to do what our innermost being or soul truly wants. As Shakespeare put it: "This above all—to thine own self be true." When you're in doubt about how to do that, the operative question is, *"What is the most loving thing I can do, both for myself and others?"*

11. *Love is stronger than fear. Pure, unconditional love emanates from your Higher Power and is at the very center of your being and all beings. All fears can be understood as different forms of separation—separation from others, ourselves, and God—separation from the love that unites all things.*

Love is stronger than fear because it goes deeper. Consciously love is the experience of feeling your heart go out toward unity with someone or something other than yourself. On a deeper level, love is the "ground state" or essential foundation of the entire universe. This is a view that is common both to Eastern and Western religions. Love isn't something we either possess or don't possess, because it literally *defines* what we are at our core and in essence. Fear may go deep, but never as deep as love, because fear only arises when we feel separate from the ground state that unifies us with everything else.

Most of the anxiety you experience may be related to specific fears of abandonment, rejection and humiliation, loss of control, confinement, injury, or death. Fear can take on any of these forms, based on your conditioning and past experience. Yet none of these fears could ever arise if you did not experience separation. The existence of fear always points to a degree of separation—separation of your conscious mind from your innermost being, separation from others, and/or separation from God. If it's true that in essence all of us are united as one, then every fear we feel—no matter how much we believe it—is, in fact, just an illusion. If we could perceive things the way they truly are, there would be no reason to have any more fear.

Love and fear constitute perhaps the most profound duality in human existence. Yet the former can always overcome the latter.

12. *Death is not an end but a transition. Our essential nature or soul survives physical death. (To fear death as "the end" is simply an illusion.)*

This basic idea is shared by all of the world's religions. They all assume that an individual's soul continues to exist after physical death, although they differ somewhat in their conceptions about the nature of the afterlife.

Actual evidence for this view has emerged in the past fifteen years from the widespread research on "near-death experiences." As you most likely already know, near-death experiences are based on reports of what people experienced between the time when their vital signs indicated imminent or clinical death and when they were subsequently revived. These reports all share several things, such as passing through a tunnel, meeting a being of light that radiates love and understanding, witnessing a scene-by-scene review of one's entire life, and sometimes meeting relatives who've already died. A smaller number of these reports describe otherworldly scenes and locales. Though the thousands of such reports that have been collected worldwide don't "prove" that consciousness survives death, they certainly make a strong case in that direction. Further evidence that near-death survivors get a peek into an afterlife comes from the fact that many of them lose their fear of death and become more deeply spiritual following their experience.

Does fear of death come up for you or underlie other fears you might have about illness or injury? If so, I would suggest that you read the literature on near-death experiences and come to your own conclusions about life after death. The book *Life After Life* (1976) by Raymond Moody is a good start, but I would especially recommend the book *Heading Toward Omega* by Kenneth Ring (1985).

YOUR PERSONAL SPIRITUAL BELIEF SYSTEM

Allow the preceding twelve spiritual ideas to be a springboard for reflecting on your own spiritual beliefs and convictions.

Of these twelve ideas, which ones do you find helpful? Are there any with which you disagree? How would believing these ideas change your view of your anxiety condition? Your view of life in general? You may wish to discuss some of these ideas with a significant other, a trusted friend, or a minister, priest, or rabbi.

The twelve ideas are briefly restated below:

Twelve Ideas Associated with Spirituality

1. Much of what we experience in life consists of lessons for our spiritual progress. Life can be understood as a "school" for spiritual growth.

2. Adversity and difficult situations in life are not random acts of fate—they are part of a larger purpose.

3. Personal limitations (including physical or mental disabilities) are not "bad luck" but challenges to be used for personal and spiritual growth.

4. Each individual's life has a creative purpose and mission.

5. A Higher Source of support and guidance is always available to us.

6. Contact with your Higher Power is directly available within your personal experience.

7. Questions sincerely asked of your Higher Power are answered.

8. Our beliefs and expectations create our reality in life. You will attract to yourself what you truly want.

9. Each of us (our souls, not our minds or egos) is an individualized expression of the Universal Spirit (God).

10. Evil is not a separate force in the universe but a misuse of human beings' creative power.

11. Love is stronger than—and can overcome—any fear.

12. Death is not the end of our existence. Some aspect of each of us (our soul) survives and continues on after physical death.

What You Can Do Now

1. Go back through the chapter and work through those exercises that are personally meaningful to you.

2. Make a commitment to add one spiritual activity or practice (for example, prayer or inspirational reading) to your daily routine starting this week.

3. Make your own list of inspirational books to read, drawing from your own religious tradition, from the list which follows, or from Appendix 4. Read one book each month.

References and Further Reading

Bohm, David, and Hiley Basil. 1993. *The Undivided Universe: An Ontological Interpretation of Quantum Theory*. New York: Routledge.

Chopra, Deepak. 1994. *The Seven Spiritual Laws of Success*. San Rafael, Calif.: New World Library.

Dossey, Larry. 1989. *Recovering the Soul: A Scientific and Spiritual Search*. New York: Bantam.

Harmon, Willis. 1988. *Global Mind Change*. New York: Warner Books.

Moody, Raymond. 1976. *Life After Life*. New York: Bantam.

Norwood, Robin. 1994. *Why Me, Why This, Why Now*. New York: Carol Southern Books.

Peck, Scott. 1978. *The Road Less Traveled*. New York: Simon & Schuster.

———. 1993. *Further Along the Road Less Traveled*. New York: Simon & Schuster.

Ring, Kenneth. 1985. *Heading Toward Omega*. New York: William Morrow.

Rodegast, Pat. 1985. *Emmanuel's Book*. New York: Bantam.

———. 1989. *Emmanuel's Book, II*. New York: Bantam.

Talbot, Michael. 1992. *The Holographic Universe*. New York: HarperCollins.

Walsh, Neale. 1996. *Conversations with God (Book I)*. New York: Putnam.

Williamson, Marianne. 1994. *Illuminata*. New York: Random House.

Zukav, Gary. 1990. *The Seat of the Soul*. New York: Fireside Books.

12

Letting Go

Most people are confronted at some time in their life with experiences that leave them feeling frightened, vulnerable, or powerless. Frequently these unpredictable events occur in childhood, such as the death or illness of a relative, the daily unpredictability of living with an alcoholic parent, or perhaps having to move frequently and change schools. In the process of trying to cope with such circumstances, it's common to acquire a strong need to maintain control, both of your environment and yourself. You become inclined to feel vulnerable and insecure if you don't seek to control everything you can. Such a need for control can take many forms. A common one is the incessant striving for perfection—the inability to tolerate mistakes or any behavior that falls short of unrealistically high standards. Another type of control is the tendency to deny or avoid uncomfortable feelings, particularly anger.

When years of seeking perfection is combined with a rigid need to discount unpleasant feelings, the end result may be panic attacks, phobias, and/or chronic anxiety. As life continues to serve up unpredictable changes—whether in the realm of job, income, health, or relationships—some of us attempt to tighten the reins of control further, with the consequence that anxiety and panic worsen.

An attitude of fundamental importance to healing fear is learning to let go. In this chapter I want to talk about two aspects of the letting-go process: 1) letting go in the face of everyday hassles and problems and 2) letting go in the face of a major life crisis.

Part 1: Letting Go in the Face of Daily Problems

How do you respond when your child misses the bus to school? The repairman doesn't complete the job? Your spouse unexpectedly goes on a business trip? The IRS says you underestimated your tax liability by $3,000? No one is immune from the almost daily twists of life that can keep us guessing what will happen next. The real question is: How do you respond to the ordinary ups and downs of living and maintain a semblance of equanimity? Someone may tell you to just "accept it" or "go with the flow"—but how do you do that? There are several approaches that can help.

Relaxation

Giving yourself ample time to relax is a most important key. Letting go of bodily tension hlps to let go of emotional concerns. A relaxed mind cannot exist in a tense body. If you're already tense when your child runs through the living room with muddy shoes, you may suddenly find yourself a lot more tense—maybe even panicky. If, on the other hand, you've been pacing yourself through the day and have made time to take breaks and to breathe deeply, you'll likely handle the latest crisis more smoothly.

Staying relaxed throughout the day takes commitment, focus, and effort. Practicing muscle relaxation or meditation on a regular basis is a good start, but it may not be enough to offset an onslaught of stressors. It's important to make time for relaxation during the entire day. *Your ability to truly take time out to relax throughout your day*, giving yourself regular "minibreaks," such as five minutes of abdominal breathing, meditation, or just sitting quietly in your chair, every hour or two, will increase your resilience and ability to cope with whatever comes along. Granted, it's not easy to slow down and take time out for relaxation in a society that moves at a breakneck pace. Giving yourself time for breaks and downtime—even five minutes every two hours—is easy to overlook when you get busy. To make relaxation and downtime a priority in your daily life takes effort and commitment. Although often difficult at first, it can become a very self-reinforcing habit after a while. The more relaxed and centered you're able to remain throughout the day, the less defensive, controlling, and fearful you'll be when circumstances suddenly don't go your way. Relaxation enhances your *flexibility*, allowing you to move through almost any difficult situation—to let go and take a fresh perspective rather than struggle with painful feelings. See Chapter 4 for more detailed guidelines on relaxation.

Humor

When your cat drags a dead mouse into the house you can either rage, panic, or laugh. Laughter is the opposite of control and closely associated with relaxation. Generally, the more perfectionistic and controlling your approach to life is, the easier it is to do anything but laugh. A sense of humor is one of the hard-won benefits of lowering perfectionistic standards. Humor is the ability to step back and get perspective when everything seems to be going out of control. It's a *choice in perception*—a choice to look at a certain situation as ridiculous or absurd as opposed to a major melodrama. When you've spent your life needing everything to be just so, it takes some intention to cultivate a sense of humor. An important first step is learning to relax the standards you impose on yourself—trying not to take yourself so seriously.

Laughter has a number of beneficial physiological effects. Research has shown that laughter reduces blood pressure and relieves muscle tension. It also stimulates the release of endorphins in the brain, leading to an overall sense of well-being. Laughter also activates the immune system by stimulating the production of white blood cells. In his well-known book, *Anatomy of an Illness* (1979), Norman Cousins recounts how a daily dose of laughter—from watching old Marx Brothers films and reruns of *Candid Camera*—helped him overcome a chronic degenerative disease. Humor certainly relieves fear and anxiety. You cannot perceive a situation as threatening (and thus anxiety-provoking) if you can find a way to laugh at it. Perhaps you can recall a situation that once made you anxious yet now, in retrospect, appears humorous.

How can you bring more humor into your life? Humor is something that can be cultivated. Find out what makes you laugh and then spend more time with it. Watching funny videos or TV shows is a good place to start. Or you may prefer reading collections of cartoons (such as Gary Larson, for example) and humor books. Some people enjoy going to comedy clubs to watch stand-up comedians. You can learn how to tell jokes by watching comedians in action. If you spend time around a friend or family member with a good sense of humor, it may tend to rub off. Finally, just smiling may be enough to trigger more positive, lighter thoughts and feelings. Whichever way you prefer, try making more time for laughter in your life. A little more laughter will go a long way to help you loosen up around daily hassles—rather than building them into major melodramas.

Patience

Patience is a close cousin of relaxation. I would define patience as a "nondriven" stance toward life, something that's only possible when you're relaxed. The stronger your tendency to push or drive yourself, the harder it is to be patient. As you learn to relax and pace yourself through life, it becomes easier to wait when something takes longer than you thought it would. A degree of striving is necessary to achieve any goal, but when striving becomes compulsive and driven, you lose the flexibility to handle temporary setbacks and obstacles. Developing your inner observing self through awareness meditation (see Chapter 9) is a wonderful way to cultivate patience. Awareness and mindfulness are the opposite of willful self-pushing because they maintain a present-centered focus rather than trying so hard to get somewhere. By staying mindfully in the present, you can be patient about delays and obstacles. The paradox is that the *less* you give energy to setbacks and obstacles, the more efficient and steady will be your progress toward your goals.

Returning to Nature

One of the best ways to let go of your troubles in daily life is to put yourself in a park or woods. Reconnecting with nature can help you to get in touch with your own body and soul in ways that can move you out beyond the confines of your worries and concerns. When you're stuck in a worry, you keep presenting the same issue to yourself over and over again. You're confined to a certain loop in your brain that keeps repeating like a broken record. From a position inside the loop it's hard to see your way out. The great outdoors provides you with a much larger context than the confines of your mind. It will often help you to move out of a closed mental circuit into a larger sense of communion with nature. There are few things more effective than taking a walk in a beautiful setting to loosen the grip of worry.

Creative Distraction

If nature is not immediately available (if you don't have time to commute to the nearest park, woods, river, lake, or beach), then the next easiest way to let go of mental overdrive is to find a creative distraction. Not all distractions work equally well. Some of us grew up with a parent or older sibling who told us, "Get your mind off of your problem"—and yet we weren't able to. In my experience, the distractions that work best are those which preoccupy body, heart, or soul (as opposed to the mind alone). It is hard to overcome the mind with the mind. As mentioned in the previous section, you need to shift to an activity or place that is larger than your mind in order to move outside your brain's tendency to loop. This can be something physical—your favorite exercise, team sport, gardening, or building project. Or it can be anything that sparks your enthusiasm. (Being moved or enthused is an activity of the soul.) Any distraction that engages body and/or soul is what I call a "creative" distraction. Examples might include:

- Your favorite hobby

- An uplifting book, video, or audio tape

- A stimulating conversation (in person or on the phone)

- Singing or playing a musical instrument

- Creative computer applications

As long as the distraction captures your enthusiasm, you'll more easily be able to let go of whatever might have preoccupied your mind.

Do Something for Someone Else

Mother Teresa once said her definition of "happiness" was finding a productive way to serve others. It's often true that a most effective way to let go of your own melodrama is to do something for someone else. Whether you listen to someone, write them a letter, pick up a gift, help someone with a task, or put in time volunteering your services, getting concerned about someone else's situation moves you out of a fixation on yourself. It also leaves you with a sense of satisfaction that you can be useful and helpful. Service to others is a most uplifting way to let go and move beyond your troubles. It is important, of course, to keep selfless concern and service in balance with caring for your own needs. Excessive devotion to others at a cost to yourself can become co-dependency or, as a friend of mine once put it, "idiot compassion."

Overcoming Perfectionism

Finally, a most important attitude to modify is perfectionism. Perfectionism keeps you on an eternal quest to meet standards that are usually set unrealistically high. When anything falls short, you become disappointed, frustrated, or critical. Perfectionism may also cause you to focus excessively on small flaws or mistakes in yourself or your accomplishments. In emphasizing what's wrong, you tend to discount and ignore what's right. In my earlier book, *The Anxiety & Phobia Workbook* (1995), I described seven ways to combat perfectionism. I repeat them here for the purpose of helping you to develop a greater capacity to let go.

1. *Let go of the idea that your achievements and accomplishments determine your worth.*

Outer accomplishment may be how society measures a person's "worth" or "social status." But are you willing to allow society to have the last word on your value as a person? Work on reinforcing the idea that your worth is a given. People ascribe inherent worth to pets and plants just by virtue of their existence. You as a human being have the same inherent worth just because you're here. Be willing to recognize and affirm that you're lovable and acceptable as you are, apart from your outer accomplishments. When self-reflective people are near death, there are usually only two things that seem to have been important to them about their lives: learning how to love others, and growing in wisdom. If you need to measure yourself against any standard, try these rather than society's definitions of value.

2. *Recognize and overcome perfectionistic thinking styles.*

Perfectionism is expressed in the way you talk to yourself. Three types of thinking characteristic of a perfectionistic attitude are "Should/Must Thinking," "All-or-Nothing Thinking," and "Overgeneralization." Below are examples of self-statements associated with each thinking style and corresponding, more realistic counterstatements.

PERFECTIONISTIC THINKING STYLES

Thinking Style	Counterstatements
Should/Must Thinking	
"I should be able to do this right."	"I'll do the best I can."
"I must not make mistakes."	"It's okay to make mistakes."
All-or-Nothing Thinking	
"This is all wrong."	"This is not *all* wrong. There are some parts of it that are okay and some that need attention."
"I feel worthless."	"Feeling worthless is just a feeling. I have many worthy traits and capabilities."

Overgeneralization

"I always foul things up."	"It's simply untrue that I always foul things up. In this particular case, I'll go back and make the necessary corrections."
"I'll *never* be able to do this."	"If I take small steps and keep making an effort, over time I'll accomplish what I set out to do."

Spend one week noticing those times when you get involved in should/must thinking, all-or-nothing thinking, or overgeneralization. Keep a notebook with you so that you can write down instances of these thoughts as they occur. Examine what you're telling yourself at times when you feel particularly anxious or stressed. Pay special attention to your use of the words "should," "must," "have to," "always," "never," "all," or "none." After you've spent a week writing down your perfectionist self-statements, compose counterstatements for each one. In subsequent weeks, read over your list of counterstatements frequently to encourage yourself to cultivate a less perfectionist approach to life.

3. Stop magnifying the importance of small errors.

One of the most problematic aspects of perfectionism is its mandate to focus on small flaws or errors. Perfectionists are prone to come down very hard on themselves for a single, minute mistake that has few or no immediate consequences, let along any long-term effects. When you really think about it, how important is a mistake you make today going to be one month from now—or one year from now? In 99.9 percent of cases, the mistake will be forgotten within a short period of time. There is no real learning without mistakes or setbacks. No great success was ever attained without many failures and mistakes along the way.

4. Focus on positives.

In dwelling on small errors or mistakes, perfectionists tend to discount their positive accomplishments. They selectively ignore anything positive they've done. A way to counter this tendency is to take inventory near the end of each day of positive things you've accomplished. Think about what ways, small or large, you've been helpful or pleasant to people during the day. Think of any small steps you've taken toward achieving your goals. What other things got done? What insights did you have?

Pay attention to whether you disqualify something positive with a "but"—for example, "I had a good practice session, *but* I became anxious near the end." Learn to leave off the "but" in your assessments of your attitudes and behavior.

5. *Work on goals that are realistic.*

Are your goals realistically attainable, or have you set them too high? Would you expect of anyone else the goals you set for yourself? Sometimes it's difficult to recognize the overly lofty nature of certain goals. It can be helpful to do a "reality check" with a friend or counselor to determine whether any particular goal is realistically attainable, or even reasonable to strive for. Are you expecting too much of yourself and the world? You may need to adjust some of your goals a bit to be in line with the limiting factors of time, energy, and resources. If your estimation of self-worth truly comes from within, rather than from what you achieve, you'll be able to do this. Acceptance of personal limitations is the ultimate act of self-love.

6. *Cultivate more pleasure and recreation in your life*

Perfectionism has a tendency to make people rigid and self-denying. Your own human needs get sacrificed in favor of the pursuit of external goals. Ultimately this tendency can lead to a stifling of vitality and creativity. Pleasure—finding the enjoyment in life—reverses this trend.

The Sioux Indians have a wise saying: "The first thing people say after their death is, 'Why was I so serious?'" Are you taking yourself too seriously and not allowing yourself time for fun, recreation, play, and rest? How can you make more time for leisure, and pleasure? You can change by taking time every day to do at least one thing you enjoy.

7. *Develop a process orientation.*

If you engage in sports, do you play to win or just to enjoy the activity of playing? In your life in general, are you "playing to win," channeling your energies into excelling at all costs, or are you enjoying the process of living day by day as you go along?

Many people find, especially as they get older, that to get the most enjoyment out of life, it works best to place value on the *process* of doing things—not just on the product or accomplishment.

Popular expressions that express this idea include: "The journey is more important than the destination," and "Stop and smell the roses."

Part 2: Letting Go in the Face of Crisis

There are situations in life where you may be confronted with something that goes far beyond the stress of everyday life and pushes you to the limit. You are suddenly faced with a crisis—perhaps a catastrophe—that doesn't respond easily or quickly to your efforts to cope. At such times you may feel frightened and up against a wall. You may despair that there doesn't seem much you can do to improve a very difficult circumstance. Examples of this type of crisis situation include: serious chronic illness, whether physical or mental; serious addiction to alcohol or drugs, where you've tried many times to stop but can't; catastrophic losses such as the loss of spouse or family to accident or disaster; loss of physical integrity due to accident or illness; sudden loss of financial resources; and so on.

When faced with this type of crisis, there are three choices you can make: 1) resignation or despair, which may lead to a sense of hopelessness; 2) continuing to struggle to control the situation on your own, which may work for a while but ultimately increases anxiety and frustration; or 3) asking for and accepting outside help in the form of support, additional knowledge, and guidance. How do these alternatives differ?

Resignation

Resignation usually involves making no further effort to resolve a challenging situation. After all your efforts on your own have failed, you decide that there's nothing further that can be done. Such a stance leads to despair and sometimes to suicide. Invariably it leads to depression.

Resignation tends to close you off from any outside help. If you're walking around with the attitude "what's the use," or "this is hopeless," you're certainly not likely to be open or willing to receive any help from others that might be available.

On occasion, resignation may develop *after* you've consistently sought help from others to no avail. Neither you nor anyone else seems to be able to offer much help for your difficulty. At this point you can choose to give way to resignation, or you can exercise a further option, to be discussed below.

Continuing to Struggle

This is the position where you believe that if you only exert enough effort, you'll be able to overcome your problem on your own. You may keep seeking ways to try to control a serious problem that stubbornly resists all of your efforts. As the struggle goes on for weeks or months, your anxiety and frustration levels can rise enormously. The problem with this position, just as with resignation, is that it closes you off to help from outside yourself. As long as you maintain the attitude "I'm the only one who can change (control) this," there is not much chance for other people to assist. Again, you may come to the point where you feel lost and bewildered about what to do.

Relying on Others

Relying on others means you let go of depending solely on yourself and have the humility and openness to ask for help—to seek out the support of family, friends, or professionals. In the case of a severe, chronic anxiety disorder, where might this help come from?

1. You may talk to a counselor and/or a therapist. Professional therapists can give you tools to manage anxiety and confront fears. They can provide empathy and unconditional acceptance that can help heal feelings of unworthiness. Finally, they can provide encouragement that empowers you to take action—to do the necessary work—to make changes in your life.

2. You can talk to others suffering from anxiety disorders, either individually or in a support group. Talking to others with anxiety can reassure you that you're not alone. Often it can give you new ideas and coping strategies to deal with your own situation (for example, hearing about someone else benefiting from medication). Also important, it can help you to stay on track with your own recovery process since you're acquainted with others who are working on getting better.

3. You can inform family and friends of your problem so they can have better understanding about it. This is especially important when you can't engage in activities you used to do effortlessly. If you're in a close, intimate relationship, you can strive to educate your partner in detail about the nature of your problem with anxiety so they can fully understand and support your recovery goals. This enables them to assist you in specific recovery tasks such as relaxation practice, graded exposure, or response prevention.

All of these sources of support together can help you to negotiate the process of recovery from a serious problem with anxiety. In fact, the combination of therapy, support groups, and family is often sufficient to help you move through nearly any major difficulty or crisis. *In some cases, however, even this is not enough.* All the help and resources available may be insufficient to heal the wound inflicted on your soul by the crisis situation or disability. After all therapy and support options have been exhausted, a problem may still not have improved enough to make life feel livable or worthwhile. This was my own situation for a period that lasted about six months, as described in Chapter 1.

Turning to a Higher Power

When all else fails, it may be the moment to look to your Higher Power (God, Spirit) for help. While some persons may incorporate spiritual beliefs and practices throughout their healing journey, others begin to do so only when pushed to the limit. It may be only after a serious or life-threatening crisis that you first awaken to the spiritual dimension of life. Or perhaps it's after such a crisis that you move from a mere intellectual belief in God to a more personal experience of the presence of a Higher Power in your life.

Turning to your Higher Power in no way diminishes the importance or necessity of relying on other sources of help. Practicing relaxation, exercise, and cognitive coping skills on a daily basis are all necessary. Having a good support system among family and friends is also vital to managing a difficult situation. However, a willingness to let go and trust in a Higher Power can add an entirely new dimension.

Deciding to ask for help from your Higher Power is a radical step because it involves relying on a resource you can neither see nor fully understand. When you turn to your Higher Power, you are not just looking for a consoling concept—a convenient idea to comfort you. Anyone who has uttered a sincere prayer for assistance from God knows it is more than simply a convenience. It is reaching out from your heart and soul for real assistance, assistance you've not been able to find to your satisfaction through everything else you have tried.

The nature of this decision to rely on a Higher Power is well summarized by the first three steps of the twelve-step program of Alcoholics Anonymous:

Step 1: Recognizing that you are powerless to resolve your issues by your own efforts

Step 2: Coming to believe that there is a Higher Power that can help

Step 3: Turning your life and your will over to that Higher Power, as
you understand it

This relinquishing of control—letting go to an Unseen Force—is an unusual and often difficult step for people in fear or anxiety. The more afraid
you are, the more you may try to struggle to exert control. To relinquish control requires humility, trust, a willingness to tolerate uncertainty, and faith.
Let's consider each of these qualities.

Humility

It's certainly humbling to turn over your sense of control to something
like a Higher Power. Perhaps you've been attached to an image of yourself as
being the master of your own life—always able to handle any situation on
your own. Perhaps you view it as a sign of weakness that you've met a problem you cannot fully master by your own efforts. Or perhaps you feel others
will regard you as weak for relying on an unseen, invisible source of help. It
certainly goes against the value system of modern, western society with its emphasis on individuality and self-determination. Particularly for men in American
society, it's often difficult to give up the belief that they can surmount any ob-
stacle by their own efforts.

It is humility that's needed first—humility to acknowledge and accept
your ultimate powerlessness in the face of a severe and unrelenting crisis. The
irony is that, once you embrace that humility and allow yourself to trust in a
Higher Power, you may be surprised to feel a tremendous sense of relief. Suddenly you're delivered from the awesome task of relying solely on yourself.
You no longer have to surmount what has seemed insurmountable on your
own. The grim determination of self-will can give way to a gentler and more
flexible attitude of accepting what gifts your Higher Power might have to offer.

Trust

If you are going to turn over—surrender—your sense of control and rely
on a Higher Power, then such a Power needs to be fully trustworthy. Such a
Power should have only your best interests in mind and be capable of offering
support, strength, or guidance in the midst of your difficulties. Your ability to
trust in a Higher Power thus depends in large part on what kind of concept
you have of God.

What is your concept of a Higher Power? Questions in Chapter 11 were
designed to help you reflect on this. To what extent is your present image of

God a result of what you learned from your family, church, or minister as a child? Is this image one with which you feel comfortable? Some people were raised with mixed messages about the nature of God. They were taught that God can be both loving and wrathful—or both forgiving and judgmental. Certainly it would seem difficult to turn over your problems to such a God. To bare your soul to a potentially judgmental or wrathful God is an uncertain, even frightening prospect.

It's also possible that your feelings toward a Higher Power, the ultimate authority, might be colored by feelings you may have toward authority figures in general, particularly parents. If your parents were abusive, critical, or dominating, you might harbor unconscious feelings of fear or anger toward not only them but authority figures in general. And your fearful images of authority may, in turn, influence your perception and image of God. Certain traditional doctrines portraying God as wrathful or punitive can serve to reinforce such an image. So you may have grown up with mixed feelings toward the idea of Deity, feeling more comfortable with an agnostic or even atheistic worldview.

How is it possible to come to a "true" understanding of the nature of a Higher Power, free of negative projections based on false teachings or traumatic experiences in childhood? There is no easy answer to such a question. Each person needs to make his or her own search, facilitated by reading, talking to others, and, above all, asking Spirit directly for insight and clear understanding. Direct revelation of the nature of God through personal experience in prayer and meditation offers the most convincing answers. Speaking from my own experience in this regard, I have come into acquaintance with a Higher Power that is all-loving, forgiving, supportive, reliable, wholly nonjudgmental, and concerned for my and everyone else's highest good. Such a power seems to me eminently trustworthy. It's a great source of strength and security to know such a Power exists.

Tolerating Uncertainty

The need to control is born out of a desire to make life predictable, orderly, and in line with your expectations. Tolerating uncertainty can be challenging because it requires the precise opposite of this: living with a degree of chaos and unpredictability. However difficult it may be, there is a gift in chaos. It's at those times when a problem situation seems most uncertain or confusing that you are most likely to experience a shift in perception toward it. As long as you're stuck in your worry, you may tend to limit yourself from perceiving new approaches or solutions. Chaos and uncertainty can shake up a rigid mind-set to allow for a fresh perspective to emerge.

Tolerating uncertainty is something that can be *learned* through practice. You might want to start with something fairly small, such as leaving certain chores undone or not opening your mail for a day or two. Then work on postponing your worry about a more serious problem situation, using exercise, relaxation, or creative distractions to deal with the tension that may be left from not worrying. Assuming you've done what you realistically can, try to extend the period of not worrying about the problem as long as possible.

Once you've increased your capacity to tolerate uncertainty, it's easier to relinquish an intractable problem to the care of your Higher Power. A little faith will also help this process greatly.

Faith

Faith is the continual renewal, over time, of your trust in a Higher Power. It's the expectancy that your requests for assistance will receive a positive response. Faith often requires some degree of courage—the courage to continue believing in the possibility of assistance from your Higher Power no matter how "discouraging" the immediate situation appears. To have faith is to persevere in your conviction of the highest possible outcome no matter what obstacles may arise along the way.

Faith is not always easy to conjure up. It develops out of direct personal experience with relying on a Higher Power to provide support, peace of mind, understanding, or guidance. It may be challenged by circumstances where adversity reigns and prayers seem to go unanswered. In my own experience, however, faith is not blind. It tends to grow with time and experience in cultivating a relationship with your Higher Power. It's something you can *learn* as you continue to practice letting go of those situations where help beyond your own means seems needed.

Keep in mind that reliance on a Higher Power does *not* mean relinquishing your responsibility for doing all you can to deal with a problem situation. Releasing your difficulty to a Higher Power in no way conflicts with developing self-responsibility. The two are on different levels. For example, working on overcoming anxiety means developing a variety of skills—abdominal breathing skills, relaxation skills, self-observation, use of constructive self-statements, exposure, accessing feelings, assertiveness, and so on. The capacity to let go and surrender to a Higher Power is of a different order. After you have made your best effort to work on your particular issues, you realize that there is an additional resource available. You learn to rely on assistance from your Higher Power *in conjunction with* your own best efforts. Specifically, you can ask for assistance from your Higher Power to help you with qualities of character—"soul qualities," if you will—that can help you in your journey toward recovery. These qualities include courage, faith, strength, perseverance, inspiration, and resourcefulness. Or you can simply leave your request open-ended: "May whatever I need come to me," "May whatever I need to know be revealed to me." None of this is in conflict with learning and practicing all of the important skills that can lead to mastery and self-reliance regarding the problem. There is a certain paradox here: relinquishing your problem to a Higher Power may actually support and enhance your own efforts to overcome it. This can be summed up in the maxim: "God helps those who help themselves."

Exercises for Letting Go

RELEASE MEDITATION

The following exercise is intended to help you get in touch with your Higher Power and obtain assistance in dealing with any issue causing you worry or anxiety. Use the exercise only if it feels appropriate to you. (You may have your own methods of prayer and meditation that you find preferable.) Give yourself time to get relaxed and centered first before working with the affirmations and visualization.

1. Get comfortable in a seated position (or lie down, if you prefer). Spend at least five minutes using any technique you wish to get relaxed. You can do abdominal breathing, use progressive muscle relaxation, visualize going to a peaceful place, or meditate.

2. If you're not already aware of it, bring to mind the situation, person, or idea that worries you. Focus on this for several moments until you have it clearly in mind. If feelings of anxiety come up, allow yourself to feel them.

3. Affirm over and over, with as much conviction as you can,
   "I turn this over to my Higher Power (or God)."
   "I release this problem to my Higher Power (or God)."

   Simply repeat these statements slowly, calmly, and with feeling as many times as you wish until you begin to feel better. While doing this, it is good to bring to mind the following ideas about your Higher Power:

- It is "all-knowing"—in other words, it has wisdom and intelligence that go beyond your conscious capacity to perceive solutions to problems.

- In its greater wisdom, your Higher Power has a solution to whatever you're worried about.

- Even though you can't see the solution to your worry right now, you can affirm faith that there is no problem that can't be resolved through the help of your Higher Power.

- If your worry is focused on another person, remember that they too have a Higher Power that is looking out for their highest good.

4. If you are visually inclined, imagine that you're going to meet your Higher Power. You might see yourself in a garden or a beautiful setting of your choice, and then imagine that you see a figure—your Higher Power—approaching you. It may be indistinct at first and then grow clearer. You may notice that this figure exudes love and wisdom. It might be a wise old man or woman, a being of light, Jesus, the Supreme Being in your particular religion, or any other presence that adequately represents your Higher Power.

5. While in the presence of your Higher Power—whether you visualize it or not—simply find a way to ask for help. For example, you might say, "I ask for your help and guidance with _____." Keep repeating your request until you feel better.

    You may want to listen to see if your Higher Power has an immediate answer or an insight to offer you about your request. It's quite all right, though, simply to make your request and ask for help without getting an answer. The purpose of this process is to develop trust and belief in your Higher Power (what has traditionally been called "faith in God").

    The key to this part of the process is an attitude of genuine humility. By asking for help from your Higher Power, you relinquish some of your conscious control of the situation, and exercise a willingness to trust.

6. Optional: If it feels appropriate, visualize a beam of white light going to that place in your body that feels anxious or worried.

Often this will be the solar plexus region (in the middle of your trunk right below the center of your rib cage) or the "pit" of your stomach. Let that area be filled with light until the anxiety dissolves or fades away. Keep directing white light to that region until it completely settles down and is free of anxiety.

Give this entire process time. It may be necessary to persist with it for as long as half an hour to forty-five minutes in order to feel a genuine connection with your Higher Power and a deeply felt trust that the problem you're worried about can truly be resolved. If, after completing this process, your worry comes back the next day, simply repeat the exercise every day until you've released your worry. To many readers, this process will appear to be a variation on traditional prayer.

RELEASE PRAYER
(Prayer to Release a Problem)

You can use the following prayer at any time you wish to turn over a problem to the care of your Higher Power. This prayer is meant to serve as one example of a type of prayer that can be used to release a difficult situation to God. Feel free to use it as it is or as a basis for writing your own prayer for release.

Speak the prayer from your heart, and then repeat it daily until you feel you have received an answer.

Dear God,
I have done all I know to heal this problem—
And have tried every resource within my knowledge and power.
I now turn this over to your care.
I acknowledge my own inability
To will this difficulty away,
As its source lies deeper than my own conscious will.
I know, however, it is not beyond Your Power,
And that nothing is impossible through God.

So I ask that You help me to heal this situation.
Bring light into this darkness
And restore peace to my mind and heart.
I am grateful that You already know the way,

Even if I do not.
I now let go in trust and faith—
Knowing that it is through your perfect love and grace
That I may be restored to wholeness. Amen.

SPIRITUAL PHRASES

You can use any of the following spiritual phrases to help let go of anxiety or worry in the moment it arises. As with any coping statement (see Chapter 6), it's good to repeat a phrase several times over the course of two or three minutes. Try using your favorite phrase in combination with abdominal breathing, repeating the phrase each time you exhale. It's particularly powerful to sit quietly, close your eyes, and silently repeat a phrase on each exhale for several minutes.

Spirit (God) is with me.
I abide in God (or Spirit).
Let go—let God.
Grant me peace.
Grant me strength.
This too will pass.
The grace of God surrounds me.
God knows the way.
My Higher Power and I can handle this together.

ALLOWING TIME FOR HEALING

The following is a guided meditation I have used with clients who have been discouraged by a protracted illness or problem with anxiety. I suggest that you record it on tape, in your own voice or someone else's. Speak slowly and deliberately when making the recording. Then listen to the entire meditation while in a relaxed state, once per day. With repetition, this meditation should help you to let go of struggling with your illness and change the way you perceive it.

A Time to Heal

This is the time your body is taking to allow itself to fully rest and heal. It's futile to try to hurry your body. It has its own natural pace—which might involve an extended time of having to let go of your normal schedule of activities. Although it's hard to sit on the sidelines and wait, be assured that it's by taking this time out now that you can reemerge feeling healthy, more vital and strong.

You must have needed this time out to fully rest, or you wouldn't have had to reduce your activities for such an extended time. Getting angry or struggling with your condition serves no purpose. It certainly is frustrating to feel ill for an extended time, yet realize that this healing crisis is needed—it's a necessary step to ensure a longer and healthier life in the years ahead. Know that when your body and soul's need for rest and healing is complete, your healing crisis will be over and you can return to all the activities and goals that give your life meaning. Allow yourself to be patient now and trust that, even in the midst of feeling distressed, you are rebuilding your strength. Let yourself trust that you'll emerge from this time with a renewed feeling of good health—health that is built from the inside out—health that is built on a solid foundation because you've been required to slow down for a period of time.

So let yourself relax and cease struggling or fighting your body and soul's own natural wisdom. Remember to occupy your days with constructive activities. Patience is a great virtue and you can use this time as an opportunity to cultivate it. Patience is usually gained only at a price. You gain patience by learning to endure through difficult times. So recognize the present time as an opportunity to grow in two important ways: first, to give your body and soul a deep rest, so that you can regroup for the months and years ahead; and second, to learn patience—the willingness to wait and persevere through adversity. With patience, you can handle all the challenges life may bring with greater ease.

So right now . . . relax, let go, and realize that a Higher Wisdom is in charge of your life. Although you may feel frustrated or distressed, this Higher Wisdom knows what it's doing, and you can trust that you're going to be fine—that you'll emerge from this time a renewed and stronger person.

Remember to have faith that there is a purpose in everything and that nothing in life remains the same for long. In time this healing crisis will be over, and you can resume all the pursuits and goals that are important to you.

So allow yourself to breathe, relax, and trust. No matter how you feel physically, your healing process is moving forward at a deep level right now. You can trust that there is an end to this, that you will be healthy and strong again—and that in the future you will look back at this time as a necessary step in your life's course.

What You Can Do Now

1. Review "Part 1: Letting Go in the Face of Daily Problems." Of the various attitudes and approaches that can help with letting go—relaxation, humor, patience, returning to nature, creative distraction, helping others—which ones might you be willing to cultivate? What specifically can you do?

2. If you feel you are overly perfectionistic, review the section "Overcoming Perfectionism." What specifically are you willing to do to lessen your tendency toward perfectionism?

3. If you feel discouraged or stuck in your problem with fear or anxiety, review "Turning to a Higher Power." Work with the "Release Meditation" or "Release Prayer" (or write your own) in order to ask your Higher Power for assistance. Use one of the spiritual phrases to address fear in the moment it arises. Record and listen to the script "A Time to Heal" to up-level your attitude toward a protracted illness or disability.

4. To help develop greater faith, you might want to keep a "faith journal." Every time you feel a prayer has been answered or you experience a small miracle in your daily life, write it down. Later, reading back over your journal entries will help to strengthen your belief in your Higher Power—not just as a concept but as an active presence in your life.

References and Further Reading

Cousins, Norman. 1979. *Anatomy of an Illness*. New York: Norton.
Jampolsky, Gerald. 1979. *Love Is Letting Go of Fear*. Berkeley, Calif.: Celestial Arts.

13

Affirming Your Recovery

For the past twenty years, cognitive therapy has made a substantial contribution to the field of psychotherapy. Originally conceived by Albert Ellis (as rational-emotive therapy) and refined by Aaron Beck, cognitive therapy revolutionized the treatment of depression during the 1970s and then the treatment of panic disorder in the 1980s. The marriage of cognitive and behavioral therapy in an integrated approach that includes relaxation training, cognitive therapy, and graded exposure (cognitive behavioral therapy) has remained the treatment of choice for panic, anxiety, and phobias up to this day.

Central to cognitive therapy is the idea that your inner thoughts, often referred to as "self-talk," play a major, if not exclusive, role in shaping your moods and the way you feel. If your thoughts imagine potential catastrophe ("What if I panic?" "What if they see me panic?" "What if I have a heart attack?"), then you're likely to make yourself anxious or even panicky. Or, if your thoughts focus on themes of hopelessness and resignation ("What's the use?" "I'm worthless"), you'll probably make yourself depressed. Underlying negative self-talk are mistaken beliefs (sometimes called *schemata* by cognitive therapists). Examples of these underlying beliefs might be: "If people really knew what I was like, they'd reject me," or "The world is a dangerous place." Such beliefs are learned from parents, society, and traumatic life circumstances. These beliefs create and perpetuate the unsupportive ways we talk to ourselves.

An important aim of cognitive therapy is to assist you to change your most deep-seated mistaken beliefs, replacing them with more hopeful and constructive beliefs about yourself, others, and life. Chapter 6 of this book provides guidelines for doing just this. To the extent that you're able to do so, your problems with anxiety, depression, anger, shame, and low self-esteem will diminish. In short, how you feel and how you see yourself are largely determined by your thinking and what you believe. The viewpoint of cognitive therapy can be illustrated as follows:

Core Beliefs ⟶ Self-Talk ⟶ Mood and Feelings

The idea that beliefs and self-talk shape moods and feelings is of fundamental importance in dealing with fear. When you learn to stop dwelling on "what-ifs" or imagining potential catastrophes, anxiety and fear do indeed tend to dissipate. Yet the assumption that beliefs and self-talk *solely* or *primarily* determine how you feel is subject to question. It might be asked, where do negative self-statements come from in the first place? Do you indulge in them simply by force of habit? Does it not also seem possible that feeling physically uncomfortable or distressed, whether due to muscle tension, underbreathing, low blood sugar, fatigue, indigestion, or neurotransmitter imbalances (to name a few possibilities) might influence you to think negative thoughts? It seems plausible that when your body is tired or stressed—or your internal physiology is out of balance—you might be more predisposed to entertain all kinds of less-than-constructive thoughts. In this instance, what happens could be illustrated as follows:

Physical Stress or ⟶ Negative Physical ⟶ Negative Thoughts
Physiological Imbalance   Sensations

Such a situation might be remedied by deep muscle relaxation (to relieve muscle tension), abdominal breathing (to correct underbreathing), improved nutrition (to correct, for example, low blood sugar or overly acidic conditions), or taking medication (to correct neurotransmitter imbalances).

An expanded cognitive behavioral approach to ameliorating anxiety might seek to integrate both the viewpoint of classical cognitive therapy along with the above model. The direction of influence between thoughts and feelings (moods) goes both ways:

Neurobiology/Physiology ⇄ Feelings/Moods ⇄ Thoughts/Beliefs

Stress can aggravate *any link in the chain*. The afternoon commute might cause you to contract muscles and underbreathe. The resulting unpleasant physical sensations could then provoke some negative thoughts. From there, you might go on to make negative judgments about the entire situation. If you think negatively about being stuck in traffic, you're likely to feel frustrated. This frustration, in turn, may add to any preexisting muscle tension. *That* increase in tension may, in turn, reinforce further negative thinking. These complex interactions between sensations of tension, emotional frustration, and negative thoughts continue to spiral until you choose to do something to relax (or exit the situation).

Help for this situation can come either from the level of mind or the level of the body. Either supportive coping statements such as, "The traffic congestion will soon pass and I'll be fine," or a physiological intervention such as abdominal breathing can reduce anxiety. This *interactive* view of the relationship between mind and body in creating anxiety was presented in great detail in my first book, *The Anxiety & Phobia Workbook*. That's why that book devoted several chapters to relaxation, exercise, nutrition, and medication as well as more cognitively oriented approaches. This same viewpoint is again presented in Part I of this book.

While fully embracing an interactive view of the relationship between thoughts and feelings, I would like in this chapter to propose an additional model. The basis for this model has no history within mainstream psychology. Indeed, it doesn't arise out of the natural sciences as they have been developed until very recently. It's necessary to look to philosophy and certain forms of spirituality to find its historical foundation. This particular model is radical because it suggests that there is a relationship—an ostensibly causal relationship—*between beliefs and external life circumstances*. This can be illustrated as follows:

$$\text{Beliefs} \longrightarrow \text{External Reality}$$

At first there may seem to be nothing surprising about this. Our beliefs and thoughts obviously influence how we behave, and our behavior obviously affects the people and circumstances that surround us. There's nothing mysterious about the everyday influence our attitudes and thoughts exert on our immediate environment. However, the idea I want to propose is that *our beliefs tend to attract to us outer circumstances that correspond to what we believe*. A different way of putting this is that outer circumstances tend to match or conform to our most strongly held beliefs. For example, if I truly believe I'm ill and dying, I will tend to attract greater illness into my life. If I'm ill and dying and consistently affirm with conviction that I'm whole, healthy, and alive, I will tend to attract wholeness and health into my life.

This idea might seem preposterous because it implies that you can actually change what happens to you simply by changing what you think and believe—without necessarily *doing* anything. Such a view flies in the face of a scientific-materialistic worldview, because it implies that we can influence the course of our personal circumstances without directly acting on them. It may even sound megalomaniac to suppose that any individual can change what happens to him or her—presuming to make the world accommodate his or her wishes.

Freud spoke of such a viewpoint as an infantile belief in the "omnipotence of thought" or "magical thinking." Small children are known to believe that just wishing for something can make it come true. "When you wish upon a star, your dreams come true" certainly seems magical to most persons educated in our rational, scientifically oriented Western society. Adults who believe such a thing may risk being viewed as very childish or worse. What do you *mean*, any reasonable person might ask, that my outer circumstances (or a physical malady within my body) can change for the better simply by affirming my belief that they can?

A brief review of Western thought in the past one hundred years reveals that the idea of attracting events according to your beliefs is not a new or particularly unusual notion. Though it was not an especially familiar concept at the beginning of this century, it's become increasingly mainstream in the past thirty years. The idea actually can be traced back to the Bible in the statements by Jesus: "As a man believeth in his heart, so is he," "It is done unto you as you believe." Goethe expressed it in the eighteenth century in his famous statement about commitment (quoted in full in Chapter 11):

The moment one definitely commits oneself,
Then Providence moves too.
All sorts of things occur to help one
That would never otherwise have occurred.

In the nineteenth century this idea was developed and promulgated first by Phineus Quimby, expressed poetically by Ralph Waldo Emerson, and then taken up by Mary Baker Eddy and Charles and Myrtle Fillmore. In the early twentieth century the idea became the foundation for a movement in American spirituality called "New Thought." Ernest Holmes and Nona Brooks were the leading exponents of this concept in the United States during the early part of this century and founded worldwide spiritual movements based on it.

In the late 1980s and 1990s this idea has entered mainstream popular thinking in the writings of Shakti Gawain (*Creative Visualization*, 1995), Wayne Dyer (*Manifest Your Destiny*, 1997), Deepak Chopra (*The Seven Spiritual Laws of Success*, 1994), Louise Hay (*You Can Heal Your Life*, 1984), and James Redfield (*The Celestine Prophecy*, 1993), to name a few. Even in basic science the idea creeps into the phenomenon known as *experimenter bias*—the tendency of the experimenter's expectations to influence the outcome of an experiment.

The purpose of this chapter is to take this idea—that your beliefs can influence and shape your outer circumstances—and demonstrate its application to healing anxiety and fear. First, I want to explain, to the best of my ability, a view of the world—a paradigm—that might form a logical basis for this idea, explaining how it works. Please regard this paradigm as hypothetical. Though it draws on a considerable amount of reading and personal experience, I suspect it's only partially correct. I offer it as an approximation of a developing worldview that I believe will be further refined, corrected, and elaborated in the twenty-first century. *It's unnecessary for you to accept, comprehend, or even read the next section in order to utilize the idea that your personal beliefs create your reality. If you're not particularly interested in an abstract speculation on how how all this might work, skip over the next section and proceed to the following, more practical section, "How to Create Your Goal," beginning on page 330.*

Creating Your Reality: How It Works
Everything Consists of Energy

All phenomena in the universe are forms of energy. According to modern physics, all of the things in the world are made of particles that also pose as waves. These "wave/particles" can be converted back and forth from matter to energy in accord with Einstein's well-known equation, $E=mc^2$. So, too, mental phenomena—your thoughts, desires, feelings, etc.—are all forms of energy. Some would argue that these phenomena are nothing more than patterns of electrical activity in the brain. However, it might be asked how a mere pattern of electrical activity can fully explain the content of a thought—for example, your thought about what you are reading or your feeling of interest or disinterest. Perhaps patterns of brain activity are necessary to "carry" the contents of your thoughts—much as radio waves are necessary to carry or transmit the content of the music you hear on the radio. Yet the meaning of the thoughts (or melody of the music) cannot be understood solely as a physical brain phenomenon. How do you derive meaning from neurophysiology or neurochemistry? There is no obvious way that an inspiration or sentiment can be fully reduced to patterns of electrical discharge in the neural networks of the brain. Still, if you assume that everything is some form of energy, even inspirations and sentiments must be energy phenomena, albeit very subtle ones.

Some people have proposed that thoughts and feelings, in essence, are actually energetic phenomena traveling faster than the speed of light. (Although Einstein held that nothing could exceed the speed of light, his theory of relativity applies only to material phenomena that exist in space and time.) That may be why we can't actually *see* thoughts and feelings objectively in our material world, where everything we do see, other than light itself, is traveling slower than the speed of light. If there are energies that travel faster than the speed of light, they must certainly be nonmaterial. Therefore, they cannot be localized in space, yet they *can* be directly experienced. You won't see them but you can, so to speak, *be* them. You won't find the feeling of anxiety by looking anywhere in your physical brain, but you can directly experience the quality anxiety. An interesting implication of this is that there may be a part of yourself—that part of you which *experiences the content or meaning inherent in your thoughts and feelings*—that exists independently of space and (linear) time. The religions of the world have referred to this aspect as the "soul" and propose that it goes on existing in a nonphysical realm ("heaven" or "nirvana") after your physical body dies.

It's not necessary to accept all of the above to imagine that thoughts (including consistently held thoughts—your beliefs and attitudes) may have an independent existence apart from your physical brain. If you can entertain this one hypothesis, what follows will be easier to understand.

Consciousness is Inherently "Nonlocal"

As indicated in the previous section, the qualitative aspects of consciousness (meanings) are not material phenomena visible in space. They cannot be precisely located in space. The question "Where—in space—is the meaning of what you are reading?" has no answer, although specific patterns of neural activity in your brain enable you to experience that meaning here and now. The term "nonlocal" is used in physics to refer to a phenomenon that can't be precisely located in space. Consciousness, in its qualitative (meaning) aspect, is inherently nonlocal. Your physical brain, on the other hand, is a very complex instrument for *localizing* the qualitative aspects of consciousness. Specific thoughts, perceptions, and feelings that you have in any instant focus or "localize" the qualitative aspects of consciousness at a particular time and place. This is necessary, for example, for you to be able to have whatever thought you are having in this moment. In sum, your brain filters nonlocal reality—the field of all possibilities—into specific thoughts at a particular time. Think of thought much like the subatomic particle studied by physicists—i.e., as having both a "wave" and a "particle" aspect. The wave-like aspect cannot be specifically located in your brain; the particle-like aspect shows up as *this* particular thought process occurring in so-and-so's brain at such-and-such time. As I see it, the nonlocal, qualitative aspects of consciousness are the "software" that organizes the neurochemistry of the brain into meaningful sequences.

Sometimes the nonlocal characteristic of consciousness "peeks through" in experiences of telepathy—where you and I, even if separated by many miles, have the same thought at the same time. Remote viewing ("seeing" what is happening far away) is another example of this.

There is an experiment in physics that actually demonstrates the existence of nonlocal phenomena. It has been shown that information associated with one electron can be transferred to another electron, many miles away, *instantaneously*. If the information were actually traveling at the speed of light, the transmission would take about forty billionths of a second. Yet, mysteriously, the second electron performs exactly as the first at virtually the same time. Whatever allows the second particle to match the first must not be dependent on space. In fact, it is from experiments demonstrating this phenomenon that physicists coined the term "nonlocal."

This and the results of other experiments have led the physicist David Bohm to propose an "implicate order" of the universe that does not exist within the physical universe but is a timeless, spaceless matrix from which the physical universe arises. If such an implicate order does exist, it's not difficult to see the parallel with traditional religious concepts of heaven or nirvana; both are realms which exist outside of space and linear time.

Microcosm Reflects Macrocosm

The basic idea of this chapter is that your thoughts, beliefs, and attitudes give shape to your outer circumstances as well as your inner world. The notion "microcosm reflects the macrocosm" suggests that this *same* relationship between "mind" and "matter" holds at the level of the entire universe. Human beings (as well as animals) are not unique in having souls, minds, and bodies that work together. It would be, in fact, rather provincial to suppose that we alone are the only place in the entire universe where mind and consciousness exist. The idea here is that our own makeup *mirrors* the way the entire universe is organized. Suppose that the whole universe has something like a "soul" and a "mind," as well as the physical aspect—ranging from atoms to galaxies—that we can see and measure. This idea may perhaps seem strange, but it's only strange if we suppose that the "universal mind" is anything like our rather limited and self-centered minds. If the entire macrocosm has its own form of consciousness, such consciousness is probably well beyond our comprehension.

However, such consciousness may have something to do with the Deity that the religions of the world have referred to by various names—"God," "Allah," "Jehovah," "Brahma," "Great Spirit," and so on. Of course, such a consciousness can only represent one aspect—or even a creation of—God, for God cannot be understood or grasped through any finite description. In sum, the idea here is not that the entire universe is like a human being, but that *the hierarchical relationship of mind to matter* occurs on all scales of size, from the cosmic down to the human, and on down to the cellular, molecular and subatomic. Mind—or intelligence—is not a unique aspect of higher animals but is an inherent aspect of all things on all levels, as the philosopher Spinoza proposed. Rather than recasting the universe to resemble man, the idea here is that man is a miniaturized version of the cosmos—the "microcosm reflects the macrocosm." Such an idea is epitomized in the saying: "As above, so below." It is also found in the Bible in the statement: "Man is made in God's image."

Form Follows Idea

The first idea presented above was that everything that exists—from atoms and molecules to thoughts and feelings—are various forms of energy. There is a philosophical tradition, which originated in the Far East, that proposes that the only difference among all these different phenomena is how "subtle vs. gross" the energy is that constitutes them. Material objects (actually the atoms out of which they're made) are more gross energy forms. Feelings and thoughts are very subtle energy forms, and spiritual awareness and inspiration are perhaps the subtlest of all.

An important assumption made by this same philosophical tradition is that subtle energy forms shape and determine gross energy forms to a much greater degree than vice versa.* For example, wind affects the movement of water more easily than water can affect the movement of air. In a similar fashion your beliefs, attitudes, and ideas tend to shape and determine the emotional and physical levels of your existence. The thought "I'm going to drive to the store" precedes actually doing so. So does the thought "I need to find a job" precede actually going out to look for one. The same principle holds *even if you do not take physical action* to bring about your idea. That is, if you sim-

---

* . The notion that ideas shape physical circumstances has also played a major role in Western philosophy, beginning with Plato. In philosophy, such a view is called "idealism" as opposed to "materialism." It is not inconsistent with causality and the physical laws of nature. Physical laws explain *how* phenomena move from one state to the next, but they do not explain the *particular* forms and patternings that happen to occur, especially for living things. Something more than physical laws is needed for that. The universe is more than a machine—an "intelligent organism" is a better metaphor to describe how the universe operates.

ply hold an idea in your mind with conviction, it will tend to attract and create corresponding physical circumstances on a material level. The popular phrase for this situation is "mind over matter." It's also expressed in the popular notion "Be careful what you wish for—you just might get it." It's demonstrated most dramatically in the phenomenon of psychokinesis, the ability to move or alter physical objects without touching them. Yet, it also takes place more subtly and imperceptibly whenever you focus or concentrate your mind with consistent desire or intention.

Thoughts/Beliefs Attract Their Physical Counterparts

With the previous four points in mind, I'll offer a speculation on how thoughts might shape material circumstances. How might this actually work? Recall that everything in the universe (including thoughts, beliefs, and attitudes) are different forms of energy. Energy, as we understand it, is not static but travels in the form of waves (visible light is a common example). Just like different colors represent different frequencies or wavelengths of light, suppose that various thoughts correspond to different "energy forms" varying possibly in frequency, wave form, or perhaps some other type of characteristic yet to be discovered. Every thought carries a particular energetic "signature." The energy forms corresponding to thoughts are not visible and possibly move faster than the speed of light, as was hypothesized above. Energies that make up physical things, on the other hand, can take on a particle form that enables us to see them in space. One thing that differentiates various forms of energy is how fast they vibrate. Very subtle energies like thoughts and feelings vibrate very fast. More gross energies or material things (actually the subatomic particles that make them up) vibrate more slowly.

Now, if thoughts in essence are nonlocal, then whenever you dwell on a particular thought, that thought—as a particular energy form—would seem likely to "line up" with all other thoughts sharing the same energy form. The more technical word for "line up" is *resonate*—as when two musical notes at the same pitch (frequency) resonate together. Thus, if you think consistently about being healthy and whole, your thought of health lines up—resonates—with all other thoughts of health everywhere. *Your thought doesn't have to "go" anywhere to do this.* The level at which your thought exists in essence—and all other similar thoughts exist in essence—is nonlocal (nonspatial). At such a level there is no separation in terms of space. Your mind simply goes to the "place" where all other similar thoughts of health exist. That is, you tune into a particular frequency or energy configuration, much like tuning a radio to a particular station.

If you happen to "stay" in such a "place"—stay focused on healthy ideas and expectations long enough—healthy circumstances will inevitably tends to show up in your life. *This is because the idea of health in your consciousness can resonate with all other ideas of health in a much more inclusive, "universal consciousness."* *

If this happens, then you simply become part of the process whereby health is being created or manifested everywhere (from nonlocal reality into material reality). As was proposed earlier, form follows idea at all levels of reality from the macrocosm down to the subatomic. If your sincere intent can embrace the highest ideas of health at the nonlocal level of reality, sooner or later healthy circumstances are likely to show up in your life, no matter how ill you may be at present.

The More "Energized" a Belief, the Greater Its Ability to Attract

The more energy I give to a thought—say of healing—the greater the power of my thought to line up with similar thoughts of healing; that is, the more it can partake of that "place" (in nonlocal consciousness) where healing is happening. If I now form an *intention* to heal, I can potentially access the energy of all the thought-forms associated with healing happening everywhere to bring about healing in my life. My own life, by my choice, becomes part and parcel of that "corner of reality" where healing is happening.

Unfortunately, the opposite is also true. The more energy I give to my fear, the more I may line up with all other thoughts of fear (in nonlocal con-

---

* The most universal level is the consciousness of the entire macrocosm, as described above. Each of our individual consciousnessess is embedded in that universal consciousness, much as a drop of the ocean is part of the larger ocean. When you hold an idea (belief) in your mind with conviction, you can potentially line up with the counterparts to that same idea in universal consciousness.

Make the further assumption now that universal consciousness is not static but continuously creative. As an active process, universal consciousness can be compared with the creative aspect of the Deity referred to in all of the religions of the world, influencing our world in subtle ways that generally converge with the laws of nature but can sometimes supersede causality and natural laws, in the instance of miracles and synchronicities.

At the point when your intention, belief, or desire for health lines up with the idea or archetype of health/wholeness in universal consciousness, you participate in the process of health/wholeness being created everywhere (from the highest, nonlocal level down to the material, spatial world). As such, healthy circumstances are bound to show up in your daily life sooner or later. In sum, *when your own mind is attuned or aligned with universal consciousness around the same ideal* (in this case, health), *the two will converge to "co-create" the highest vision of your goal.*

sciousness). In short, the more I may tune in to that "place" in nonlocal consciousness where "fear" is happening. And, the more likely I may draw to me exactly what I fear. My fear becomes a self-fulfilling prophecy.

How can a thought, belief, or intention become energized or strengthened?

- *Repetition*—by dwelling on it repeatedly. Repeating an idea over and over strengthens it in your mind.

- By *putting your "heart and soul" into it*. Just thinking about something doesn't energize it, because you don't invest the deeper levels of your being in it. However, if you put your "heart and soul" into it, you are bringing that larger, more inclusive, more "nonlocal" aspect of consciousness to bear. When the thought is held from the more universal, nonlocal aspect of your own inner being, it enters energetically into discourse with all other thoughts like it. This gives it tremendous energy to attract/manifest corresponding circumstances.

- By *forming a clear intention*. Just thinking about something or even wishing and hoping for it only energizes it to a degree. However, when you form a specific intention, and a clear commitment to go after it, you're *focusing* your energy. And energy that's focused is generally more powerful. This is not hard to see when you think of a laser beam versus an incandescent light bulb. Light that's highly focused (the laser) is considerably more intense and powerful than light which is more diffuse. If thoughts and beliefs are indeed *energetic* phenomena, the laser analogy may well apply. As I mentioned in Chapter 11, a clear intention and commitment, from the wholeness of your heart, will tend to draw to you what you seek. The power of intention is strengthened when you put your heart and soul into it. When repetition is added, when you hold your intention with conviction over time, you have what is called *commitment*. Sustained commitment to a goal is the strongest (most energized) way to actually bring that goal about.

- *"Spiritualizing" your intention*. A clear, committed intention can be energized and strengthened even further by evoking or relying on spiritual resources. There are many ways to do this, though prayer is traditionally the most popular and widely practiced. When you not only have a strong intention, but ask for spiritual assistance in bringing it about, you may access unlimited energy—the energy associated with your Higher Power or God. Later in this chapter I will offer a five-step method for creating healing (or any other positive goal) that relies on spiritual attunement or assistance.

Your Life Is an "Outpicturing" of Your Beliefs

The popular sayings "You get back what you put out" and "What goes around comes around" epitomize this idea. This simply puts the ideas expressed in the previous two sections together. If you put a lot of energy into something you believe in, you will tend to bring it into being. If you believe you can heal from a chronic illness and put a lot of time and energy into that belief, you will tend to draw healing to yourself. The healing might take one of three forms: First, you might actually experience—suddenly or over time—a miraculous healing; the condition is simply lifted. There are numerous records of miraculous healings in the past as well as in recent times. Second, you might draw to yourself resources that assist you in the process of bringing about healing. For example, you might read a certain magazine article, hear about a healing modality you hadn't known about, find a particular healing practitioner, or read a quote that moves you to alter some aspect of your life. All of these unforeseen events would contribute to an eventual healing of your illness. In the third form of healing your condition persists. The condition itself does not go away but your attitude changes so much that you can live with it peacefully, without the struggle and distress you once had. The "healing" is on a psychological rather than physical level.

The "good news" is that you have the capacity to recreate your life, for the better, on the basis of your intentions and beliefs, no matter how adverse the circumstances you happen to face.

The "bad news" is that if you dwell on negativity—if you keep "feeding" what you fear—you may tend to draw *that* outcome to yourself also. The popular term for this is "self-fulfilling prophecy."

Most of the time, most of us harbor a mix of hopes and fears, a combination of faith and doubt, optimism and pessimism. The result is that we don't create anything especially positive or negative because our conflicting beliefs tend to cancel each other out. When, however, you energize a *positive* belief, in the ways described in the preceding section, you can *recreate* a new life apart from whatever fears, doubts, resentments, or guilt may have been obstructing your progress. The purpose of this chapter is to provide a framework to assist you with recreating what you want in your life.

Not Everything That Happens to You Is the Result of Your Beliefs

There is an unfortunate tendency on the part of some people to believe that whatever happens to them is simply the result of their beliefs. If you're hit by a drunk driver, somehow you "created" that misfortune or "drew it to you." Even worse, if a small child is brutally abused, somehow the child created it. The assumption is that *anything* that happens to you is created by your beliefs.

In my opinion, this is carrying the idea of creating your reality too far. It is, in fact, a gross and unfortunate oversimplification. There are two kinds of circumstances that you don't, in fact, create in accord with your thoughts, desires, and beliefs: 1) those which are the result of the beliefs in the collective consciousness of society or humanity, and 2) those that are in the "consciousness" of, for lack of a better word, "God" or the "universe." If the government decides to raise taxes, I did not single-handedly create that circumstance, but the collective consciousness of my society did. If I'm injured in an accident with an intoxicated driver, I may not have "drawn" that to me, but I am a participant in a society (a collective consciousness) where drunkenness and drunk driving happen to occur fairly often. The collective beliefs of the larger group created it, and I, as a member of that group, happen to participate in it. If it rains on my picnic, I did not personally create that outcome—a low-pressure system related to changes in atmospheric conditions did. Being born to my parents is not something I created but is a given—something I have to work with. So may many other things that simply come into my life outside of my conscious will. A scientific-materialistic worldview would say these events are just random occurrences. A Christian viewpoint would speak of tests and trials, while a Hindu or Buddhist would speak of karma accrued from previous lifetimes. Rather than taking a position here, I would simply call such events "life circumstances"—and speculate that such events are not random but are, indeed, the outpicturing of some consciousness or intelligence incomprehensibly greater than my personal ego. Like Job, none of us can fully know the reasons for all the circumstances that happen to come our way.

In conclusion, some of what happens in my life is a result of my particular beliefs, attitudes, desires—and some is not. What is most important is that I have free will—*the ability to change my attitude and beliefs in response to whatever happens in my life, even the most unfortunate*. It is in this sense that I am the author of my destiny, even if I did not single-handedly create or attract all of the events that happen to come into my life.

You Are Endowed with Free Will

Human beings are endowed with free will. Thus, each person is free to choose experiences of freedom or restriction, abundance or lack, joy or misery—according to the most cherished thoughts and beliefs they hold. Your life will tend to reflect those thoughts and beliefs you hold in mind and give energy to. What you believe in, for good or ill, does tend to come to you: "It is done unto you as you believe."

When you don't like the way your life is going, it's most important to examine self-limiting beliefs and attitudes that might be contributing to your circumstances. Then you can resolve to make a new choice—to think differently and more constructively. Free will is an awesome responsibility, but it also implies that you always have the power to *recreate* your life and circumstances, in accord with the way you think and believe.

How to Create Your Goal

The first step in creating something you want is to truly believe that you can do so. That means you need to set aside any fears, doubts, feelings of resignation, or hopelessness you may have about the possibility of attaining what you seek. You need to stop focusing on the problem itself and refocus your attention and energy on creating *what you want instead* of the problem. This requires an open mind, as well as courage and tenacity. If you've derived a sense of identity from having your problem—or being victimized by it—you need to be willing to give up that identity. If you are in considerable distress over the problem, you need the courage to look past your distress and pain and focus primarily on what you'd rather have in your life. Finally, since the process of creating a goal usually takes time—often weeks or months—you need tenacity to keep visioning and revisioning the goal that you seek, no matter what setbacks and discouragement arise along the way.

In order to have the courage and tenacity to keep affirming your goal, you need to be willing at least to *entertain* the idea that what you believe in will actually manifest. While you may or may not accept the ideas in the previous section about how it all works, you need to be open-minded about the basic principle, "It is done unto you as you believe." If you regard this idea as a naive, "pie-in-the-sky" viewpoint, then you may get easily discouraged when what you visualize or affirm does not immediately come about.

I must admit that when I first encountered the idea that beliefs can create reality, I was skeptical. If this notion were true, why did so many people have unfulfilled dreams and unanswered prayers? If overcoming adversity were simply a matter of choosing to believe differently, why didn't more people "choose" their way out of their predicaments in life? If a new belief could actually pay the rent or put food on the table, this certainly wasn't immediately obvious or evident to me. Three things have subsequently led me to lose my skepticism, and to actually give some credence to the idea that what happens in your life reflects your beliefs. The first and most important was that when I put the idea to the test, it actually worked for me. Many times in my life I have chosen to visualize and affirm a goal that, on the face of it, seemed unlikely or impossible. Yet if I continued my visualization long enough, the goal did in fact manifest, quite to my surprise. This has happened often enough that I've come to believe that there really *is* something to it. Believing in the process of creating a new life has, I feel, played a *major* role in overcoming the severe problem I had with my own anxiety disorder a few years ago. The degree of recovery that I've experienced seems miraculous to me now. I doubt that it would have occurred had I not consistently affirmed that it could.

Second, I've found that "creating your reality" is not a pie-in-the-sky notion or a form of "magical thinking" because you *still have to do all the footwork*. Entertaining a visualization of prosperity is not going to pay the rent or put food on the table unless you also take action, such as going out and looking for a job. What it might do, however, is make your job search easier by encouraging a confluence of events that bring you in touch with persons or situations that lead to the "right job." Affirming your recovery *by itself* will not lead to healing your anxiety disorder. You still need to make a conscientious effort to change your self-talk, practice relaxation and exercise, use *in vivo* exposure, or improve assertiveness as the case may be. However, sincere visualizations and affirmations of your goal may "attract" you to the right therapist, medication, or other supportive resources in ways that you would not have foreseen or even attempted otherwise. If you affirm healing *in conjunction with doing all the necessary footwork*, outside circumstances tend to conspire to promote your achieving a high degree of recovery.

Finally, I have come to realize that when you choose to create a positive goal, it may not manifest in quite the way or form you expected. There may be some modifications in your goal along the way to bringing it into reality. For example, you may visualize the goal of a loving relationship, but instead of attracting a new partner you wind up with a child to nurture and care for. Or you may affirm 100 percent recovery from a particular anxiety disorder, and the result is that you attain 80 percent recovery yet also acquire a whole new attitude and greater peace of mind to bring to handling the residual 20 percent of symptoms that remain. It's important not to be too attached to the exact form in which a goal manifests. Just be clear that your goal is attainable in its essence or *spirit*, if not in the *form* you originally conceived it. If you want more peace in your life, you can create it—in time.

Really trusting the idea that it's possible to create what you believe is the most liberating realization I've gained along the path to my own recovery. In essence, it means there is no adversity in life that cannot be overcome. You do not have to be a victim of any circumstance, no matter how difficult it *appears*, because you can recreate an altogether new circumstance. The power of mind and spirit always exceeds the power of *any* adverse situation. Just knowing that has given me a tremendous sense of hope and optimism. I hope it will for you, too.

With all this in mind, I ask you now to consider the following seven-step process for creating your goals. You can use these steps for visualizing or affirming your recovery from anxiety—or for any other goal you seek. These steps have worked well for me and for many of my clients. Be sure to see the sections following these steps on how to develop visualizations and affirmations as well as clearing resistance and self-limiting beliefs. These sections will assist you with steps two and three. For further assistance beyond this chapter in creating your goals, I highly recommend the book *Creative Visualization* by Shakti Gawain (1995). Twenty years after its original publication, it's still the clearest, most articulate, and most practical description of the creative process I know of.

The Process of Creating Your Goal

1. *Set your goal.*

   Decide what it is you would like to change or realize in your life. Most likely this will be overcoming your problem with anxiety. However, your goal can be on any level—physical, emotional, mental, or spiritual. You might want a new job, a new or better relationship, clarity about making an important decision, or peace of mind. To illustrate how the process of creation works, let's suppose you want to overcome a condition of chronic anxiety or fear and achieve a state of wholeness and health.

2. *Develop a visualization or affirmation of your goal (or both).*

   Create a mental picture—or a statement—of your goal exactly as you'd like to achieve it. Think of it as if it were already realized or fulfilled. If you design a visualization, describe what your life would look and feel like if you attained your goal, in as much detail as you can. If you design one or more affirmations, they should be positive statements in the present tense, worded as though you'd already achieved your goal. If you seek wholeness and health, for example, you might say, "I am fully whole and healthy in body and mind." See the sections on developing visualizations and affirmations below for more details on writing your own.

3. *Acknowledge and detach from any doubts or fears.*

This is an important step. If you have any doubts or fears about being able to have what you truly want, take time to acknowledge them but don't give them any additional energy or attention. Let yourself detach emotionally from them as best you can. If they come up, you might want to write them down to give them expression, and then resolve to move past them and refocus on your goal. The less energy you give them, the weaker such fears become until they eventually die of neglect. For example, if you're dealing with a chronic anxiety disorder, you might have doubts or fears such as, "I've had this problem twenty years; I'll never get better," or "This problem is so old and familiar that I'm scared to embrace the possibility of a new life without it." Simply notice that these attitudes come up, give them a moment of acknowledgment, and then resolve to look past them and refocus on the goal of creating wholeness and wellness. See the section below on "Overcoming Fears, Doubts, and Self-Limiting Beliefs" for further assistance with this step. It's helpful to work through self-limiting beliefs and attitudes before you sit down to practice a creative visualization or affirmation.

4. *Relax.*

Relaxation helps you to put more energy and presence behind your visualization or affirmation. If you try to visualize or affirm something while your mind is scattered, it's hard to focus conscious energy on it because your consciousness itself is scattered. Relaxation helps you to quiet and focus your mind. Then you can hold the visualization or affirmative statement in your mind easily. Research has confirmed, in fact, that visualizations for healing illness are far more effective in a relaxed, reverie-like state than in a more active, analytical state of mind.

Before doing a visualization or working with affirmations, you might want to use progressive muscle relaxation, a guided relaxation tape, calming music, or meditation to relax.

5. *Focus on your visualization or affirmation clearly.*

While relaxed, give yourself time to focus on your visualization in full detail. Or repeat your affirmation several times slowly, with full presence of mind. Try to be in the present moment, bringing your full, undistracted awareness to this process. This is the time to be clear and deliberate about what you are visualizing/affirming without rushing.

6. *Energize it.*

The more you can get behind your visualization or affirmation with your whole being, the more you empower it. To put your heart and soul into it gives your visualization or affirmative statement increased power to attract exactly what you seek. Think about your goal in a positive, uplifting way and build your conviction that you truly can have it, and that it is now coming to you. As you put deeper levels of yourself (your inner being) behind your intention, you may begin to draw on resources beyond yourself (i.e., your Higher Power or God) to bring it about.

7. *Repeat the process of visualization or affirmation daily (or until your goal manifests).*

Repetition of your visualization/affirmation strengthens it. First, the process of persisting in refocusing away from doubts and fears toward whatever you seek helps you to release those doubts. Your conviction and commitment toward your goal increase. Second, repetition actually increases the capacity of your belief—your own picture or statement of your goal—to attract its real-life equivalent on a physical level. The principle of "mind over matter" is reinforced by perseverance.

It's important to persevere with the process of visualizing or affirming a goal until you achieve it. This may take days, week, months, or even years.

Developing a Visualization

You may be concerned that it's difficult to visualize your goal because you don't readily "see" mental pictures in your mind. Realize that you don't need to see images in detail to utilize visualization. Some people are naturally visual, while others tend to favor auditory or kinesthetic channels of sensory experience. More important than seeing your goal in detail is your ability to *feel* a sense of conviction about it when you imagine it. The strength of your belief and commitment to your goal is the best measure of your ability to actually create it.

If you're still concerned about your capacity to visualize, work with the script below until you feel satisfied with your ability to "see" the scene involved. Have a friend read it to you or record it on tape so you can be fully relaxed when you visualize it. The more you relax, the easier it will be for you to visualize the scene in detail.

The Beach

You're walking down a long wooden stairway to a very beautiful, expansive beach. It looks almost deserted and stretches off into the distance as far as you can see. The sand is very fine and light in appearance. You step onto the sand in your bare feet and rub it between your toes. It feels so good to walk slowly along this beautiful beach. The roaring sound of the surf is so soothing that you can just let go of anything on your mind. You're watching the waves ebb and flow ... they're slowly coming in ... breaking over each other ... and then slowly flowing back out again. The ocean itself is very beautiful and so relaxing just to look at. You look out over the surface of the ocean all the way to the horizon and then follow the horizon as far as you can see, noticing how it bends slightly downward as it follows the curvature of the earth. As you scan the ocean you can see, many miles offshore, a tiny sailboat skimming along the surface of the water. And all these sights help you to just let go and relax even more. As you continue walking down the beach, you become aware of the fresh, salty smell of the sea air. You take in a deep breath ... breathe out ... and feel very refreshed and even more relaxed. Overhead you notice two seagulls flying out to sea ... looking very graceful as they soar into the wind ... and you imagine how you might feel yourself if you had the freedom to fly. You find yourself settling into a deep state of relaxation as you continue walking down the beach. You feel the sea breeze blowing gently against your cheek and the warmth of the sun overhead penetrating your neck and shoulders. The warm, liquid sensation of the sun just relaxes you even more ... and you're beginning to feel perfectly content on this beautiful beach. It's such a lovely day. In a moment, up ahead, you see a comfortable-looking beach chair. Slowly, you begin to approach the beach chair ... and when you finally reach it, you sit back and settle in. Easing back in this comfortable beach chair, you let go and relax even more, drifting even deeper into relaxation. In a little while you might close your eyes and just listen to the sound of the surf, the unending cycle of waves ebbing and flowing. And the rhythmic sound of the surf carries you even deeper ... deeper still ... into a wonderful state of quietness and peace.

Now, write a script in which you picture yourself having achieved your goal in as much vivid detail as possible. What would a day in your life look like if you had realized your goal? What new things would you do? How would you feel? Would there be changes in your environment, and, if so, what would they look like? How would you act toward significant others in your life? How would they act toward you?

When you have developed a detailed script answering as many of these questions as are relevant, have a friend read it to you or listen to a tape recording of it while you're in a relaxed state. With practice, you should find that your ability to visualize it in detail increases.

The following is an example of a detailed visualization of an ideal day developed by one of my clients.

It's 5 a.m. and I am up and moving comfortably, without dizziness and anxiety, to the kitchen to fix breakfast for my husband Steve and me. My mind is clear, and I am thinking at a normal pace and moving without pain or stiffness. As I move I am talking to myself with affirmations and mentally planning my day. As I sit down to breakfast, I talk about my plans for the day and watch the animals outside our window. I am calm and enjoying breakfast at a normal pace. It is 6:15 and Steve is leaving for work. I wish him a good day and comfortably move into my early morning exercise routine. I'm looking forward to doing my daily program: yoga is helping me become stronger, more flexible, and more relaxed; aerobics is giving me stamina, strength, and energy; and relaxation and meditation are giving me inner peace and calm. I find that I have boundless energy. I'm feeling calm, at peace with the world and myself, energetic, and comfortable in my body. I'm enjoying and desiring healthy food and am preparing a healthy snack. As I dress slowly, I am doing abdominal breathing and using affirmations to calm any anticipatory anxiety or racing thoughts. This helps me stay in the moment ... Now I imagine that I'm at my desk, enjoying the sunlight and the view, as I plan and prioritize my day. Decision-making is easy, as is scheduling. My schedule allows me to balance all of my activities. I am excited with these items on my agenda for today and at peace with each of them. After lunch I'll give myself time to rest, read or nap, if I want to. I find it easy to move through the day comfortably, calmly, and with self-confidence. I know I am ready to handle the unusual or unexpected and can reprioritize if needed ... Now I see myself calmly walking to the

*car to go to the grocery store and I feel happy to be going out. As
I begin my drive, I move comfortably and with purpose, ready to
do what I need to do. As I drive I remain calm and relaxed. The
entire trip is easy to negotiate. It is getting easier every time to
handle driving and going to the grocery store. I do fine both on the
trip out and on the return trip ... Now I see myself getting ready
to go to the golf course to practice. This is something I like to do.
I enjoy what the game of golf teaches me about myself. Today I
will learn more about life from golf—things such as "easy does it,"
"go with the flow," "laugh and enjoy," "less is more," and "life is
an ongoing process, not a task to always be completed." I'll watch
my childlike, playful self get stronger. What a nice way to meet and
talk with people in a peaceful setting ... On my way home I plan
dinner, the evening, and think about what I might do to help others
through my experience with anxiety/panic/depression. I'm excited
that I might help someone overcome or cope better with anxiety
through my experiences. Walking through the door to our house, I
thank God for a wonderful day and the blessings I have. I calmly
move through my tasks after being out for the day. I'm sitting on
the floor, having a mini-break and playing with my dog, Boggs.
What a good and loving friend he is. He makes me laugh and
think often that life's greatest pleasures are the little things. As I fix
dinner I think of what I experienced today, what lessons I learned
and what I can glean from those lessons. I have had a full, productive, and enjoyable day and am enjoying dinner with Steve. After
dinner, I'll get ready for bed and read or listen to the tapes I've
been working with. Or I may just take a long, relaxing bath or sit
on the patio and watch the animals in the yard.*

Please note that if your healing visualization involves overcoming a phobia, you may need to do *imagery desensitization* first. This will be necessary if
you find that you become anxious when you first imagine approaching your
phobic situation. Break the visualization down into a series of steps, starting
with the easiest and proceeding to the most difficult. For example, if you have
a fear of flying, you might visualize going to the airport first, then checking in
your bags, and then going to the gate. When you're comfortable with these
scenes, visualize each aspect of a flight separately, beginning with boarding the
plane, then finding your seat, then waiting until the door to the aircraft is
closed, then taxiing down the runway, then taking off, etc. Visualize each
scene repeatedly until you get fully comfortable with it, then proceed to the

next scene. For detailed instructions on how to do imagery desensitization, see Chapter 7 in *The Anxiety & Phobia Workbook*.

Developing Affirmations

Much of what goes on in your mind is based on the basic or "core" beliefs that you've gained from parents, peers, and society at large. Many of these beliefs can be counterproductive—in fact, such beliefs are often the source of much of the anxiety and stress you experience. Beliefs such as "I'm powerless to change my circumstances," "There is something very wrong with me," or "I don't really deserve to have what I want" are common examples of such unhelpful beliefs.

An affirmation is a way to "make firm" something you would *like* to believe. The practice of using affirmations enables you to begin replacing some of the negative, conditioned beliefs from your past with more constructive ideas about yourself, others, and life in general. Utilizing affirmations will help you, first, to overcome any depressed or anxious feelings that stem from your negative beliefs. More than this, *affirmations will help draw to you circumstances that reflect their positive content.* You can use them to help you create the goals you seek.

Here are some examples of affirmations:

- I am becoming prosperous.

- I have all the financial resources I need.

- I now have a well-paying, satisfying job.

- I now have a loving, fulfilling relationship.

- I am vibrantly healthy and whole.

- I love myself the way I am.

- I respect and believe in myself.

- My relationship with _____ is growing happier and more fulfilling all the time.

- Whatever I truly need comes to me.

In writing an affirmation to reflect a goal you wish to attain, observe the following guidelines:

1. Keep affirmations in the *present tense* ("I am prosperous") or *present progressive tense* ("I am becoming prosperous"). Telling yourself that

some change you desire will happen in the future always keeps it one step removed.

2. *Avoid negations.* Instead of saying "I'm no longer afraid of public speaking," try "I am learning to enjoy public speaking" or "Public speaking comes easily to me."

3. An affirmation should be *short, simple,* and *positive.* "My mind and body are healthy and whole" is preferable to "I am overcoming my problem with panic attacks."

4. An affirmation should be framed in terms of a new goal rather than an old problem. As in the preceding example, state the goal you wish to achieve rather than overcoming some problem in the past.

5. It's important that you have *some* belief in—or at least a willingness to believe in—your affirmations. It's by no means necessary, however, to believe in an affirmation 100 percent when you first start out. The whole point is to shift your beliefs and attitudes in the direction of the affirmation.

Ways to Work with Affirmations

Once you have developed one—or preferably several—affirmations that reflect your goal, you can work with them in one of three ways:

1. Write the affirmation slowly, with your awareness fully present, five to ten times. Try to build conviction about your positive statement as you write it again and again. On the opposite side of the paper, write down any doubts or fears that come up in the process (if they do). See the following section on "Overcoming Fears, Doubts, and Self-Limiting Beliefs" to deal with these.

2. Record the affirmation on tape, five times in the first person—e.g., "I am healthy and whole," and five times in the second person, "You are healthy and whole." Leave five to ten seconds between each reiteration of the affirmation so that you have time to reflect and meditate on it. Your recording should take about a minute or two. Listen to this recording once or twice per day when you are in a relaxed, focused state for at least thirty days. It's okay to play the tape at any time, while you're cleaning the house or driving your car. However, doing so in a relaxed, aware state will increase the power of the process considerably.

3. Take one affirmation describing your goal into quiet meditation. Repeat this affirmation slowly and with conviction when you feel relaxed and centered. Continue this process for five to ten minutes. The more you can put your deepest conviction—your "heart and soul"—behind your affirmation, the more you empower it to attract what you seek. Should doubts or fears come up, clear them (using the guidelines in the following section) before you repeat the process.

Overcoming Fears, Doubts, and Self-Limiting Beliefs

Many of us want to heal limiting circumstances in our bodies, minds, and lives, and yet we harbor doubts and fears. Various forms of resistance stand in our way. You may be afraid to have what you truly want or else you feel you don't deserve to have it. Often your doubts and fears are unconscious. By making them conscious, you can work through them and free the way for your visualizations or affirmations to be effective.

Some of the most common ways you can obstruct your own progress follow:

1. *Fear of change.*

    It may feel safer to cling to what's familiar, even if it's uncomfortable, than to venture into unknown territory (which is always necessary if you truly want to change). Living with panic and phobias—or obsessions and compulsions—can be miserable, but at least it's familiar. To imagine yourself without them might be such a major change that you balk (perhaps unconsciously) at the prospect.

2. *Reluctance to give up a problem's hidden benefit or "payoff".*

    Remaining ill often affords the opportunity to receive a lot of attention and be taken care of. It may also provide reasons not to have to work, not to have to deal with the outside world, or not to have to leave an unhappy relationship and risk being alone. In short, there can be many hidden (or not so hidden) benefits to staying ill. In such cases it becomes easy to complain and imagine that you would *like* to recover, when deep inside you don't really want to.

3. *Being "lost" without your problem.*

    Perhaps you derive your sense of identity from having an anxiety disorder or from some other misfortune such as strained family relations, financial problems, or job dissatisfaction. You might ask yourself whether you feel like a "victim" of your circumstances. If you get your sense of who you are from your problem, it may be difficult to let it go. To do so would mean giving up your very identity. To truly change means relinquishing your habitual way of seeing yourself.

4. *Fear of giving up control.*

A close cousin to the fear of losing your sense of self is the fear of giving up control. If you're always busy trying to manipulate circumstances in order to "conquer" your problem, it may be difficult to relinquish control to allow others or your Higher Power to assist. It's certainly important to develop a sense of responsibility for yourself in order to overcome an anxiety disorder (or any other problem). However, a sense of responsibility can be carried to an extreme when you become unwilling to relinquish control enough to accept outside help. The chapter on "Letting Go" addresses this issue in depth.

5. *Low self-esteem.*

If you haven't learned to accept, respect, and believe in yourself, you may unconsciously feel that you don't deserve what you want most. Often it's important to deal with guilt or shame from the past, to forgive yourself for what you perceive to be past mistakes or failings. As you let go of shame and learn to truly love yourself, you can begin to believe in your right to be well, happy, and successful. See Chapter 8, "Addressing Personality Issues," for further assistance with this.

6. *Specific mistaken beliefs.*

All of the above points of resistance involve certain mistaken, limiting beliefs that can interfere with your capacity to attain your goals and resolve your problems in general. What follows are examples of specific mistaken beliefs that can obstruct the process of visualizing or affirming your goal. The list was adapted in part from Louise Hay's *You Can Heal Your Life* (1984), a book I highly recommend if you are serious about healing your anxiety or any other problem.

Beliefs That Hold You Back from Growth and Change

- It's not right for me to try that.

- It's too much work.

- It's too expensive.

- It will take too long.

- It's not practical.

- My family never did that.

- Ordinary people don't do that.

- Ordinary men/women don't do that.

Others Won't Let Me

- It isn't the right environment.

- They won't let me change.

- My doctor doesn't want me to.

- I can't get time off from work.

- *They* have to change first.

- My spouse, family, friends . . . wouldn't approve.

- I don't want to hurt them.

Negative Self-Concept

- I'm too: old   weak   lazy
  young   dumb   stuck
  fat   smart
  thin   poor
  short   messed up
  tall   scattered

Stalling Tactics

- I'll do it later.

- I don't have the time right now.

- I have too many other things to do.

- As soon as _____ happens, I'll do it.

Fear

- I might fail.

- They might reject me.

- I might get hurt.

- What would my spouse, friends, boss, etc., think?

- I might have to change.

- I don't have the energy.

- Who knows where I might end up?

- It might hurt my image.

- I'm not good enough (don't deserve it).

- God doesn't care about my little problem.

General Self-Limiting Beliefs

- I feel powerless or helpless.

- Often I feel like a victim of outside circumstances.

- Life is very difficult—it's a struggle.

- I am unworthy. I feel that I'm not good enough.

- My condition seems hopeless.

- There is something fundamentally wrong with me.

- I feel like I'm nothing (or can't make it) unless I'm loved.

- What others think of me is very important.

- People won't like me if they see who I really am.

- I can't rely on others for help.

- If I let someone get too close, I'm afraid of being controlled.

- I'm the only one who can solve my problems.

- I'm just the way I am—I can't really change.

How to Clear Self-Limiting Beliefs

After having reviewed the preceding list, you may have a better idea about those negative attitudes and beliefs that might obstruct your ability to create your goal. To get even more specific, try the following exercise.

RELEASING LIMITING BELIEFS EXERCISE

Take a piece of paper. At the top write the statement, "The reason I can't have _____ *(your goal)* _____ is . . ." Then list all of the reasons that come to mind. When you are done, take some time to think about what you've written. *How strongly do you believe it?* The more energy and conviction you give to negative attitudes that are contrary to attaining your goal, the harder it will be to realize that goal. Identify the particular attitudes and beliefs that you think are most getting in your way and jot them down on a separate piece of paper. Add any additional negative beliefs from the list of self-limiting beliefs above. Now you're ready to work on clearing and releasing your problem beliefs. You may be surprised to find how well the following process works if you follow it carefully and with sincere intention.

1. *Accept that you have the negative belief.*

   Don't try to deny it or "beat yourself up" for having it. You probably didn't consciously choose the belief but were conditioned to believe it long ago by your parents, peers, or society at large. Before you can let a belief go, it's important to simply accept that it's been a part of your life.

2. *Acknowledge any fearful or hurtful feelings you have around the belief.*

   Painful feelings have a way of holding a negative belief in place. If, for example, you've held a belief that you don't deserve to have your goal, you need to identify and *express* any feelings of guilt or shame that surround that belief. Or, if you are afraid to truly have what you want, it's important that you express that fear. Of all the steps in the clearing process, this is the one where you're most likely to benefit from working with a counselor or a trusted friend. It's often easier to acknowledge long-standing, painful feelings in the presence of a supportive other. If you choose to do clearing on your own, however, you can express your feelings on paper or into a tape recorder.

   A key to expressing your painful feelings is to have compassion toward yourself—to forgive yourself—especially for any negative feelings of fear, shame, or anger that may have blocked your ability to believe in yourself. Again, having a compassionate counselor or friend to assist may help this process along.

3. *Ask yourself whether you're ready and willing to let go of the negative belief.*

Is there some way in which holding on to the self-limiting belief(s) can still serve you? Is there some unconscious benefit or payoff you get from keeping the belief(s)? Can you accept—are you ready for—a life that is not based on such a belief? Review the list of reasons for resisting change above and decide whether you are fully *ready* and *willing* to let go of your self-limiting belief(s). Realize that while you may or may not release a long-standing, negative belief in an instant, your sincere readiness and *willingness* to let it go will assure that you do so—sooner or later.

4. *Perform a ritual to release the negative belief.*

To symbolize the process of releasing a negative belief, you can tear up the piece of paper on which it is written—or perhaps throw that piece of paper into a fire. In addition, you can repeat affirmations to encourage letting go, for example:

"I now dissolve any negative, self-limiting beliefs."

"I release and let go of any fear, shame, or guilt that stands in my way."

"I am now free and clear of any attitude that I don't need."

"All of my negative attitudes are now fully dissolved and released."

By going through the preceding steps, you have prepared a "place" in your mind and heart to go forward with visualizing or affirming the goal you wish to create. Keep in mind that the process of creating something new in your life may take place over time. It may be necessary to repeat the clearing process frequently until you feel you've completely released a particular limiting belief. Think of it as if you were pulling weeds from a garden. You may need to do weeding more than once in the process of watching your "plants" grow to full maturity.

Including Your Higher Power in the Creative Process

Relying on the presence of your Higher Power can deepen the process of creating your goal. By putting your heart and soul behind what you visualize or affirm, you're already moving it to a deeper level within yourself. However, the process can be taken even further by including your Higher Power as a resource to assist you. What I'm talking about is very close, if not the same, as common prayer. When you pray with conviction, consistency, and faith for something that you truly want, you have a great likelihood of bringing it about. In praying, you solicit the energy of your Higher Power to help you create something. It's my impression that *sincere* prayers are answered (see Chapter 11), *if* the request is for the highest good of the person making the prayer *and* for the highest good of everyone else involved. However, the *form* in which a prayer is answered may be unexpected and possibly differ in some ways from what was originally requested (in order to assure that it's for the highest good of everyone). It's not for any of us to fully know in advance how a given prayer might be answered.

The process outlined below is the one I've often used when I want to create a particular goal. It's not necessary for you to utilize this process in creating your own goal, but, in my own experience, I've found it to be quite powerful. The process has been called "affirmative prayer" by many people, because it *affirms* a desired outcome instead of asking for it. Other terms often used for this process are "spiritual manifestation" and "cocreation," the latter because God or Spirit is invoked to participate in the process of creating a goal. I prefer to think of the process simply as bringing God into the creative process.

Before using the following five-step process, it's important to have worked through all of the steps outlined in the previous section "How to Create Your Goal." Identifying and releasing your own self-limiting beliefs is important at the outset. Relaxing and centering yourself before you begin the process greatly increases its effectiveness. Finally, this process should be repeated daily until you're satisfied with the results.

Affirmative Prayer Process

1. *Identify the spiritual "quality" that can best overcome your problem situation.*

   What is the highest possible good you could ask for to heal or resolve the problem situation you face? What spiritual quality is needed in the situation to fully remedy it?

"Spiritual qualities" are experienced subjectively. They are those qualities of experience through which you might experience reverence, awe, or a sense of something larger than yourself: the love of a small child, the wisdom of a famous poem, the beauty of a magnificent sunset, the peace of an alpine meadow or deep meditation, or those moments of joy when life seems nearly perfect. What makes these qualities spiritual is that they contain a certain element of perfection. In experiencing them, we are moved beyond our everyday concerns into a deeper, wider state of appreciation. Like the sun penetrating clouds, they are points through which a larger, universal reality breaks through into our personal world.

Spiritual qualities include ideal love, peace, wholeness, harmony, order, wisdom, abundance, joy, and beauty. Recognizing the spiritual quality that could best heal or overcome a difficult situation is the first step in turning it around. In simply recognizing that quality, you turn away from the immediate appearance of the situation toward a higher reality. For example, to affirm perfect love in the midst of conflict, or perfect peace in the midst of turmoil is to invite the presence of your Higher Power (God) to help overcome your own limited beliefs and perceptions about the situation. In the case of illness, perfect wholeness (in mind and body) might be the spiritual quality that overcomes the condition.

2. *Unify in consciousness with your Higher Power.*

In this step you enter into an attunement with your Higher Power. This can be done by meditating, in which you become silent and simply ask to enter into the presence of God. For example, you might say to yourself, "Great Spirit, I ask for your support and guidance in this moment." (The Lord's Prayer and the Twenty-third Psalm are well-known forms of coming into the presence of your Higher Power in the Judeo-Christian tradition.)

Another way to facilitate unification is to write out statements that affirm a state of oneness with Spirit, such as "I know that I am in the perfect presence of Spirit now," or "God is working in my life right now for my highest good." It's helpful to write several of these affirmative statements until you actually feel a deepening sense of connection with your Higher Power.

3. *Affirm the spiritual quality that overcomes your problem.*

At this point you simply affirm the spiritual quality you identified in the first step. This can be done silently in meditation or by writing out two or three affirmative statements. For example, if you're ill, the divine attribute you might want to affirm is Wholeness. You might say: "I know that I'm whole and healthy in mind and body. I am well, strong, and vital in every respect. In this moment, I realize my right to be fully healthy and whole."

It's important at this stage to put aside, as far as possible, any fear or worry about whatever circumstances you face. No matter what circumstances and limitations you confront, you turn your attention away from them and resolve to affirm the highest good. This does not mean you deny or ignore the limitations of your situation. The point is to stop giving undue attention and energy to the problem. Instead, you focus on affirming the highest good in the situation. In so doing you line up with the creative power of your Higher Power—the universal resource that is God—to effect a change for the better.

4. Express gratitude.

At this point you give thanks to God (your Higher Power) in advance for the fulfillment of whatever you've affirmed. Remember that from the standpoint of your Higher Power, there is no time. To give thanks in advance for wholeness, peace, abundance, or love is to strengthen your conviction that it's already present at the highest level (i.e., in Universal Consciousness). Expressing gratitude gives impetus to the process whereby whatever good you've affirmed can actually manifest in the physical world.

Expressing gratitude also acknowledges, in humility, that your personal will or ego is not the ultimate source of healing and resolution.

5. Release.

After giving thanks, it's time to let the process go. You do not, at this point, need to hold on in anxious concern about whether the process will "work." Having affirmed the highest good in faith, you can now relinquish the fulfillment of your affirmation to your Higher Power.

For example, you might say:

- "I now entrust this affirmation to the Creative Spirit."

- "I let go and allow God to work on the realization of this goal, for the highest good of everyone concerned."

It's time to simply trust the process of creation by letting go and getting on with the business at hand. However, it's appropriate, whenever you feel your conviction wavering, to repeat the preceding five steps. It's important to persist in the process until you actually experience a healing or resolution of the problem, whether this takes days, weeks, months, or even years. Your persistence will eventually bear fruit.

The following example comes from an affirmative prayer I used in the process of my own recovery from a severe anxiety disorder a few years ago. I have separated out the five steps just described.

AN AFFIRMATION FOR RESTORING WHOLENESS

There is One Healing Power in the Universe—
a pattern for Perfect Wholeness that exists beyond all separation or
discord.
I acknowledge this One Omnipresent Power—
present in all things and in myself.
Spirit is a force for wholeness that knows no obstacles or limits.

I now experience this all-loving presence of Spirit.
Right where I am, God is working in my life for my highest good.
I now let go of all perceptions and judgments of limitation and
allow my will to align fully with the Divine Will.

I am steadfast in faith regardless of what appears in my life.
No matter what has happened in the past, I now realize, as I speak
these words, a renewed conviction and confidence that healing is
taking place in my life.
I am becoming whole and at peace in all aspects of my life.
I reclaim my Divine inheritance, which is wholeness and the fullness
of life in body, mind, and spirit.

I give thanks to Spirit for the power to disperse all appearances and
bring healing into my life.
I give thanks to the power of Spirit to release doubt and fear and
restore my faith.
I am grateful for the new directions in my life, which are revealed
through Spirit.

I now release this affirmation to the universe, knowing that its per-
fect realization is in process.
I let go and allow Spirit to move in new and mysterious ways for

my highest good and the highest good of all others.
And so it is.

Feel free to use this prayer to affirm your own recovery, or write your own prayer incorporating the five steps just described. For an outstanding collection of short affirmative prayers, see the book *Heart Steps* (1997).

Summary: Attitudes That Empower Creating Your Goal

The following six attitudes will help you to succeed in affirming your recovery or creating any other goal in your life.

Acknowledge and Release Feelings

Fear, anger, and feelings of victimization about a problem tie you to it rather than opening the door to healing and resolution. For this reason it's very important to *acknowledge* and *express* your feelings about a difficult situation. Do this with a counselor, a trusted friend, or your journal or tape recorder. Then you can clear a space for the kind of serenity or quietness from which your affirmation or visualization can be powerful.

Meditation practice can be very helpful in the process of learning to acknowledge and release feelings. See the chapter "Developing Your Observing Self" for a discussion of the usefulness of meditation.

Courage

When a problem frightens you, it takes courage to affirm the possibility of healing and resolution. Courage means that after being frightened or even overwhelmed by some difficult situation, you don't knuckle under. Instead you get back up on your feet and believe in the possibility of moving forward no matter how tough the road has been. To affirm your belief in your goal in spite of fear, despair, or outrage takes considerable courage. Yet it is also one of the most empowering things you can do. Asking for assistance from your Higher Power when you experience a setback will help to keep you on course and likely ease your journey.

Trust

Genuine trust means you *believe* in the possibility of creating—and recreating—your reality. You trust that your visualization or affirmation actually helps to attract your goal, even though you can't *see* how it does. Earlier in this chapter I presented a model of how the creative process might actually work. However, this model is far from complete, and it may or may not be particularly convincing or plausible to you. In the last analysis, none of us can fully understand exactly how the process of creating your reality works. Trusting that it does ultimately needs to come not from an intellectual understanding but from personal experience.

If you feel skeptical about the possibility of creative visualization or affirmation being effective, I invite you to try it out for yourself, following all the guidelines suggested in this chapter. To give it a fair trial, be willing to keep working with the process toward a specific goal until you obtain what you regard as genuine results. The direct experience of success with the creative process is the best way to gain trust in its potential.

Perseverance

Repeating what was just said, it's important to persevere with a visualization or affirmation until a problem resolves in one way or another. It's especially important to persevere at those times when worry or doubt cloud the initial resolution you felt at the time you first initiated your visualization, affirmation, or prayer. It took time to manifest the negative problem situation that you seek to overcome. And so it may take time to create something new. For example, if your struggle with anxiety involves not only conditioned thoughts and reactions but also a long-standing neurobiological problem, it may take time to create a high level of recovery. Months or even years may pass for the complete realization of healing to occur, but your willingness to persist over time—both in direct efforts (the "footwork" part) as well as consistently affirming your recovery—will assure the highest possible outcome.

Faith

Faith can help perseverance. Faith means believing in the ultimate triumph of "good" over limitation in the long run, no matter what happens. Much has been written on the subject of faith, but in essence it simply means believing you live in a benevolent universe where, despite appearances, all things ultimately work out for the highest good. There is no way to logically argue the case for a benevolent universe. Such a belief develops from personal experience and direct intuitive perception in relation to your Higher Power.

Being Proactive

Taking action—doing what you can—to realize your goal is a way in which you strengthen and empower your intention. You're not merely fantasizing or talking about your goal; you're sincerely going after it. When you do your part, you make yourself available to receive assistance and guidance from your Higher Power in new ways. When you take the first step toward a goal, ideas about the next step often will come to you. The proverbial saying "God helps those who help themselves" reflects a fundamental truth about the creative process.

In closing, I would like to offer an example that illustrates the power of intention. This excerpt was written by a physician who has explored Native American healing practices, and it demonstrates what's possible when an intention to heal is held with courage, perseverance, and faith.

> *Wesley was a Native American living in Duluth, about one hundred miles from the reservation where he had grown up. When I met him, Wesley's face was gaunt and he moved very slowly, wincing at the effort of rising from his chair. He looked like a man in his late sixties.*
>
> *Doctors at the University Medical Center in Duluth had diagnosed Wesley's illness as lymphoma, cancer of the lymph nodes. Wesley's had spread rapidly into his abdomen and chest, and his doctors told him he had no more than six months to live. They advised him to put his affairs in order. Wesley sought out an Ojibway medicine woman from northern Minnesota and asked her to conduct a ceremony for him. Carolyn, the woman, told him to come at the waxing of the moon. She told him to bring anyone who might help with his healing.*
>
> *At first Carolyn worked alone with Wesley, using what psychologists would call hypnosis to prepare him for the ceremony. The Arikara of North Dakota have a phrase for Carolyn's brand of hypnosis; literally it means "putting him to sleep so he thinks he sleeps when he's really awake."*
>
> *After she had prepared Wesley, Carolyn took us all into the sweat lodge to pray for four straight nights. On the fifth day she took Wesley outside and walked with him. She told him that he*

might not think so yet, but he would still bend many bows before he died. She told him an eagle would be his sign of wellness.

When Wesley spotted an eagle later that day, he was ecstatic. Carolyn performed a ceremony on the spot, sanctifying the ground by sprinkling tobacco and cornmeal. Then she burned sage to chase away evil, singing sacred songs and smoking the sacred pipe and speaking to the spirits. Finally, she told Wesley that the White Buffalo Woman had told her he was well. When he returned to the city, Wesley's doctors could find no trace of his lymphoma—and they could give no explanation of its disappearance, which was simply recorded on his chart as one of those rare, baffling spontaneous remissions. The doctors were not as quick as Carolyn had been to declare him well; because lymphomas sometimes go into remission and then reappear, judgment on a lymphoma cure is withheld for five years. When Wesley had remained cancer-free for the required five-year interval, his physicians came around to the White Buffalo Woman's position and declared Wesley well.

What You Can Do Now

1. Decide on a goal that you'd like to create. Use the seven-step process in the section "Creating Your Goal" to begin working on bringing it into your life. Develop a visualization, a series of affirmations, or both, to define your goal. Repeat the process on a regular basis until you achieve the results you seek.

2. Review the section "Overcoming Fears, Doubts, and Self-Limiting Beliefs." Think about what obstacles you might be putting in the way of achieving whatever goal you seek. Work through the four-step process in the section "How To Clear Self-Limiting Beliefs" to release unhelpful attitudes. Repeat this process two or three times when letting go of attitudes or beliefs you've held for many years. Seek out the assistance of a counselor if you need help working through feelings of sadness, anger, or shame that surround particular negative beliefs.

3. If you feel inclined, use the five-step process in the section "Including Your Higher Power in the Creative Process" to create your goal. I have found this to be a very powerful approach when used on a regular basis. Write out an affirmative statement that corresponds to each step at first. Then read through what you've written in a

relaxed, focused state each time you repeat the process. Work on building conviction and faith that you will eventually attain the goal you seek. See the following references to increase your understanding about the process of creating goals.

References and Further Reading

Bohm, David. 1980. *Wholeness and the Implicate Order.* London: Routledge and Kegan Paul.

Cameron, Julia. 1997. *Heart Steps.* New York: Tarcher/Putnam. (More than one hundred affirmative prayers for all purposes.)

Chopra, Deepak. 1994. *The Seven Spiritual Laws of Success.* San Rafael, Calif.: New World Library. (A concise summary of Dr. Chopra's spiritual philosophy.)

Dyer, Wayne. 1997. *Manifest Your Destiny.* New York: HarperCollins.

Gawain, Shakti. 1995. *Creative Visualization, Revised Edition.* San Rafael, Calif.: New World Library.

Hay, Louise. 1984. *You Can Heal Your Life.* Santa Monica, Calif.: Hay House.

Holmes, Ernest. 1988. *The Science of Mind.* New York: Putnam. (The classic text on affirmative prayer.)

Holmes, Ernest. 1995. *How to Use the Science of Mind.* Los Angeles: Science of Mind Publications.

Mehl-Madrona, Lewis. 1997. *Coyote Medicine.* New York: Scribner. (A Stanford-trained physician bridges conventional medicine with Native American healing. Excellent reading.)

Redfield, James. 1993. *The Celestine Prophecy.* New York: Warner Books.

Talbot, Michael. 1992. *The Holographic Universe.* New York: HarperCollins. (A fascinating exploration of the interface between modern physics and spirituality.)

14

Learning to Love

Love and fear are opposites. Fundamentally, they move in opposite directions. In love, we are drawn to connect with someone or something other than ourselves. In fear, we want to move away from or avoid the object of our fear. None of us exists in total isolation; we all live in relationship to loved ones, community, nature, and the Cosmos. Love is an innate force in the human heart that moves us toward unity with the "Other" in its multiple forms.

Fear, on the other hand, is a part of our instinctive nature that propels us away from a perceived threat. It's a separating force intended to preserve our individual integrity from threats to survival. In some cases fear serves us, but in many more cases it's a false alarm. Fear debars us from feeling either love or peace whenever we imagine a threat, whether or not that threat actually exists. Because we've been hurt—even traumatized—before, we're conditioned to easily project imaginary scenarios of disaster. Such fearful projections take us away from the immediate moment, from our deeper selves, and from the matrix of life that supports us. Unfounded fears separate and alienate us, while genuine love reunites us with others and heals our fear.

In a sense, this chapter's title "Learning to Love" is a misnomer. Love, in its most essential form, is not something you have to learn. It's a gift of the soul—an innate potential within you that's always there no matter what is going on nearer the surface of your awareness. What *can* be learned and practiced are ways to bring out and reveal the love that lies within. *Learning* to love means learning how to release the obstacles to the natural, innate flow of love within your heart—a potential that you brought with you into the world. That potential was very visible when you were an infant, coexisting with your more instinctive needs. No matter what has happened to you since infancy, your potential to give and receive love is still there, always ready to be evoked and nurtured.

Fear can run deep, but not as deep as your potential for love. Love is at the very core of your innermost being and ultimately derives, I believe, from your Higher Power, God, Spirit, the Infinite Field of Possibilities—whatever you choose to call it. I'm not talking about human forms of love such as romance, passion, or affection (although these certainly may be exalted to a high level), but the highest forms of love that you experience in moments of genuine forgiveness, compassion, kindness, or altruism. Sometimes this kind of love is referred to as "unconditional love"—a spontaneous love for another that has no conditions or expectations attached to it. In a manner of speaking, you might view unconditional love as a "gift from heaven"—a bit of God reflected in each human's soul. Fear, on the other hand, is not part of our inheritance from heaven. It's a survival mechanism that all animals need to thrive in a physical world. It's a part of our earthly existence that may help or hinder us. Fear may reside deep in your subconscious, but not at the very source of your being. Love, however, does exist at the source. Because it lies deeper, love can ultimately overcome any form of fear, no matter how entrenched. When you call upon love to help you heal fear, you are bound, sooner or later, to succeed.

There is much more to be said about the various forms of love. The Greeks distinguished two forms of love: Eros and agape. *Eros* referred to the passionate or romantic love you feel when physically attracted to another. *Agape* is the kind of love you feel when you genuinely care for someone, apart from any personal attraction to them. Either form of love can take on spiritual dimensions when it moves you beyond yourself into something larger. (Just because Eros is more physical does not render it less potentially "divine" than agape, in the Greek view of things.) Other forms of love include filial love—the love between close friends or brothers and sisters—and maternal love, which has certain elements in common with agape. Compassion, a form of love that plays an important role in Eastern philosophy, particularly Buddhism, is also closely related to agape. Compassion is an unselfish concern for another born out of empathy or understanding of their particular life situation (especially if that situation involves suffering). Any of these forms of love can be conditional or unconditional, depending on whether there is any personal agenda or expectations involved in extending one's love. True compassion closely approximates unconditional love; when you feel compassion you are not usually concerned about taking care of your own needs. Conditional love falls short of this ideal. If you extend your love primarily out of a need to get something from another, or out of a motive to control or manipulate them, your love is less likely to have a healing impact on the other person or yourself. The other person will likely experience your own personal agenda mixed in with whatever apparent love you offer.

How Love Can Heal Fear

If extending your love arises out of a self-imposed expectation that you "should" give—rather than out of a spontaneous desire—once again your act is less likely to heal or empower. Codependent or selfishly motivated acts of love are distortions of genuine love that ultimately create resentment within you. If you sacrifice yourself too much in the process of giving to another, you'll eventually resent it. It is the unconditional forms of love—compassion, kindness, forgiveness, generosity and altruism—that can heal fear. Opening your heart to cultivate such forms of love in your life is a very powerful way to move beyond fear.

How can you do this? *It begins with learning to love yourself.* If you're lacking love for yourself, how can you possibly extend love toward others? *Genuine* love for others cannot be willed—it cannot arise out of a self-imposed "should." It is a spontaneous overflow of whatever love you feel within and toward yourself. What you give to yourself first is what you have to give to others.

Loving Yourself

Loving yourself can be defined as *accepting*, *respecting*, and *believing* in yourself. *Accepting* yourself means you can live comfortably with both your personal strengths and weaknesses without excessive self-criticism. You can be okay with yourself just the way you are. *Respecting* yourself means you know your own worth and dignity as a unique human being. You value yourself and do not allow anyone to use or take advantage of you. *Believing* in yourself means you feel you deserve to have what you want out of life. You feel confident that you can fulfill your personal dreams and goals.

To love yourself is the opposite of being selfish or self-centered. Selfishness comes from a feeling of insufficiency or inadequacy within yourself that leads you to try to grab or manipulate to get what you want. Loving yourself, on the other hand, is associated with an inner confidence and self-regard that naturally overflows into expressions of caring toward others. Selfishness is associated with inner lack; self-love with inner fullness and security.

You begin life with a limitless capacity to give and receive love. As you go through childhood, you make decisions about yourself that often cause you to lose that capacity. If your parents overly criticized you, you may have made a decision such as "I'm unlovable." If you lost a parent due to death or divorce, you may have decided "I've got to go it alone—it's too painful to get close and then lose someone I love." Or, if you were physically abused, your decision might have been "It's dangerous to trust." Trauma and mistreatment close down our hearts and propel us to defend and withhold our inner selves from others. We may grow up finding it difficult to love anyone, least of all ourselves.

Fortunately, loving yourself is something that can be *learned*—or relearned, since you had the capacity at the outset of your life. You can learn to love yourself through specific changes in the way you perceive, think about, talk to, and act toward yourself. You can also learn through having close relationships with other persons who *model healthy self-love*. This can include partners, friends, counselors, or mentors. At least ten approaches to building healthy self-love are described elsewhere in this book. They include:

- Taking good care of your physical body

- Changing unhealthy self-talk (especially unfair self-criticism)

- Befriending your inner child

- Practicing small acts of kindness toward yourself each day

- Discovering and expressing your unique talents and gifts

- Recognizing your personal needs and giving them equal time relative to others' needs

- Becoming assertive: asking for what you want; saying "no" to what you don't want (having boundaries)

- Letting go of perfectionism—setting realistic standards

- Building a healthy support system in your community; cultivating relationships with people who have healthy self-regard

- Recognizing that your beauty and worth as a unique human being is a gift from your Higher Power

I'll say a little about each of these and indicate the section of this book where you can find some further discussion.

Taking good care of your physical body means you make time to give your body adequate rest, relaxation, exercise, and nutrition. Your body will respond to your efforts by giving you more energy, pleasure, and an enhanced feeling of well-being. See Chapters 4 and 5: "Caring for Your Body: Relaxation, Exercise, and Energy Balance" and "Caring for Your Body: Nutrition."

Changing unhealthy self-talk begins with identifying four inner voices (subpersonalities) that tend to undermine your sense of self-worth: the "Worrier," "Critic," "Victim," and "Perfectionist." You can determine the specific self-talk that each of the voices uses against you and learn how to counter with constructive, supportive statements to yourself. The four inner voices are discussed in Chapter 8, "Addressing Personality Issues" in the section "Overcoming the Fear of Abandonment or Isolation." Detailed guidelines and exercises for working with the negative self-talk of each of these four voices can be found in Chapter 9 ("Self-Talk") of *The Anxiety & Phobia Workbook.*

Befriending your inner child means learning to tune into another subpersonality within yourself—your "inner child." This is the part of you that feels childlike, expresses your deepest emotional needs, and may still carry leftover pain or trauma from your childhood. The previously mentioned section in Chapter 8, "Overcoming the Fear of Abandonment or Isolation," describes several ways to cultivate a closer relationship with your inner child.

Practicing small acts of kindness toward yourself on a daily basis is a simple but powerful way to cultivate a more loving relationship with yourself. Loving yourself is quite similar to loving another person—the relationship prospers when you give it time and attention. See the list of self-nurturing activities in Chapter 8.

Discovering and expressing your unique gifts and talents. Each of us has a unique purpose—something we came here to do and can offer to others. When you're expressing your unique purpose, you will feel more alive, creative, and fulfilled within yourself. See Chapter 10, "Finding Your Unique Purpose" if you feel this is an area you wish to work on.

Recognizing your personal needs—and giving them equal time relative to others' needs—is certainly one way you might define the concept of "self-love." As long as pleasing others is more important than pleasing yourself, you'll likely have low regard and respect for yourself. If you tend to be a "people pleaser" at your own expense, see the section "Overcoming the Fear of Rejection or Embarrassment" in Chapter 8.

Becoming assertive means you not only give attention to your personal needs but are willing to ask others to help you meet them. Assertiveness also implies an ability to set limits in response to unreasonable demands or requests—the ability to say "no" when you need to. It's hard to build self-respect unless you recognize and can exercise your basic rights as a human being. Again, the section "Overcoming the Fear of Rejection or Embarrassment" in Chapter 8 has more information on developing assertiveness. So does the chapter "Asserting Yourself" in *The Anxiety & Phobia Workbook.*

Letting go of perfectionism and setting realistic standards is an important part of learning to love yourself. As long as you are never quite satisfied with your own achievements or actions, it's difficult to be comfortable with yourself. Being overly critical of yourself about mistakes and errors also tends to undermine your self-worth. There are several ways to ease up with perfectionism, including creating more fun and recreation in your life, cultivating a sense of humor, learning to enjoy the journey as much as the destination, and countering "should" and "must" self-talk. See Chapter 12, "Letting Go," for further discussion.

Building a healthy support system means you have a circle of friends beyond your immediate family. These are people you can trust and confide in. Such friends can provide objectivity, feedback, support, and validation in ways that may not be possible with intimate family members. They also are likely to be reliably there, through crises or major transitions in your life. Having a healthy support system is an important way in which you can better care for yourself. If you don't presently have such a group, you can build one through getting more involved with a church, service organizations in your community, or intentional support groups for persons dealing with anxiety, codependency, recovery from an abusive childhood, or twelve-step "anonymous" groups.

Recognizing that your value is inherent can go a long way toward fostering a greater sense of self-worth and self-respect. Ultimately you did not create yourself—you were born into this world with a unique value and purpose. Your own judgments of yourself, however negative, do not change your inherent worth as a person. Even your behavior, no matter how unenlightened, does not alter your innate worth. Believing that there is a higher purpose to your life will help you to see your own limitations and mistakes not as failings, but as part of a greater plan for the evolution of your soul. See Chapter 11, "Enlarging Your View of Life," for further discussion about how spirituality can transform your estimation of yourself.

Use the following guided meditation to help you affirm the power and significance of love in your life. Have someone read it to you or else record it. You may also want to try it with "I" statements instead of "you" statements.

GUIDED MEDITATION

You deserve love.

You deserve to feel loved, accepted, and valued for the good person you are.

As you come to understand that you deserve love, you're more and more willing to receive love from others.

You find yourself increasingly willing to be open to receive love from those people you're closest to.

As you release and let go of old hurts and defenses, you discover a growing awareness of love inside. For you have much love to give.

There is no need to struggle for love—it exists completely and perfectly within you.

Each day you are learning more how to love yourself.

And as you love yourself, you experience more natural ability to love others. No longer do you deprive yourself of the free expression of love. You find you feel wonderful when you express love.

As you heal the past and learn to love yourself, you find it easier to give and receive love.

You find how much the special people in your life want to give you love, and you find it easier to allow them to.

It is becoming easier to open to more love in your life.

In this moment, you are willing and ready to embrace more love in your life.

If you have learned how to love yourself—to accept, respect, and believe in yourself—then opening your heart to various forms of unconditional love becomes easier. The remainder of this chapter considers three forms of love which, when unconditional, carry a tremendous capacity to heal both yourself and others: forgiveness, compassion, and generosity. At the end of the description of each type of love there is an exercise to help cultivate that particular form. Doing the exercises will ensure you get the most benefit out of this chapter.

Forgiveness

Forgiveness is one of the greatest acts of healing possible between two persons. It opens channels for love to be expressed again, no matter what has gone before. In forgiving another, you liberate yourself from any resentment or hurt you may have been withholding—painful emotions that only result in causing you further stress. In forgiving yourself (for past or present mistakes), you come to accept and respect your own worth. You make a space in your life to move toward a positive future unfettered by your past.

Why is it so often difficult to forgive? One of the biggest obstacles, I believe, is in trying to forgive someone or something before you feel ready to. It's impossible to genuinely forgive another when it's something you feel you *should* do. Forgiveness can't be forced—it's an experience that needs to emerge naturally after you've had the opportunity to acknowledge and express any feelings of anger or hurt. If I'm angry with you over something you said, I'm unlikely to be ready to forgive you until I've communicated my angry feelings. This is best done in a nonblaming way; I simply let you know that what you did made me angry (and perhaps hurt me as well), without putting you down. Then I can come to a place of clarity where it is possible to forgive.

If the person you need to forgive is no longer around or alive, you can still work through any unresolved anger or pain by writing a letter to that person disclosing all of your feelings in detail. It doesn't matter whether they ever receive the letter—what's important is expressing your unfinished feelings. Only then can you be open to the possibility of genuine forgiveness.

Another aid to forgiveness is empathy. It's easier to forgive if you can take the role of the other person and understand where they are (or were) coming from. Forgiveness is difficult when another person's hurtful action is unintelligible. If you don't understand them, what they did may seem arbitrary, unfeeling, or possibly even cruel. In attempting to understand what led another to act as they did, you may not agree with their position, but at least their behavior becomes comprehensible. Perhaps what they did arose out of considerable suffering on their part—in which case you may be able to feel some compassion.

Understanding the abusive backgrounds of unhappy parents who abuse their children does not condone their ugly behavior. Yet it may allow enough insight to open the door to compassion and eventually forgiveness. Sometimes, of course, even understanding may not be sufficient to allow for forgiveness. In such cases it's important simply to *accept* that what happened did happen. Acceptance is the first step. Then you can grieve your consequent loss and put what happened in the past, where it belongs, so that you're free to go on with the present.

For example, if you were physically harmed or sexually molested by a parent, you may still be angry to the point that it feels difficult to forgive. Simply acknowledging and expressing your anger about the past in the presence of a counselor or a supportive friend can help you to accept that what happened—happened. Then you can grieve the fact of your parent's inability to offer you the love you needed. Perhaps you can even have some understanding of your parent's predicament based on knowledge about their childhood.

Whether or not you get to forgiveness, going through such a process empowers you to finish with your past so that you can get on with your life in the present.

Coming to terms with your past is a powerful means for opening yourself to a greater experience of love in your life. In truth, the past cannot be changed—it can only be released.

When you do reach the point where you can forgive another, you're no longer likely to be angry or afraid of them. Forgiveness frees you of inner stress or turmoil you've felt toward someone and also frees them to make amends to you. Forgiveness is a sacred act—it reaches beyond the limitations of human personality and behavior to the spiritual essence that all of us share.

FORGIVENESS EXERCISE

- Think about a person who hurt you or did something you find difficult to forgive (whether this person is alive or dead).

- What did this person do that you find most difficult to forgive? If there are many things, start with the most difficult first.

- Write a letter to this person, speaking from your heart about all of your feelings toward them and toward what they did. Take time to do this and do not hold anything back—you may need several pages. It isn't necessary and may not be appropriate to send the letter.

- When your letter is done, share it with a person you're close to and trust (or else a professional counselor). Feel free to express any feelings that come up aloud to the person you're confiding in. Give yourself at least one hour for this.

- Now think about the person who hurt you again. Do you feel ready to forgive them—in all sincerity—or do you feel you're not ready? If you're not ready to forgive, it's time to work on *accepting* the fact of what happened so that you can let go of the past and move on. Working with statements such as "It happened and it's over" or "It's in the past and I can go on" may facilitate the process. If you feel sadness and grief in the process of doing this, accept that it's part of the healing.

- If you feel you're ready to forgive the person, take time to relax, close your eyes and visualize that person (whether they're alive or not) standing before you. Then speak to them as *if* they were *present right now*, telling them that you forgive them for what they did in whatever words feel appropriate. If you're able to truly forgive them, you will feel as though a weight has been lifted. (Note: If you feel you need to forgive yourself for something in the past, visualize yourself and follow the same instructions.)

Compassion

Compassion involves having concern for another person's difficulty. You feel for another's suffering—and wish that they might be free of that suffering—without judging them.

The path to developing compassion is simple, although it's not always easy. Compassion begins with *acknowledging that adversity exists for everyone.* Although suffering certainly is not all there is to life, no one is immune to times of hardship and challenge. Much of our current society appears to be based on the need to deny pain and suffering as much as possible. Material consumption, TV, overeating, analgesics, and alcohol are some of the many strategies used to avoid pain. Those persons who are ill, disabled, and elderly are consigned to places where they are largely forgotten and out of sight. Youthful vitality, beauty, and virility are the ideals promoted by the media. A willingness to look beyond surface appearances and acknowledge the fragility and mortality of life is where compassion begins.

True compassion requires not just acknowledging the mortality and limitations of life but opening your heart to it. The ability to do so is something that develops with maturity and life experience. (Sometimes it happens only after having gone through a period of personal suffering.) In the moment when you stop running from your own inner pain—letting go of persons, substances, or activities that shield you from it—you find that you have more space to open your heart. To be sure, life is full of moments of joy and beauty where your heart opens naturally, without perceiving any pain. Yet, in my experience, opening deeply to compassion for others requires a willingness to bear witness to your own personal afflictions. When you have acknowledged and accepted your own difficulties in life, you can be fully present for another's. Having compassion for others is a gift to yourself. In bearing witness to your own inner discomfort, you allow it to emerge and move on. You release it instead of holding it—or hiding it—within your soul.

Beyond acknowledging suffering and opening your heart, compassion requires *understanding* another. You seek to understand the conditions that led the person into their predicament. You try seeing their situation from *their* point of view rather than your own. This particular aspect of compassion is closely related to empathy—the ability to take another person's perspective—to "walk in their shoes." Once you genuinely understand another's difficulty, you can stop judging them and feel concern for them instead. Even the most reprehensible behavior can be understood (although not condoned) if you fully understand the conditions that led up to it. As your capacity for compassion grows, you learn to stop judging people so quickly and seek instead to understand them.

When you fully understand someone—to the point where you're truly able to feel for their predicament—then that person is no longer likely to threaten you. Compassion for another diminishes the possibility of being afraid of them. Instead you see them as another fallible human being who has suffered just like yourself. To be compassionate, however, does not mean you allow another to take advantage of you or wield their inner distress in destructive ways at your expense. Compassion always comes from a position of strength. It may require you to set limits, and even use force, if necessary, to redirect another away from hostile or destructive behavior. In being compassionate you hold the highest vision for another; you see their suffering and acknowledge their potential. If another person's behavior is destructive or violent, the most compassionate act toward them is one that calls them to change their ways. You call them to take responsibility for being true to their full potential as a human being—anything less is unacceptable. A popular expression for this form of compassion is "tough love." Concern for another's distress does not include allowing destructive expressions of that distress to hurt you. Compassion for yourself is always included in compassion for another.

COMPASSION EXERCISE

Close your eyes and take a few deep breaths until you feel relaxed and centered. Now think about a person you know who is experiencing physical or mental suffering. Reflect on their situation without judgment and allow your heart to open to them. Do this for two or three minutes. If it helps, you might want to silently repeat a phrase such as "May you be free of your pain and suffering" or perhaps "May you be at peace." (Pick your own phrase if you prefer.) If feelings other than compassion arise, such as fear, despair, anger, or sorrow, focus on your breathing and allow these feelings to arise and move through. You may want to write them down if they start to distract you. When your feelings pass, refocus on the person you've chosen and allow yourself to settle down into a place where you simply feel concern for their ultimate well-being. In learning to perceive another's adversity without getting lost in fear or sorrow, you will begin to transform the way you relate to your own pain. Developing compassion leads to more equanimity within yourself.

Optional: Try this same exercise with someone you strongly dislike, or even someone who is causing harm in the world. As you reflect on this person, make an effort to understand what kind of conditions/circumstances might have led them to behave the way they do. Even if there is no way to know the background of this particular person, acknowledge that there are certain reasons and conditions that led them to act as they do. Reflect on the truth that hurtful behavior usually arises out of suffering (often fear) and ultimately only adds further suffering to the perpetrator's situation.

If you find judgment of—or anger at—the person coming up, focus on your breathing and allow the judgments to arise and pass through you, while staying with the exercise. If you need to write down your negative feelings do so, but then return to the exercise. See if you can reframe the way you perceive the other person. Instead of judging them as "bad" or "evil," try instead seeing their *behavior*—what they did—as unenlightened or ignorant. Imagine how this person might act if they lived up to their full potential as a human being—if they could learn to act from a position of love instead of fear or anger.

Generosity

Generosity is the desire to extend yourself in order to benefit or bring joy to someone else. It is one of the earliest expressions of unconditional love. Small children are known to engage in simple acts of generosity spontaneously. Generosity usually arises from a feeling of contentment, joy, or love within yourself. It's an overflowing of an inner abundance you already feel, not something done out of a sense of obligation or compulsion.

Generosity is not emphasized in modern society, except perhaps at holidays and birthdays. The prevalence of consumer values conditions most of us to want, need, and seek to acquire things rather than to think about giving. True generosity requires a fundamental shift in perception: to move from a stance of "What can I get?" to one of "How can I help or give to someone else?" This shift from getting to giving in fact brings joy to the giver. Whether giving is a spontaneous impulse or a conscious choice, acts of generosity often lighten your spirit by moving you beyond immediate preoccupation with your own concerns. This is how generosity (like other forms of unconditional love) can free you from fear. Fear is a defensive posture where you contract—or move away—from something you perceive to be threatening. Generosity reverses the sequence—you transcend your own avoidance and contraction in the moment you give to someone else. Generosity overcomes separation and reconnects you with someone or something larger than yourself.

You can cultivate generosity with practice. Each of us has an innate potential to be generous, but sometimes that potential needs to be nurtured. The place to begin is to stop stifling your impulses to be generous out of fear. Sometimes you may worry about another's reaction to your generous act or perhaps whether they'll like what you plan to give. The adage we all grew up with, "It's the thought that counts," still holds true. People generally respond more to your thought of them than to what you give. When you think of giving something away, you might also worry about whether you really want to part with it. Remember always to check in with yourself first with the question: "Do I really need this?" If the answer is "no," you'll likely benefit both the other person as well as yourself by giving. Developing generosity means following through with spontaneous desires to give, in spite of any resistance your mind tries to throw up. In this respect it's not unlike developing courage; you learn by simply moving past your resistance and doing it anyway.

There are many different ways to be generous. The simplest is to be present for another person—to genuinely listen to what they have to say. Hearing a person out without interrupting them, advising them, or judging them lets the other know that you value what they have to say and, by extension, that you value them. Listening is one of the simplest of gifts, but it takes presence of mind and skill to do it well. Beyond listening, you can praise, support, encourage, validate, uplift, amuse, serve, and help others in a variety of ways. You also give to someone on a more physical level by hugging them, touching them, giving them material gifts, anticipating their needs, cooking for them, and so on. Others seem to appreciate our gifts most when we surprise them—offering them something other than what they might expect to receive.

Unexpected gifts are sometimes called "random acts of kindness." As you look down the following list, think about which items you would consider giving to 1) your partner or spouse, 2) your child, 3) your parent(s), 4) other relatives, 5) friends, 6) an acquaintance at work, and 7) your community. Which ones are you willing to take action on this week? this month?

Random Acts of Kindness

- Listen to someone well—be present for them.

- Buy someone a special gift.

- Give someone a hug.

- Offer to help someone with a chore.

- Show interest in someone's favorite pastime.

- Give someone a back rub.

- Make something for someone.

- Cook for them.

- Spend time outdoors with them (taking a walk, going to a park).

- Offer support when they're upset.

- Praise someone for an accomplishment.

- Offer them encouragement when they're feeling challenged.

- Teach someone what they need to know.

- Thank someone for doing something you usually take for granted.

- Smile and say something pleasant to a stranger or a clerk.

- Put money in a parking meter for someone whose time ran out.

- Make a donation to your favorite charity or cause.

- Donate time to a volunteer organization or project.

- Donate things you don't need anymore.

- Your own idea of a generous act.

In bringing out your own potential for generosity, there are two important things to keep in mind. First, don't worry if you don't always feel a spontaneous desire to give. Try giving just to give. Sometimes by doing the behavior first without the feeling, the feeling comes along later. Be willing to "prime the pump" by doing random acts of kindness even at times when you don't feel like it. Second, it's self-contradictory to act generously out of a motive for personal gain or out of a sense of obligation. Be careful to distinguish true generosity from co-dependency. If you do something for someone because you want to win their approval, placate them, or avoid their anger, your action is primarily for yourself rather than the other. If you give because you think you should, but your heart's not in it, you're merely satisfying your own internalized standard rather than truly extending yourself. There is always some element of desire—"I want to"—in a generous act, even in the instance where you simply want to cultivate your capacity to give by practicing it. There is also usually an element of altruism—"I want to do it for them."

Remember that any sincere gift to another is always a gift to yourself. When you shift your perception from yourself to how you can benefit another, you transcend your own personal needs and the concerns that go with them. This is how practicing generosity can overcome fear. Fear and anxiety are based on separation from others—generosity reconnects you with them.

In fact, all forms of unconditional love—forgiveness, compassion, generosity, caring, kindness, and unconditional affection—overcome fear by reconnecting you with a larger sense of life that begins with your nearest loved ones and extends to your friends, community, country, the entire planet, and ultimately the cosmos. Fear is only an illusion of separation that you temporarily believe. Acts of genuine love reconnect you with a Source to which you've always belonged and which forever exists beyond all types of fear. As was said long ago: "Perfect love casts out fear."

What You Can Do Now

1. Review the section "Loving Yourself." Several different ways to care for and value yourself were described. Which one(s) would you be willing to make time to work on?

2. Choose one of the three forms of unconditional love discussed in this chapter: forgiveness, compassion, or generosity. Make a commitment to work on cultivating that particular form for one month, beginning with doing the relevant exercise in this chapter.

3. Love begins at home. Perhaps the best place to start opening your heart is with your closest relationship—your spouse or partner (or perhaps a parent, child, or close friend). Consider the following ways that you might cultivate greater love toward that person.

   • Be willing to share all of your deepest feelings and thoughts (including your greatest fears) with them openly. Let go of withholding yourself from them out of fear.

   • Be willing to make time to really listen to them. Hear what they say for fifteen minutes without interrupting them, judging them, or advising them. Repeat back to them the most important elements of what they say so that they know you've truly heard them. Do this at least once per week.

- Show an interest in those activities and goals they most value. Support them in developing and expressing their creative gifts—their "life purpose(s)."

- Hug them spontaneously at a time when they're not expecting it. Tell them you love them.

- Help them with a project or chore prior to their asking you. Only offer help, of course, if they truly want it.

- Offer to go with them to a special place they'd like to visit. Do something playful or fun with them.

- Give them special time or attention when they're upset or having a "bad day."

- Praise them for an accomplishment.

Think about at least one thing you can do each day to demonstrate your love for this special person. Keep in mind, however, the two guidelines mentioned above. First, showing your love is something you want to do for another; not something you do for yourself, and not something you do out of a sense of obligation. Second, avoid giving more of yourself than feels natural. Giving too much at your own expense will only lead you to feel frustrated or resentful.

Finally, notice each day the ways in which the other person demonstrates love for you—however small—and let yourself feel grateful for this gift of love in your life.

References and Further Reading

Buscaglia, Leo. 1972. *Love*. New York: Fawcett Publishing.

Hendricks, Gay. 1993. *Learning to Love Yourself*. New York: Fireside Press.

Keyes, Ken. 1990. *The Power of Unconditional Love*. Coos Bay, Oregon: Loveline Books.

Jampolsky, Gerald. 1979. *Love Is Letting Go of Fear*. Berkeley: Celestial Arts.

Salzberg, Sharon. 1997. *Loving-Kindness: The Revolutionary Art of Happiness*. Boston: Shambhala.

Williamson, Marianne. 1992. *A Return to Love*. New York: HarperCollins.

15

Conclusion: Acquiring Courage

Healing fear requires courage—the courage to accept, even embrace what might be easier to avoid. What does it mean to have courage? How do you acquire courage in the face of what you fear? The word "courage" derives from the word *coeur*, the French word for heart. To have courage, I believe, is closely related to what we speak of as "taking heart" or "having heart." Fear and cowardice—the opposite of courage—are sometimes referred to as being weak or "faint" of heart. By contrast, one who has courage is sometimes spoken of as being "strong-hearted" or even "lion-hearted." What does it mean, then, to be *strong of heart*?

To have strength of heart means to act from the fullness of your heart—not just your head. And also not just from your body. If you're afraid of something and "stuck" in your head thinking about it, it's easy to get lost in fearful, even catastrophic thoughts and imaginings that can paralyze action. Likewise, if you're frightened and fixated on your body, preoccupied with physical symptoms such as shaking, trembling, dizziness, heart palpitations, or shortness of breath, you can "freeze" and be unable to move forward. The moment you're able to "take heart," you move out of just your head or just your body into a wider space within yourself—a space where you have greater freedom to choose constructive action. It seems evident that the "heart"—defined not just as an organ but a place in your inner being—*is something that underlies and unifies mind and body*. Coming from your heart means to come from a larger place in yourself than just your conscious mind—

a place closer to what might be called your "whole being." The heart is associated with passion, love, deep sentiment, aspiration, inspiration as well as courage. All are states of being that are larger than your mind—states where you typically feel more whole and more unified. (Such states are also more than mere emotions.) In short, the heart is a place in your being that can unify disparate parts of yourself into one.

Perhaps this inner place is very close to what is called the *soul*. The words *heart* and *soul*, in fact, are often used together, and I believe they are closely related. Feeling something "deep in your heart" or "deep in your soul" are not so far apart. Both involve experience that can go beyond your ordinary consciousness, and from which the highest states of being (pure love, peace, joy, creativity, as well as courage) can arise. I believe this "heart and soul" place deep within is your inner point of connection with Spirit. It has existed since you were born and cannot be diminished or limited by anything that happens in your life. Yet it's often hidden underneath a morass of reactions, thoughts, images, and judgments that make up the ordinary, moment-to-moment activity of your mind. Anxiety and irrational fear are reactions that arise whenever your conscious mind *believes in the possibility of danger*. When you can move into this larger place within yourself, you move beyond your conscious mind—outside the field of imagination where fearful thoughts can arise. Outside of fear, courage—the ability to move toward rather than avoid whatever frightens you—will come more naturally.

The capacity to "take heart"—to move from conditioned thoughts and reactions into a larger, more unified place in yourself—depends on how connected (some would call it integrated) you are within yourself. In fact, living from your heart and being connected or unified within yourself are really two ways of describing the same thing. The more connected you feel with your deeper self, the easier it is to overcome fear in all forms. The greater the distance that you live from your heart and soul, the more alienated you will feel and the more vulnerable you will be to fear.

In concluding this book, I want to restate the basic theme expressed in Chapter 2:

Fear—especially irrational fear—arises from separation, alienation, or disconnection from yourself, as well as from others, nature, and the cosmos.

Courage, unconditional love, and serenity are different faces of the same thing: a state of being which is the opposite of fear. They all arise from the same place—a place where you feel connected and unified with your own deeper self as well as with others, nature, and the cosmos.

Restating these ideas more simply:

Anxiety and irrational fear arise out of separation from what is real, and are themselves ultimately unreal.

Reconnecting with what is real, within your deepest self and within others, will heal anxiety and irrational fear.

What I'm referring to as "real" here is not the so-called "real world" of adult society but something much deeper—something beyond the conditioned thoughts, perceptions, and reactions of your mind. It's not something you can see with your eyes; rather, it's a reality you experience in those moments when you return to your true heart and soul. You'll know it to be real when you're there.

The individual chapters of this book describe a variety of ways of returning to this inner place—ways of reconnecting with yourself and with others. All of these approaches address how to restore lost connections and overcome self-alienation. The more of these approaches you can embrace, the more naturally you will find courage—and perhaps serenity as well—to face and ultimately heal whatever may frighten you.

What follows is a summary of the major perspectives described in this book, with a brief description of how each can help you reconnect with yourself and the larger world around you.

Simplifying your life can give you the *time* to reconnect with your deeper self and live more in the moment. Fewer complications in your life allow you greater opportunities to spend quality time both in the presence of yourself and with those you care about.

Relaxation has a similar effect. Any form of stress creates internal tensions that obstruct being in touch with your inner self. When you relax and slow down, you'll find it easier to access your inner being. You'll feel your true feelings and more easily be in touch with the inspirations and intuitions that can guide you to take care of yourself and make wise decisions. *Regular aerobic exercise* also reduces stress, helping to clear muscle tension as well as fatigue, with the result that you feel more alive, whole, and connected with yourself. *Energy balance* modalities such as yoga and Tai Chi (as well as healing arts such as acupuncture and massage) can *directly* release blocks to the flow of life energy and restore the integrity—the psychophysical integration—of mind and body.

Taking care of what you eat will also contribute to reducing stress and help you to feel more light, fluid, and energetic. Avoiding foods and substances that cause indigestion, allergy, toxicity, and congestion in your body will enable you to feel more alive and vital. And when you feel energetic and alive, you're not only more connected with yourself but with larger rhythms of nature and the universe. You are empowered by not only your own physical bodily energies but by a matrix of subtler energies that influence all living things.

Right thinking (a term that originated in Buddhist philosophy) means to know and believe what is true and avoid what is false. The aim of cognitive therapy, described in the chapter "Tools That Work," is essentially to achieve right thinking. You challenge erroneous beliefs and self-talk and cultivate attitudes, beliefs, and thoughts which construe things as they truly are. Seeing things accurately is a way to live more closely connected with yourself and the world about you. Irrational fears and anxious thoughts only serve to alienate you from the immediacy of the present moment; they separate you from the reality of your ongoing experience. When you can see yourself, others, and the world around you *just as they are*—without elaborating on them with fearful thoughts—there is no more reason to avoid or flee them. You will avoid only those situations where fear is a legitimate and appropriate reaction.

Medication may not initially seem to provide a means of restoring a closer connection with yourself. Certainly *some* medications (the benzodiazepines in particular) can have the unwanted effect of distancing you more from your true feelings. In reducing anxiety they may suppress other feelings as well. On the other hand, if your anxiety is so strong that it prevents you from thinking clearly, perhaps medication is needed for a while to help you get your feet back on the ground. Some medications, particularly the SSRIs, may correct neurotransmitter imbalances in the brain, allowing you to experience *more* of the normal range of your feelings—instead of anxiety and depression. Such medications can serve to *restore* your psychophysical integrity instead of disrupting it. Medication can be a powerful aid to healing, yet its appropriate use must be weighed carefully in each individual case.

Developing your observing self, through the regular practice of meditation, allows you to connect with your inner self directly. Meditation very effectively moves you to deeper ground beyond the constant play of emotional reactions, judgments, and thoughts that make up your moment-to-moment experience. When you meditate, you reconnect with a place of peace and integrity within yourself that always remains calm. The more you can connect with that still place inside, the more you will move beyond anxiety; and the more freedom you will experience simply to act in your own best interest without conflict and doubt.

Learning to let go helps you to stop struggling so much for control. You begin to develop an ability to trust the natural rhythms of life. In so doing, you learn to accept life's inevitable ups and downs, realizing that nearly all problems work themselves out in time. When you can let go of the struggle for control, you create much less resistance and conflict within yourself, making room for higher wisdom and intelligence to speak to you. At such times you may receive assistance from your Higher Power, if you choose to ask. Often it's easier to find courage when you can let go and trust in the possibility of resources beyond your own conscious mind to overcome a problem situation.

To affirm your recovery is to believe firmly in the highest vision of yourself and your life. You do this no matter what present circumstances look like. In so doing, you stop moving to the beat of your conscious mind's fears and limitations. Instead, you align yourself with a universal intelligence that holds greater wisdom and a more hopeful intention for your life. It's my personal conviction that there is a higher purpose or "plan" for each individual's life. When you hold the highest possible vision of what you can be—whole, healthy, vital, and fulfilling your life's deepest purpose(s)—you line up with that plan. When you consistently affirm the highest vision of your life, you'll receive assistance from resources beyond your conscious mind and will. Anyone who has worked deeply with prayer or a twelve-step program will attest to this.

Learning to love is the simplest and most direct way to come more from your heart—and thus from your whole being. Love cancels out fear because love is fear's opposite. Genuine love arises from a desire to overcome the separation that creates fear. It arises from a place deeper than the "mind field" where you perceive threat and imagine fear. Love always leads you to reconnect with someone or something larger than yourself. In that reconnecting you will not only feel more safe, but more in touch with who you truly are.

Each of the pathways described in this book ultimately leads to the same destination—a place of integration and self-connection where you can find the courage to face whatever you fear. The more of these paths you embrace, the more easy it will be to live in alignment with your deeper self, others, and the world around you. In so doing, you line up with the rhythm and intelligence of nature and the larger universe. You find yourself more a part of the "whole" of life rather than apart from it. In truth, you never really were apart. Fear and anxiety are illusions of separation each of us creates in our minds. At the deepest level we are all safe—all parts of a common ground which knows only love and peace.

Since much of the above has tended toward the abstract, I would like to conclude with something practical. Healing fear is not a philosophy but a daily practice that requires effort and application on your part. The list that follows enumerates ten daily practices that can all help you to overcome your anxiety and fears. You may find it helpful to photocopy the list and post it.

Ten Ways to Heal Fear Daily

1. Spend one-half hour in deep relaxation (progressive muscle relaxation, guided visualization, or meditation).

2. Engage in twenty to thirty minutes of aerobic exercise (forty to sixty minutes of walking).

3. Practice active coping or cognitive coping techniques as needed (see Chapter 6, Part 4).

4. Avoid caffeine, all forms of sugar, and processed foods as much as possible.

5. Pace yourself slowly throughout the day. Give yourself more time to do fewer activities than you (or others) think you should do. Practice living simply.

6. Make quality time to be with your significant others among family or friends (remember to hug them).

7. Spend one-half hour reading inspirational or uplifting material (see Appendix 4).

8. Make time for a few minutes of prayer. Your prayer can be asking for support, strength, or guidance. Or it can simply be to let something go.

9. Make time for a few minutes to affirm your recovery, using an affirmative statement, prayer, or a visualization.

10. Find humor in something (comics in the newspaper, a video, or yourself). Lighten up.

Appendices

1

Descriptions of the Anxiety Disorders

In this short appendix, I have included only basic descriptions of the seven most common anxiety disorders. For additional information on how these disorders can be treated, please see Chapter 1 of *The Anxiety & Phobia Workbook* (1995).

Panic Disorder

Panic disorder is characterized by sudden episodes of acute apprehension or intense fear that occur "out of the blue," without any apparent cause. Intense panic usually lasts no more than a few minutes but, in some instances, can return in "waves" for a period of up to an hour or longer. During the panic itself, any of the following symptoms can occur:

- Shortness of breath or a feeling of being smothered

- Heart palpitations, pounding heart, or accelerated heart rate

- Dizziness, unsteadiness, or faintness

- Trembling or shaking

- Feeling of choking

- Sweating

- Nausea or abdominal distress

- Feelings of unreality—as if you're "not all there" (*depersonalization*)

- Numbness or tingling in hands and feet

- Hot and cold flashes

- Chest pain or discomfort

- Fears of going crazy or losing control

- Fears of dying

At least four of these symptoms are present in a full-blown panic attack, while having two or three of them is referred to as a *limited-symptom attack*.

Your symptoms would be diagnosed as panic disorder if you: 1) have had two or more panic attacks and 2) at least one of these attacks has been followed by one month (or more) of persistent concern about having another panic attack, or worry about the possible implications of having another panic attack. It's important to recognize that panic disorder, by itself, does not involve any phobias. The panic doesn't occur because you are thinking about, approaching, or actually entering a phobic situation. Instead, it occurs spontaneously and unexpectedly for no apparent reason.

A diagnosis of panic disorder is made only after possible medical causes—including hypoglycemia, hyperthyroidism, reaction to excess caffeine, or withdrawal from alcohol, tranquilizers, or sedatives—have been ruled out. The causes of panic disorder involve a combination of heredity, chemical imbalances in the brain, and personal stress. Sudden losses or major life changes may trigger the onset of panic attacks. So can the use of recreational drugs, especially cocaine or methamphetamine ("crank").

People tend to develop panic disorder during late adolescence or their twenties. In many cases, panic is complicated by the development of agoraphobia (as described in the following section). Between 1 and 2 percent of the population has "pure" panic disorder, while about 5 percent, or one in every twenty people, suffer from panic attacks complicated by agoraphobia.

Agoraphobia

Of all the anxiety disorders, agoraphobia (usually referred to as "panic disorder with agoraphobia") is the most prevalent. About 5 percent of the general population suffer from varying degrees of agoraphobia. The only long-term psychological disorder that affects a greater number of people in the United States is alcoholism.

The word *agoraphobia* means fear of open spaces; however, the essence of agoraphobia is a fear of panic attacks. If you suffer from agoraphobia, you're afraid of being in situations from which escape might be difficult—or in which help might be unavailable—if you suddenly had a panic attack. You may avoid grocery stores or freeways, for example, not so much because of their inherent characteristics, but because these are situations from which escape might be difficult or embarrassing in the event of panic. Fear of embarrassment also plays a key role. Most agoraphobics fear not only having panic attacks but *what other people will think* should they be seen having a panic attack.

It's common for the agoraphobic to avoid a variety of situations. Some of the more common ones include:

- Crowded public places such as grocery stores, department stores, restaurants

- Enclosed or confined places such as tunnels, bridges, or the hairdresser's chair

- Public transportation such as trains, buses, subways, planes

- Being at home alone

Perhaps the most common feature of agoraphobia is anxiety about being far away from home or far from a "safe person" (usually your spouse, partner, a parent, or anyone to whom you have a primary attachment). You may completely avoid driving alone or may be afraid of driving alone beyond a certain short distance from home. In more severe cases, you might be able to walk alone only a few yards from home or you might be housebound altogether.

Agoraphobia affects people in all walks of life and at all levels of the socioeconomic scale. Approximately 80 percent of agoraphobics are women, although this percentage has been dropping recently. It's possible that as more women are expected to hold down full-time jobs (making a housebound lifestyle less socially acceptable), the percentage of women and men with agoraphobia may tend to equalize.

Social Phobia

Social phobia is one of the more common anxiety disorders. It involves fear of embarrassment or humiliation in situations where you are exposed to the scrutiny of others or must perform. This fear is much stronger than the normal anxiety most nonphobic people experience in social or performance situations. Usually it's so strong that it causes you to avoid the situation altogether, although some people with social phobia endure social situations, albeit with considerable anxiety. Typically, your concern is that you'll say or do something that will cause others to judge you as being anxious, weak, "crazy," or stupid. Your concern is generally out of proportion to the situation, and you recognize that it's excessive (children with social phobia, however, do not recognize the excessiveness of their fear).

The most common social phobia is fear of public speaking. In fact, this is the most common of all phobias and affects performers, speakers, people whose jobs require them to make presentations, and students who have to speak before their class. Public speaking phobia affects a large percentage of the population and is equally prevalent among men and women.

Other common social phobias include:

- Fear of blushing in public

- Fear of choking on or spilling food while in public

- Fear of being watched at work

- Fear of using public toilets

- Fear of writing or signing documents in the presence of others

- Fear of crowds

- Fear of taking examinations

Sometimes social phobia is less specific and involves a generalized fear of *any* social or group situation where you feel that you might be watched or evaluated. When your fear is of a wide range of social situations (for example, initiating conversations, participating in small groups, speaking to authority figures, dating, attending parties, and so on), the condition is referred to as *generalized social phobia*.

While social anxieties are common, you would be given a formal diagnosis of social phobia only if your avoidance interferes with work, social activities, or important relationships, and/or it causes you considerable distress. As with agoraphobia, panic attacks can accompany social phobia, although your panic is related more to being embarrassed or humiliated than to being confined or trapped. Also the panic arises only in connection with specific types of social situations.

Social phobias tend to develop earlier than agoraphobia and can begin in late childhood or adolescence. They often develop in shy children around the time they're faced with increased peer pressure at school. Typically these phobias persist (without treatment) through adolescence and young adulthood, but have a tendency to decrease in severity later in life. Recent studies suggest that social phobia affects 3 to 13 percent of adults in the U.S. at some time in their life (the prevalence rates vary dependening on the threshold used to evaluate distress).

Specific Phobia

Specific phobia typically involves a strong fear and avoidance of *one particular* type of object or situation. Most often the phobic situation is avoided, though in some instances it may be endured with dread. Confronting the object or situation almost always provokes anxiety.

With specific phobia, fear is generally focused on the *phobic situation* itself and only secondarily, if at all, on having a panic attack. This is unlike agoraphobia, where the primary focus of fear tends to be on panic attacks. There is also no fear of humiliation or embarrassment in social situations, as in social phobia. Panic attacks may occur with specific phobia, but only upon confronting the feared object or situation.

While fears are pervasive, a diagnosis of specific phobia is made only when the fear and avoidance are strong enough to interfere with normal routines, work, relationships and/or to cause significant distress.

Specific phobias are classified into five different types:

- *Animal phobias* consist of fears of animals such as snakes, mice, or dogs; or insects such as bees or spiders. Typically, animal phobias originate in childhood.

- *Natural environment type*—These phobias consist of fears related to the natural environment such as heights (sometimes referred to as acrophobia), fire or water; or natural occurrences such as thunderstorms, tornadoes, or earthquakes.

- *Blood-injection-injury type*—In this category are fears evoked by the sight of blood or seeing someone injured. Phobias of receiving an injection or other invasive medical procedure are also included. These phobias are grouped together because they're all characterized by the possibility of fainting, in addition to panic or anxiety. Blood-injection-injury phobias can develop at any age.

- *Situational type*—Situational phobias relate to a variety of situations in which a fear of being enclosed, trapped, and/or unable to exit plays a dominant role. Such situations include flying, elevators, driving, public transportation, tunnels, bridges, and other enclosed places such as shopping malls. Situational phobias tend to develop in childhood or in early adulthood (twenties).

- *Other type*—This is a residual category for specific phobias not falling into the previous four types. Included here are fears of contracting illness (such as AIDS or cancer), avoidance of situations that might lead to choking or vomiting (for example, eating solid foods), and the fear of open spaces.

Specific phobias are common and affect approximately 10 percent of the population. However, since they do not always result in severe impairment, only a minority of people with specific phobias actually seek treatment. These types of phobias occur in men and women about equally. Animal phobias tend to be more common in women, while illness phobias are more common in men.

As previously mentioned, specific phobias are often childhood fears that were never outgrown. In other instances, they may develop after a traumatic event, such as an accident, natural disaster, illness, or visit to the dentist—in other words, as a result of conditioning. A final cause is childhood *modeling*. Repeated observation of a parent with a specific phobia can lead a child to develop it as well.

Generalized Anxiety Disorder

Generalized anxiety disorder is characterized by chronic anxiety that persists for at least six months *but is unaccompanied by panic attacks, phobias, or obsessions.* You simply experience persistent anxiety and worry without the complicating features of other anxiety disorders. To be given a diagnosis of generalized anxiety disorder, your anxiety and worry must focus on two or more stressful life circumstances (such as finances, relationships, health, or school performance) a majority of days during a six-month period. It's common, if you're dealing with generalized anxiety disorder, to have a large number of worries, and to spend a lot of your time worrying. Yet you find it difficult to exercise much control over your worrying. Moreover, the intensity and frequency of the worry are always out of proportion to the actual likelihood of the feared events happening.

In addition to frequent worry, generalized anxiety disorder involves having at least three of the following six symptoms (with at least one symptom present more days than not over a period of six months):

- Restlessness—feeling keyed up

- Being easily fatigued

- Difficulty concentrating

- Irritability

- Muscle tension

- Difficulties with sleep

Finally, you're likely to receive a diagnosis of generalized anxiety disorder if your worry and associated symptoms cause you significant distress and/or interfere with your ability to function occupationally, socially, or in other important areas.

If a doctor tells you that you suffer from generalized anxiety disorder, he or she has probably ruled out possible medical causes of chronic anxiety, such as hyperventilation, thyroid problems, or drug-induced anxiety. Generalized anxiety disorder often occurs together with depression: a competent therapist can usually determine which disorder is primary and which is secondary. In some cases, though, it's difficult to say which came first.

Generalized anxiety disorder can develop at any age. In children and adolescents, the focus of worry often tends to be on performance in school or sports events. In adults, the focus can vary. This disorder affects approximately 4 percent of the American population, and may be slightly more common in females than males (55 to 60 percent of those diagnosed with the disorder are female).

Obsessive-Compulsive Disorder

Some people naturally tend to be more neat, tidy, and orderly than others. These traits can in fact be useful in many situations, both at work and at home. In obsessive-compulsive disorder, however, they are carried to an extreme and disruptive degree. Persons with obsessive-compulsive disorder can spend many hours cleaning, tidying, checking, or ordering—to the point where these activities interfere with the rest of the business of their lives.

Obsessions are recurring ideas, thoughts, images, or impulses that seem senseless but nonetheless continue to intrude into your mind. Examples include images of violence, thoughts of doing violence to someone else, or fears of leaving on lights or the stove or leaving your door unlocked. You recognize that these thoughts or fears are irrational and try to suppress them, but they continue to intrude into your mind for hours, days, weeks, or longer. These thoughts or images are not merely excessive worries about real-life problems and are usually unrelated to a real-life problem.

Compulsions are behaviors or rituals that you perform to dispel the anxiety brought up by obsessions. For example, you may wash your hands numerous times to dispel a fear of being contaminated, check the stove again and again to see if it's turned off, or look continually in your rearview mirror while driving to assuage anxiety about having hit somebody. You realize that these rituals are unreasonable. Yet you feel compelled to perform them to ward off the anxiety associated with your particular obsession. The conflict between your wish to be free of the compulsive ritual and the irresistible desire to perform it is a source of anxiety, shame, and even despair. Eventually you may cease struggling with your compulsions and give over to them entirely.

Obsessions may occur by themselves, without necessarily being accompanied by compulsions. In fact, about 25 percent of the people who suffer from obsessive-compulsive disorder only have obsessions.

The most common compulsions include washing, checking, and counting. If you're a washer, you're constantly concerned about avoiding contamination. You avoid touching doorknobs, shaking hands, or coming into contact with any object you associate with germs, filth, or a toxic substance. You can spend literally hours washing hands or showering to reduce anxiety about being contaminated. Women more often have this compulsion than men do. Men outnumber women as checkers, however. Doors have to be repeatedly checked to dispel obsessions about being robbed; stoves are repeatedly checked to dispel obsessions about starting a fire; or roads repeatedly checked to dispel obsessions about having hit someone. In the counting compulsion, you feel you must count up to a certain number or repeat a word a certain number of times to dispel anxiety about harm befalling you or someone else.

Obsessive-compulsive disorder is often accompanied by depression. Preoccupation with obsessions, in fact, tends to wax and wane with depression. This disorder may also be accompanied by phobic avoidance—such as when a person with an obsession about dirt avoids public restrooms or touching doorknobs.

It's very important to realize that as bizarre as obsessive-compulsive behavior may sound, it has nothing to do with "being crazy." You always recognize the irrationality and senselessness of your thoughts and behavior and you're very frustrated (as well as depressed) about your inability to control them.

Obsessive-compulsive disorder used to be considered a rare behavior disturbance. However, recent studies have shown that as many as *2 to 3 percent of the general population* may suffer, to varying degrees, from obsessive-compulsive disorder. The reason prevalence rates have been underestimated up to now is that most sufferers have been reluctant to tell anyone about their problem. This disorder appears to affect men and women in equal numbers. Although many cases of obsessive-compulsive disorder begin in adolescence and young adulthood, about half begin in childhood. The age of onset tends to be earlier in males than females.

The causes of obsessive-compulsive disorder are unclear. There is some evidence that an imbalance of a neurotransmitter in the brain known as serotonin, or a disturbance in serotonin metabolism, is associated with the disorder. This is borne out by the fact that many sufferers improve when they take medications that increase brain serotonin levels, such as clomipramine (Anafranil) or specific serotonin-enhancing antidepressants such as fluoxetine (Prozac), sertraline (Zoloft), and paroxetine (Paxil). Further research needs to be done.

Post-Traumatic Stress Disorder

The essential feature of post-traumatic stress disorder is the development of disabling psychological symptoms following a traumatic event. It was first identified during World War I, when soldiers were observed to suffer chronic anxiety, nightmares, and flashbacks for weeks, months, or even years following combat. This condition came to be known as "shell shock."

Post-traumatic stress disorder can occur to anyone in the wake of a severe trauma outside the normal range of human experience. These are traumas that would produce intense fear, terror, and feelings of helplessness in anyone and include natural disasters such as earthquakes or tornadoes, car or plane crashes, rape, assault, or other violent crimes against yourself or your immediate family. It appears that the symptoms are more intense and persistent when the trauma is personal, as in rape or other violent crimes.

Among the variety of symptoms that can occur with post-traumatic stress disorder, the following nine are particularly common:

- Repetitive, distressing thoughts about the event

- Nightmares related to the event

- Flashbacks so intense that you feel or act as though the trauma were occurring all over again

- An attempt to avoid thoughts or feelings associated with the trauma

- An attempt to avoid activities or external situations associated with the trauma—such as a phobia about driving after you have been in an auto accident

- Emotional numbness—being out of touch with your feelings

- Feelings of detachment or estrangement from others

- Losing interest in activities that used to give you pleasure

- Persistent symptoms of increased anxiety, such as difficulty falling or staying asleep, difficulty concentrating, startling easily, irritability, and outbursts of anger

For you to receive a diagnosis of post-traumatic stress disorder, these symptoms need to have persisted for at least one month (with less than one month's duration, the appropriate diagnosis is "acute stress disorder"). In addition, the disturbance must be causing you significant distress, interfering with social, vocational, or other important areas of your life.

If you suffer from post-traumatic stress disorder, you tend to be anxious and depressed. Sometimes you will find yourself acting impulsively, suddenly changing residence or going on a trip with hardly any plans. If you have been through a trauma where others around you died, you may suffer from guilt about having survived.

Post-traumatic stress disorder can affect people at any age. Children with the disorder tend not to relive the trauma consciously but continually reenact it in their play or in distressing dreams.

2

Resources

The Anxiety Disorders Association of America

The Anxiety Disorders Association of America (ADAA) is a nonprofit, charitable organization founded in 1980 by leaders in the field of treatment for phobias, agoraphobia, and panic/anxiety disorders. Its purpose is to promote public awareness about anxiety disorders, stimulate research and development of effective treatments, and offer assistance to sufferers and their families in gaining access to available specialists and treatment programs.

The association publishes a quarterly newsletter and a *National Treatment Directory*, which lists professionals and programs throughout the United States and Canada specializing in the treatment of anxiety disorders. It also publishes several relevant books and pamphlets.

For further information about the Anxiety Disorders Association of America, its services, publications, and annual conference, as well as how to join, please contact:

The Anxiety Disorders Association of America
    11900 Parklawn Drive, Suite 100
    Rockville, MD 20852-2624
    (301) 231-9350

Other Resources

Agoraphobic Foundation of Canada
    P.O. Box 132
    Chomedey, Laval, Quebec
    H7W 4K2, Canada

Agoraphobics in Action, Inc.
    P.O. Box 1662
    Antioch, TN 37011-1662
    (615) 831-2383

Agoraphobics in Motion-A.I.M.
    1729 Crooks Street
    Royal Oaks, MI 48067
    (248) 547-0400

Anxiety Disorders Network
    1848 Liverpool Rd., Ste 199
    Pickering, Ontario
    LIV 6M3, Canada
    (905) 831-3877

CHAANGE
    128 Country Club Drive
    Chula Vista, CA 91911
    (619) 425-3992

ENcourage Newsletter
    13610 North Scottsdale Road, Suite 10-126
    Scottsdale, AZ 85254

National Institute of Mental Health-Information Service
    Call 1-800-64-PANIC for free information on the nature and treatment of
    panic disorder

Obsessive Compulsive Foundation, Inc.
    P.O. Box 70
    Milford, CT 06460
    (203) 878-5669

Phobics Anonymous
    P.O. Box 1180
    Palm Springs, CA 92263
    (760) 322-COPE

Terrap
    932 Evelyn Street
    Menlo Park, CA 94025
    (800) 274-6242

3

Progressive Muscle Relaxation

Progressive muscle relaxation involves tensing and relaxing sixteen different muscle groups of the body. The idea is to tense each muscle group hard (not so hard that you strain, however) for about ten seconds, and then to let go of it suddenly. You then give yourself fifteen to twenty seconds to relax, noticing how the muscle group feels when relaxed in contrast to how it felt when tensed, before going on to the next group of muscles. You might also say to yourself "I am relaxing," "Letting go," "Let the tension flow away," or any other relaxing phrase during each relaxation period between successive muscle groups. Throughout the exercise, maintain your focus on your muscles. When your attention wanders, bring it back to the particular muscle group you're working on. The guidelines below describe progressive muscle relaxation in detail:

- Make sure you're in a setting that's quiet and comfortable.

- It is preferable to practice on an empty stomach—before or one hour after a meal.

- It's preferable to be seated in a recliner or lying down, with your head supported.

- When you tense a particular muscle group, do so vigorously, without straining, for seven to ten seconds. You may want to count "one-thousand-one," "one-thousand-two," and so on, as a way of marking off seconds.

- Concentrate on what is happening. Feel the buildup of tension in each particular muscle group. It's often helpful to visualize the particular muscle group being tensed.

- When you release the muscles, do so abruptly, and then relax, enjoying the sudden feeling of limpness. Allow the relaxation to develop for at least fifteen to twenty seconds before going on to the next group of muscles.

- Allow all the *other* muscles in your body to remain relaxed, as far as possible, while tensing a particular muscle group.

- Tense and relax each muscle group once. If a particular area feels especially tight, you can tense and relax it two or three times, waiting about twenty seconds between each cycle.

Once you are comfortably supported in a quiet place, follow the detailed instructions below:

1. To begin, take three deep abdominal breaths, inhaling and exhaling slowly through your nose each time. As you exhale, imagine that the tension throughout your body begins to flow away.

2. Clench your fists. Hold for seven to ten seconds and then release for fifteen to twenty seconds. *Use these same time intervals for all other muscle groups.*

3. Tighten your biceps by drawing your forearms up toward your shoulders and "making a muscle" with both arms. Hold . . . and then relax.

4. Tighten your *triceps*—the muscles on the undersides of your upper arms—by extending your arms out straight and locking your elbows. Hold . . . and then relax.

5. Tense the muscles in your forehead by raising your eyebrows as far as you can. Hold . . . and then relax. Imagine your forehead muscles becoming smooth and limp as they relax.

6. Tense the muscles around your eyes by clenching your eyelids tightly shut. Hold . . . and then relax. Imagine sensations of deep relaxation spreading all around the area of your eyes.

7. Tighten your jaws by opening your mouth widely so that you stretch the muscles around the hinges of your jaw. Hold . . . and then relax. Allow your jaw to hang loose.

8. Tighten the muscles in the back of your neck by pulling your head way back, as if you were going to touch your head to your back (be gentle with this muscle group to avoid injury). Focus only on tensing the muscles in your neck. Hold . . . and then relax. Since this area is often especially tight, it's good to do the tense-relax cycle twice.

9. Take a few deep breaths and tune in to the weight of your head sinking into whatever surface it's resting on.

10. Tighten your shoulders by raising them up as if you were going to touch your ears. Hold . . . and then relax.

11. Tighten the muscles around your shoulder blades by pushing back your shoulder blades as if you were going to touch them together. Hold the tension in your shoulder blades . . . and then relax. Since this area is often especially tense, you might repeat the tense-relax sequence twice.

12. Tighten the muscles of your chest by taking in a deep breath. Hold for up to ten seconds . . . and then release slowly. Imagine any excess tension in your chest flowing away with the exhalation.

13. Tighten your stomach muscles by sucking your stomach in. Hold . . . and then release. Imagine a wave of relaxation spreading through your abdomen.

14. Tighten your lower back muscles by arching your back. (You can omit this exercise if you have lower back pain.) Hold . . . and then relax.

15. Tighten your buttock muscles by pulling them together. Hold . . . and then relax. Imagine the muscles in your hips going loose and limp.

16. Squeeze the muscles in your thighs all the way down to your knees. You will probably have to tighten your buttocks along with your thighs, since the thigh muscles attach at the pelvis. Hold . . . and then relax. Feel your thigh muscles smoothing out and relaxing completely.

17. Tighten your calf muscles by pulling your toes toward you (flex carefully to avoid cramps). Hold . . . and then relax.

18. Tighten your feet by curling your toes downward. Hold . . . and then relax.

19. Mentally scan your body for any residual tension. If a particular area remains tense, repeat one or two tense-relax cycles for that group of muscles.

20. Now imagine a wave of relaxation gradually spreading throughout your body, starting at your head and slowly penetrating every muscle group all the way down to your toes.

The entire progressive muscle-relaxation sequence should take you twenty to thirty minutes the first time. With practice you may decrease the time needed to fifteen to twenty minutes.

You might want to record the above exercises on an audiocassette to expedite your early practice sessions. Or you may wish to obtain a professionally made tape of progressive muscle relaxation. Some people always prefer to use a tape, while others have the exercises so well learned after a few weeks of practice that they prefer doing them from memory.

4

Inspirational Books

The following books have been uplifting to me personally and to a number of my clients.

Beattie, Melody. 1990. *The Language of Letting Go.* New York: Harper/Hazeldon.

Borysenko, Joan. 1993. *Fire in the Soul.* New York: Warner Books.

Caddy, Eileen. 1979. *The Dawn of Change.* Forres, Scotland: Findhorn Publications. (Inspired messages from the author's Higher Power.)

Hay, Louise. 1984. *You Can Heal Your Life.* Santa Monica, Calif.: Hay House. (Helpful tools and affirmations for developing self-worth.)

Jampolsky, Gerald. 1979. *Love Is Letting Go of Fear.* Berkeley, Calif.: Celestial Arts.

Miller, Carolyn. 1995. *Creating Miracles.* Tiburon, Calif.: H.J. Kramer, Inc. (As the title implies, this insightful book has many useful ideas about how to create miraculous outcomes in ordinary life.)

Mitchell, Stephen, ed. 1989. *The Enlightened Heart: An Anthology of Sacred Poetry.* New York: Harper Perennial.

Moody, Raymond. 1976. *Life After Life.* New York: Bantam. (The classic book on near-death experiences.)

Nelson, Martia. 1993. *Coming Home.* Novato, Calif.: Nataraj Publishing. (Offers deep insight into the human condition.)

Norwood, Robin. 1994. *Why Me. Why Now. Why This.* New York: Carol Southern Books. (Makes a strong case that what happens to us in life are lessons for our growth.)

Redfield, James. 1993. *The Celestine Prophecy*. New York: Warner Books.

Rodegast, Pat. 1985. *Emmanuel's Book*. New York: Bantam. (Very inspiring communications from a Higher Source. A personal favorite.)

——. 1989. *Emmanuel's Book II*. New York: Bantam.

Roman, Sanaya. 1989. *Spiritual Growth*. Tiburon, Calif.: H.J. Kramer.

Walsch, Neale. 1996. *Conversations with God, Book 1*. New York: Putnam. (Inspiring presentation of the author's "conversation" with his Higher Power.)

Weiss, Brian. 1996. *Only Love Is Real*. New York: Warner Books..

Williamson, Marianne. 1994. *Illuminata*. New York: Random House. (An outstanding collection of reflections and prayers for modern times.)

Zukav, Gary. 1990. *The Seat of the Soul*. New York: Fireside Books.

5

Helpful Counterstatements

You may find the following counterstatements helpful when you're going through a particularly difficult time with anxiety.

Negative Self-Talk	Positive Counterstatements
This is unbearable.	I can learn how to cope better with this.
What if this goes on without letting up?	I'll deal with this one day at a time. I don't have to project into the future.
I feel damaged, inadequate relative to others.	Some of us have steeper paths to walk than others. That doesn't make me less valuable as a human being—even if I accomplish less in the outer world.
Why do I have to deal with this? Other people seem freer to enjoy their lives.	Life is a school. For whatever reasons, at least for now, I've been given a steeper path—a tougher curriculum. That doesn't make me wrong. In fact, adversity develops qualities of strength and compassion.

Having this condition seems unfair.	Life can appear unfair from a human perspective. If we could see the bigger picture, we'd see that everything is proceeding according to plan.
I don't know how to cope with this.	I can *learn* to cope better—with this and any difficulty life brings.
I feel so inadequate relative to others.	Let people do what they do in the outer world. I'm following a path of inner growth and transformation, which is at least equally valuable. Finding peace in myself can be a gift to others.
Each day seems like a major challenge.	I'm learning to take things more slowly. I make time to take care of myself. I make time to do small things to nurture myself.
I don't understand why I'm this way—why this happened to me.	The causes are many, including heredity, early environment, and cumulative stress. Understanding causes satisfies the intellect, but it's not what heals.
I feel like I'm going crazy.	When anxiety is high, I *feel* like I'm losing control. But that feeling has nothing to do with going crazy. Anxiety disorders are a long way from the category of disorders labeled "crazy."
I have to really fight this.	Struggling with a problem won't help so much as making more time in my life to better care for myself.
I shouldn't have let this happen to me.	The long-term causes of this problem lie in heredity and childhood environment, so I didn't cause this condition. I *can* take responsibility for learning how to better deal with it.

About the Author

Dr. Edmund ("Ed") Bourne, Ph.D., has specialized in treating anxiety disorders and related problems for two decades. He is author of the highly regarded *Anxiety & Phobia Workbook*, which has helped hundreds of thousands of persons in the United States and other countries. For many years, Dr. Bourne was director of The Anxiety Treatment Center in San Jose and Santa Rosa, California. Currently he resides and practices in Kona, Hawaii and California.

Personal telephone consultations with Dr. Bourne may be arranged by calling 808-334-1847. Information on intensive therapy programs in Kona, Hawaii is also available by calling this number. If you would like to find a therapist who specializes in treating anxiety disorders in your local area, please contact The Anxiety Disorders Association of America for a referral (301-231-9350).

Some Other New Harbinger Self-Help Titles

High on Stress: A Woman's Guide to Optimizing the Stress in Her Life, $13.95
Infidelity: A Survival Guide, $13.95
Stop Walking on Eggshells, $14.95
Consumer's Guide to Psychiatric Drugs, $13.95
The Fibromyalgia Advocate: Getting the Support You Need to Cope with Fibromyalgia and Myofascial Pain, $18.95
Healing Fear: New Approaches to Overcoming Anxiety, $16.95
Working Anger: Preventing and Resolving Conflict on the Job, $12.95
Sex Smart: How Your Childhood Shaped Your Sexual Life and What to Do About It, $14.95
You Can Free Yourself From Alcohol & Drugs, $13.95
Amongst Ourselves: A Self-Help Guide to Living with Dissociative Identity Disorder, $14.95
Healthy Living with Diabetes, $13.95
Dr. Carl Robinson's Basic Baby Care, $10.95
Better Boundaries: Owning and Treasuring Your Life, $13.95
Goodbye Good Girl, $12.95
Being, Belonging, Doing, $10.95
Thoughts & Feelings, Second Edition, $18.95
Depression: How It Happens, How It's Healed, $14.95
Trust After Trauma, $13.95
The Chemotherapy & Radiation Survival Guide, Second Edition, $14.95
Heart Therapy, $13.95
Surviving Childhood Cancer, $12.95
The Headache & Neck Pain Workbook, $14.95
Perimenopause, $13.95
The Self-Forgiveness Handbook, $12.95
A Woman's Guide to Overcoming Sexual Fear and Pain, $14.95
Mind Over Malignancy, $12.95
Treating Panic Disorder and Agoraphobia, $44.95
Scarred Soul, $13.95
The Angry Heart, $14.95
Don't Take It Personally, $12.95
Becoming a Wise Parent For Your Grown Child, $12.95
Clear Your Past, Change Your Future, $13.95
Preparing for Surgery, $17.95
The Power of Two, $12.95
It's Not OK Anymore, $13.95
The Daily Relaxer, $12.95
The Body Image Workbook, $17.95
Living with ADD, $17.95
Taking the Anxiety Out of Taking Tests, $12.95
Five Weeks to Healing Stress: The Wellness Option, $17.95
Why Children Misbehave and What to Do About It, $14.95
When Anger Hurts Your Kids, $12.95
The Addiction Workbook, $17.95
The Chronic Pain Control Workbook, Second Edition, $17.95
Fibromyalgia & Chronic Myofascial Pain Syndrome, $19.95
Flying Without Fear, $13.95
Kid Cooperation: How to Stop Yelling, Nagging & Pleading and Get Kids to Cooperate, $13.95
The Stop Smoking Workbook: Your Guide to Healthy Quitting, $17.95
Conquering Carpal Tunnel Syndrome and Other Repetitive Strain Injuries, $17.95
An End to Panic: Breakthrough Techniques for Overcoming Panic Disorder, Second Edition, $18.95
Letting Go of Anger: The 10 Most Common Anger Styles and What to Do About Them, $12.95
Messages: The Communication Skills Workbook, Second Edition, $13.95
Coping With Chronic Fatigue Syndrome: Nine Things You Can Do, $13.95
The Anxiety & Phobia Workbook, Second Edition, $18.95
The Relaxation & Stress Reduction Workbook, Fourth Edition, $17.95
Living Without Depression & Manic Depression: A Workbook for Maintaining Mood Stability, $17.95
Coping With Schizophrenia: A Guide For Families, $15.95
Visualization for Change, Second Edition, $15.95
Postpartum Survival Guide, $13.95
Angry All the Time: An Emergency Guide to Anger Control, $12.95
Couple Skills: Making Your Relationship Work, $13.95
Self-Esteem, Second Edition, $13.95
I Can't Get Over It, A Handbook for Trauma Survivors, Second Edition, $16.95
Dying of Embarrassment: Help for Social Anxiety and Social Phobia, $13.95
The Depression Workbook: Living With Depression and Manic Depression, $17.95
Men & Grief: A Guide for Men Surviving the Death of a Loved One, $14.95
When Once Is Not Enough: Help for Obsessive Compulsives, $13.95
Beyond Grief: A Guide for Recovering from the Death of a Loved One, $13.95
Hypnosis for Change: A Manual of Proven Techniques, Third Edition, $15.95
When Anger Hurts, $13.95

Call **toll free, 1-800-748-6273,** to order. Have your Visa or Mastercard number ready. Or send a check for the titles you want to New Harbinger Publications, Inc., 5674 Shattuck Ave., Oakland, CA 94609. Include $3.80 for the first book and 75¢ for each additional book, to cover shipping and handling. (California residents please include appropriate sales tax.) Allow two to five weeks for delivery.

Prices subject to change without notice.